Bureaucrats and Politicians
in
Western Democracies

# Bureaucrats and Politicians in Western Democracies

Joel D. Aberbach

Robert D. Putnam

Bert A. Rockman

WITH THE COLLABORATION OF

Thomas J. Anton

Samuel J. Eldersveld

Ronald Inglehart

Harvard University Press

*Cambridge, Massachusetts, and London, England   1981*

Library of Congress Cataloging in Publication Data

Aberbach, Joel D.
    Bureaucrats and politicians in western democracies.

    Includes bibliographical references and index.
    1. Government executives—Europe.  2. Government
executives—United States.  3. Politicians—Europe.
4. Politicians—United States.  I. Putnam, Robert D.
II. Rockman, Bert A.  III. Title.
JN94.A69E92      351′.001′094      81-2899
ISBN 0-674-08625-2              AACR2

*For our wives*

# Preface

In uneasy partnership at the helm of the modern state stand elected party politicians and appointed professional bureaucrats. At least since Max Weber, political observers have theorized about the relationship between politicians and bureaucrats, about their contrasting approaches to public policymaking. This volume confronts these theories with evidence from systematic interviews with more than 1,400 senior civil servants and members of parliament in the United States, Britain, France, Germany, Italy, the Netherlands, and Sweden.

The central question of our book is this: How do senior bureaucrats and parliamentary politicians differ from one another and, conversely, how are they alike? Complementing this question are two others: What explains the differences and similarities between bureaucrats and politicians? and What do these differences and similarities mean for policymaking?

In addressing these questions, Chapter 1 states our guiding concepts. Here we outline four images of bureaucrats and politicians that correspond roughly to the evolution of their roles in Western polities over the past century. These images anchor our analyses throughout the book.

Chapter 2 details our methods of study, with primary focus on the techniques employed in the cross-national elite surveys and in the data analyses. The chapter also describes the political contexts of the various countries at the time of our surveys.

Our empirical analysis begins in Chapter 3, which charts the paths that

Western bureaucratic and political elites take to the top. We look at who they are and how they differ from one another and from the public. We also examine the explanations for and implications of background and career differences between bureaucrats and politicians.

We turn our attention in Chapter 4 to the related questions of how senior bureaucrats and parliamentary politicians interpret their respective roles and how they approach governance and policymaking. Here, as elsewhere in the book, we discover the peculiar effects of American political institutions, which seem to blur the differences between bureaucrats and politicians that are so sharp in Europe.

Chapter 5 examines the structure, content, and origins of ideological thinking among bureaucrats and politicians. We investigate how their ideological commitments differ, and why, and what difference it makes to the governing process.

In Chapter 6 we inquire into the outlooks that bureaucrats and politicians have toward key dimensions of democracy—liberty and pluralism, equality and participation—and we seek to explain the origins of these commitments.

From what bureaucrats and politicians believe, we move in Chapter 7 to how they behave, exploring the interactions of senior bureaucrats and parliamentary politicians with one another and with other participants in the policy process. These contact patterns turn out to reflect differences in role, in personal attitude, and in national institutional setting.

Finally, Chapter 8 pulls our findings together and considers their implications for effective democratic government. How can the inevitable tensions between politician and bureaucrat be made more creative, so that the modern state can be both effective and responsive, both stable and innovative?

In a fundamental intellectual sense, this volume is a product of a thirteen-year collaborative project sponsored by the University of Michigan and directed by Samuel J. Eldersveld. The project would never have come to fruition without the guiding force of Professor Eldersveld, and the book reflects the efforts and ideas of the project team. In recognition of the depth and importance of this collaboration, our title page lists all the members of the team as full collaborators.

In the summer of 1968 a group of Michigan faculty members met to discuss the study of elite political culture. We were interested in the attitudes, values, and beliefs of top officials and soon decided that an empirical study in a variety of national settings would answer many of our questions and stimulate new ones. The University of Michigan generously provided us with funds from its Ford Foundation Grant in Comparative and International Studies, and this was followed by a sizable award from the National Science Foundation, which provided the core support for our project.

Funds in hand, we embarked on an odyssey that turned out to be rather longer than anticipated. After pretesting the basic questions we wanted to ask members of the elite, we undertook fieldwork in nine countries in the period 1970 to 1974. Joel Aberbach and Bert Rockman directed work in the United States; Robert Putnam had responsibility for three countries—Great Britain, Germany, and Italy; Thomas Anton led the Swedish part of the study; Samuel Eldersveld managed the study in the Netherlands; and Ronald Inglehart had charge of the work in France. (Archibald Singham and John Waterbury conducted related studies in Jamaica and Morocco, respectively.)

The fieldwork was only the beginning of our task. We next had to develop a coding procedure to convert our conversational interviews into quantitative data—an extremely delicate job. Our goal was to capture as much of the nuance and complexity in the conversations as possible, at the same time using standard coding categories suitable for comparative analysis. This process took another two years to complete.

Our hopes for a volume covering all aspects of the research were repeatedly thwarted because of the immense cost of coordinating the efforts and perspectives of a large team of researchers. In the interim, three books focusing on individual countries, and numerous articles, were produced by various researchers in our group. (All the publications emanating from the project are listed at the back of this book.) The three of us eventually decided to try our hand at an integrative work on a more limited set of topics, drawing on data from the seven industrialized democracies in the study. The book we have written, therefore, covers only part of the material developed in the project.

A project of the magnitude of this one requires the assistance of large numbers of people. First and foremost, we owe a huge debt of gratitude to all of the parliamentarians and administrators who took time from their busy schedules to talk with us. They were our teachers.

"Money," an American elected official once said, "is the mother's milk of politics." It is also the mother's milk of research. We owe much to the

National Science Foundation; the Ford Foundation; the Institute of Public Policy Studies, the Rackham School of Graduate Studies, and the Vice President for Research at the University of Michigan; Harvard's Center for International Affairs; the University Center for International Studies, as well as the Provost's Research Fund, at the University of Pittsburgh; and the James K. Pollock Research Program at DATUM (Bonn). Besides Michigan, Pittsburgh, and Harvard, we are grateful to the other institutions that have hosted us during the past thirteen years—the Brookings Institution and the Woodrow Wilson International Center for Scholars in Washington, D.C., the Department of Political Science at the University of Stockholm, and the Center for Advanced Study in the Behavioral Sciences in Palo Alto, California. We also wish to acknowledge the permission of Tulane University to draw on material previously published in Robert D. Putnam, "Bureaucrats and Politicians: Contending Elites in the Policy Process," in *Perspectives on Public Policy-Making,* ed. William B. Gwyn and George C. Edwards III, Tulane Studies in Political Science, vol. 15 (New Orleans: Tulane University Press, 1975), pp. 179–202.

A few individuals played special roles in improving the quality of our country studies and, in fact, of the overall project. The late Carl Beck, director of the University Center for International Studies at the University of Pittsburgh, generously gave his support and enthusiasm at key moments. James D. Chesney did much of the congressional interviewing in the United States and in excellent fashion directed the coding of that part of the study. Nancy Brussolo was indefatigable as transcriber, coder, and expediter on the American project. Klaus Liepelt of DATUM-INFAS in Bad Godesberg and Alberto Spreafico of the Italian Social Science Committee in Rome were cordial hosts and thoughtful counselors. Hugh Grambau invested nearly two years in directing a vast multilingual coding team with superb skill and unending good humor. Hans Daalder was a key to the success of the Dutch study, along with Jan Kooiman and Theo van der Tak, who were Professor Eldersveld's coworkers. Hans Meijer, rector of the University of Linköping, was an early sponsor of the Swedish portion of the project, and Olof Ruin of the University of Stockholm gave it a home and the value of his knowledge of the Swedish system. Michel Crozier, Dusan Sidjanski, and Ezra Suleiman provided particularly helpful advice and suggestions on the French part of the project, and Suleiman later provided a useful critique of the present manuscript. To all these people we owe particular thanks.

We held two major international conferences in the course of our research, one sponsored by the Council on European Studies and held at Airlie House in March 1975, the other sponsored by the European Cultural Foundation and held at the Netherlands Institute of Advanced Studies in November 1977. We wish to thank the sponsors and all those who attended for their time and helpful comments: Allen H. Barton, Jorgen Christensen, Giuseppe Di Palma, Pierre Gremion, Jack E. S. Hayward, Bruce Headey, Jan Kooiman, Claes Linde, Maurizio Meschino, Uwe Schleth, Ezra Suleiman, Daniel Tarschys, and Theo van der Tak.

A large number of people helped to interview the elites, code and analyze the data, or revise drafts of the manuscript. We list them alphabetically because we are indebted to them all: Iris Aberbach, Pauline Aberbach, Iride Amadio, Arlene Apfel, Paul Allen Beck, Jacqueline Bissery, Claude Blanquet, Rossana Brichetti, Eleanor Brown, June Brown, Marie-Elisabeth de Bussy, Gabriella Carosio, Franco Cazzola, Fanny Colonomos, Cindy Currens, Linda Kroll Davoli, Bernd Dirks, Carla Dugo, John Echols, Bryan Ford, Lucy Fox, Alice Fram, Robert Friedrich, Gerald Gaus, Aulo Gonano, William T. Gormley, Jr., Anne-Mieke Halbrook, Khondaker E. Haque, Kai Hildebrandt, Raymond Hinnebusch, Judith Jackson, M. J. Jonkers, Daniel Kalcevik, Jack Katosh, Celinda Lake, Françoise de La Serre, Robert Leonardi, Claes Linde, Gunnar Lönnqvist, Lee Luskin, Robert Luskin, Antonio Maccanico, Bill McGee, Antje McNaughton, Anders Mellbourn, Roy Meyers, Elena Milillo, Harris Miller, Jeanne Moore, Janet Morgan, Raffaella Nanetti, Jeffery Nurre, Arnold Paradise, Yolande Parris, Christine Penitzka, Pamela Poulter, Robert Rickards, David Roger, Richard Rose, Wendy Roth, Alberta Sbragia, Marie-France Seylaz, W. J. Soullié, Kendall Stanley, Jean Thiel, Horst Tiefenbach, S. Van Esterik, Carl Van Horn, G. Van Tign, Carla Venditti, and A. Wolterbeek.

Some groups actually owe *us* thanks, and we speak for them here. Without us the telephone company, the airlines, and numerous duplicating firms would all be much the poorer.

It is customary to close with thanks to the authors' spouses and children; in our case, we truly owe them an extraordinary debt. For thirteen years they put up with us as we traveled hither and yon preoccupied with the study. They showed great forbearance when we gathered at one home or another for our periodic meetings, spreading papers everywhere and generally disrupting the household we had invaded. They were patient when we tied up the phone for hours, debating single words and large themes with equal passion. Their good humor and gentle reminders helped us to complete this project as good friends. On publication day they will wear their "I Survived the Comparative Elites Project" buttons with the special understanding of veterans of team research.

J.D.A.

R.D.P.

B.A.R.

# Contents

Bureaucrats and Politicians
in
Western Democracies

# Introduction

## 1

In the tumultuous Munich winter of 1918, toward the end of his notable career as a social theorist, Max Weber was asked by his students to speak on the political choices facing postwar Germany. Before commenting on the issues of the day, he set out to describe two powerful currents of history that ran beneath the flickering surface of events. Contemporary politics, Weber claimed, was being shaped, first, by the emergence of modern bureaucracy—most especially the growing state apparatus, increasingly led by technically trained, professional career administrators. The second trend Weber saw, to some extent oblique to the first, was the rise of a new class of professional politicians, their influence based not on inherited social status, but rather on mass political parties claiming the membership and the suffrage of millions of ordinary citizens. Weber's own monarchical and individualistic sympathies caused him to view both trends with some distaste and distrust, but he was convinced that inexorable historical tendencies would make this the century of the professional party politician and of the professional state bureaucrat.[1]

Looking back more than a half-century later, we can see that Weber's insights were remarkably prescient. In the advanced nations of the West, the century from 1870 to 1970 saw innumerable social and political changes, but in terms of the policymaking process the most significant of these has been precisely the steadily growing power of professional party politicians and of permanent civil servants. These twin trends have unfolded at different rates and in somewhat different phases in the several

*1*

countries of Europe and North America, but in broad outline the patterns are visible everywhere.

On the political side, the parliaments and cabinets of mid-Victorian Europe were still largely the preserves of aristocrats and local gentry, amateurs who (as Weber said) lived for politics, but not from politics. A century later a few such figures can still be found in the European political elites, but they are now vastly outnumbered by new men and women of power, risen mostly from middle-class (and occasionally working-class) backgrounds, well-educated, committed to a lifetime in politics, dependent on the electoral fortunes of their particular party and on their own success in playing the game of party politics. In the career lines of politicians, party and legislative ladders have increasingly merged. If the first half of the period (1870 to 1920) saw the capture of European parliaments by parties, in the sense that access to legislative (and hence cabinet) leadership became controlled by parties, the half-century after 1920 saw a complementary "parliamentarization" of party leadership.[2]

The change in the character and power of civil servants over these hundred years is even more striking. The scope of the liberal state of 1870 was still relatively small, and the tasks of civil servants were still largely clerical. Policy decisions could reasonably be taken by the leisured amateurs around the cabinet table, and the highest posts in the civil service were filled as often by patronage appointments as by competitive examination. By 1970 the state had expanded fantastically in both size and task. Real total public expenditure had increased twentyfold to thirtyfold in ten decades. The gross national product was also growing, to be sure, but the share spent by the state was rising several times faster. The inevitable concomitant was an explosion in the size of the government bureaucracy. In 1870 the staff of the British civil service, for example, totaled just over 50,000 men and women. By 1970 this figure had risen to nearly 800,000. The one permanent growth industry of the modern world, it seems, is the state.

The tasks of the bureaucracy increased in complexity as well. By 1970 civil servants throughout the West were deciding how to restructure the steel industry, how to design an actuarially sound pension scheme, where to locate airports, how to brake inflation, and a thousand other such issues. Throughout this century the tendency toward governmental omnicompetence has accelerated virtually everywhere in the West. In tiny Denmark, for example, the annual output of pages of laws and regulations increased about tenfold from 1911 to 1971, and in the United States the size of the *Federal Register* (the official publication of administrative regulations) quadrupled in barely a decade, from 1966 to 1975.[3] To accommodate these trends, Western civil services have become increasingly specialized, highly professionalized, and unquestionably powerful—a cadre of experts in the running of the modern state.

Weber's thesis—part chronicle and part prophecy—thus has been strikingly confirmed: at the levers of power in the modern state stand these two uncertain partners, the elected party politician and the professional state bureaucrat. Indeed, so familiar is this pattern that some effort is required to recognize that in historical terms it is far from "normal." Outside nineteenth- and twentieth-century Europe and North America, leadership in most political systems has not reflected this division of labor between elected politicians and career bureaucrats. "Aylmer in his study of Stuart administration points out that as late as the reign of Charles I there were not even rudimentary distinctions between politicians and administrators; 'policy in the modern sense scarcely existed.' "[4] Similarly, although most countries of the Third World today have organizations labeled "legislatures," "parties," and "bureaucracies," in few of these systems is power actually divided between elected politicians and career administrators. In fact, institutionalization of mass-based parties and of professionally staffed bureaucracies is widely taken to be the hallmark of a modern political system. The problematic relationship between these two institutions is perhaps the distinctive puzzle of the contemporary state, reflecting as it does the clash between the dual and conflicting imperatives of technical effectiveness and democratic responsiveness.[5]

On no single dilemma has more ink been spilled by political scientists in the last quarter-century than on the relative power and roles of the bureaucracy, on the one hand, and of representative institutions, such as parties and legislatures, on the other. Much of the debate quite appropriately has stressed normative issues, while the empirical contributions have emphasized institutional analysis.[6] Our focus in what follows is complementary, but different; for we want to ask not about bureaucratic and political institutions, but about bureaucrats and politicians as policymakers. How are they different? Indeed, *are* they different? Do they come from different backgrounds? Have they different priorities? Do they consider different criteria when making decisions? Do they regard public affairs and the process of policymaking differently? Have they different world views? What do these differences, if any, imply for their relationships and for their performance as policymakers? What difference would it make if all important government decisions were made by civil servants instead of by party politicians, or vice versa?

We fully recognize that answers to such questions turn in part on institutional and structural issues—on the organizational frameworks within which bureaucrats and politicians act, struggle, calculate, seek advantage and advancement. But we seek to move the discussion forward by examining bureaucrats and politicians as individual policymakers, drawing on national surveys of elected politicians and senior civil servants in seven advanced countries: Britain, France, Germany, Italy, the Netherlands, Sweden, and the United States. Before describing our methods of inquiry in detail, let us first—as a way of orienting our inquiry—consider several possible images of the relationship between politicians and bureaucrats.

## Image I: Policy/Administration

The earliest theory about the relationship between politicians and bureaucrats was in many ways the simplest: politicians make policy; civil servants administer. Politicians make decisions; bureaucrats merely implement them.

On the Continent, this traditional identification of politics and policy (in contradistinction to administration) is embodied in language itself (*politique, Politik, politica*). In the United States, an early generation of progressive reformers emphasized the sharp distinction between the spheres of politics and administration. Woodrow Wilson, for example, wrote:

> Administration lies outside the proper sphere of politics. Administrative questions are not political questions . . . The field of administration is a field of business. It is removed from the hurry and strife of politics . . . It is a part of political life only as the methods of the counting-house are a part of the life of society; only as machinery is part of the manufactured product.[7]

Frank Goodnow spoke for the dominant view at the turn of this century, arguing that the functions of the state are naturally divided into the expression of the public will (politics) and the execution of that will (administration),[8] and Luther Gulick added that these functions must be kept institutionally separate: "We are faced by two heterogeneous functions, 'politics' and 'administration,' the combination of which cannot be undertaken within the structure of the administration without producing inefficiency."[9]

The official norm in every state is that civil servants obediently serve their political "masters."[10] This image of the division of labor between politicians and bureaucrats exalts the glittering authority of the former and cloaks the role of the latter in gray robes of anonymous neutrality. It is congenial for both figures, and not surprisingly it remains a prominent part of the mythology of practitioners, particularly in Europe. As B. Guy Peters has noted, "For administrators, this presumed separation of administration and politics allows them to engage in politics without the bother of being held accountable politically for the outcomes of their actions, [and] without the interference of political actors who might otherwise make demands upon them for the modification of those policies . . . The separation of politics and administration also allows a certain latitude to politicians . . . [permitting] many of the difficult decisions of modern government to be made by individuals who will not have to face the public at a subsequent election."[11] In fact, this image does reflect the formal contrast between what happens on the floor of parliament, as major issues are debated and "decided," and what happens instead in bureaucratic warrens, as routine applications for permits and pensions are processed.

Weber himself thought that what we have termed Image I was the ideal relationship between politicians and administrators, but he recognized that it was an improbable one, for the distinction between discretionary (political) and nondiscretionary (administrative) decisions is ultimately untenable. "Every problem, no matter how technical it might seem, can assume political significance and its solution can be decisively influenced by political considerations."[12] The distinction between policy and administration, between deciding and implementing, resembles the fabled Cheshire cat—upon examination, its substance fades, leaving only a mocking smirk.[13]

Moreover, even if civil servants wanted merely to follow orders—and there is some evidence that many honestly do—that is a practical impossibility. Politicians lack the expertise, the information, and even the time to decide all the thousands of policy questions that face a modern government each year. As one frustrated British politician has written, "Ministers may bring with them broad ideas of how future policy should develop. But in the transformation of policy goals into realistic plans, in the execution of those plans, and still more, in policy responses to new and unexpected developments, Ministers are largely, if not wholly, dependent on their official [civil service] advisers."[14] And where bureaucrats are less self-effacing than in Britain, their propensity to work at cross-purposes from party politicians is greater still. Weber saw the point very clearly: "Under normal conditions, the power position of a fully developed bureaucracy is always overtowering. The 'political master' finds himself in the position of a 'dilettante' who stands opposite the 'expert' facing the trained official who stands within the management of administration."[15]

In short, Image I assumes a degree of hierarchy of authority, of simplicity of decision, and of effective political supremacy that now seems unrealistic to students of modern government. Discretion, not merely for deciding individual cases, but for crafting the content of most legislation, has passed from the legislature to the executive. In most countries (though not in the United States) initiation of major bills is effectively a monopoly of the executive, and within the executive branch elected politicians are everywhere outnumbered and outlasted by career civil servants.[16] Skilled and experienced bureaucrats have gained a predominant influence over the evolution of the agenda for decision. "As a result," some even claim, "bureaucratic politics rather than party politics has become the dominant theater of decision in the modern state."[17] Whether or not this extreme view is accurate, even the most conventionally minded participants in the process admit that bureaucrats today do more than merely implement decisions taken elsewhere. Only 1 percent of the senior civil servants we interviewed and only 15 percent of the members of parliament agreed unreservedly with the view that "a senior civil servant should limit his activity to the precise application of the law."[18] He should not, because as a practical matter, he cannot. At least at the more senior levels of government, Image I is not an adequate account of the division of labor between politicians and bureaucrats.

## Image II: Facts/Interests

This second image assumes that *both* politicians and civil servants participate in making policy, but that they make distinctive contributions. Civil servants bring facts and knowledge; politicians, interests and values. Civil servants bring neutral expertise—will it work?—while politicians bring political sensitivity—will it fly? Civil servants thus emphasize the technical efficacy of policy, while politicians emphasize its responsiveness to relevant constituencies.

The logic behind this image has been most clearly articulated by Herbert Simon. He suggests that we regard "the process of human choice as a process of 'drawing conclusions from premises.' It is therefore the *premise* (and a large number of these are combined in every decision) rather than the whole *decision* that serves as the smallest unit of analysis." Arguing that the premises involved in policymaking can be classified as either factual (descriptive) or evaluative (preferential), he proposes that we seek "procedural devices permitting a more effective separation of the factual and ethical elements in decisions," and "a more effective division of labor between the policy-forming and administrative agencies." In this division of labor administrators provide expertise, while "democratic institutions [composed of elected politicians] find their principal justification as a procedure for the validation of value judgments."[19]

Image II finds expression in contrasts between "political rationality" and "administrative rationality." Fritz Morstein Marx, for example, observed that

> administrative rationality often has little appeal to the political mind, whether in the executive branch or in the legislative body. The political decision-maker, bent upon his aims, is often impatient with dispassionate reasoning, except in small doses. He does not like to face the dreadful array of pertinent facts, especially when he is cast in the role of the special pleader ... Exceptional political maturity is required for public opinion and party leaders to welcome the role of the bureaucracy in putting proposed policy to the acid test of cause-and-effect relationships.

The role of bureaucratic expertise, as Morstein Marx saw it, is to supplement the "unrestrained interaction of political forces" and the "crude test of political influence" as a basis for public policy.[20] Karl Mannheim put a more critical twist on the same fundamental distinction in his passing, but insightful, observation that "the fundamental tendency of all bureaucratic thought is to turn all problems of politics into problems of administration."[21] To this others have replied (referring to politicians' concerns with patronage, logrolling, and special interests) that the fundamental tendency of political thought is to turn problems of administration into problems of politics.

Image II is related to typologies of policymakers in nondemocratic states too, as in the common distinction in Communist regimes between "reds" and "experts." But in the case of democracies, Image II assigns to politicians the special task of articulating and balancing and mediating diverse claims and divergent interests, of formulating and reformulating and resolving social conflicts. As expressed in Image II, the work of politicians reflects a conception of the public interest based on the rights of contending interests to put forth their demands, whereas the work of civil servants entails a holistic conception of the public interest based on objectively fixed standards and informed judgment.[22] In this theory, while bureaucrats should be responsive to political direction, their responsiveness

> is not intended to make the bureaucracy a partisan fighter for politically defined policy. Of course, insofar as government functions as the coordinator of interests in accordance with its program, it is bound to favor certain interests and to show itself indifferent or hostile toward others. That is a matter of the political course and properly within the responsibility of the government in power . . . For itself, however, the bureaucracy is not entitled to acknowledge or even to cultivate friends and foes among the organized interests. If it did, it could not be impartial. It must seek to advance the general interest and to guard its neutrality toward the special interests.[23]

As later chapters will show, Image II finds some resonance in our empirical evidence, including in particular our findings about the distinctive sorts of criteria that politicians and bureaucrats bring to bear on discussions of public issues. However, a number of students of government and policymaking have adduced evidence in recent years that seriously calls into question the accuracy of this image as a comprehensive account of the division of labor between bureaucrats and politicians. On the one hand, the increasing educational standards and professionalization of politicians reduces the plausibility of Image II's suggestion that bureaucrats monopolize expertise.[24] More importantly, numerous studies have called attention to the role of bureaucratic agencies in mobilizing and mediating sectoral interests.

"In the quest for power," writes Francis E. Rourke, "every executive agency is heavily dependent upon its skill at cultivating public support. The administrator, like the politician, must nurse his constituency to ensure his own survival, and the task of creating a continuing fund of public support is an indispensable part of bureaucratic statecraft."[25] Quite apart from these perhaps self-serving efforts of bureaucratic entrepreneurs, contemporary administrators, some have argued, are inevitably thrust into the role of interest management. Legislators unable to reach consensus on general policy often effectively delegate the reconciliation of conflicting interests to administrative agencies—for example, in the bland charge to grant licenses "in the public interest." As Rourke has said, "bureaucratic policy making in domestic areas commonly represents a reconciliation of conflicting group interests as much as it does the application of expertise toward the solution of particular problems."[26] As early as 1936, Pendleton Herring claimed that "the solution of the liberal democratic state must lie in establishing a working relationship between the bureaucrats and the special interests—a relationship that will enable the former to carry out the purpose of the state and the latter to realize their own ends."[27] Some American scholars have traced this more "political" function of bureaucrats to peculiar features of American national politics, such as the fragmentation of authority,[28] and we shall return to this theme of American exceptionalism later. But it is relevant here to note that observers of the European scene have described a comparable phenomenon. Renate Mayntz and Fritz Scharpf, referring to policymaking in Germany, for example, claim that "it is the ministries and not parliament or the political parties to which organized interests turn first, where they argue their demands in detail, and to whom they present information in support of their claims."[29] In responding to these representations, European bureaucrats are hardly engaged in the neutral exercise of antiseptic expertise. James B. Christoph has said of the British case, "While part of the job of civil servants is to analyze, verify, and cost the claims of such groups, and forward them to higher centers of decision, it would be unnatural if officials did not identify in some way with the interests of their clienteles, and within the overall framework of current government policy advance claims finding favor in the department."[30] To accommodate such observations, we need to formulate yet a third account of the relationship between politicians and bureaucrats.

## Image III: Energy/Equilibrium

According to Image III, *both* bureaucrats and politicians engage in policymaking, and *both* are concerned with politics. The real distinction between them is this: whereas politicians articulate broad, diffuse interests of unorganized individuals, bureaucrats mediate narrow, focused interests of organized clienteles. In this interpretation of the division of labor, politicians are passionate, partisan, idealistic, even ideological; bureaucrats are, by contrast, prudent, centrist, practical, pragmatic. Politicians seek publicity, raise innovative issues, and are energizing to the policy system, whereas bureaucrats prefer the back room, manage incremental adjustments, and provide policy equilibrium (per Webster's, "a state of balance between opposing forces or actions"). Let us explore this image in more detail.

Reflecting on British policymaking, Richard Rose has noted: "In theory, ministers are meant to communicate the ends of policy to civil servants, who then devise administrative means to carry out the wishes of their minister. In this formulation, the roles of politician and civil servant are separate and complementary. In practice, policymaking usually develops dialectically; both politicians and civil servants review political and administrative implications of a major policy."[31] For this reason sensitivity to political interests is a necessary part of the job of a senior civil servant. But the interests to which civil servants are sensitive are generally quite focused, for their world is mostly defined by departmental boundaries, and thus the interests of the department's organized clientele bulk particularly large. As a Canadian civil servant has observed bluntly, "That's part of the department's job, to advocate the case of the groups it works with."[32]

The role of a civil servant brings him into frequent contact with his department's clientele. The following description of British civil servants could easily be applied to their counterparts in other countries: "[In] both the pre- and post-legislative stages civil servants are in steady contact with those pressure groups likely to be affected by proposed changes—obtaining technical information on the anticipated effects of new rules, bargaining from the knowledge of what is apt to be their minister's final position, getting consent in advance whenever possible, satisfying the unwritten British requirement that consultation with interests precede government action, testing for their minister the temperature of the political water about to be stirred up."[33] In many countries this process of consultation has spawned hundreds of specialized consultative committees dominated by civil servants and private members often nominated by civil servants. On these committees party politicians are most notable by their relative absence. Through such channels civil servants and interest groups enter into a symbiotic relationship.[34] From it emerges what in Britain is termed the "Whitehall consensus," in which it becomes quite unclear whether the primary initiative comes from the bureaucrats or the interest groups.

In sum, in Image III the role of civil servants is one of registering the resultant of the parallelogram of organized political forces. It is important to note three limitations on this administrative process of interest aggregation. First, unorganized interests are largely ignored. As Mayntz and Scharpf remark about the German case, for example: "Because of their limited work capacity, the federal departments restrict their search for relevant situational information to contacts with the major organized interests. This means that they can [not] and do not systematically inquire into the situation and wishes of socioeconomic groups which are not organized and have a low potential of engaging in conflict with the administration, or of creating political difficulties."[35] Politicians, by contrast, have some incentive to articulate unorganized interests in their unending search for novel and attractive electoral appeals. Samuel Huntington has noted, in the case of the United States, "Congress's position as the representative of unorganized interests of individuals."[36] In Europe, where party strength reduces the need for individual politicians to engage in retail coalition building, their capacity for attending to broader, mass-based interests is greater still.

The second limitation on interest aggregation by bureaucrats is that typically they do not bridge the divisions between functional sectors. Damgaard's description of administrative policymaking in Denmark is typical: "Most ministries have well-organized clientele, such as farmers, workers, businessmen, students, teachers, or retired people. The overall political function involves making decisions affecting those groups' diverse interests. In carrying out this function, politicians get only a little help from their civil servants because the latter usually identify with a certain section of society or, at least, do not want any trouble with the groups in question . . . Therefore, what we actually find is not rational policymaking, but 'segmented incrementalism' in terms of the allocation of resources and services."[37] Civil servants necessarily are tuned to a rather narrow band of the spectrum of political interests, whereas politicians receive and transmit over a somewhat broader band. Mediating among interests within a single sector is largely the responsibility of bureaucrats, but cross-sector aggregation of interests—farmers and consumers or labor unions and management—is typically the province of politicians.

The third distinctive limitation of administrative interest aggregation is that bureaucrats typically take the existing parallelogram of political forces as a given, whereas politicians can and often do relax that constraint. The more extensive political contacts and skills of the politician enable him or her to mobilize a wider range of potentially destabilizing political forces. Moreover, political ideals and ideologies can provide politicians with a point of critical leverage beyond the existing correlation of forces—a sense of how society might be organized differently, some notion of how to get there, and an emotional commitment that is sometimes infectious.

Indeed, one striking difference that many observers have noted between politicians and bureaucrats is one of temperament. Politicians—at least many of them—have ideals and partisan passions in a degree quite alien to most civil servants. For instance, more than twice as many British MPs, as contrasted with their civil service compatriots, agree unreservedly with the view that "only when a person devotes himself to an ideal or cause does life become meaningful."[38] One civil servant has written: "There is no need for the administrator to be a man of ideas. His distinguishing quality should be rather a certain freedom from ideas. The idealism and the most vicious appetites of the populace are equal before him."[39]

Prudence, practicality, moderation, and avoidance of risk are the preferred traits of a civil servant; only a politician could have termed extremism a virtue and moderation a vice. The difference in temperament can be traced in large part to career channeling. "The merit bureaucracy is not the place for those who want . . . to rise fast, to venture far, or to stand on their own."[40] On the other hand, electoral and party politics reward one who will dare greatly and become identified with larger passions and ideals, "a tribune of the people," as Aneurin Bevan said, "coming to make his voice heard in the seats of power."[41] Short-run political feasibility is a much greater constraint for the bureaucratic mind than for this breed of politician.

Both politicians and bureaucrats, in Image III, need political skills, but not the same political skills. They may be of the same genus, but they are not the same species. The natural habitat of the politician is the public podium, whereas the bureaucrat is found seated at a committee table. Christoph's observation about Britain applies more widely: "The committee is the chief instrument of government . . . Civil servants lubricate this process in their own special way: they are renowned as masters of the arts of committeemanship, of achieving consensus whenever possible through compromise behind closed doors."[42]

A British civil servant summarizes his criterion for political success (and by implicit contrast, the criterion that politicians would use instead): "The administrator steers what may appear to be a craven course among the various pressures of public and still more of semi-public opinion and the opinion of groups, and his concern is to come off with victory, not in the sense that his opinion prevails, for he has no right to one, but in the sense that at the end he is still upright, and the forces around him have achieved a momentary balance."[43]

How do these differences between politicians and bureaucrats, as embodied in Image III, affect their performances as policymakers? In the first place, the two groups are likely to place somewhat different issues on the public agenda, for issues arise for them in somewhat different ways. As Mayntz and Scharpf report from their study of policymaking in the German bureaucracy, "the impulses for initiatives originating in the [administrative] section come from the observation of developments in the field, from contact with the clientele, or from the feedback produced by presently operating programs."[44] Politicians, on the other hand, have political antennae that are sensitive to more diffuse sorts of public discontent. Moreover, their more fully developed partisan ideologies mean that their attention is apt to be aroused by discrepancies between social realities and political ideals. They are more likely than bureaucrats to nominate for the public agenda problems that are highlighted by philosophical principles, such as equality or liberty, even though those problems lie beyond the bounds of the current social consensus. Though bureaucrats are in some senses political, they could hardly have produced the neoconservative policies of Britain's prime minister Margaret Thatcher, nor would they have come up with the populist proposals of the Labour radical Anthony Wedgwood Benn. As Richard Rose has asserted, "The distinctive claim of parties is to review questions of public choice in the light of more general values and principles."[45]

Inherent in administrative policymaking as described by Image III is a sense of the near inevitability of the status quo, likely produced more by procedural or temperamental conservatism than by conservative political ideology. A close observer of British policymakers reports that "in the absence of contrary instructions from their political masters, officials normally frame policy programs which fit within the context of the existing objectives pursued by their department. Innovation and radical change are not commonly the product of proposals generated within the Civil Service."[46] This special sensitivity of bureaucrats to precedent and continuity is hardly peculiar to Britain. A study of high-level civil servants in Germany, for example, concludes that policymaking for them "means overwhelmingly to improve on existing policy rather than starting something entirely new."[47]

It is not merely a preference for the quiet life that biases administrative decision making against radical change. Because of their close interaction with relevant interests and their aversion to public controversy, civil servants are particularly prone to engage in anticipatory conflict management, seeking consensus among the relevant participants before a proposal is actually put forward. "This means in effect that the operative units of the bureaucracy will minimize the conflict potential of their projects by adjusting their content to the opposition they meet or anticipate. More often than not, the result of such adjustments is a reactive and incremental rather than active policy."[48] Administrative policymaking is thus a kind of *liberum veto* group politics, in which strenuous objections from any quarter are likely to be accepted.[49]

> Bureaucrats may, from a sense of professionalism and public spirit, strive to achieve the public interest. But if they are left to live with organized groups without political supervision, they may find it impractical, politically dangerous, and finally unnecessary and uncivil to define the public interest in ways offensive to the most active, powerful, even cooperative participants.[50]

Richard Rose has aptly termed this type of politics "government by directionless consensus . . . In the absence of a forceful partisan initiative, providing both protection and direction, the simplest course of action is for administrators to seek out the lowest common denominator of opinions among affected interests . . . The process of building consensus becomes the end toward which government works."[51] Of course, the consensus of opinion may change, allowing policy to follow in its train, but lacking partisan ideologies or political contacts outside the narrow range of organized interests, bureaucrats are unlikely themselves to stimulate this sort of change. Because the pattern of "consultation" is designed to provide stability for the existing equilibrium among the affected interests, the result is more likely to be what Beer has termed "pluralistic stagnation" and what others have labeled "liberal corporatism."[52]

It would, of course, be a mistake to assume that politicians are wholly immune to this type of policymaking. But Image III asserts that broader, longer-range, more controversial issues are likely to be addressed, if at all, only by politicians. This is particularly true of issues that involve some redistribution in the underlying social allocation of power. For example, Gerhard Lehmbruch has contrasted the patterns of German policymaking on cartel legislation, which involved marginal adjustments within the business sector, and on codetermination, which involved a fundamental clash between the interests of labor and management. In the former case, "the essential bargaining took place between the administration and business representatives and largely outside the party system," while in the latter case, "it was no longer the administration that served as the 'turntable,' but rather the party system." Lehmbruch summarizes:

On the one hand, if there exists a high level of conflict (particularly on "redistributive" issues), it is probable that the party system possesses a greater capacity for consensus-building, since its flexibility is greater and thresholds of consensus are lower. To put it the other way around, consensus-building and problem-solving in a corporatist subsystem of interest representation depend on a rather low level of conflict intensity because of the high threshold imposed by (de facto or de jure) unanimity rules which are essential to its functioning.[53]

For these reasons, Image III asserts, the policymaking influence of civil servants tends to diminish or even vanish at moments of acute social crisis or major reforms. Bernard Gournay notes: "The high administration seems to have had no major or direct influence on the outcome of political crises in France during the last decades."[54] Mayntz and Scharpf report from Germany that

policy initiatives which are long-range in time perspective, of broad scope, and deal with controversial questions, are usually of central origin. If one traces the genesis of those policy decisions made in the past few years which possess these characteristics of an active policy, they are found to originate quite often within the political executive (cabinet) or parliament.[55]

Mattei Dogan concludes that

most major reforms, some of a revolutionary nature, introduced throughout liberated Europe just after the war, were neither inspired nor formulated by the high administration, even though there were a few important exceptions such as the Beveridge plan for British social security. The directing staffs of political parties were, at that time, the principal actors and enactors.[56]

The role of policy innovator and energizer might seem to be peculiarly cast for left-wing politicians. Richard Crossman, a leading Labour party minister, argued for example that "if a politician enters Whitehall without a manifesto, without a programme, he is lost; and they [the civil service] will tell him what to do, although the only point of his being there is to be a catalytic irritant in the departments."[57] But a strikingly similar analysis was offered by one of his Conservative opponents: "The minister should offer philosophical, intellectual leadership . . . Only ministers can make major changes; proposals generated by civil servants are bound to put safety first."[58] Canadian prime minister Pierre Trudeau put the matter with characteristic directness: "We aren't here just to manage departments; we want to see change."[59]

It is occasionally supposed that in some Continental cases, such as France, administrators can provide this sort of impetus for major reform. But after a careful review, Alfred Diamant concluded: "The French experience would indicate that, in fact, during periods of political indecision the *grand corps* do not really govern the country, they simply continue routine operations, maintain the status quo, and protect their own interests. It would seem, particularly from the experience of the Fourth Republic, that under then prevailing conditions the administration could carry on from day to day, but it could not carry through radical innovations. There was no lack of ideas, plans, proposals, but in the absence of a determined political will these plans remained dormant."[60] This, then, is the division of labor between politicians and bureaucrats as portrayed in Image III. We shall see that in certain important respects it is consistent with the evidence from our surveys.

### Image IV: The Pure Hybrid

It will not have escaped the attentive reader that our first three images suggest a progressively greater degree of overlap between the roles of bureaucrat and politician, nor that the intellectual origins of the three conceptions are progressively more recent. Image I, which offers the starkest differentiation, emerged in the last half of the nineteenth century, as the Weberian distinction between professional bureaucrats and party politicians was itself crystallizing. Image II, which admits a certain policymaking role for civil servants, can be roughly dated to the first half of the twentieth century, whereas Image III, which concedes to bureaucrats a rather more "political" role, has been extracted primarily from writings of the last several decades. Assuming a rough, if lagged, correspondence between government realities and scholarly interpretations, this progression is at least consistent with the notion that in behavioral terms the two roles have been converging—perhaps reflecting, as some have argued, a "politicization" of the bureaucracy and a "bureaucratization" of politics.[61] Carrying this notion to its logical conclusion, Image IV suggests speculatively that the last quarter of this century is witnessing the virtual disappearance of the Weberian distinction between the roles of politician and bureaucrat, producing what we might label a "pure hybrid."

To be sure, ever since the appearance of cabinets responsible to parliaments (or presidents), ministers have occupied a Janus-like role at the top of departments, facing simultaneously inward as administrators and outward as political leaders, though perhaps giving special attention to one or the other facet of their complex role. But the trend that we are here addressing extends well beyond the long-established dualistic position of the minister.

The organizational format for this trend varies from country to country. In some systems such as France and Japan, a key factor is the high rate of personnel circulation between the political and administrative career ladders. An increasingly common pattern in the Fifth Republic, for example, has been for a bright and ambitious civil servant to enter a ministerial *cabinet,* where his political skills are honed, followed some years later by a move into the political elite (typically, though not always, in the ranks of the ruling party).[62] One such figure—President Giscard—has, of course, reached the very pinnacle of the French political system. A roughly similar syndrome has characterized career patterns in postwar Japan.[63]

In Britain and Germany, harbingers of the hybrid figure may be found in the introduction of politically sympathetic "outsiders" or "irregulars" into positions once reserved for career civil servants. In 1964 Harold Wilson imported into the central administration a small but potentially significant number of partisan appointees who were neither career civil servants nor MPs. The government of Edward Heath that followed created the post of "political secretary" to individual ministers and introduced a Central Policy Review Staff, peopled by numbers of what Americans would term "in-and-outers." None of these experiments were judged wholly successful by their sponsors, but all are symptomatic of a need felt by both parties for a type of official who combines substantive expertise with political commitment.[64]

In the German case, active party membership among senior civil servants has long been common, as has the presence of a substantial number of ex-bureaucrats in the Bundestag. A further step was taken by Willy Brandt's government after 1969, when it brought into the top layers of the Socialist-Liberal administration a sizable number of *Aussenseiter,* experts with long-standing ties to one of the coalition parties. Mayntz and Scharpf maintain that the function of such figures

> can be defined as the integration of politics with administration. More exactly, the divisional leaders have to articulate two sets of decision criteria with each other: those of technical knowledge and

substantive expertise with those of political strategy . . . To be able to perform this integrating function, divisional leaders must be able to speak the language of the politician as well as of the bureaucrat, they must be men of two worlds as it were . . . This is in fact asking too much of many career civil servants and gives a distinct advantage to the external recruit with an unusual career, the marginal type with multiple reference groups—provided he is able to develop a second identity as a bureaucrat.[65]

In a number of countries the appearance of pure hybrids has been associated with an expansion of key central agencies, such as the cabinet office, the chancellery, and the White House staff, which have absorbed increasing numbers of political administrators in virtually every country of the West over the last decade. The best study of these "superbureaucrats" is the research of Colin Campbell and George Szablowski, initially in Canada and now being extended to Britain, the United States, and Switzerland. In the Canadian case, the staff members of these central agencies differ from more traditional civil servants in the broader, more flexible authority they enjoy; in their greater social representativeness and substantive innovativeness; and in their recognition of the legitimacy of politics—not merely in the sense of responsiveness to clientele interests, but in the broader sense that Image III ascribes to politicians alone. One intriguing organizational sign of the merging of the roles of politician and bureaucrat in Canada is the growing custom of ministers' delegating their attendance at cabinet committee meetings to their civil service aides.[66]

Still another interesting variation on this theme is the distinction within the Swedish central government between "ministries," small policymaking staffs working directly with cabinet ministers, and "administrative boards," much larger agencies charged with the day-to-day implementation of existing policies. Evidence from our own survey in Sweden verifies that ministry officials are significantly more "political" in background and outlook than their counterparts on the administrative boards.[67]

The line between political and administrative leadership has been traditionally more blurred in the United States than in Europe. Hugh Heclo's study of executive politics in Washington makes it clear that this blurring has accelerated in recent years. "If anything, the position of higher civil servants and the lines between political and career appointments have become even more complex and uncertain. 'In my mind,' said an intimate White House aide of a former President, 'the whole political-bureaucracy thing is all mixed up. I don't have a strong sense of where the line's drawn.' "[68]

Like us, Heclo finds that career officials hold nominally political positions, and conversely, that there is political influence over appointments to nominally civil service slots. "Whatever the intricacies of body counts in the personnel system, the major point is that somewhere in this smudgy zone between top presidential appointees and the several thousand officials below them, the vital interface of political administration occurs."[69] Heclo concludes:

> Political appointments to positions of executive leadership (once the domain of party men) have taken on more of the enlarged, specialized, and layered characteristics of the bureaucracy. Old-fashioned patronage influences in the civil service have been augmented by increased attention not only to controlling the bureaucracy but to identifying the higher civil service with the particular policies and purposes of the White House.[70]

In short: the bureaucratization of politics and the politicization of bureaucracy.

At the opposite end of Pennsylvania Avenue, further evidence for the emergence of our pure hybrid type could doubtless be found in the exploding profusion of congressional staffers, bound more tightly to their political patrons than most political executives, but increasingly expert and involved in substantive policymaking. The expansion of legislative staffs in this country and (to a much smaller degree) elsewhere has been justified as a way of enabling politicians to counterbalance the growing influence of the permanent executive. Some keen observers fear, however, that the real danger may lie in the subordination of political judgment in both branches of government to the overriding perspective of expertise.[71] In any event, the trend seems consistent with our tentative hypothesis about the convergence of the roles of bureaucrat and politician.

If this sort of convergence is indeed under way, it may mark the demise of what we may call the Weberian epoch of modern government, the analytic construct from which our study began. On the other hand, these conjectures remain speculative. Throughout the industrialized democracies today most policymakers still fall rather naturally into one or the other of our two basic categories—politicians and bureaucrats. While straining for a glimpse of the future, we should not mistake it for the present.

Precisely because most of the figures that we have tentatively classified as pure hybrids are still relatively rare in most countries, and are typically found in novel niches such as cabinet offices, ministerial *cabinets,* and legislative staffs, our own surveys of more conventionally defined senior civil servants and parliamentary politicians are not aptly designed to test the hypotheses embodied in Image IV.[72] Nevertheless, recognition of this hypothetical merger of the roles of bureaucrat and politician can sensitize us to possible convergences in the backgrounds, outlooks, and behavior of the groups we have surveyed.

We have carefully chosen to refer to four "images" of the relationship between bureaucrats and politicians, rather than "models" or "theories." We do *not* propose to "test" these images in any rigorous way, rejecting some and perhaps confirming one or another. Rather, we intend to use these four interpretations of the division of labor between politicians and bureaucrats as searchlights for illuminating empirical patterns in our data. Our basic question, to repeat, is this: in what ways are bureaucrats and politicians, as policymakers, similar and in what ways are they different?

We stress our interest in bureaucrats and politicians *as policymakers,* because each group also engages in activities that are only indirectly related to their joint concern with policy. Bureaucrats, for example, often have substantial responsibilities for managing the administrative machinery of government and for routine implementation of past decisions. They may spend much of their time letting contracts, hiring subordinates, redrawing organization charts, writing regulations, and so on. On the other hand, politicians spend much of their energies on electoral and party affairs—mending fences, mapping tactics, meeting the media, and so on. Despite the importance of such entries in the daily agendas of politicians and bureaucrats, these activities usually fall clearly into the province of one group or the other. We have chosen to concentrate instead on shared functions and "contested territory," that is, on those policymaking activities that involve both groups, at least potentially. We shall explore the more specialized or distinctive features of each role only insofar as those activities affect each group's policymaking behavior. We also emphasize that our respondents occupy senior positions in their national policymaking communities, for as we noted earlier, the appropriateness of one or another of the four images is quite likely to vary from level to level within the governmental apparatus. In general, we conjecture that Image I and perhaps Image II are particularly appropriate at lower levels in the government hierarchy, whereas Image III and perhaps Image IV are more accurate at higher levels.

Because our study design and to some extent our language here impose a formal dichotomy on the universe of government policymakers, it is important to clarify that we do *not* assume that the two sets of officials are internally homogeneous and externally competitive. We recognize, and our data confirm, that both bureaucrats and politicians are rather heterogeneous lots of individuals. This heterogeneity characterizes the sorts of variables that will be at the center of our analysis, such as political sensitivity and role conceptions, and it is also characteristic of the positions of these policymakers on concrete policy issues. Rare indeed are issues that pit politicians as a group against bureaucrats as a group. Much more common are alliances that cut across the two roles. We accept as generally true of modern government Ezra Suleiman's conclusion in the French case that policy outcomes reflect, not domination by civil servants, nor by politicians, but rather, shifting coalitions that include members of both groups.[73] Similarly, we do not assume that relations between bureaucrats and politicians are necessarily competitive and antagonistic. On the contrary, for some (though not all) of our countries, we could borrow the following description of relations between civil service and political elites in postwar Norway: "This relation has been characterized more by cooperation and a mutually satisfactory division of labor than by conflict and encroachment on one another's domain."[74]

In order to generalize about the comparison between bureaucrats and politicians in modern government, unobscured by national idiosyncracies or institutional peculiarities, it was essential that our analysis include a number of different countries. Some scholars, for example, have suggested that U.S. congressmen tend to be more parochial in orientation than federal executives, but it seems at least possible that this localism, rather than being endemic to the role of politician, might result instead from the extraordinarily decentralized American party system.[75] We felt that this possibility could be checked by including in our survey countries such as Britain, with its highly centralized party system.

Because our data cover several countries, they reveal many interesting cross-national differences among bureaucrats and among politicians. It would be tempting to explore these cross-national comparisons in some detail, for they often suggest fascinating insights into comparative politics and comparative administration. For reasons of time and space, however, we shall for the most part resist the temptation to wander down these byways, except insofar as they are directly relevant to our central concern: the relationship between bureaucrats and politicians.[76]

In that context one important contrast to keep in mind is that between the United States and Europe. Historically, sociologically, and constitutionally, European systems share more common traits than any of them does with the United States. We cannot here synthesize the voluminous literature on American exceptionalism. It will be useful, nonetheless, to review briefly some American peculiarities that bear on the relationship between bureaucrats and politicians.

Constitutionally, American government is usually described as embodying a "division of powers," but in practice, as Richard E. Neustadt has noted, American government is more accurately described as "separated institutions sharing powers [in other words, functions]."[77] The relatively clear division of labor between parliament and the executive that characterizes European governments is absent on this side of the Atlantic. In consequence, public authority here is institutionally fragmented and shared. Samuel Huntington has said, "America perpetuated [from the model of Tudor England] a fusion of functions and a division of power, while Europe developed a differentiation of functions and a centralization of power."[78]

Congress plays a more powerful and independent role in formulating policy and overseeing its implementation than do its sister legislatures in Europe. Whereas the legislative agenda of European parliaments is typically under the control of the government of the day, "half of the major legislation enacted by Congress in the last century has, in its entirety or in large part, been the result of congressional initiative and innovativeness."[79] Moreover, congressional oversight is substantially more detailed and effective than in Europe; indeed, it has been claimed that "many administrative officials now receive a good deal more day-to-day guidance from Congressmen than they get from the President."[80] The swollen staffs of Congress, occasionally the envy of European parliamentarians, are the natural concomitant of this expansive congressional role in national policymaking.

The American electoral and party systems are also distinctive. Single-member districts and party weakness require congressmen to articulate and respond to short-term demands and particularistic interests to a degree unusual among European legislators. Conversely, the less unified American parties have a weaker capacity than have the European parties to transform the articulation of demands into a coherent political force.

Another result of congressional strength and party weakness is that the pattern of consultation that in Europe links interest groups and civil servants is expanded in the United States to include congressional committees, producing the famous (or infamous) "iron triangles" that are at the heart of policymaking and policy implementation in many functional sectors of American government.[81] Weak parties and shared responsibilities mean that "the American system of politics does not generate enough power at any focal point of leadership to provide the conditions for an even partially successful divorce of politics from administration."[82]

On the administrative side, the American bureaucracy lacks the predemocratic legitimacy that attaches to the monarchical, ex-monarchical, or Napoleonic bureaucracies of Europe. "Partly because they enjoyed a security of position that American bureaucracies lacked, and partly because of the conventions of the parliamentary system, executive agencies in European states have historically had less reason and less opportunity to engage in direct political activity of the sort that is common in the United States."[83] We have already noted one consequence of this contrast, namely, that the distinction between civil servants and political appointees is much more blurred in this country than in Europe. Moreover, American administrators have long had responsibility for promoting their policies and mobilizing their constituencies with an overtness and an intensity that is foreign to the European tradition. This practice, together with the weakness of American parties, has meant ironically that the U.S. bureaucracy has been recognized as a channel of representation rivaling Congress and, moreover, one that aggregates interests in a manner that is hardly less comprehensive or progressive.[84]

Thus, history has bequeathed to American policymakers a system that minimizes institutional distinctiveness and maximizes the propensity for officials throughout the system to share skills and outlooks across the formal boundary between politician and bureaucrat. The institutional division of labor is far less tidy in America than in Europe, and we should expect this contrast to be mirrored in our surveys of bureaucrats and politicians.[85]

# Strategy of Inquiry

## 2

Individually and together, senior bureaucrats and politicians have a substantial impact on what gets proposed for consideration by governments, what gets passed into law, and how laws get implemented.[1] Both groups are more or less continuously involved with the processes of proposing, making, and implementing public policy, although they differ typically in the scope of their concerns and the specialization of their knowledge.

How the particular functions of policy involvement are allocated among civil servants and politicians is likely to vary at least somewhat from nation to nation. For example, because of the independent powers of the legislative body in the United States, politicians tend to play a larger role than elsewhere in overseeing the implementation of public policy. Our inquiry is motivated, though, by the belief that high-level bureaucrats and parliamentary politicians are both significant actors in the policy process. And for this reason alone it is worth knowing more about their characteristic perspectives, the potential tensions between them that are in some measure inherent in their roles, and the basic issues of responsiveness, popular accountability, and effectiveness that are raised by their responsibilities.

### The Samples

We felt that the best way to learn more about the administrative and political elites of the industrial democracies was to talk to them. We did so in six West European nations (Britain, France, Germany, Italy, the Netherlands, and Sweden) and in the United States.

For three reasons our professional politicians are sampled from national parliaments. We noted early in Chapter 1 that the professional politician discussed by Max Weber is above all a party politician. As parliamentary bodies have come to be the supreme arena of partisan politics, it is not surprising that they are "home" to professional party politicians. Party leaders in virtually all modern democratic systems are to be found in their national parliamentary bodies. (The United States has a formal, but impotent, party leadership located in the national party committees. To the American respondents in our survey, bureaucrats as well as members of Congress, "party leaders" were thought of as being congressional leaders.) The overlap between party officials and parliamentary membership, if not always total, is at a minimum very great. In order to sample professional party politicians, therefore, parliament is a good place to begin.

Secondly, parliaments almost always breed cabinet ministers, even in those countries that do not require cabinet ministers to be in parliament during their tenure in the government. France is a partial exception to this generalization because of the presidentialist features of the constitution of the Fifth Republic. The United States is a larger exception, but one reflecting the separation of powers doctrine that makes Congress an especially powerful body. Still, it is worth pointing out that nearly 60 percent of all American presidents have been members of Congress, a proportion that has been maintained across the eight presidencies since World War II. Parliamentary bodies at any given time include in their membership those who will ascend to the highest pinnacle of leadership in their systems. There is, in other words, no more reliable arena from which to sample those who are likely to get to the very top of the political elite.

A third reason for our sampling from among parliamentary bodies is that they are influential in shaping public policy, though their influence varies in degree from country to country. Our respondents appear to concur with this assumption. When we asked our civil servant and politician respondents to rate the influence of senior civil servants and of members of parliament over policy, the two groups were perceived as roughly equal. In three of the five countries where the data are basically comparable, members of parliament are seen to be more influential than senior civil servants, although civil servants are accorded a slight advantage in

*Table 2-1*  Sample sizes.

| Country | Senior bureaucrats | Parliamentary politicians | Bureaucratic high-fliers |
|---|---|---|---|
| Britain | 96 | 97 | 29 |
| France | 76 | 92 | 40 |
| Germany | 97 | 104 | 41 |
| Italy | 85 | 58 | 30 |
| Netherlands | 76 | 44 | 17 |
| Sweden | 317[a] | 44 | — |
| United States | 126[b] | 77 | — |
| | 873 | 516 | 157 |

[a] Of the Swedish senior bureaucrats, 210 serve in the administrative boards, 48 administer public authorities, and 59 are in the small, policymaking ministries.

[b] Of the American senior bureaucrats, 61 are nontenured appointees, hereafter referred to as political executives, whereas 65 are supergrade career civil servants.

the averaged (five-country) influence score. If a major eclipse of parliament is presumed to be taking place in Western democracies, it is barely visible to most of our respondents.

National parliamentary bodies are the arenas from which we choose our politician samples, then, because they house party politicians, because they almost invariably breed cabinet ministers, and because they continue to influence policy, if variably, in their respective countries. It is a relatively straightforward matter to define and then select representative samples of parliamentary politicians, whatever differences may exist in parliamentary powers across the nations. It is more complicated, however, to define and then select representative samples of high-ranking administrative officials, a matter we shall discuss shortly. In all, over 500 parliamentary politicians, nearly 900 senior bureaucrats, and more than 150 younger administrators ("high-fliers") were interviewed (Table 2-1).[2] Our response rate varied somewhat from sample to sample—slightly lower in Italy and France, for example—but on average we actually interviewed about four-fifths of all the politicians and bureaucrats we contacted.

Except as otherwise noted, only the populations of senior bureaucrats and parliamentary politicians serve as the empirical base for the analyses reported in this book. The high-flier samples of especially promising young civil servants rarely differ dramatically from the senior officials in their countries on matters relevant to their administrative role. Their more junior status, of course, does affect their range of contacts, and to some extent they tend to be more accepting of politics than are their senior colleagues—a difference that is most pronounced, oddly, in Britain. For the most part, however, there is far more similarity than difference across the senior–high-flier strata—testimony, perhaps, to the durability of bureaucratic cultures.[3]

Among the senior officials our sampling frame reflected a rough attempt to combine some measure of structural equivalence with a measure of functional equivalence across the national samples. As a result, our samples cannot be defined in a simple manner. The first and simplest characteristic is that all of the bureaucrats we interviewed were located in their nation's capital. Second, our sampling frame encompassed a broad range of ministries but specifically excluded administrators from the foreign affairs and defense ministries.[4] Those who performed obvious staff functions were also eliminated, though this distinction often was far sharper on paper than in reality.

In general, our sampling net was targeted to catch civil servants one to two rungs below the top administrative official in a department. Roughly speaking, our samples were drawn from a population of 300 to 600 such officials in each country. However, the level at which our samples were taken is the most complex facet of our sampling procedure. No straightforward rule applies here, because of the organizational differences that occur across administrative systems and because of our efforts to combine formal structural equivalence with informal functional equivalence. The approximate counterpart in the American system of the British under secretary, for example, would be a politically appointed official such as a deputy assistant secretary. An additional complicating factor is that each national sample was undertaken with an eye to intranational analysis as well as cross-national comparison. In brief, our net sometimes caught bigger fish and, less commonly, smaller fish than we originally targeted.[5]

The peculiarities of the American and Swedish samples require special attention. Because there is deep layering of nontenured appointments throughout the American federal bureaucracy, two American samples were taken. One was composed of senior career officials defined by their supergrade status and operational responsibilities for administering a subunit; the other was composed of political executives, ranging from assistant secretaries to deputy assistant secretaries and some bureau chiefs, all of whom formally were serving at the pleasure of the incumbent presidential administration. Our American bureaucratic sample divides virtually in half between the two groups of officials.

In Sweden, sampling was targeted toward three groups of administrative officials. One group, a bit less than one-fifth of the total Swedish bureaucratic sample, comprises ministerial civil servants. Their functions inside the small Swedish ministries largely fall into policy-formulating activities without specific operational responsibilities. Structural parallels across administrative systems often are perilous, but these ministerial civil servants can be thought of as occupying roles that are akin to those of the American political executives, except that the Swedes have civil service tenure. As we shall see, the American political executives and the Swedish ministerial civil servants resemble one another in important ways. The great bulk of the Swedish administrative sample (approximately two-thirds) is drawn from officials who populate the administrative boards that perform the principal policy-implementing and fine-tuning functions. They are supplemented by another group of officials, largely technical in their backgrounds, who administer the public authorities in Sweden. Public-authority executives account for approximately 15 percent of the Swedish administrative sample. Since they closely resemble the civil servants working for the boards, for the most part they are treated together in our analyses.

The central point here is that parallels across administrative systems inevitably are inexact; our objective, therefore, was to produce samples for each country that were as comparable hierarchically and functionally as possible, even at the cost of simple rules. Because of the unusual "political" status of the American political executives and the Swedish ministerial civil servants, separate samples were drawn. We shall note where they differ in substantial ways from the more traditionally defined professional bureaucrats in their countries.[6]

Except for the constraints already mentioned, we sampled randomly from the vast array of responsibilities carried out by civil servants in the modern state—from collecting taxes to scheduling airlines and from purchasing pencils to planning hospitals. This diversity in functional responsibilities, which is reflected in our samples, increases our confidence in the generalizability of our findings about bureaucrats as a group, even as we recognize that bureaucrats are not stamped from a single mold.

Sample sizes, as we have seen in Table 2–1, are not uniform across nations. This causes a mild complication. The large Swedish sample, for instance, constitutes about 44 percent of the total sampling of senior bureaucrats. Many of the findings presented in subsequent chapters display the results of analyses using pooled but unweighted samples. We have done this primarily for reasons of economy in data presentation. These pooled analyses are presented only where we have substantial evidence of empirical convergence from having performed the same analyses separately for each national sample. In instances where any of these separate analyses depart in a noteworthy way from the pooled results, the country samples have been weighted so that especially large or small samples do not bias the results. It should be stressed, however, that these divergences are rare. In some instances we have drawn explicit cross-national comparisons, and in these the various subsamples within the American and Swedish samples are themselves compared if there are substantial differences between them. Finally, when univariate distributions or summary parameters from distributions are presented, we show the weighted average across the national samples. The reason for this is straightforward: it is more likely that univariate distributions will fluctuate across national samples as a result of instrument or coding variance than will the structure of relationships between variables.

With the subjects of our inquiry identified and the boundaries of our study sketched, we turn now to the logic of our analysis and to the issues posed by the particular techniques we employed.

## Paths of Comparative Analysis

The fundamental logic of all science lies in comparison. But the logic of comparative inquiry itself leads us down two disparate paths, which we call the cross-national approach and the cross-role approach. A journey down the first path begins with an elaboration of differences across various political entities. From the standpoint of our investigation this cross-national approach translates into showing that the characteristics and perspectives of bureaucrats and parliamentary politicians vary from one political system to another. But if our fundamental purpose is to explain why these characteristics vary across political systems, then we must be concerned with extracting those variables for which the national political system is but a portmanteau. That is, to be able to assess what lies beneath political system differences, factors commonly measured across all systems but varying in the values they assume must be explicitly built into the research design. Such an undertaking, it should be stressed, is exceedingly ambitious, for it means that comparative analysis in this sense is not defined merely as a set of univariate comparisons across national systems. Instead, comparative analysis requires a multilevel explanatory structure in which "indicators are matched across systems and their behavior with regard to hypothesized dimensions is observed."[7] Defined in these terms, the logic of comparative inquiry requires a highly elaborated theoretical structure prior to commencing fieldwork.

The focus of our own inquiries, however, has taken a different route. For the most part, though not exclusively, we concentrate on one level of analysis, that of the individual. Our efforts have been invested in trying to illuminate consistent features characteristic of bureaucrats and parliamentary politicians. The generalizability of these features is strengthened by their persistence across several political systems—hence the cross-role label. From time to time throughout this book, national differences become important to our analysis. This is especially so in Chapter 7, which focuses on the web of elite interactions. Furthermore, we are struck by the frequent dissimilarities between American administrative and political elites and their counterparts in Europe. Still, our attention is mainly directed at generic characteristics of bureaucrats and politicians in industrial democracies and the similarities and differences between those occupying the two roles. Our focus is on the characteristic ways by which they arrive at their respective positions, the ways in which they think about their roles, the structure and content of their political thinking, and their patterns of interaction. The extent to which these characteristics can be found across political systems is a measure of their generalizability. For instance, the authors of a recent cross-national study of political participation have observed that similarities found individually across nations provide a basis for believing that similar processes are at work within each nation.[8] As we emphasize elsewhere in this chapter, this point is relevant primarily to the relationships that emerge rather than to the absolute magnitudes of individual characteristics, a matter subject to some instrument and coding variation across national samples.

### Beliefs and Behavior

If high-level bureaucrats and parliamentary politicians are both important in the policy process, then the perspectives they bring to that process are prima facie important. But how are we to inquire into these perspectives as they affect policymakers' behavior?

One method is to examine the behavior of bureaucrats and politicians through systematic case studies across comparable policy arenas and nations.[9] Well-executed case studies can specify the roles that various actors have played in the policy process and can elucidate the operative context in which choices are made. However, inferences from the observed behavior patterns to the presumed values and perspectives that help explain those patterns remain difficult, particularly if we are seeking generalizations valid across nations and policy domains.

For our purposes, then, we are better off inquiring directly into the beliefs of administrative and political elites. The link between beliefs and behavior, however, is inevitably problematic.[10] This problem is not resolved theoretically merely by starting with behavior and inferring backward, for behavior always reflects a compound of beliefs—cognitions, evaluations, and motivations—and situations—options, incentives, and structural constraints. Situational variations and the difficulty in generalizing across them help to account for the lack of resolution in the behavior-belief nexus at whichever end of the problem one begins. Moreover, if it is often very difficult to locate parallel behavioral settings across political systems, it is also very hard to find parallel forms of behavior between bureaucrats and politicians. For while legislators vote, bureaucrats write memos. At least superficially it is relatively easy to measure and therefore compare parliamentary behavior, but comparison of bureaucratic behavior is another matter.

Although contextual factors often inhibit a direct translation of a policymaker's beliefs into behavior, beliefs and behavior certainly are not just randomly associated. A particularly clear illustration of the joint effects of context and belief on behavior emerged from our interviews with British politicians. In the fall of 1971, eight months after our interviews, the House of Commons addressed the question of Common Market membership. The leaders of the Labour party strongly opposed the pro-Market policy of the Conservative cabinet. Although each party was sharply divided internally on the issue, party whips on both sides of the aisle demanded loyal support from their back-benchers. In the event, as Table 2-2 shows, the votes of individual members of Parliament were about equally determined by the contextual constraints of party discipline and the imperatives of personal conviction (as measured in our interviews). This example illustrates both the substantial power of beliefs to affect behavior and the limits of that power when constrained by strong institutional forces.

Moreover, at least among elites, there is evidence of impressive consistency between a person's abstract values and his operational application

*Table 2-2*    Role and beliefs as determinants of elite behavior: vote of British members of Parliament on the Common Market.

| | | Party | | |
|---|---|---|---|---|
| | | Conservative | | Labour |
| Personal attitude toward European unity:[a] | | *Pro* | *Con* | *Pro* | *Con* |
| Vote on Common Market | Yes | 100% | 59% | 55% | 11% |
| entry: | No | 0 | 41 | 45 | 89 |
| | | 100% | 100% | 100% | 100% |
| | | N = (24) | N = (22) | N = (22)[b] | N = (9) |

*Source:* Robert D. Putnam, *The Comparative Study of Political Elites,* © 1976, p. 104. Reprinted by permission of Prentice-Hall, Inc., Englewood Cliffs, N.J.

[a] Attitude measured by agreement or disagreement with the statements "It is desirable that the Common Market evolve toward the political formation of the United States of Europe" and "It is acceptable to me that there be, over the British government, a European government responsible for foreign affairs, defense, and the economy."

[b] Two pro-European Labourites who abstained on the vote are excluded from this table.

of these values, even when these two types of attitude are measured through different media.[11] Opportunities permitting, consistent beliefs are likely to be salient, and salient beliefs are more likely to impact upon behavior.[12] Ceteris paribus, it is quite plausible to assume that even rather abstract attitudes and values can help predict behavior. The difficulty of testing this assumption rigorously, of course, is that in the real world of policymaking ceteris is hardly ever paribus.

We are not centrally concerned, however, with predicting who will do what tomorrow on the basis of the beliefs that they express today. We seek to understand the generic behavior patterns of politicians and bureaucrats as policymakers. We shall see that these two groups are frequently differentiated both by the content and by the form of their beliefs. We focus upon beliefs because they provide us with the broadest vista from which to assess the contemporary roles of Western politicians and bureaucrats.[13] A better understanding of the cognitive worlds of these types of policymakers will, we believe, complement the results of more intensive case studies of policy processes.

What beliefs have we, in fact, focused on? And to what extent is our choice of instrument related to the focus of our analysis? Our principal objectives lie in uncovering both role-related and culturally influenced patterns of elite thinking about the policymaking process, and a spectrum of relationships between administrative and political elites and between those who govern and the public. More specifically, our inquiry probes such areas of elite belief as the following:

(1) Social and political conflict and its management;
(2) Issues of democratic politics, including political representation, interest articulation, citizen involvement, political tolerance, acceptance of pluralism, relations between government and politics, and popular control of government;
(3) Relations between administrative and political activity, and between administrators and politicians;
(4) The role of government in social and economic affairs;
(5) The need for social and political change;
(6) The operation and the need for governmental reforms;
(7) Major problems and public-policy issues affecting society now and in the future.

Obviously, we secured background and career information during our interviews, but our principal purpose was to explore the thinking of bureaucrats and politicians about society, politics, the process of governing, and their roles in this process. *How* bureaucrats and politicians think was as important for us as *what* they think. In part, this is so because, as Chapter 5 especially demonstrates, the two are not unrelated. Moreover, *how* they think could reveal to us what is most likely to distinguish bureaucrats from elected politicians in the industrial democracies. In addition, there is reason to believe that the basic ideological and structural features of the belief systems of bureaucrats and politicians are less susceptible to the vagaries of ephemeral circumstance than are their views on the issues of the day.[14] We attempted, therefore, to uncover a deep structure and pattern of beliefs on the part of our respondents, and still subject our discoveries to systematic quantitative analysis.

**Surveying Elites**

In order to probe the nuances of individual responses to our questions— the manner in which responses are framed and organized, the extent to which elements are interrelated, and the salience of particular ideas—we required an instrument that would permit us to listen, capture, then codify these subtleties. For this reason we employed an open-ended, yet largely structured, interview instrument, supplemented in several countries with a short-answer questionnaire. The discussions frequently were wide-ranging and the interviews typically were conducted in a conversational style, facilitated in turn by the use of a tape recorder. The virtue of open-ended procedures for elite interviewing, especially with regard to our particular interests, is that they "emphasize the contextual richness of response and allow for the exploration of subtlety and nuance," and most especially, they allow for an assessment of "not just the surface content of a response but also the reasoning and premises underlying it."[15] Indeed, investigators who conducted a survey of elites in Norway have contended "that the *manner* in which respondents react to general, philosophical questions can be an important datum concerning the role ideological models play in the thinking of elites [and that] what is *not* said in response to questions probing ideological constructs may equal in importance what is said."[16] They conclude moreover, as we did, "that this search for ideologically significant lacunae in elite thinking can be better conducted with the general, philosophical questions ... than with the seemingly more sophisticated fixed-response questions typical of mass surveys [since] the former facilitate an often fruitful *post hoc* analysis of what was left out [whereas] the latter type of questions prevent this by deciding *a priori* what will not be said."[17]

In addition, Sidney Verba has noted that a particular advantage of open-ended questions in cross-national survey research lies in the potentially different meaning that respondents in different cultures attach to a similar-sounding item. "The openness of the responses [therefore] provides the researcher with a body of material out of which one can more easily locate lack of equivalence than one can in a response to a fixed choice question."[18]

Despite initial reservations regarding close-ended questions, in four countries (Britain, Germany, Italy, and the Netherlands) a short-answer questionnaire was used to supplement, and in some respects validate, responses from the open-ended questions. The open-ended questions, we thought, would have the virtue of greater response validity, if also the liability of greater coding error. Although we have no conclusive way of distinguishing whether the open-ended or close-ended materials from our interviews were more reliable, there is evidence from our study and others that more structured or more focused open-ended questions produced more reliable responses than less structured or less focused ones.[19] In addition, evidence from another study involving one of the present authors has shown that there is a high level of test-retest reliability on close-ended attitude questions among political elites.[20] Responses to open-ended questions are far richer, often more interesting, and certainly more amenable to ascertaining nuance—but they introduce far more complexity in coding the responses and result in lower levels of intercoder reliability than do close-ended responses. Had we known then what we have subsequently learned, we very likely would have standardized more short-answer questions across a wider array of samples. For our purposes, however, neither technique alone could have yielded the combination of nuance gleaned from open-ended materials and the highly standardized data developed from the short-answer questions.

## Data Collection: Implications for Analysis

The coding of open-ended questions is an inherently difficult task. For comparative inquiry the difficulty is compounded by the fact that coding of some of our national studies was done over different points in time and by different coders. The consequences are twofold. First, a number of items used to indicate the structure of a respondent's beliefs were not coded in all samples. The coding process was a learning experience, so that more indicators are available for countries coded later in the process. As a result, we lack data for some countries on a few items that we have since discovered to be especially useful.

A second consequence of the fact that coding was not undertaken by a common community of coders is that no common base point was available for measuring intensities on comparable items. Thresholds for measuring intensity, then, surely differ to some degree across our various coding communities.[21] The upshot is that relational findings—including the comparison between politicians and bureaucrats that is at the heart of this volume—are bound to be more trustworthy than univariate comparisons across the national samples. This is why, in general, we have averaged univariate distributions or parameters derived from them across the national samples.

Coding procedures are of great importance when semistructured open-ended interviews are used to generate systematic data. Clear descriptions of conceptual criteria and unambiguous code categories are essential, as is rigorous training of the coders, but the judgmental element is so central to the enterprise that a rigorous technique for ensuring high-quality, reliable data is critical. Independent, double-coding procedures were employed to maximize the reliability and validity of the data. While procedures varied slightly from country to country, the basic technique was to have each interview coded twice separately and then to discuss and reconcile any coding discrepancies.[22] As a result, we were able to calculate the reliability for each variable (by correlating the results of the separate coding efforts) and to use the coding process as a mechanism for building a better understanding among the coders of the concepts underlying each variable and of the criteria for scoring the interview contents. The process of reconciling discrepancies produced final data that are more reliable than the coefficients indicate because differences were carefully reviewed prior to a final decision on the "proper" code category.[23]

Each national study explored issues that were of common concern to the comparative inquiry, but each was also designed as a self-contained investigation. We began at various times over a four-year period with a core set of concerns focusing on the capacities of elites to meet the twin challenges of legitimacy and effectiveness, and with a core set of common operational questions. While interviews were completed in France by the spring of 1970, those in Holland were only begun in 1973. Because of these variations in timing and also in coding, the national data sets are not always precisely comparable. The British, German, Italian, and Dutch data sets are the most nearly so; for example, each of these four includes data from the short-answer questionnaire, and each is based on the most fully developed coding scheme for the open-ended questions. The French, Swedish, and American data sets, while substantially comparable, are less so than the others. Put another way, our data presentations in this book always include, at a minimum, the British, German, Italian, and Dutch samples; often they include one or more from among the Swedish, American, and French samples; sometimes they include samples from all seven countries.

Although the design of this book is intended to minimize those features of our data that are a product of ephemeral circumstance and to stress those that are durable and of generic significance, we need to return to the environment of our respondents during the time they were being interviewed. An appreciation of this context is helpful for placing in perspective what may appear to be national idiosyncracies in our data.

## The Political Context

The early 1970s, when our interviews took place, was a time of some turbulence throughout much of Europe as well as in America. Yet the atmosphere and turmoil of the period were very different from those that gripped Europe and America throughout the 1930s. The earlier era produced an unrest bred from profound economic crisis, exacerbated in much of Europe by the fragility of parliamentary institutions. In the early 1970s, by contrast, parliamentary institutions were relatively strong and it was a period of unprecedented prosperity in both Western Europe and the United States, although there were ominous harbingers of economic and industrial difficulties to follow. Despite regional variations in prosperity and rates of economic transformation, greater in some countries than in others, the social structure of every nation had been transformed as a consequence of the vast economic changes of the postwar period.

From the perspective of the early seventies, therefore, many of the issues affecting all these countries originated in abundance: the thrust for greater democratization and control over institutions of authority, the advancement and enlargement of benefits from the social welfare state, the emergence of new constituencies pushing for sociocultural reforms on issues such as women's rights, abortion, divorce laws, and, especially in the United States, environmentalism. At universities and oftentimes in the streets demonstrations against authority took place, some of them violent. It was a period in which Rudi (the Red) Dutshke, Daniel Cohn-Bendit, and Mark Rudd became exaggerated symbols of the disaffection of student communities from authority. Enveloping these trends was the specter of American military involvement in Vietnam. Its effect, while surely greater in the United States than in Europe, was to precipitate many challenges to authority throughout the industrialized world.

The period during which these interviews took place, then, was one of ferment, of challenge to authority and to the structures and institutions of authority. For the most part these challenges were not readily acceptable to broad-based voting publics, as the 1968 elections in France and the United States and the 1970 elections in Britain indicated. In subsequent years other issues arose, as both Europe and the United States were confronted with their economic vulnerabilities. Europeans and Americans were lashed with high rates of inflation and unemployment. If the early 1970s was a time when abundance created issues and constituencies new to the public agenda, the late 1970s, a time of limits, generated a more familiar politics of interests—one that in Britain at least has become notably bitter. The displacement of prior political environments, however, is rarely complete. The effects of past responses linger and in subtle ways may alter the political culture.

One of our collaborators, writing in the late 1970s and analyzing the Swedish data developed as part of this study, observed that the likelihood of greater political instability and leadership turnover in Sweden "compounded by unsolvable economic and social problems, perhaps accompanied by a more visible social unrest" will create a far more turbulent environment and confront officials there with special challenges.[24] In this context the Swedish general strike in the spring of 1980 is less surprising, for it undoubtedly reflects the shock waves of a society whose emphasis upon equality and high wages was thwarted by increasingly high inflation, public indebtedness, and lowered productivity. Similarly, a British analyst comparing Swedish and British policy responses in transportation concludes that Swedish policy management has become more politicized than it was in the late 1960s, perhaps a consequence of the drive in the 1970s toward democratization of all decision-making channels in Sweden.[25] In brief, while the agendas of the late 1970s have been vastly altered, the issues that evolved in the early 1970s, the constituencies that became mobilized, and the ideas that were generated about participation and authority have affected how the issues of the 1980s are likely to be confronted.

If it is fair to characterize the early 1970s as a time of experimentation and conflict, the issues that were raised were not uniformly presented everywhere, nor were they uniformly interpreted.[26] Moreover, they often arrived at different times and their effects were felt at different rates in different places. Let us look then at the particular political environments that characterized the time during which each of our national samples of bureaucratic and political elites was interviewed.[27]

BRITAIN    Interviews with civil servants and MPs in Britain were conducted during the first half of 1971. A new Conservative government, led by Edward Heath, had been elected in the spring of 1970 to supplant the Labour government of Harold Wilson. Inflation and strikes were the two most prominent issues of the Tory campaign, and on the domestic scene the Heath government concentrated almost exclusively on them. Industrial unrest earlier in the year had been recorded as the second greatest in nearly forty years, and the new government's efforts to tame the labor unions remained problematic. Prior to and during the period of interviewing, the government presented proposals to reduce taxes on income and corporations—at the expense of reduction in some social services, increased charges for others, and denationalization of several industries. The proposals were vehemently attacked by the Labour opposition.

Aside from other major issues involving the fate of Northern Ireland and British defense policy east of Suez, the principal focus of the government was on inflation, strikes, changes in industrial relations, and a reduced rate of government spending. An immediate consequence was the creation of a highly polarized political environment (which in some respects has been reproduced at the start of the eighties with even more vigor by the forcefulness with which the Thatcher government has pressed its policies). The Heath government, in the face of the greatest labor unrest since 1926, introduced an omnibus bill to regulate labor-industrial relations, with a major provision that would institute a compulsory cooling-down period for strikes that threatened serious risk to the community or constituted a potential national emergency.

These issues struck to the core of prevailing British political alignments. The data from our interviews indicate a high level of polarization by party among MPs. The strength of party-based correlations in our British data bear witness to the intensity of the political debate and the fundamental relationship between core party ideologies and the issues cast as the centerpiece of the Tory agenda. In the midst of the strong alignments evident in our British MP interviews, the durability of the nonpartisan culture of the British administrative elite was singularly impressive. The debates and issues that urgently beckoned Tory and Labour MPs to their respective battle stations seemed barely to touch the senior administrative officials who were interviewed, testimony perhaps to a view of bureaucrats as inveterate incrementalizers.

FRANCE    Interviews with French civil servants and assembly deputies were conducted during the autumn of 1969 and the first quarter of 1970. Like Britain, France was experiencing considerable strife, but of a somewhat different sort. Industrial unrest and fundamental economic issues were at the core of social conflict in Britain and at the base of the Labour government's defeat in the 1970 elections. In France, the events of May 1968, precipitated by disaffected radical students at the University of Nanterre, quickly turned into a fundamental challenge to the regime. The historic theme of isolated leftist challenges to the legitimacy of a "bourgeois" regime was reiterated. An equally historic response to such challenges is a crushing defeat of the Left. Repeating this pattern, the Gaullist coalition won overwhelmingly in the elections that followed the

Paris tumult of 1968. The triumph of the Right and Right-Center produced a strangely depoliticized period in French politics. It also had an unfortunate impact on our study: Communist deputies are underrepresented in our sample, in part because their response rate was low, but equally because their numbers were temporarily reduced in the parliament. The fact, therefore, that the French deputies in our analyses seem less polarized than those in Britain, for instance, is at least in part an artifact of the time during which the sample was interviewed—a time during which there simply were not very many leftist deputies. The replacement of de Gaulle himself in the presidency by the Gaullist prime minister, Georges Pompidou, did not in any way alter these essential facts.

GERMANY   Our interviews with civil servants and members of the Bundestag were undertaken in the fall and winter of 1970. As a result of the federal elections of 1969, the Social Democrats (SPD) led the government in Bonn as the dominant element of a governing coalition after three years of partnership in a grand coalition with the Christian Democrats (CDU) under the chancellorship of Kurt Georg Kiesinger. The SPD government, in coalition with the small but pivotal Free Democrats (FDP), was led by Willy Brandt. The new government's priorities were directed to foreign policy, to social reform, and to gaining greater control of the administrative machinery of government after uninterrupted (except for the preceding three years of the grand coalition) dominance by the Christian Democrats.

There are strong hints from our data that in the period prior to our interviewing in Bonn the SPD sought to promote those officials sympathetic to its reformist outlook. Bureaucrats in the Federal Republic seem to hold attitudes, for example, that are significantly different from those that had been described a mere decade and a half earlier. Many had arrived at their positions shortly before our interviews, an indication of the SPD's effort, as opportunities presented themselves, to remold the Bonn bureaucracy into a more politically sympathetic apparatus. To some degree, therefore, the activist and reformist orientations of the Bonn bureaucrats reflect SPD efforts to transform the federal bureaucracy.

These orientations also reflect a more basic change in the age structure of the German bureaucracy. A rapid generational shift occurred in the period prior to our interviewing, as men who retired were replaced by significantly younger bureaucrats (men in their early fifties) because of the "missing" World War II generation in Germany. And these younger men were more activist and reformist than their predecessors, even allowing for party sympathies. This leads us to think that the return of a CDU government, though it might slow the process, could probably not reverse the trend toward a more activist and reformist orientation in the bureaucracy.[28]

ITALY    Italian civil servants and deputies were interviewed during the first half of 1970. From the perspective of the 1960s, rather than of the 1980s, this seemed to be a particularly turbulent period in Italy. The dramatic economic growth of the sixties, which pushed Italy forward into the ranks of the major industrial nations, began to slow. This helped precipitate a series of strikes throughout the spring of 1970. Equally as important, the *apertura alla sinistra* crafted in the early 1960s to provide reform with stability to Italian politics unraveled nearly a decade later as the junior Socialist coalition partner in the dominant Christian Democratic alliance split over the relations between the government and the powerful Italian Communist party. The ruling coalition dominated by the Christian Democrats (DC) was torn by the divorce bill before Parliament—between the Socialists (PSI) and other secular parties who supported it, and the Vatican, which opposed it. Uneasiness in the DC-PSI coalition was further exacerbated by the willingness of the PSI to form governing coalitions of the Left with the Communists (PCI) in several regional councils after the inaugural regional elections in 1970.

From the more recent perspectives of terrorist activity in Italy, these anxieties and the continued fragility of the government seem to be tame stuff indeed. Nonetheless, the long-standing inability to develop stable governments with both popular legitimacy and the capacity to formulate and implement policy agendas remained the prominent feature of the Italian political landscape. The fractiousness of Italian politics and the fragmentation of Italian society that it reinforces continue to breed alienation from the normal processes of pluralist politics. Insofar as the dominant elements of the Italian political culture are concerned, the *Zeitgeist* effects on our interviews would be best described as "plus ça change, plus c'est la même chose."

THE NETHERLANDS    Interviews took place in the Netherlands during 1973. For nearly all of the first part of the year and the last months of the previous year, the Netherlands was under caretaker government—the result of indecisive, even polarizing elections in the fall of 1972. The hiatus between governments was the lengthiest on record. Further, the results of the election strengthened both the secular Left and Right at the expense of the confessional (religious) parties.

The tone of Dutch politics appeared to be undergoing change during this period: agreements became more difficult to reach and coalitions necessarily more fragile, the popular base of confessional political strength weakened, and the consociational glue holding together a highly fractionated politics became less adhesive in the face of the growing secularization of Dutch society and politics. Yet these events were taking place during a period of great affluence, strong economic prospects, and a meteoric growth in public expenditures for the welfare state, proportionately second only to Sweden.

Dutch society was showing signs of growing radicalization manifested in the Dutch Catholic Church and in the attitudes of mass publics.[29] Whether (as seems likely) precipitated by elites or merely reflected by them, these trends are also evident in our elite data. The youngest of the politicians in our samples, the Dutch MPs also are the most radical in many respects. At the same time, there is considerable evidence within the Dutch MP sample of strong cross-party differences despite the ambiguous positioning of Dutch parties from left to right. The differences between MPs of the various socialist parties and those of the confessional and bourgeois parties are as strong as those found anywhere. Despite the complicating fragmentation of the Dutch parties, left-right party differences are sharp. This polarization, however, has a different explanation than the comparable polarization in Britain during the interviewing period there. Whereas in Britain the Right put forth an agenda that provoked strong reaction from the Left, in Holland, especially during the late 1960s and early 1970s, the Left began increasingly to dominate the agenda, provoking strong reactions from the nonsocialist parties.

In short, it appears that our fieldwork in the Netherlands commenced at a time of special ferment, but as the even lengthier government crisis of 1977 indicates, there is no reason to believe that there was anything especially idiosyncratic about the period. There *is* reason to think, however, that it may have capped the earlier more consensual, more deferential, and less secular political epoch.

SWEDEN   Interviews were conducted in Sweden during the last half of 1970 and the first half of 1971. Rapid inflation, especially of food prices, and the costliest industrial strike since the end of World War II boded ill for the ruling Social Democrats in the elections held in September 1970. Although they lost their majority in the Riksdag, the Social Democrats remained by far the largest party bloc and continued to rule alone.

Under the government of Prime Minister Olof Palme, the egalitarian revolution in Sweden continued unabated, as did the economic growth that made the expansive Swedish welfare state possible. In stark contrast to Italy, neither a largely conservative administrative elite nor a more radical political elite felt particularly disaffected from their political system.[30] Indeed, among social reformers, Sweden often was held up as a model of democratic social reform and equality, and also as a model of democratic participation within work institutions.

Since our interviews, of course, the Social Democrats have fallen from power altogether and Sweden has shown itself to be vulnerable to the same ailments that afflict the other economies of Europe—inflation, low growth, steep wages, lessened productivity, energy concerns, and trade imbalances. It is probable that some of the egalitarian zest of Swedish elites has diminished and that some fears of an omniscient state have become sharper. If Sweden in 1970–1971 was a society where radical policies were conservatively managed, the principal shift subsequently may have been to a society where a penchant for reform persists, where veto-group corporatism in policymaking has become more prominent, and where the importance of prudent management of the economy and of social reform has grown as the discretionary prospects for such management have diminished.

UNITED STATES   Interviewing took place in the United States during 1970 and 1971. Washington at the time was a capital with divided political control over government. The White House was held by a Republican president with strong designs for gaining control over the executive machinery of government. On the other hand, the Congress continued to be at least nominally controlled by the Democrats after the 1970 elections, when we interviewed members of the new House of Representatives.

Although some of the turbulence that had affected the country during the last few years of the administration of Lyndon Johnson was winding down, much of it was still present—but to some extent transformed. While racial explosions in big cities abated, unrest and sizable demonstrations continued over the involvement of American forces in Vietnam, and within the universities over a variety of other issues as well. Moreover, small bands of radical groups began to engage in violent activity including street melees and bombings. During our interviews, for instance, bombings took place inside the Justice Department and the Capitol. On the economic front, the United States continued to experience growth, but suffered persistent inflationary effects dating from the Johnson years, a harbinger of worse things to come. In the summer of 1971, indeed, President Nixon announced a wage-price freeze.

From the perspective of the early 1980s, the period of our interviews seems to have been an interesting time of transition in American politics and society. Some of the issues of the day emanated from the disaffection amid affluence of the 1960s, while there were also signs of the gestating problems of hyperinflation, economic stagnation, and supply shortages that would influence the late 1970s. Many of the concerns of the early 1970s, moreover, became institutionalized in government policies and agencies and thus left a large imprint on responses to later problems.

Ordinarily, the White House and the Congress are attuned to different political forces and constituencies even without divided party control. The Nixon administration was intent, however, on turning a sparring match into a championship bout by challenging both the Democratic Congress and the Washington bureaucracy. The roundhouse blows were not to be delivered until after President Nixon's reelection in 1972, but by the time our interviews took place, White House jabs at Congress and the bureaucracy seemed to presage the more lethal and ultimately self-destructive blows to come. Had we interviewed among White House staff personnel during this time, we undoubtedly would have picked up many of the frustrations (since they were later recorded via the Watergate hearings and tapes) that led to these exceptional reactions.

Because our interviews among American senior bureaucrats were divided into those who were political (noncareer) executives and those who were career civil servants, we discovered sharp partisan divisions between the two groups—a result of Republican control of the White House. As expected, the political executives were overwhelmingly Republican (81 percent for high political appointees). It would be best to describe the career officials as underwhelmingly so (17 percent were Republicans).[31] Such a split, of course, is purely a product of circumstance, though it is a frequently recurring one.

*    *    *

To summarize, these were interesting, but not especially atypical times. Tensions generated by social, economic, and political change brought to each country special problems, and unique events occurred in each. But it was not a period of global war or revolution or depression. It was, in short, a reasonably good time to study the beliefs, values, and experiences of top bureaucrats and politicians in Western nations.

# Paths to the Top

## 3

The basic question we confront is deceptively simple: In what ways are top bureaucrats and politicians similar and in what ways are they different, especially as policy actors? Some answers emerge from looking at their social and political origins and at their career patterns. We can first ask two straightforward descriptive questions about origins and career patterns: (1) How do bureaucrats and politicians differ from the publics they govern? (2) How, if at all, do they differ from one another? Answers to these simple queries, however, stimulate two further and more analytically complicated questions: (1) How do differences in the *ways* that bureaucrats and politicians are chosen *lead* to differences between them and the public and to differences between each of them? (2) What is the significance of their origins and career paths for their attitudes and behavior?

Why are these questions important? First, answers to them provide us with information about the extent to which access to the elite is biased and the ways in which it is biased. In addition, knowledge of the different paths to the top can tell us about the processes of selection—processes that may favor some while eliminating others—and thus about the possibilities for opening the channels of recruitment to people from more diverse backgrounds, and ultimately for influencing the attitudes and behavior of administrative and parliamentary elites. Lastly, we need to know whether or not the attitudes of these elites favor the interests of the social groups from which they are drawn or whether there is a process of socialization both before and after joining the policymaking elite that lessens the ties binding its members' political allegiances to those of their parents and social peers.

Our discussion loosely follows the issues raised here in outlining the reasons for our interest in social origins and career patterns. We begin with a broad treatment of the social background and training of top officials, turn to a description and analysis of their career patterns, discuss their political origins and current party loyalties, and conclude with a brief description of changes likely to take place in the near future.

## Social Origins

Research on the composition of elites in virtually every polity has shown a disproportionate representation of educated, high-status males, particularly at the top of the political and administrative hierarchy.[1] Our evidence, too, strongly confirms this "law of increasing disproportion," particularly in the case of administrative elites. Indeed, our elites are drawn from unusual backgrounds, not merely by comparison with mass publics in their respective countries, but even by comparison with those we shall call their "recruitment-pool peers"—people of similar occupational status, age, and sex, but who are not in the governmental sector.

In terms of gender, our samples illustrate the "iron law of andrarchy" (rule by males). Women constitute barely 7 percent of our parliamentary samples, ranging from a low of 4 percent in Britain and Italy to a high of only 14 percent in the Netherlands. Males dominate the administrative elites even more completely, for fewer than 1 percent of our senior civil servants are female. Woman constitute 4 percent of our supplementary samples of administrative high-fliers (especially promising, younger bureaucrats), a finding that perhaps augurs some slight modification of the sexual composition of future administrative elites. But for the moment, the world of power remains essentially a man's world. Being a male may not have been a sufficient condition for attaining positions of power in the early 1970s, but it was little short of a necessary condition.[2]

Apart from sex, our evidence suggests that *education* is the crucial credential for those who reach parliament or the top rungs of the bureaucracy. Table 3–1 displays the educational attainments of our elite samples, along with four samples intended to provide standards of comparison. The first is simply a random sample of the adult population, while the succeeding subsamples are progressively more restricted to provide a

Table 3-1 Educational attainments of mass and elite samples.[a]

| Educational attainment of group sampled | Britain[b] | France | Germany | Italy | Netherlands | United States | Six-nation average |
|---|---|---|---|---|---|---|---|
| | | | | Country | | | |
| **A. Mass samples[c]** | | | | | | | |
| Total | | | | | | | |
| Primary | 98 } | 75 | 34 | 71 | 31 | 9 | 93 } |
| Secondary | | 19 | 62 | 25 | 66 | 66 | |
| University[d] | 2 | 6 | 4 | 4 | 3 | 26 | 8 |
| N = | 100 (1829) | 100 (1968) | 100 (2039) | 100 (1838) | 100 (1823) | 101 (1573) | 101 |
| Males, 35–70 years | | | | | | | |
| Primary | 97 } | 77 | 20 | 66 | 30 | 12 | 92 } |
| Secondary | | 17 | 75 | 29 | 65 | 64 | |
| University | 3 | 7 | 5 | 6 | 5 | 23 | 8 |
| N = | 100 (559) | 101 (637) | 100 (547) | 101 (590) | 100 (611) | 99 (411) | 100 |
| Males, 35–70 years, management/professional | | | | | | | |
| Primary | 90 } | 25 | 0 | 17 | 4 | 5 | 64 } |
| Secondary | | 27 | 71 | 34 | 65 | 47 | |
| University | 10 | 48 | 29 | 48 | 31 | 48 | 36 |
| N = | 100 (94) | 100 (79) | 100 (89) | 99 (29) | 100 (51) | 100 (133) | 100 |

Males, 35–70 years, high management/professional

| Education | | | | | | | |
|---|---|---|---|---|---|---|---|
| Primary | ⎱ 84 | 21 | 0 | 50 | 4 | 2 | ⎱ 54 |
| Secondary | ⎰ | 21 | 35 | 30 | 65 | 12 | ⎰ |
| University | 16 | 58 | 66 | 20 | 31 | 86 | 46 |
| N = | 100 (38) | 100 (52) | 101 (29) | 100 (10) | 100 (51)[e] | 100 (42) | 100 |
| | | | | | | | (42) |

B. Administrative and parliamentary elite samples[f]

| Education | CS | MP | CS | MP | CS | MP | CS | MP | CS | MP | CS | PE | MP | CS[g] | MP |
|---|---|---|---|---|---|---|---|---|---|---|---|---|---|---|---|
| Primary   | 0 | 5  | 0  | 5  | 0  | 1  | 0   | 2  | 0  | 0  | 0   | 0  | 0  | 0   | 2  |
| Secondary | 16 | 24 | 3  | 16 | 1  | 32 | 0   | 14 | 5  | 20 | 0   | 3  | 9  | 4   | 19 |
| University| 83 | 71 | 97 | 79 | 99 | 67 | 100 | 84 | 95 | 80 | 100 | 97 | 90 | 96  | 79 |
|           | 99 | 100| 100| 100| 100| 100| 100 | 100| 100| 100| 100 | 100| 99 | 100 | 100|
| N =       | (91)|(97)|(69)|(81)|(94)|(99)|(82)|(57)|(74)|(44)|(65)|(61)|(75)| | |

[a] Entries are percentages; because of rounding, they do not always sum to 100.

[b] The coding of the British mass sample does not permit a clear division between primary and secondary education.

[c] Mass data are drawn from the archives of the Interuniversity Consortium for Political and Social Research, based on the Butler and Stokes 1966 British electoral study, the Converse and Pierce 1967 French electoral study, the 1972 German election panel study, the Barnes and Sani 1972 Italian study, the Stouthard 1970 Dutch electoral study, and the Center for Political Studies 1970 U.S. election study.

[d] Persons who attended university are included in this category, whether or not they actually graduated.

[e] The coding of occupational status for the Dutch mass sample does not permit us to separate out a category of *high* management and professionals, as we have done for the other samples.

[f] CS = civil servant; MP = member of parliament (or Congress); PE = political executive.

[g] Averages for the civil service samples exclude the American political executives.

closer match to the characteristics of our elite samples. The first subsample consists of males between 35 and 70 years old, the age cohorts from which 95 percent of our elite samples are drawn. The second subsample is further restricted to males of this age range in managerial or professional occupations.[3] Finally, the third subsample includes only males of the same age from higher-level managerial or professional positions. This subsample—roughly 2 percent of the national population—is as close to a sample of the recruitment-pool peers of our elites as we can obtain from survey data, although its rarefied character means that the number of respondents in some of the national subsamples is undesirably low.[4]

The evidence in Table 3–1 reveals the unusual educational achievements of political and administrative elites. Whereas the average rate of university attendance among the general public is only about 8 percent— 4 percent for the European nations—the average figure for our elites is 88 percent. Even the peer subsamples of older, upper-status males average only 46 percent university attendance, while the average figure for the larger (and more reliable) subsamples that include lower-ranking managers and professionals is only 36 percent. In fact, these comparisons somewhat understate the differences between elites and nonelites, for almost all the elites are actually university graduates, whereas the figures for the nonelites include substantial minorities who attended but did not complete a university degree. As expected, politicians and bureaucrats in the countries we surveyed are extraordinarily well educated compared to their countrymen. Especially impressive, however, is the fact that they are also far more educated than those occupying roughly comparable positions in the private sector.

When we examine the elite samples in more detail, some clear differences are apparent among countries and between roles. First, in every country bureaucrats have more formal education than parliamentarians. While 96 percent of the bureaucrats have attended a university, the comparable figure for the political elites is 79 percent. Individuals without a university education have at least a small chance of entering parliament, but virtually none of entering the higher bureaucratic strata.[5] The largest numbers of politicians with less than a university education are found in the parliaments of Britain and Germany, having reached there (as we shall see later) primarily via the Labour and the Social Democratic parties. A small number of so-called class-to-class recruits to the British administrative class, promoted from the ranks of the clerical civil service, provide the only visible numbers of nonuniversity graduates in any of these administrative elites. Though intrinsically interesting, these national peculiarities should not detract from the primary finding: in advanced industrial nations virtually the only significant path to the top of the polity passes through the university.[6] This central fact has implications not merely for the skills and perspectives of the decision-making elite but also, as we shall see later, for the social composition of this elite.

Turning briefly to the type of university training these elites have received, we examine their fields of study in Table 3–2. Most notable is the contrasting role played by legal education in common-law and Roman-law countries. In the continental countries, where legal training is essentially training for administrative roles, legal backgrounds are much more common among bureaucrats than in the two common-law countries, where the advocacy skills and adversarial demeanor gained in legal training make the law a likely spawning ground for elected politicians. Second, in all countries, bureaucrats are more likely than politicians to have had training in the natural and social sciences. Among bureaucrats, the balance between social sciences and natural sciences varies somewhat from country to country, with hard science most common among American career officials, followed by the British and the Dutch. Not unexpectedly, British bureaucrats are particularly likely to have studied humanities.[7]

American political executives are distinguished here and elsewhere in this volume from career civil servants, who comprise a substantial share of the top levels of the American bureaucracy. As we shall see, these two groups have quite different social and political profiles, in part because at the time of our interviewing the ranks of the political executives were filled primarily by Republican appointees drawn from outside the federal government.[8] Table 3–2 shows that in terms of their education, these political appointees were much less likely than the career officials to have studied the natural or technical sciences.

By education, as well as by current occupational status, our samples of political and administrative leaders rank in the very highest strata of their respective societies. Perhaps even more remarkable is the exceptionally high level of their social origins. We can see the extent to which this is true by examining evidence in Table 3–3 on class origins, as measured by father's occupation. As in Table 3–1, we also provide comparable evidence from nested subsamples of the national population. On average, 12 percent of our full mass samples had fathers in managerial or professional occupations, the top two levels in our status classification. By contrast, 66 percent of our political and bureaucratic elites came from

Table 3-2 Major field of university study of elites.[a]

| | Country | | | | | | | | | | | | | Five-nation average | |
|---|---|---|---|---|---|---|---|---|---|---|---|---|---|---|---|
| | Britain | | Germany | | Italy | | Netherlands | | United States | | | | | | |
| Field | CS | MP | CS | MP | CS | MP | CS | MP | CS | PE | MP | | | CS[b] | MP |
| No university | 16 | 29 | 1 | 33 | 0 | 16 | 5 | 20 | 0 | 3 | 9 | | | 4 | 21 |
| Law | 3 | 21 | 66 | 33 | 54 | 30 | 39 | 23 | 18 | 28 | 51 | | | 36 | 32 |
| Humanities, including history | 40 | 5 | 2 | 7 | 0 | 23 | 0 | 5 | 6 | 7 | 0 | | | 10 | 8 |
| Social science | 12 | 6 | 17 | 15 | 37 | 11 | 24 | 18 | 29 | 38 | 0 | | | 24 | 10 |
| Technology and natural science | 26 | 6 | 14 | 9 | 10 | 14 | 22 | 11 | 42 | 10 | 0 | | | 23 | 8 |
| Major unknown | 2 | 33 | 0 | 2 | 0 | 7 | 9 | 23 | 5 | 15 | 40 | | | 3 | 21 |
| | 99 | 100 | 100 | 99 | 101 | 101 | 99 | 100 | 100 | 101 | 100 | | | 100 | 100 |
| N = | (91) | (97) | (94) | (99) | (82) | (57) | (74) | (44) | (65) | (61) | (75) | | | | |

[a] Entries are percentages; because of rounding, they do not always sum to 100. CS = civil servant; MP = member of parliament (or Congress); PE = political executive.
[b] Averages for the civil service samples exclude the American political executives.

Table 3-3  Father's occupational status of mass and elite samples.[a]

| Father's occupational status of group sampled[b] | Country | | | | | | Six-nation average |
|---|---|---|---|---|---|---|---|
| | Britain | France[c] | Germany | Italy | Netherlands[d] | United States | |
| **A. Mass samples[e]** | | | | | | | |
| **Total** | | | | | | | |
| High management or professional | 7 | 4 | 3 | 1 | 5 | 7 | 12 |
| Low management or professional | 7 | 3 | 20 | 2 | | 16 | |
| Skilled nonmanual | 11 | 42 | 13 | 18 | 48 | 35 | 36 |
| Lower nonmanual | 10 | 13 | 16 | 9 | | 3 | |
| Skilled manual | 39 | 7 | 32 | 13 | 48 | 21 | 52 |
| Semiskilled or unskilled | 26 | 32 | 16 | 58 | | 18 | |
| | 100 | 101 | 100 | 101 | 101 | 100 | 100 |
| N = | (536) | (1903) | (1189) | (1782) | (1794) | (1356) | |
| **Males, 35–70 years** | | | | | | | |
| High management or professional | 7 | 4 | 2 | 1 | 4 | 5 | 11 |
| Low management or professional | 4 | 2 | 19 | 1 | | 18 | |
| Other nonmanual | 21 | 59 | 25 | 29 | 50 | 42 | 38 |
| All manual | 67 | 36 | 55 | 70 | 46 | 35 | 51 |
| | 99 | 101 | 101 | 101 | 100 | 100 | 100 |
| N = | (115) | (618) | (328) | (568) | (605) | (358) | |

(continued)

Table 3-3 (continued)

| Father's occupational status of group sampled[b] | Country | | | | | | Six-nation average |
|---|---|---|---|---|---|---|---|
| | Britain | France[c] | Germany | Italy | Netherlands[d] | United States | |
| **Males, 35–70 years, management/professional** | | | | | | | |
| High management or professional | 21 | 19 | 7 | 4 | } 18 | 11 | } 34 |
| Low management or professional | 16 | 8 | 47 | 19 | | 33 | |
| Other nonmanual | 21 | 62 | 24 | 56 | 71 | 30 | 44 |
| All manual | 42 | 12 | 21 | 22 | 12 | 25 | 22 |
| | 100 | 101 | 99 | 101 | 101 | 99 | 100 |
| N = | (19) | (78) | (70) | (27) | (51) | (114) | |
| **Males, 35–70 years, high management/professional** | | | | | | | |
| High management or professional | 22 | 19 | 30 | 10 | } 18 | 25 | } 41 |
| Low management or professional | 33 | 12 | 30 | 10 | | 39 | |
| Other nonmanual | 22 | 58 | 20 | 60 | 71 | 20 | 42 |
| All manual | 22 | 12 | 20 | 20 | 12 | 17 | 17 |
| | 99 | 101 | 100 | 100 | 101 | 101 | 100 |
| N = | (9) | (52) | (10) | (10) | (51)[d] | (36) | |

B. Administrative and parliamentary elite samples[f]

| | CS | MP | CS | MP | CS | MP | CS | MP | CS | MP | CS | PE | MP | CS[g] | MP |
|---|---|---|---|---|---|---|---|---|---|---|---|---|---|---|---|
| High management or professional | 51 | 55 | 66 | 54 | 46 | 36 | 46 | 29 | 37 | 27 | 39 | 49 | 32 | 48 | 39 |
| Low management or professional | 17 | 9 | 30 | 22 | 21 | 15 | 36 | 12 | 23 | 18 | 30 | 27 | 30 | 26 | 18 |
| Skilled nonmanual | 16 | 11 | 3 | 18 | 19 | 11 | 16 | 21 | 26 | 14 | 11 | 11 | 18 | 15 | 16 |
| Lower nonmanual | 5 | 1 | 0 | 0 | 2 | 9 | 0 | 6 | 11 | 32 | 7 | 7 | 2 | 4 | 8 |
| Skilled manual | 5 | 16 | 1 | 6 | 11 | 15 | 3 | 10 | 0 | 0 | 7 | 4 | 14 | 4 | 10 |
| Semiskilled or unskilled | 8 | 9 | 0 | 0 | 1 | 14 | 0 | 23 | 4 | 9 | 7 | 2 | 4 | 3 | 10 |
| | 102 | 101 | 100 | 100 | 100 | 100 | 101 | 101 | 101 | 100 | 101 | 100 | 100 | 100 | 101 |
| N = | (89) | (94) | (73) | (83) | (91) | (88) | (81) | (52) | (74) | (44) | (57) | (45) | (50) | | |

[a] Entries are percentages; because of rounding, they do not always sum to 100.

[b] The coding scheme comes from Butler and Stokes, 1969 (see note 4). Because of operational differences among these independent mass surveys, cross-national comparisons should be drawn only with caution.

[c] The French code for father's occupational status in the original study is as follows: (1) industrialist, large merchant, liberal professions; (2) higher managerial jobs; (3) small merchant, artisan, farmer; (4) middle managerial or administrative jobs; (5) agricultural worker; (6) worker, service personnel.

[d] The coding of occupational status for the Dutch mass sample permits only a threefold classification: managerial or professional; other nonmanual; all manual.

[e] Mass data are drawn from the archives of the Interuniversity Consortium for Political and Social Research, based on the Butler and Stokes 1966 British electoral study, the Converse and Pierce 1967 French electoral study, the 1972 German election panel study, the Barnes and Sani 1972 Italian study, the Stouthard 1970 Dutch electoral study, and the Center for Political Studies 1970 U.S. election study.

[f] CS = civil servant; MP = member of parliament (or Congress); PE = political executive.

[g] Averages for the civil service samples exclude the American political executives.

homes in that privileged slice of the social hierarchy. This finding is all
the more striking when compared to the figure of 41 percent for the most
select of our peer samples, that is, males between 35 and 70 who themselves hold higher managerial or professional jobs. In terms of their social
origins, our bureaucrats and politicians are the *crème de la crème* of their
societies.[9]

We noted earlier the uniformly higher educational credentials of bureaucrats as compared to members of parliament. Thus, it is not surprising to learn in Table 3–3 that bureaucrats are drawn from more uniformly privileged social origins than politicians. Among bureaucrats, 74
percent were sons of managers or professionals, compared to 57 percent
of the politicians. At the other end of the social hierarchy, more than one
in four of our politicians are the sons of manual or low-ranking clerical
workers, compared to fewer than one in eight of the bureaucrats. The
maximum difference in the proportions of scions of the upper-middle
class (categories 1 and 2 in Table 3–3) between bureaucrats and politicians is found in Italy (41 percent), the minimum difference between the
roles is found in Britain (4 percent) and the United States (7 percent,
comparing congressmen and career officials). Bureaucrats and politicians
in France, sampled at the peak of the Gaullist era, came from the highest-
status backgrounds, with 86 percent of them the sons of managers and
professionals, whereas the Dutch elite as a whole had the most modest
origins, with "only" 52 percent from that category. By any measure the
governmental elites of these countries, both bureaucrats and politicians,
represent a most exclusive social group.

The importance of educational credentials for elite recruitment might
be seen as the mark of meritocracy. But if access to education is itself dependent on social status, then selecting a well-educated elite may be tantamount to selecting an elite from the upper social strata.[10] In fact, of
course, study after study has demonstrated a ubiquitous link between social origins and educational attainments. During the years when today's
elites were educated, children of professional families in the West were
between five and five hundred times more likely to attend a university
than were the children of manual workers.[11]

So at least part of the bias in the social composition of elites must be
attributed to the operation of the educational system, for even a random
sample of university graduates would overrepresent individuals from
upper-class backgrounds. But do social origins have a more direct impact
on elite recruitment processes, apart from that mediated through the

*Figure 3-1*   Social origins, education, and elite recruitment.

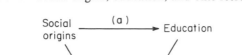

educational system? Figure 3-1 may help to clarify this issue. Arrow (*a*) represents the impact of social origins on educational opportunities, while arrow (*b*) represents the impact of educational achievements on access to elite posts. Thus, the indirect effects of social origins on elite recruitment may be interpreted as the product of (*a*) and (*b*). Arrow (*c*), on the other hand, represents the direct effect of social origins on elite recruitment. If this effect is weak, a lower-class youth who manages to slip past the social barriers in the educational system finds himself competing on even terms with his colleagues from more privileged backgrounds. However, if the effect symbolized by arrow (*c*) is strong, then he will find further special hurdles in his path toward political and administrative power, hurdles in the elite recruitment process itself that favor sons of the upper classes.

We know from the work of educational sociologists that arrow (*a*) is generally strong in our countries, and we know from evidence presented earlier in this chapter that arrow (*b*) is extremely strong. What can we say about the strength of arrow (*c*)? Methodologically, this question may be answered by comparing the social origins of the university graduates among our elites with the social origins of a random sample of university graduates in their respective nations, and, similarly, by comparing the social origins of the few nongraduates among our elites with the social origins of nongraduates in the population as a whole. Obtaining appropriate data for these tests is not simple, for the number of university graduates in the mass surveys of these countries is quite small; we have therefore supplemented such evidence by an examination of data from the Organization for Economic Cooperation and Development on the social composition of university student populations in the 1950s.[12] Slight differences in timing and in operational definitions of class boundaries make precise comparisons unreliable, but in broad outline the results are clear.

First of all, among nonuniversity graduates social discrimination in the elite recruitment process is quite strong, particularly for administrative elites. Among nongraduates in the general population, fewer than 25 percent are from middle-class homes; but among the nongraduates in our samples of parliamentary elites, roughly 60 percent are from middle-class homes, while among the handful of nongraduates in our samples of administrative elites, more than 80 percent are from the middle class. Without educational credentials, children of the working class are at a marked disadvantage compared even to nongraduates from middle-class backgrounds, though of course both groups are considerably less well off than university graduates of whatever social origin. This bias against working-class nongraduates is particularly marked in the case of the administrative elite. (The flow of class-to-class recruits to the administrative class in Britain has provided an opening for a minority of exceptionally qualified nongraduates, but this channel nevertheless has favored sons of the middle and lower middle classes rather than the working class.)

Second, social discrimination in elite recruitment is also visible among university graduates, although social bias is much less marked among graduates than among nongraduates, particularly in the case of parliamentary recruitment. Roughly two-thirds of the general pool of university graduates in these six countries are from middle-class homes, compared to roughly 75 percent of graduates in the political elite and roughly 90 percent of graduates in the administrative elite. Working-class children who make it through the university face some additional social hurdles, but these hurdles are not so sharply discriminatory as the educational system itself.

Table 3–4 summarizes these findings and makes clear the intensity of the effects of direct social bias—arrow (c) in Figure 3–1—on access to the administrative and parliamentary elites. Receiving a university degree partially offsets the bias against those of lower-class origins, particularly for parliamentarians. Direct social bias is greatest for recruitment to top administrative positions, and especially strong for those who have not

*Table 3-4*    Direct social bias in access to the elite.

| Type of elite | Level of education | |
|---|---|---|
| | Nonuniversity graduate | University graduate |
| Civil service | Highest bias | Medium bias |
| Parliament | Medium bias | Lowest bias |

graduated from a university. In the administrative world the sons of the upper middle class still stand a slight chance even when they have not graduated from a university, but the sons of those lower in social status had better gain educational credentials or they stand almost no chance of making it to the top.[13]

Another generalization supported by these somewhat fragile data is this: recruitment of European parliamentarians from the pool of university graduates is essentially unbiased in social terms, although of course admission *to* that pool is socially biased.[14] Graduates from working-class backgrounds find as much opportunity for advancement in the political hierarchy as do middle-class graduates. To understand why this is so, we must consider the role of leftist and, to a lesser degree, Christian Democratic political parties in elite recruitment.

Table 3–5 presents evidence on the social origins of our parliamentary samples, disaggregated into major-party groupings. The data show quite clearly the special effects of the socialist and communist parties of Western Europe. Despite their varying degrees of ideological revisionism, these leftist parties continue to provide a significant channel into the national political elite for working-class recruits. To be sure, the parliamentary representatives of these parties more and more are university graduates, and they no longer include large numbers of manual workers. However, the parties do offer an avenue of advancement for ambitious and well-educated sons of the working class—a role that, as our data clearly show, is not played by their American counterpart, the Democratic party. The European leftist parties serve, in the parlance of contemporary America, as a kind of affirmative-action institution for the working class, mitigating some of the sociological bias against it in the elite recruitment process. Americans of working-class origins have no such champion. Parties in America are more correctly categorized as coalitions of freelancers than as organized bodies. Individuals with monetary resources of their own have a great advantage in such a system. Ironically, the fluidity of the American party system helps to inhibit the rise of those of working-class origins.

A second phenomenon of more than passing interest reflected in these data concerns the various Catholic parties—the CDU in Germany, the DC in Italy, and the KVP in the Netherlands. Although these parties are moderate to conservative in terms of ideology and public policy, they appear to be significantly more open to sons of the working class than are secular conservative parties. The most plausible explanation for this

Table 3-5  Social-class origins of political elites, by party.[a]

| Father's social class | Country | | | | | | | | | | | | | |
|---|---|---|---|---|---|---|---|---|---|---|---|---|---|---|
| | Britain | | France | | Germany | | Italy | | | Netherlands | | | United States | |
| | Lab | Con | PCF | PS (Center and Right) | SPD | CDU (CSU) | PCI / PSI / PSIUP | DC | Other (Center and Right) | PVDA / Other (Left) | KVP | Other (Center and Right) | Dem | Rep |
| Middle and upper middle | 54 | 96 | 80 | 97 | 48 | 70 | 39 | 62 | 100 | 45 | 33 | 93 | 86 | 75 |
| Lower middle and working | 46 | 4 | 20 | 3 | 52 | 30 | 61 | 38 | 0 | 55 | 66 | 7 | 14 | 25 |
| | 100 | 100 | 100 | 100 | 100 | 100 | 100 | 100 | 100 | 100 | 100 | 100 | 100 | 100 |
| N = | (46) | (48) | (15) | (64) | (44) | (43) | (23) | (24) | (9) | (20) | (9) | (14) | (22) | (28) |

[a] Entries are percentages. Party abbreviations are as follows: Lab = Labour; Con = Conservative; PCF = Communist; PS = Socialist; SPD = Social Democratic; CDU = Christian Democratic Union; CSU = Christian Social Union; PCI = Communist; PSI = Socialist; PSIUP = Proletarian Socialist; DC = Christian Democratic; PVDA = Labor; KVP = Catholic People's; Dem = Democratic; Rep = Republican.

somewhat surprising finding is their traditional ties to segments of the working class, ties embodied historically in Christian socialism. It is striking that at least in recruitment patterns these bonds seem to have survived the ideological and organizational changes that the parties have undergone in the last half-century.

All the top civil service bodies, European and American, appear to resist institutional affirmative action of the sort promoted by left wing and, to a lesser degree, Christian Democratic parties. The very mechanisms that are meant to protect the civil service from undue political influence—merit systems, slow movement up the career ladder, insulation from publicity—ironically seem also, for better or worse, to shelter the higher civil service from the broader forces in the society. The procedures used in recruitment and promotion—written tests and small-group interviews—favor the advancement of those who are most like their predecessors. Additionally, the long apprenticeship required means that the bureaucratic elites of today reflect the criteria of those who recruited them into the civil service many years ago.[15]

If political parties wish to promote demographic democratization, however, they can do so relatively easily and rapidly. Even if the party selectorates wish to keep the social circle of recruitment closed, the political process is relatively open to public view, which makes it harder to hide bias and less likely that it will be exercised. There *is* bias in parliamentary recruitment, of course, and it is particularly shown in conservative parties, but it is harder to sustain in the more public world of politics than in the more insulated world of bureaucracy.

Our argument has been phrased in terms of "bias," but obviously our research provides no direct evidence of the mechanisms that might underlie these statistical biases. To some extent they might result from intentionally discriminatory choices made during the selection of bureaucratic and political elites. Another possibility is unintentional discrimination, as would be exemplified if personnel managers favored poised candidates, and poise in turn was correlated with social origin. Finally, the biasing mechanism might be self-selective; perhaps children from working-class homes rarely aspire to top-level political or administrative positions, for whatever complex set of reasons. We suspect that all these interpretations are accurate in some degree, and our use of the term *bias* is meant to leave open this question.

To summarize, in the recruitment of European administrative elites a university education is crucial, and this creates a very strong bias in favor of the sons of the middle and upper classes who are the most likely to advance this far up the educational ladder. Among nonuniversity graduates there is a clear and direct bias against those of working-class origins, especially in France and Italy. In the recruitment of European parliamentary elites, securing a university education is also quite important and again creates a definite bias in favor of the middle and upper classes. Among these politicians the direct effect of social origins—arrow (c) in Figure 3–1—is quite weak, however. One practical consequence is that should arrow (a), the effect of social origins on educational achievement, be significantly weakened—by expanding educational opportunities for working-class children, for example—the social composition of European political elites, ceteris paribus, might become reasonably representative of the populations as a whole, at least in terms of family background. Yet because there is no direct equivalent of a working-class affirmative-action party in the administrative sector, our evidence suggests that administrative elites might prove to be more resistant to demographic democratization.

American patterns of recruitment are rather different. In the first place, the historically greater accessibility of higher education in the United States means that the social composition of the pool of university graduates is significantly less biased than in Europe; thus, the direct effect of social class on education, arrow (a), is weaker in this country. Secondly, this greater accessibility of higher education also means that the educational credentials necessary for recruitment to the elite are more widely available; hence arrow (b), the effect of higher education on access to the elite, is *relatively* weaker in the United States. On the other hand, the absence of a working-class party means that politically ambitious university graduates from modest backgrounds encounter hurdles not faced by their counterparts in Europe; in short, the relative openness of the American educational system is offset to an extent by the relatively less open political recruitment system.

We can assess more directly the consequences of these differing patterns by examining summary indexes of educational and social inequality in elite recruitment. Figure 3–2 represents in graphic form Gini coefficients for our several elite samples; these indexes, based on the data of Tables 3–1 and 3–3, measure the degree of disparity between the socioeducational profiles of our elite groups and the profiles of comparable mass samples.[16] Unavoidable deficiencies and unreliabilities in the data that underlie these indexes counsel prudence in their interpretation.

*Figure 3-2*   Indexes of inequality (Gini coefficients).

| PARENTAL SOCIAL CLASS | | OWN EDUCATION |
|---|---|---|
| | 1.00 | |
| | | Italian civil servants (.96) |
| | | German civil servants (.95) |
| | | Dutch civil servants (.94) |
| Italian civil servants (.92) | | French civil servants (.93) |
| French civil servants (.91) | | |
| | | Italian politicians (.90) |
| | .90 | British civil servants (.89) |
| | | American civil servants (.89) |
| | | American politicians (.87) |
| | | American political executives (.86) |
| | | Dutch politicians (.83) |
| | | French politicians (.82) |
| | .80 | |
| French politicians (.78) | | British politicians (.77) |
| | | |
| Dutch civil servants (.70) | .70 | German politicians (.69) |
| British civil servants (.66) | | |
| German civil servants (.63) | | |
| American political executives (.62) | | |
| | .60 | |
| Dutch politicians (.58) | | |
| British politicians (.58) | | |
| | .50 | |
| American civil servants (.48) | | |
| Italian politicians (.46) | | |
| American politicians (.44) | | |
| | .40 | |
| German politicians (.33) | | |
| | .30 | |

NOTE: Gini coefficients are calculated from a comparison of elite and mass surveys. Parental social class is a six-level measure based on father's occupation. Own education is a three-level measure of primary, secondary, and university education.

Nevertheless, a cautious assessment of the evidence in Figure 3–2 supports the following conclusions.

(1) In all cases, access to the elite is considerably more biased in educational terms than in social terms. Higher social origins are helpful in gaining access to the elite, but higher education is a virtual necessity.

(2) In all cases, access to the political elite is more egalitarian (or less inegalitarian) than access to the administrative elite. In part this results from the more demanding educational credentials required of high-ranking civil servants; but as we have seen, it also results from more subtle sorts of posteducational social discrimination. In fact, the indexes of social inequality—summing, as they do, both direct and indirect effects—show a considerably greater disparity between political and administrative elites than do the indexes of educational inequality. (The mean index of educational inequality is .81 for the political elites and .92 for the administrative elites. On the other hand, the mean index of social inequality is .53 for the politicians and .71 for the bureaucrats.) The central point here is that recruitment resting ultimately on electoral mechanisms produces an elite more representative in social terms than does recruitment resting on appointment and examination.

(3) Despite the higher average educational levels and the higher average social origins of the American elites compared to their European counterparts, American indexes of inequality generally are lower than most European indexes. The reason for this seeming paradox is that the educational and social profile of the American population is also skewed upward in comparison with the European profiles. There are more sons of the middle class among the American elites, but at least in the previous generation the American middle class was proportionately larger than the European middle classes.

On the other hand, this relative American egalitarianism is much more marked in the administrative than in the political sphere, for American political recruitment is marked by the absence of a strong working-class party. (The index of social inequality for the career administrative elite in America is .48, whereas the European administrative average is .76. The index of social inequality for the American congressional elite is .44, compared to an average of .54 for the European parliamentary elites, or .49 if we exclude the anomalous French case.)

(4) The Italian and French administrative elites are distinctively unrepresentative in social origins, as is the French parliamentary elite. As

we indicated in Chapter 2, our sample of French politicians is probably unrepresentative of the current French political class, but no such simple artifact can explain away the findings for the two administrative elites. Something about the Latin bureaucracies has made them significantly less open to recruits from the lower classes than even the (not terribly egalitarian) bureaucracies of northern Europe. Since the Italian political elite is among the least inegalitarian in social terms, the disparity between politicians and bureaucrats is far higher in Italy than it is in any other country.

It is not completely clear why recruitment to the Latin bureaucracies is so especially biased, but one possible explanation is that there has never been a long-standing left-wing government in either of the Latin countries. If left-wing control brings with it both a relatively more egalitarian climate and a tempering of class conflict, then the civil service system is more likely to have been pressed to broaden its recruitment base. On the other hand, where the left-wing has never been in control for very long, there seems to be a strong climate of social and political conflict and an unusually strong level of social bias in administrative recruitment. In these societies the Right sees little reason to democratize the civil service system and in addition may fear leftist political contamination by opening the system. The result, in any case, is a more virulent inegalitarianism in bureaucratic recruitment.

(5) Finally, German politicians appear to be unusually egalitarian both educationally and socially. In party terms this pattern seems to derive from the coincidence of one major party with socialist roots and another major party with Catholic roots. To be sure, by their own occupational status German politicians are solid members of the middle class, but our data reveal a surprising degree of intergenerational mobility, fed in part by a relatively high degree of openness to nonuniversity political recruits.

Thus, we have seen that our elites, like elites studied elsewhere, are drawn quite disproportionately from well-educated, upper-status segments of the population. But we have also seen that the degree of sociological representativeness varies significantly from country to country and between politicians and bureaucrats. We can add one final note to this account of the social context of elite recruitment by considering briefly the geographic origins of our respondents.

Table 3–6 shows that whereas successful national politicians are produced in only slightly disproportionate numbers by urban areas, leading

*Table 3-6*    Urbanism and elite recruitment.[a]

| Country | | Civil servants | Political executives | Members of parliament | Mass[b] |
|---|---|---|---|---|---|
| Britain | | 64 | | 52 | 39 |
| | N = | (83) | | (66) | |
| Germany | | 64 | | 42 | 30 |
| | N = | (86) | | (85) | |
| Italy | | 74 | | 39 | 18 |
| | N = | (77) | | (46) | |
| Netherlands | | 43 | | 32 | 35 |
| | N = | (72) | | (41) | |
| United States | | 60 | 52 | 31 | 30 |
| | N = | (48) | (48) | (52) | |
| Five-nation average | | 61 | | 39 | 30 |

[a] Entry is percentage of each category who were raised in cities over 100,000 population.

[b] Data based on population distribution in censuses for 1930 to 1935.

bureaucrats are mostly urban bred. Moreover, we find that whereas the regional distribution of future politicians generally mirrors quite faithfully the distribution of the national population, regional concentrations of bureaucratic recruitment are found in nearly every country. Roughly three-fifths of the British bureaucrats were raised in London, the Southeast, and the Midlands, but only two-fifths of the parliamentarians. The northeastern United States produced roughly one-fifth of the congressional sample, but more than a third of the career civil servants. In the Netherlands the megalopolis encompassing the Randstat and Utrecht supplied 43 percent of the parliamentary elite, but 64 percent of the bureaucratic elite. Although we have no data on the geographic origins of our French samples, other studies have found large cities in general, and the Paris region in particular, to be overrepresented among the French administrative elite.[17] The peculiar history and geography of the German Federal Republic seem to have blurred geographic concentrations of bureaucratic recruitment; we find only a faint overrepresentation of Berlin and the eastern territories, along with a slight underrepresentation of Bavaria.

In all five of these cases bureaucratic recruitment tends to be concentrated in the "center" rather than on the "periphery," but the Italian pattern is considerably different. While regional concentration of bureaucratic recruitment is extreme in Italy, it is centered in the less developed regions. More than four-fifths of our Italian bureaucratic respondents were raised in the South (including Lazio), as contrasted with less than one-third of the deputies. The traditional absence of attractive opportunities for employment in the private sector in the Mezzogiorno seems to account for this phenomenon, widely reported in previous studies.

Thus, in general, bureaucrats tend to come from the more urban, usually more cosmopolitan, areas of their countries, whereas politicians as a group do not differ significantly from the national population. Two complementary explanations of this pattern seem reasonable. First, political recruitment is considerably more decentralized than administrative recruitment, and the geographic basis of electoral representation in most of the countries sampled tends to promote home-grown politicians. Second, the greater importance of educational credentials for bureaucratic recruitment gives a special advantage to areas of greater educational opportunity, which tend to be urban. Italy offers one interesting illustration of this phenomenon. When our Italian officials were growing up, secondary schools were nonexistent in most of the smaller towns of the South, so that the ambitious sons of the local gentry were apt to move to the larger cities for their schooling. In fact, only 35 percent of our senior Italian officials were born in cities over 100,000 in population, but 74 percent grew up in such cities. In no other sample in our surveys—not even among Italian politicians—does such a pattern of massive adolescent migration appear, although Suleiman reports a similar phenomenon for the French administrative elite.[18] The economic requirements implicit in this pattern probably help explain the severe underrepresentation of lower middle-class and working-class recruits to the administrative elites of these two countries. Over the long run the representativeness of administrative elites probably would be increased if educational opportunities in rural and provincial areas were improved.

### Careers in National Government

When examining the career lines of bureaucratic and political elites, we find it useful to consider two ideal types of recruitment systems, differing in the permeability of the recruitment channels.[19] At one extreme are what we may term *guild systems,* which require long apprenticeship within a single institution as a prerequisite for admission to the elite. At the other extreme are *entrepreneurial systems,* characterized by a high degree of lateral entry into the elite from outside careers and institutions. Guild systems ensure that elites will be more experienced and more fully

*Figure 3-3*  Age and tenure in national government.

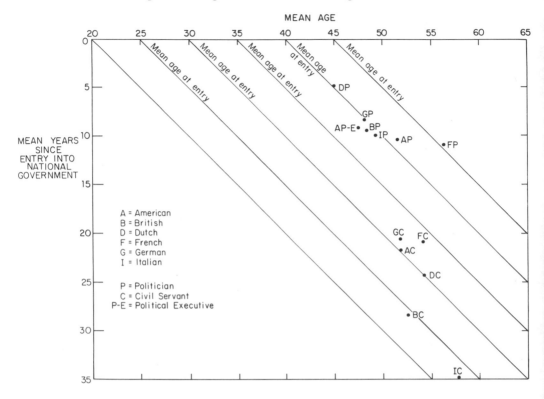

socialized into the norms of the elite institution. On the other hand, entrepreneurial systems provide the elite with freshets of new ideas and with exposure to the skills and experiences of other social institutions. In short, guild systems maximize internal integration within the elite, whereas entrepreneurial systems maximize integration of the elite and other parts of society. Personnel turnover is likely to be higher in entrepreneurial systems than in guild systems, although in principle one could combine relatively high turnover at the top with long periods of prior apprenticeship.

What does our evidence have to say about the career patterns of parliamentary and administrative elites in modern democracies? Figure 3–3 synthesizes much of the relevant information. Measured along the horizontal axis is the average age of each of our samples, with the average number of years since the respondents first entered national government given along the vertical axis.[20] Samples in the lower right-hand section of the graph are relatively old with rather high tenure, whereas samples in the upper left-hand quadrant are heavily composed of younger, more recent arrivals. From these two bits of data we can readily deduce the average age at which members of each sample first entered national government; this information is read off the diagonal lines. For example, British civil servants in our survey averaged 52.5 years of age and had served an average of 28.5 years in national government; they had entered the civil service, then, at an average age of 24.

The most obvious pattern in Figure 3–3 is the clear distinction between politicians and bureaucrats. The average member of parliament in these six samples was 50 years old and had entered parliament ten years earlier at the age of 40. By contrast, the average senior civil servant was 53 years old and had entered national government 25 years earlier at the age of 28. The average member of parliament had spent roughly 70 percent of his adult life (after the age of 25) outside national government, the average top administrator less than 20 percent. Nearly two-thirds of the politicians had served less than a decade in national government, compared to only about one-eighth of the civil servants. (It is notable and significant that by these measures the American political executives are more appropriately grouped with politicians than with the other administrators.) Since career patterns are one key indicator of the appearance of the "pure hybrid" type of political-bureaucratic relationship described in Chapter 1, we can see that hybrids are not yet dominant in the bureaucracies of any of our systems, except perhaps in the section of the American bureaucracy reserved for appointees, where significant numbers of politically sympathetic outsiders are regularly introduced into the upper reaches of the bureaucracy.

These data reflect the obvious fact that national government is a lifetime career for most civil servants, but not for most politicians. It is plausible to theorize that the difference in career patterns described above produces different degrees of expertise in national policymaking. In an era of complexity, this difference may also be related to shifts in the balance of effective power between parliament and the executive. And the difference is also compatible with the energy/equilibrium image (III) of the role of bureaucrats and elected politicians in policymaking, where the generally slow and steady rise in position of the bureaucrat and his cultivation of expertise through long service is thought to give him a more prudent, practical, and moderate approach to policy design and implementation than the politician takes, even though both sets of actors need and use political skills. (In later chapters, we return to this issue of ideological and stylistic differences between politicians and bureaucrats.)

In addition, the difference between political and administrative career patterns reflects a difference between entrepreneurial and guild forms of recruitment. This distinction is supported by the fact that in virtually every country the variance in mean age is considerably higher for politicians than for bureaucrats; politicians are less likely to have taken a single-speed escalator to the top. Of course, many of these politicians served an apprenticeship in party and local politics before entering parliament. Parliamentary recruitment is somewhat more guildlike than these figures suggest. Nevertheless, political recruitment channels assuredly are more permeable to lateral entry than bureaucratic recruitment channels.

National differences among the political elites are extraordinarily slight. Dutch parliamentarians at the time of our interviews were slightly younger and less experienced in national government than the other samples, and French members of parliament were a bit older than average, having entered parliament at a slightly more advanced age. But all in all, the clustering of the political samples is remarkable, particularly since the formal institutions of government and party organization in our six countries are quite different.

Contrasts among the national bureaucratic samples are more significant. The data in Figure 3–3 may be usefully supplemented by the evidence on career mobility presented in Table 3–7. At one extreme we find the sclerotic Italian bureaucratic elite, older and with much higher tenure than any other sample in the study. This bureaucracy fits the model of guild recruitment almost perfectly. The average senior Italian bureaucrat entered the civil service at the age of 22, and there he has stayed for thirty-five years. More than 90 percent of the members of this gerontocracy have spent their entire adult lives in national government and more than 80 percent have spent all this time in a single ministry. Lateral entrants into the Italian bureaucratic elite are virtually nonexistent.

Next most guildlike in its recruitment patterns is the British civil service. On average, British officials in our study had entered national government at the age of 24, although a minority of 12 percent had spent at least a quarter of their adult life in some other career before entering national government. The apprenticeship pattern in the British civil service is also signaled by the relatively low variance in its age and tenure profiles, although in neither case is this uniformity so great as in Italy. The fact that the average senior British official is six years younger than his Italian counterpart (Figure 3–3) indicates a lower retirement age and consequently higher turnover rates. Finally, the much higher level of in-

*Table 3-7*   Career mobility of bureaucratic elites.

| Country | Percentage who have spent 25% or more of adult life[a] outside national government | | Percentage who have served in a ministry other than present one |
|---|---|---|---|
| Britain | | 12 | 51 |
| | N = | (91) | (92) |
| France | | 37 | No data |
| | N = | (75) | |
| Germany | | 49 | 31 |
| | N = | (87) | (90) |
| Italy | | 2 | 18 |
| | N = | (84) | (84) |
| Netherlands | | 35 | No data |
| | N = | (75) | |
| United States | | | |
| Civil servants | | 30 | 22 |
| | N = | (64) | (64) |
| Political executives | | 78 | 18 |
| | N – | (60) | (61) |

[a] Defined as age 25 and over.

terministerial mobility in Britain than in any other country for which we have relevant information marks an important idiosyncracy of British administrative career patterns.

The recruitment patterns of the other four bureaucratic elites are much more similar. In each case, basically apprenticeship systems are leavened by a significant degree of lateral entry, so that the average age at entry is significantly higher than in Britain and Italy. Interestingly, the American career civil service is shown to be quite similar to its counterparts in most of Western Europe. The prominence of political appointees in the most visible posts has tended to obscure the cadre of permanent officials within American national government, whose career patterns are much like those of a typical European bureaucracy.

The degree of lateral entry characteristic of the Bonn bureaucracy is perhaps somewhat unexpected. Our data suggest that this pattern may be attributed primarily to the advent of the SPD to national government. The SPD supporters in our sample had spent an average of 49 percent of their adult lives outside national government, compared to a figure of 20 percent for the Christian Democratic supporters and independents, although the Social Democrats were significantly younger. These figures, together with other evidence on their political outlook and behavior, suggest that many of the Social Democrats in the Bonn ministries in the early 1970s might be seen as the functional equivalents of the American political executives.[21] In any event, the contemporary German bureaucratic recruitment process seems much more permeable than has been traditionally assumed.

### Political Origins and Current Loyalties

It is well known that high-level elected officials and civil servants are drawn disproportionately from upper-status groups, but it is not clear what difference this makes for politics and policy. Drawn most starkly, the issue is whether elites favor the interests of the social groups from which they are drawn or whether there is a process of socialization both before and after joining the policymaking elite that significantly loosens the ties binding its members' political views to those of their parents and peers. Our examination of these issues begins with the unique family traditions of political activity and administrative service that have influenced Western elites.

Reviewing studies which confirm that political and administrative elites are drawn disproportionately from the top of the socioeconomic hierarchy, Kenneth Prewitt has pointed out that "the correlation between social status and political power, though consistently positive, is not grounds for assuming that the former is a sufficient or necessary condition for the latter." Seeking a supplementary explanation for patterns of elite recruitment, Prewitt suggests that

> as a result of political socialization experiences, a small segment of the population are "overexposed" to public affairs; this group of persons are exposed more frequently and intimately to politics than is the case for the average member of society. A tenable hypothesis is that this group contributes heavily to the leadership class. What the politician shares with his colleagues is a familiarity with politics that reaches back into his early adulthood, adolescence, or, in many cases, his childhood.[22]

In short, the hypothesis is that elite members tend to have inherited, if not their public posts, then at least their proclivity for public service.

A rigorous test of this overexposure hypothesis requires directly comparable evidence on the socialization of both elite and nonelite members, evidence that is unfortunately not yet available. However, some data from our elite surveys tend to support Prewitt's suggestion strongly. Table 3–8 presents some of the relevant information. Nearly half of all our politicians and more than a quarter of our bureaucrats report having immediate relatives actively involved in politics, either now or in the past. Analogously, more than half of the bureaucrats and more than a third of the politicians report one or more relatives in the civil service. Indeed, 16 percent of the European politicians and 33 percent of the European bureaucrats report that their father's primary occupation was in government service; the U.S. figures are considerably lower. All in all, 58 percent of the European politicians and 62 percent of the European bureaucrats report relatives actively involved in politics or government, while in the United States slightly more than a third of the respondents report relatives in politics or government. In response to a question posed only in Europe, 65 percent of the politicians and 54 percent of the bureaucrats reported that political affairs were discussed reasonably often in their parents' home. Further analysis confirms that political discussions were more common in the homes of those respondents with politically active relatives. It is highly unlikely that comparable samples of mass publics in these nations would report such high levels of family political and governmental involvement.

Particularly in Europe, these data provide strong if indirect evidence for the existence of what Mosca termed "the political class," that is, a stratum of the population in which a tradition of participation in politics and government is passed from generation to generation. More precisely, a comparison of the somewhat contrasting responses from politicians and bureaucrats suggests two partially overlapping strata: one especially involved in politics and producing a relatively high proportion of today's political elite, and a second with a tradition of government service and producing a relatively high proportion of today's administrative elite.

The social exclusiveness of these strata should not be exaggerated, for the parental social standing of our respondents from political or administrative families is only slightly higher than that of their colleagues without such family traditions. Rarely did the fathers of our respondents hold positions in national politics and government as senior as those of their sons. For the most part, our members of parliament are the sons, not of members of parliament, but of local political activists. Our directors gen-

Table 3-8  Family background in politics and government.

| Measure of family involvement in politics and government | Britain CS[a] | Britain MP | France CS | France MP | Germany CS | Germany MP | Italy CS | Italy MP | Netherlands CS | Netherlands MP | United States CS | United States PE | United States MP | Six-nation average CS[b] | Six-nation average MP |
|---|---|---|---|---|---|---|---|---|---|---|---|---|---|---|---|
| Percentage with one or more relatives active in politics now or in the past | 16 | 41 | No data | | 43 | 57 | 25 | 36 | 30 | 50 | No data | | | 28 | 46 |
| N = | (90) | (96) | | | (90) | (99) | (52) | (50) | (74) | (44) | | | | | |
| Percentage with one or more relatives in the civil service now or in the past | 46 | 29 | No data | | 64 | 35 | 69 | 40 | 41 | 34 | No data | | | 55 | 35 |
| N = | (88) | (96) | | | (90) | (99) | (58) | (50) | (74) | (44) | | | | | |
| Percentage with father employed in government | 20 | 17 | No data | | 32 | 10 | 41 | 17 | 37 | 21 | 9 | 0 | 2 | 28 | 13 |
| N = | (89) | (94) | | | (91) | (88) | (81) | (52) | (74) | (44) | (57) | (45) | (50) | | |
| Percentage with one or more relatives in politics and/or the civil service now or in the past | 54 | 57 | 50 | 51 | 80 | 65 | 75 | 57 | 51 | 61 | 37 | 33 | 38 | 58 | 55 |
| N = | (87) | (79) | (70) | (53) | (89) | (77) | (52) | (44) | (74) | (44) | (56) | (55) | (26) | | |
| Frequency of political discussion at home in childhood (percentage) | | | | | | | | | | | | | | | |
| A great deal | 30 | 46 | No data | | 46 | 59 | 46 | 44 | 26 | 42 | No data | | | 37 | 48 |
| Occasionally | 11 | 10 | No data | | 18 | 14 | 15 | 19 | 25 | 24 | No data | | | 17 | 17 |
| Rarely or never | 59 | 44 | No data | | 36 | 27 | 39 | 36 | 49 | 34 | No data | | | 46 | 35 |
| | 100 | 100 | | | 100 | 100 | 100 | 99 | 100 | 100 | | | | 100 | 100 |
| N = | (87) | (82) | | | (83) | (85) | (59) | (36) | (72) | (41) | | | | | |

[a] CS = civil servant; MP = member of parliament (or Congress); PE = political executive.
[b] Averages for the civil service samples exclude the American political executives.

eral are the sons, not of directors general, but of middle-ranking officials. Cross-nationally speaking, it is interesting to note that this pattern of political inheritance is much less marked among American elites. As observers since Tocqueville have noted, public affairs in America—for better or worse—are not the special preserve of individuals who have been bequeathed traditions of public service, at least not to the same degree as in Europe.

Thus there is strong circumstantial evidence that especially in Europe our elites have inherited a peculiar propensity for politics and government. It is quite striking that when we turn to partisan affiliations, we discover that inherited loyalties only moderately govern political behavior. The transmission of parental partisanship is particularly weak among our bureaucratic samples. In our six nations the mean correlation (tau-beta) between father's reported party preference and respondent's party preference is .54 among the mass public, .40 among our political elites, and .25 among our administrative elites.[23] In some important respects, therefore, politicians and bureaucrats seem to have imbibed their parents' special interest in public affairs without necessarily accepting their political views. We turn now to further evidence that at least in terms of partisan politics these elites, but especially bureaucrats, are peculiarly independent of the social and family milieu in which they were raised. Such evidence modifies the otherwise abundant proof of social and political inheritance that we have presented thus far.

We have seen that our bureaucratic and parliamentary elites are unusually well educated and come from extraordinarily high social origins, even when compared to their recruitment-pool peers in professional and managerial positions. These characteristics would ordinarily lead us to expect them to be rather conservative politically, especially when compared to the average citizens of their countries and even when compared to their professional and managerial peers. In most of these countries a major basis of political conflict is class. Indeed, this is the reason why people are so concerned about the social biases of elite recruitment: if class determines political outlook, administrative and parliamentary elites drawn from a very socially biased pool presumably will be politically biased as well. We find that quite the contrary is true, at least in terms of partisanship.

Before we get to our findings, we need to say a word about our procedures for testing the impact of social backgrounds on elite attitudes and behavior. Ordinarily correlation coefficients would be used. However,

*Figure 3-4*  Own and fathers' Left-Right party preferences for mass, peer, and elite samples.[a]

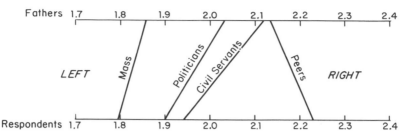

[a] Mean scores are based on equally weighted samples from Britain, Germany, the Netherlands, and the United States. Party scores: Left = 1; Center = 2; Right = 3.

because of the recruitment biases we have described, variance on the independent variable—social origins—is truncated, with the result that the correlation coefficients are artificially depressed. It is, therefore, more informative to compare the aggregate party preferences of the parliamentary and administrative elites with the party preferences of the relevant mass publics and the party preferences of recruitment-pool peers. The question addressed here is simply this: Compared to the electorate as a whole (or the recruitment pool), does social bias in elite recruitment entail a bias in partisan terms?[24]

Figure 3–4 displays the weighted average of scores on a measure of party preference for respondents from mass samples, recruitment-pool peer samples, and politician and civil servant samples for four of the countries for which we have data on the party preferences of bureaucratic elites.[25] The mean scores for each country were derived from a trichotomized variable on which left parties were coded 1, center parties were coded 2, and parties of the right coded 3. Since the parties were classified country by country, we do not assume that the categories have precisely the same meaning cross-nationally; our interest here is not cross-national, but intranational comparison.[26] The means have been pooled for clarity of presentation. Points on the lower axis represent the weighted average of the party preferences of our respondents, and points on the upper axis represent the weighted average of reported party preferences of their fathers. Lines linking pairs of points represent the degree and direction of change in party sympathies from fathers to sons.

These data show, first, that political elites are to the left of their peer groups and, in fact, politicians are relatively close to the mass of citizens in their party affiliations. Second, and more surprising, senior civil servants also are well to the left of their peers in party identification and are not far from the average voter. The bureaucrats and their peers come from families with virtually identical conservative sympathies, and both bureaucrats and peers now occupy social niches even higher, on average, than did their fathers. However, whereas the peers have typically moved to the right of their fathers, the bureaucrats have moved sharply to the left. This finding is all the more remarkable because the civil servants are in fact higher in occupational status, educational attainment, and social origin than most of the respondents in the peer samples. In most of our countries, to be sure, bureaucratic elites are on average more conservative in party loyalties than the citizenry at large, but these elites are much more representative of public party preferences than one might guess from their social backgrounds.

Why are high-ranking civil servants typically to the left of their social peers? Our data do not provide a final answer, but they do negate one possible explanation: senior officials do *not* come from unusually leftist families—they do not inherit their relatively progressive party allegiances from their family and childhood social milieus. Some possible explanations of this phenomenon, which will be examined in our discussion of the structure of elite ideology in Chapter 5, involve self-selection, selective recruitment, and experience in government. People who choose a career in the civil service may be more likely than their peers and their parents to look with favor on governmental involvement in social and economic affairs, a view more commonly held by leftist parties. At least in some of our countries, the relatively representative political complexion of the administrative elite may reflect subtle (or not so subtle) selective devices that tend to exclude persons of immoderate political loyalties from positions of leadership. Given the social and political origins of most civil servants, such selective devices would tend to exclude larger numbers of conservatives. Finally, respondents who have spent a lifetime in government working with politicians of all major parties may over time become less wholeheartedly committed to the relatively conservative faiths of their fathers.

While the French administrative elite is an exception to the general description we have offered, it is not an inexplicable one. Members of the higher levels of the Gaullist bureaucracy are exceptionally biased in social terms and were probably recruited with special attention to their political affiliations and partisan tendencies. In this respect they probably resemble to some degree the American political executives of the Nixon administration, for in reported party preferences both the American political executives and the French bureaucrats are well to the right of their recruitment-pool peers as well as their fathers.[27] Perhaps both Gaullist administrators and Nixon appointees were chosen as agents of right-wing change. For whatever reason, they are clearly unlike the career civil servants in the United States and in our other countries.

Even aside from the special case of France, we do not wish to claim that the higher ranks of the civil services in these countries are filled with radical social reformers. Our point is that neither the parliamentary nor the administrative elites in these countries are so out of tune with the electorate's political views as one might expect from the elites' social backgrounds. Some simple statistics may clarify the point. Among the fathers of today's voters in Britain, Germany, Holland, and the United States, an average of 46 percent were supporters of leftist parties, compared with 35 percent of the fathers of today's politicians, 29 percent of the fathers of today's bureaucrats, and 29 percent of the fathers of the elite's social peers. In the present generation, on the other hand, 52 percent of the electorate are supporters of leftist parties, compared to 50 percent of the political elite, 46 percent of the administrative elite, and 28 percent of their social peers. Notwithstanding class theories of politics and allied notions about representative bureaucracy, both elites (except in France) have moved away from the partisan preferences of their fathers, and even more sharply away from those of their social peers, and gravitated closer to those of the mass public.

## The Face of the Future

Change in the social and political composition of elites is, of course, best analyzed with genuinely longitudinal data. However, it may be of passing interest to contrast the characteristics of the senior officials and members of parliament discussed up to this point with comparable characteristics of our special samples of younger politicians and bureaucrats, selected to represent, at least in part, the elites of the future.[28]

Our primary finding is quite simple: there are very few differences in the social and political backgrounds of younger versus older elite generations. They do not differ, for example, in parental social status or in geographic origin. As we have reported, women are slightly more common among the administrative high-fliers than among senior officials, but the younger group remains 96 percent male.

We have discovered only two significant, cross-nationally consistent differences between our younger and older samples. First, university education is more common among the younger cadres. In part, this difference may represent a genuine generational transformation of elite composition; some longitudinal research supports that view.[29] On the other hand, evidence from our own senior samples shows that, in the past at least, university graduates have entered the national elites earlier than their less-educated colleagues, who must work their way up a longer ladder. Hence, our samples of high-fliers, precociously visible in national affairs, may slightly overestimate the proportion of university graduates who will compose their cohort when it finally reaches the top. Nevertheless, the comparison of high-fliers and senior incumbents strongly suggests that the unique importance of educational credentials for elite recruitment is not likely to diminish.

The second difference between older and younger cohorts is a tendency, at least on the Continent, for offspring of government families to be even more common among the high-fliers than among their senior colleagues. This finding may simply reflect the general growth in government employment in recent decades, and therefore the greater likelihood that anyone would have a relative in government. Alternatively, it may represent a tendency for scions of the political class to climb the recruitment ladder faster than their colleagues without family ties to the government. We do not interpret this apparent intergenerational difference as evidence that the hold of the political class on elite recruitment is actually increasing over time, but certainly there is no evidence that the grip is slackening. In sum, our analysis of intergenerational similarities and differences in the social and political composition of elites strongly suggests that the immediate future will be much like the immediate past.[30]

## Summary and Conclusions

At the beginning of this chapter we posed two general descriptive questions about the social and political origins and career patterns of top administrators and politicians. First, how do they differ from the publics they govern? Second, how do they differ from one another? We then posed two more complex questions: (1) How do differences in the *ways* in which they are chosen *lead* to differences from the public and from one another? (2) What is the significance of their origins and career paths for their attitudes and behavior?

A broad summary of the answers to the first two questions is seen in

*Figure 3-5*   Entering the elite: a sociological flowchart.

For a child (R) born in the 1920s, which characteristics affect his chances of entering the political or bureaucratic elite in the 1970s?

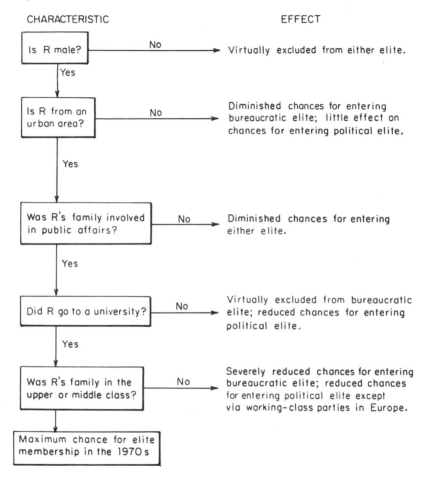

CHARACTERISTIC

Is R male? — No → Virtually excluded from either elite.

Is R from an urban area? — No → Diminished chances for entering bureaucratic elite; little effect on chances for entering political elite.

Was R's family involved in public affairs? — No → Diminished chances for entering either elite.

Did R go to a university? — No → Virtually excluded from bureaucratic elite; reduced chances for entering political elite.

Was R's family in the upper or middle class? — No → Severely reduced chances for entering bureaucratic elite; reduced chances for entering political elite except via working-class parties in Europe.

Maximum chance for elite membership in the 1970s

EFFECT

Figure 3–5, which is a flow diagram showing the conditions maximizing the chances that a person born around 1920 would be in our 1970–1971 political elite samples:

(1) The female half of the population is virtually excluded at the outset from both the administrative and parliamentary elites.

(2) In general, bureaucrats tend to come from the more urban, generally more cosmopolitan, areas of their countries, but parliamentarians as a group do not differ significantly from the national population in this regard.

(3) Both sets of elites, particularly in Europe, appear to have inherited a propensity for politics and government, for their relatives were unusually involved in political activities or were in government employ. Thus, the minority of the general population whose families have a public affairs orientation have a very disproportionate chance for elite status. Those from the apolitical majority are mostly excluded.

(4) Parliamentary politicians and, even more, high-level administrators are extraordinarily better educated than their countrymen of any social stratum, including those who are their recruitment-pool peers. Only a small minority of the public in the six countries examined has been to a university. Those in the nonuniversity majority by and large are excluded from the elite, especially from the higher levels of the bureaucracy.

(5) Persons from working-class and lower-middle-class backgrounds are largely excluded from the elite, in part by social filters built into the educational system, but also in part by more direct social bias. This sort of bias is partially attenuated among university graduates, particularly in parliamentary recruitment. In most of Western Europe a university degree assures a son of the working class as much opportunity for advancement in the political hierarchy as his middle-class fellow graduates have. The leftist parties—and, to an extent, the Christian Democratic parties—are responsible for this, whereas in America the Democratic party does not play such a role. Overall access to American elites, however, is more egalitarian than in Europe, both because the social and educational profile of the American population is skewed upward and because the American educational system is more egalitarian.

Thus, two groups highly unrepresentative in demographic terms emerge as members of the administrative and political elites. Top administrators come from the tiny minority of the population that is male, urban, university educated, upper middle class in origin, and public affairs oriented. Parliamentary elites are drawn mainly from the pool of male university graduates from public-affairs-oriented families. But they are less unrepresentative demographically than bureaucrats because they are joined by a small number of nonuniversity graduates, and also because the party system fosters a certain amount of mobility from the lower middle and working classes.

The ways in which they are chosen and reach the top seem to account for some of the differences between the two elites. The guild systems that dominate the administrative world tend to produce highly experienced top elites who are well socialized into the norms of their institutions. Most members of the administrative elite were originally selected by examinations and small-group interviews that one could not easily pass without a university education. (For those without a university education, a fine preparatory education and the graces learned in an upper-class family would seem to be the best substitutes.) Once in the bureaucracy, the social and educational biases of those already at the top and the exams and interviews used to promote from within also subtly favor men from upper-status backgrounds. Turnover at the top is generally slow, so that even if the criteria for admission to and advancement within the civil service were to become more "liberal" in terms of educational and experiential backgrounds (with a greater emphasis on technical skills and experience), those presently at the pinnacle of the bureaucratic hierarchy would still have been selected by the criteria and norms that dominated the organization many years before. National government is a lifetime career for most civil servants. The desire to protect civil service systems by insulating them from political meddling, and the emphasis on seniority and interpersonal skills, makes it difficult to secure rapid changes in the social biases at the top of the system. These biases, as we have seen, are strongest in societies where the Left has had little opportunity to govern.

Parliamentary systems are much more entrepreneurial in their recruitment and advancement practices. People enter at a later age and stay a shorter time. Recruitment is more open to public scrutiny and control, and party leaders are interested in presenting candidates with whom their electorates can identify. Reinforcing this is the fact that the ideologies of certain parties seem to favor people from lower-middle-class and working-class backgrounds. So while the secular conservative parties are bastions of those with upper-status backgrounds, the left wing especially seeks people from lower-status backgrounds to present to the electorate. The fact that parties usually seek support from all geographic regions helps explain why elected officials come less predominantly from urban areas than do top administrators. In addition, articulateness is a trait valued by those who select and those who elect candidates for public office. University education promotes facility with words and thus becomes an important filter in the recruitment of political elites. Moreover, to the politically ambitious, securing a university education improves prospects for being recruited. The end result is a less biased, but still highly biased, set of elected officials.

While both sets of elites are basically unrepresentative socially, and while both come from families with unusually high levels of political involvement and government employment, inherited loyalties do not fully determine their partisan attachments. Neither the parliamentary nor the administrative elites are as out of tune with the electorate's political views as one might expect from their social backgrounds. With the exception of France, elites in our six countries have moved away from their fathers and their recruitment-pool peers and toward the mass publics. The reason why elected politicians resemble the public's partisan preferences is obvious, but the process by which members of the top bureaucratic elite come to resemble the public more than one might expect is surely complex. Self-selection for an administrative role, selective recruitment, and experience in government are probably all important. Our surmise is that the administrator's typically lengthy tenure in government, working with politicians of all major parties, may moderate previously held political views and that those at the top who winnow out candidates for succession to their posts usually eliminate persons of immoderate political loyalties. Ironically, it may well be the slow and measured pace of advancement up the administrative ladder and the tests and skills required in that arena that keep administrators almost as representative in partisan terms as the more uncertain and rapidly changing environment of the elected official.

# Roles and Styles in Policymaking

## 4

Classical writings on the relationship between bureaucracy and politics leave little doubt that administration and politics are distinctly separable, that the demands placed upon administrators and politicians differ sharply, and that different skills and orientations are required for each role. Max Weber, for instance, observed that the bureaucratic official "functions more exactly, from a technical point of view, because . . . it is more likely that purely functional points of consideration and qualities will determine his selection and career." On the other hand, Weber notes that political recruitment gives "decisive weight not to expert considerations but to the services"[1] that the official renders to his political organization. In this formulation, which resonates with Image II as proposed in Chapter 1, Weber concisely expresses the distinction between the bureaucrat who responds to facts and the politician who responds to interests and acts on behalf of ideals.

The onset of "scientific management" in the United States further solidified the distinction between administration and politics, if in a different form than Weber had proposed.[2] As we noted in Chapter 1, such influential American scholars as Woodrow Wilson, Luther Gulick, and Frank Goodnow argued vigorously that it was necessary to divide the worlds of politics and administration.[3] Image I captures the dichotomy they advocated: bureaucrats ought to manage, and politicians ought to make policy.

The notion that bureaucratic activity and political activity can be sharply separated from each other is increasingly challenged by the growing complexity of governmental activities, by the surge in demands from recently mobilized constituencies, and by the consequent requirement that bureaucrats develop political support on behalf of interventionist policies whatever their particular nature. The enlarged scope of administrative activity in the positive state means also a larger array of responsibilities and burdens, which may compel administrators to forge consent for concrete policies, to represent interests, and to reconcile or broker conflicting claims—all activities which, according to Images I and II, had been thought to lie in the sphere of political rather than administrative activity.

Yet the likelihood is that administrators and politicians are both involved in policymaking activities and, thus, in inherently political activities. Such notions are readily assimilated by what we have called Image III. What critically distinguishes bureaucrats and politicians according to Image III is that they are engaged in policymaking in different settings linked to different constituencies—one relatively narrow and more concretely specified; the other broader and less easily defined. Moreover, the characteristics that distinguish the bureaucrat's setting from that of the elected politician should lead to different ways of looking at policy and different behavioral styles. The politician gives to policy general direction inspired by principles or interests or sometimes both. The bureaucrat, on the other hand, gives to policy concrete meaning derived in part from an understanding of its technical aspects and in part from negotiation with those interests immediately affected by administrative interpretation.

If circumstances perhaps have led bureaucrats in the industrial democracies to become more sensitized to political concerns, they also may have moved political leaders to become increasingly familiar with administrative and technical aspects of policy problems. The ascendancy of technocratically trained political leaders such as Valéry Giscard d'Estaing and Raymond Barre in France, Helmut Schmidt in West Germany, and Jimmy Carter in the United States is perhaps indicative of such a trend. In such cases the relevance of the hybrid career (Image IV) as a path to the very top can hardly be overlooked. Criteria traditionally associated with bureaucratic orientations—the mastery of specialized technical skills, analytic problem solving, the temperance of passion, and above all a tendency to define reform in terms of efficiency—may be coming to play a more significant role in the styles of political leaders.

Although the issue of convergent outlooks raises a number of interesting questions about the relative influence and institutional power of bureaucrats and parliamentary politicians, these are questions about which we can only speculate. A discussion of "who controls"—bureaucrats or politicians—is often pointless because alliances rarely form along such clear-cut lines. In Chapter 7, however, by examining the contact networks of bureaucrats and politicians, we shall discuss and illuminate the character of institutional interdependencies.

For now we begin with a prior question: in what respects do bureaucrats and politicians think and act in distinctive or similar ways? We address this question from several angles. Initially we identify some key dimensions of role focus among our respondents—what do they emphasize about their own jobs?—and we compare and contrast bureaucrats and politicians in these terms. We then explore some characteristic differences in the ways bureaucrats and politicians approach decision making, especially from the standpoint of political ideals, conflict management, and technical efficiency. Briefly, we examine some important national differences in how bureaucrats and politicians define their roles; here an important subtheme of our analysis—the contrast between the United States and Europe—is highlighted. We examine what characteristics bureaucrats and politicians think are essential for the conduct of each job, and the extent to which they agree about them. Finally, we analyze the criteria by which bureaucrats and politicians look at policy: how do they think about it, and what standards do they apply?

In short, we can now move from an armchair elaboration of possible differences and convergent tendencies of bureaucrats and politicians to an empirical, and thus more complicated, evaluation of their roles and styles as policymakers.

## Role Focus

Our measurement of role focus derives from attitudes expressed throughout the interviews, but it taps especially those aspects of the interviews that touch upon the respondents' jobs and responsibilities. Admittedly, there is no guarantee that the behavior of respondents follows directly from their characterization of their jobs or from related attitudes. Nonetheless, few areas of discussion are so likely to reflect behavioral experiences as the way one talks about one's job.

We asked our coders, then, to judge whether the respondents emphasized in their jobs: (1) *technical* aspects, which focus on solving technical

*Table 4-1*   Principal-factor analysis of role focus (all respondents).[a]

| Role focus | Factor loadings | | |
|---|---|---|---|
| | $F_1$: Politics/ technics | $F_2$: Authority/ responsiveness | $F_3$: Umpire/ player |
| Technician | **−.66**[b] | −.08 | .06 |
| Advocate | **.73** | −.01 | .04 |
| Legalist | −.17 | **.37** | **.68** |
| Broker | .10 | **.65** | **−.36** |
| Trustee | .07 | **.54** | **.43** |
| Facilitator | **.45** | −.22 | −.02 |
| Partisan | **.73** | −.08 | .02 |
| Policymaker | .29 | **.59** | **−.30** |
| Ombudsman | **.60** | −.18 | **.36** |
| Total variance explained | 24% | 14% | 11% |

[a] Because American respondents were not coded on the ombudsman role focus, the results reported above exclude them. If we eliminate the ombudsman focus and include the American respondents, we obtain a two-dimensional factor structure employing Kaiser's criterion.

[b] Loadings of .3 and above are shown in bold face for emphasis.

policy problems and applying specialized knowledge; (2) *advocacy* aspects, which focus on fighting for or representing the interests of a broad social group, class, or cause, or protesting injustice; (3) *brokering* aspects, which focus on mediating or resolving conflicts of interest and political conflict; (4) *facilitator* aspects, which focus on protecting the interests of specific clientele groups or constituents; (5) *partisan* aspects, which focus on partisan politics; (6) *policymaker* aspects, which focus on formulating policy; (7) *trustee* aspects, which focus on one's role as a representative of the state; (8) *legalist* aspects, which focus on legal processes or legalistic definitions of one's responsibilities; and/or (9) *ombudsman* aspects, which focus on undertaking case work for protecting and defending the interests of individual constituents or clients. It is important to note that these role foci were not treated as mutually exclusive, so that any particular respondent may have been coded as giving emphasis to more than one.[4]

How are our respondents' emphases on these aspects of their roles patterned? When we factor-analyze the role foci on which both bureaucrats and politicians have been coded, to discover the underlying similarities and dissimilarities in their role definitions, three dimensions emerge (Table 4-1). The first factor defines a politics/technics dimension: speaking about their own work, some respondents emphasize advocacy, partisanship, and the defense of more or less specific constituencies, whereas others stress instead the solution of technical policy problems. In general, we expect that bureaucrats are likely to be at the technics pole of this first dimension and politicians (naturally enough) at the politics pole. In other words, this should be the dimension that most sharply distinguishes bureaucrats from politicians. As we shall show in Chapter 5, this distinction also represents a basis upon which Leftists differ from Rightists. This dimension seems to fit most congruently with Image II—the traditional facts versus interests-and-values dichotomy.

The second factor defines an authority/responsiveness dimension, bringing together those variables that measure the respondents' relative commitment to a "top-down" role perspective—the brokering of conflict, the making of policy, the representation of the national interest above the claims of particular interests. This dimension seems to accord most readily with our Image III, the equilibrium versus energy distinction, and it too should distinguish politicians from bureaucrats, though less sharply than the first dimension.

The third factor is less clear, but this dimension seems to distinguish a relatively passive or "umpire" view of one's role (with the modest exception of the ombudsman focus) from a more active or "player" conception. This dimension seems less likely to distinguish civil servants from politicians than to differentiate members of each group from one another. A distant echo of Image I—administration versus policy—may be detected here.

The factor analysis shown in Table 4–1 provides us with significant clues to how bureaucrats and politicians think about their functions. But these clues are at best broad-gauged, and our search must continue.

### Role Focus and Functional Specialization

What most sharply characterizes parliamentary politicians, according to Max Weber, is their interest "in the possibility of inter-local electoral compromises, in vigorous and unified programs endorsed by broad circles and in a unified agitation throughout the country."[5] Although Weber cautiously noted that the results of political action often stand in contrast to their original intent, it was, he thought, service on behalf of a cause that is at the core of political action.[6] These observations are well substantiated by the evidence presented in Figure 4–1. Of the nine role foci on which both bureaucrats and politicians were coded, the three showing the largest differences are *partisan, advocate,* and *technician*—precisely

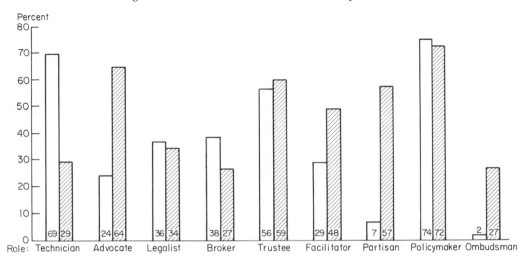

*Figure 4-1*    Role focus of bureaucrats and politicians.

NOTE: Open bars represent bureaucrats; cross-hatched bars represent politicians Percentages are means across seven nations, except that the calculation for the ombudsman role excludes the United States.

the role foci with the highest loadings on the politics/technics dimension of the factor analysis shown in Table 4 1. Politicians especially orient themselves toward partisan politics, toward representing groups, and toward advocating causes, role foci that are largely foreign to bureaucrats. Bureaucrats are far more apt to focus instead on applying technical expertise to the solution of problems, a role with little resonance among politicians. From these data the Weberian distinction between the world of the bureaucrat and that of the politician (Image II) is well sustained. For politicians focus upon serving as advocates of causes and proponents of partisan programs, while bureaucrats largely focus upon problem solving based upon technical (or fact-oriented) criteria. In these large distinctions Image II, which posits that bureaucrats deal with facts and politicians with causes and interests, seems to be corroborated.

Similarly, politicians give more weight to the representational function (facilitator) and the casework function (ombudsman) than do bureaucrats. This is, of course, an expected finding, since bureaucrats do not pass tests at the ballot box as politicians do and thus need not be responsive in the same sense that politicians must be. But while bureaucrats rarely claim to see their responsibilities in terms of defending or representing the interests of clientele groups, they often recognize that they serve specialized constituencies.[7] As we shall note later, in fact, administrators do not disclaim the facilitator role in all countries.

While politicians emphasize advocacy, partisanship, and representation, they are far less inclined to define their responsibilities in terms of mediating and reconciling interests (the broker focus). Members of parliaments, of course, represent only one species of the genus known as politician. Probably the primary responsibility for reconciling interests falls on cabinet ministers and on the political-administrative hybrids responsible for conjoining technical and political considerations in policymaking. Still, it is striking that bureaucrats are more likely to focus on brokering than are legislators. To the extent that such brokering activities involve negotiations with interests directly affected by policy, these activities do represent a departure from the classical expectations of Images I and II. According to Image III, bureaucrats have come to assume this responsibility because they are more deeply involved with the concrete details of policy decisions than are legislative politicians. For it is civil servants who define through administrative interpretations the concrete meanings that policies have for affected groups. As a consequence, it is understandable that bureaucrats are continually engaged with representatives of affected groups, a matter that we shall firmly establish in Chapter 7.

Members of parliaments are often importuned by interest groups, of course, but the pressures they are subject to are more sporadic and usually more diffuse. As generalists, they rarely get involved in a sustained mediating or bargaining relationship with specific interest groups as bureaucrats necessarily do. Instead, as partisans, MPs articulate the interests of those groups which form the core constituency of their parties, playing the role of advocate rather than mediator. Bureaucrats, by contrast, inhabit an environment in which there are close and continuing relationships with organizations directly affected by administrative actions. With continuous interest-group penetration, the bureaucrat is required to mediate between interests—those of various private interests as well as between private interests and those of government.[8] Most importantly, this process of reconciling interests is relatively immune from the mass political pressures with which the politician must cope.

As suggested by Image III, then, both bureaucrats and politicians in industrial democracies must cope with external political pressures, but those that affect bureaucrats are more precisely focused and more clearly organized than those that influence politicians. The logic of their roles leads parliamentary politicians to articulate broad demands and thus to act as advocates, whereas bureaucrats more frequently are compelled to reconcile in fine print the specific interests of the organized clienteles affected by their actions. Each performs a political role. But for the bureaucrat this role entails nudging well-established interests toward agreements within the context of a limited pluralism; for the politician it more often means representing either broad currents of public opinion or ideological principles. This conclusion—that civil servants, more than parliamentary politicians, are interest brokers in national politics—is one of our most striking and unexpected findings. We shall see further evidence for it later.

### Energizers and Equilibrators in the Policy Process

From the evidence examined thus far, we can conclude that bureaucrats and politicians do conceive their responsibilities in distinctive ways, so that a division of labor clearly exists. These distinctions, however, fail to accord with the Wilsonian administration versus policy dichotomy of Image I. And, indeed, although these empirical differences often fit the facts versus interests-and-values dichotomy of Image II, this image too fails to capture fully the ways in which the roles of senior civil servants and parliamentary politicians have evolved in the industrial democracies.

In Image I, policymaking was viewed as an activity undertaken by politicians, not by administrators. Policy preferences were to be arrived at through a clearly defined political process, and the technical execution of these preferences was to be accomplished through an equally clearly defined administrative process. But, in fact, nearly three-quarters of the bureaucrats in these political systems see themselves as actively involved in the policy-formulating process. Administrators today evidently are not hearty subscribers to Image I. On the other hand, despite the frequent claim that parliamentary power has been shrinking before the technical authority of civil servants, it is significant that a virtually equal proportion of MPs believe that *their* responsibilities involve the formulation of public policy. Members of parliaments do not view themselves solely as representatives or as caseworkers. Nor do they see themselves as limited to pursuing partisan causes and political ideals. First and foremost, they see themselves as involved in the making of policy.

Bureaucrats and politicians each affect policy, but they do so in distinctive ways. As Table 4–2 indicates, in responding to a set of short-

*Table 4-2*   Attitudes toward decision making of civil servants and members of parliament.

| Statement on questionnaire | Mean percent agreement[a] | |
|---|---|---|
| | Civil servants | Members of parliament |
| In contemporary social and economic affairs it is essential that technical considerations be given more weight than political factors. | 46 | 25 |
| Only when a person devotes himself to an ideal or cause does life become meaningful. | 69 | 86 |
| Generally speaking, in political controversies extreme positions should be avoided, since the right answer usually lies in the middle. | 82 | 64 |
| Although parties play an important role in a democracy, often they uselessly exacerbate political conflicts. | 64 | 48 |
| It is social conflicts which bring about progress in modern society. | 52 | 64 |
| The strength and efficiency of a government are more important than its specific programs. | 60 | 39 |

[a] Responses exclude French, Swedish, and American samples, where short-answer items were not administered.

answer questions politicians are more likely to be stimulated by ideals and programs and conflict in their approach to public life than are bureaucrats. Politicians represent the nerve ends of the policy process by imparting partisan commitment and ideological direction to public policy. Their role in the main is to define the politically desirable and acceptable compass of policy directions. Moreover, politicians are more likely than bureaucrats to look at the policy world downside-up or outside-in. As Image III suggests, they are the energizers of the policymaking process. They bring visions and conceptions to the policy process rather than detailed blueprints. (We shall explore in Chapter 5 the substance of the ideologies that guide politicians and bureaucrats.)

If the message of Table 4-2 is that politicians energize the policy process, it is equally true from these data that bureaucrats seek to equilibrate and accommodate, to avoid conflict, to avoid extremes. The authority to manage takes precedence over the purposes for which authority is to be exercised. As suggested by the second dimension of our factor analysis (Table 4-1), bureaucrats see the policy process topside-down or inside-out. The details of policy both in formulation and in implementation fall to them, and they are apt to be discomfited by visible political interference that forces them to recalculate their basic, if often implicit, assumptions. Nevertheless, bureaucrats do not operate in a political vacuum. They continually interact with organized interest groups and mediate among established interests. Indeed, because they provide concrete definition to policy and strike the complicated bargains that must be reached between affected interests and the government, bureaucrats are apt to be especially disconcerted by politically inspired unraveling of packages they have gone to such pains to wrap.

In sum, bureaucrats spotlight the technical aspects of public policy and attempt to develop agreements among a limited number of actors with continuous and specialized interests in clearly defined functional arenas. Left to their own devices, civil servants—in the memorable phrase of Richard Rose—would govern by "directionless consensus," accepting that course which is least resisted by those directly involved.[9] By contrast, politicians, like lightning rods, attract the sparks of sporadic but vociferous claimants. They advance broad policy claims based on party program, ideology, and constituency demands. They are, in other words, not so much interest reconcilers as they are interest articulators.

Our analysis confirms that bureaucrats and politicians play distinctive roles, but we reject Image I, the pristine administration/policy distinction, as a basis for this difference. Further, Image II, the facts/ideals-and-interests distinction, seems partially accurate, but incomplete in its characterization of bureaucrat-politician differences. It is true that bureaucrats are more "fact" oriented than politicians, and that politicians are more apt to be motivated by ideals and more likely to be responsive than bureaucrats. Image III, however, permits us to close the circle: bureaucrats and politicians are both active participants in the policy process, but each responds to an audience different both in character and in size, and each imparts a distinctive orientation to the policy process. Bureaucrats are integrators, preferring tranquility, predictability, manageability, and tidiness. Politicians, on the other hand, are partisans who bring both visionary and particularistic elements to the process. They bring general direction, but rarely a concern for detail. Bureaucrats at times must persuade politicians to confront vague goals with intractable facts, and politicians, in turn, sometimes must stretch the incrementalist instincts of bureaucrats. These distinctions express the contemporary division of labor between bureaucrats and politicians.[10]

Whatever the modal differences between bureaucrats and politicians, neither the role of politician nor that of civil servant is of a single piece. Politicians, after all, may be cabinet ministers and executives. In such posts they are as likely to be reconcilers and managers as articulators and advocates—activities so emphasized by MPs. Moreover, the contemporary complexity of governmental responsibilities has produced a diversity of bureaucratic functions—the analysis and evaluation of policy and the coordination of line departments, as well as the more traditional administration of programs, regulations, and laws. These considerations complicate, but do not detract from, the essential division of labor evident in our data. Naturally enough, as we shall see even more clearly in Chapter 5, parliamentary politicians see the world of public affairs in the form of politics, whereas bureaucrats see it in the form of governance.

## The American Aberration

Although we have stressed the generic differences between the roles of bureaucrats and parliamentary politicians in the contemporary industrial democracies, American exceptionalism dogs our quest for uniformity and uninhibited generalization. The distinctiveness in role focus between civil servants and legislators throughout Europe is conspicuously absent in America. For instance, Figure 4-2 summarizes the rank-order similarity between the role foci of bureaucrats and the role foci of politicians within each country. This evidence makes clear that whereas bureaucrats and politicians in Europe conceive their roles quite differently, bureaucrats and politicians in America conceive their roles quite similarly.

Furthermore, this high level of agreement in role focus between American bureaucrats and congressmen cannot be attributed to the fact that nearly half of the American bureaucrat sample are noncareer appointees. In the first place, the American political executives and the senior civil servants differ substantially on only two of the foci. The civil servants are twice as likely (79 percent to 41 percent) to indicate a "technician" role focus than the political executives, and the latter are twice as likely (33 percent to 17 percent) to cite a partisan role focus than the civil servants. But ranking the two sets of U.S. bureaucrats' role foci by their frequency of adoption produces an extremely high rank-order coefficient (Spearman's rho = .91).[11] Additionally, the role focus rankings of each of the two sets of bureaucrats are highly and nearly equivalently correlated with the rankings obtained for congressional politicians. The evidence is overwhelming, therefore, that the high level of agreement in

*Figure 4-2*  Rank-order similarities in bureaucratic and political role focus, by
country.

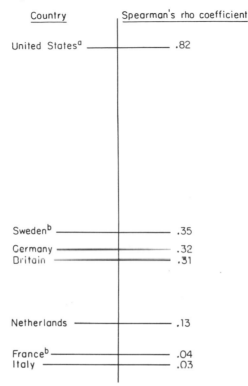

[a] Spearman's rho coefficient between American career civil servants only and members of Congress is .84. The American rankings are based on eight role foci.
[b] Only seven common role foci are coded for Swedish and French bureaucrats and politicians.

role focus between American bureaucrats and congressmen is not merely an artifact of the existence of a large dose of "politically" appointed executives in the American sample.

What is responsible for the startling extent to which role foci are shared across elite sectors in the United States?[12] To answer this question requires that we begin with institutions, for institutions are in large part responsible for this remarkable fusion. American bureaucrats, to a degree unmatched elsewhere, are responsible for shoring up their own bases of political support. Fragmented accountability forces American bureaucrats to be risk takers and forceful advocates for positions they hold privately. The risks accompanying this style, as Wallace Sayre once noted, are large but so too are the potential gains.[13] In a political system that rewards entrepreneurs, neither protected by anonymity nor clearly serving a single master, American bureaucrats must find allies where they can. This, in turn, generates an entrepreneurial style of behavior that encourages bureaucratic commitments to clienteles. To be sure, bureaucratic politics, properly understood, exists everywhere. But outside the United States the game typically is played with a narrower range of actors and a far more determinate, if not wholly definitive, set of rules. Bureaucratic politics in Europe typically is episodic; in the United States it is ceaseless.[14]

The absence of ministerial responsibility and "team" government in the United States is a double-edged sword insofar as the advantages and vulnerabilities of bureaucrats are concerned. The same process that makes bureaucrats into targets of sharp political criticism, even outright deprecation at times, also provides resources for them to pursue their programmatic objectives and to play off various would-be masters against one another. The constitutional framers, fearing the power of a single faction, designed a government with many veto points. Such a system could rarely achieve the unity necessary for action. This political structure, as Rose observed, is built upon a foundation of distrust.[15] The system has no clearly defined decisional apparatus. Thus, to the extent that the classical administrative theory of Image I was predicated on the assumption that the function of the bureaucrat is merely to implement authoritative decisions, the basic conditions for the theory, however tenuously held in all governments, are nowhere so frail as in the United States. Even with respect to Image III, the greater distinction in Europe between the process of politics and that of governing demarcates bureaucratic and political roles more securely than in the American system, where the political process is more or less unbounded.

By institutional necessity, and also because of the historic absence of socialization as an administrative elite, American bureaucrats are more oriented toward traditionally political roles than bureaucrats in Europe. Yet the overlap in role focus between bureaucrats and politicians in America is not attributable exclusively to differences between American bureaucrats and their European peers. American politicians are also different from European politicians. For example, as Table 4–3 shows, the technician role focus ranks higher among legislative politicians in the United States than in any other country. Much of this emphasis stems from the singular importance of the legislative body in America. Con-

*Table 4-3*  Role focus of civil servants and members of parliament by country.[a]

| | Country | | | | | | | | | | | | | |
| Role focus | Britain | | France | | Germany | | Italy | | Netherlands | | Sweden | | United States | |
| | CS | MP | CS | MP | CS | MP | CS | MP | CS | MP | CS | MP | CS | MP |
| --- | --- | --- | --- | --- | --- | --- | --- | --- | --- | --- | --- | --- | --- | --- |
| (1) Technician | 66 | 19 | 59 | 17 | 82 | 33 | 84 | 29 | 59 | 33 | 82 | No data | 61 | 45 |
| (2) Advocate | 13 | 73 | 32 | 76 | 23 | 68 | 22 | 61 | 24 | 69 | 11 | 47 | 40 | 54 |
| (3) Broker | 64 | 27 | 44 | 38 | 52 | 47 | 28 | 40 | 40 | 7 | 12 | 7 | 28 | 23 |
| (4) Facilitator | 31 | 62 | No | data | 23 | 32 | 40 | 27 | 7 | 32 | 21 | 46 | 53 | 89 |
| (5) Partisan | 4 | 83 | 1 | 52 | 12 | 74 | 3 | 75 | 0 | 44 | 23 | No data | 24 | 13 |
| (6) Policymaker | 84 | 77 | 82 | 72 | 87 | 87 | 57 | 58 | 90 | 83 | 42 | 54 | No data | |
| (7) Trustee | 58 | 49 | 77 | 96 | 48 | 36 | 65 | 62 | 57 | 54 | 16 | 30 | 74 | 83 |
| (8) Legalist | 21 | 19 | 10 | 78 | 61 | 36 | 47 | 37 | 52 | 34 | 24 | 5 | 39 | 28 |
| (9) Ombudsman | 1 | 47 | No | data | 1 | 16 | 1 | 9 | 1 | 59 | 5 | 5 | No data | |
| Minimum *N* = | (123) | (96) | (116) | (89) | (138) | (102) | (111) | (57) | (75) | (39) | (313) | (44) | (126) | (77) |

[a] Entries are percentages of respondents from each sample who gave at least some emphasis to each type of role orientation. The responses of senior officials and high-fliers are merged because the differences between them are negligible. CS = civil servant; MP = member of parliament (or Congress).

gress plays a prominent agenda-setting and policymaking role and its work is mostly done within a highly specialized committee and subcommittee structure rather than within the party caucus. In contrast with other parliamentary bodies, Congress is laden with staff specialists. Politicians are likely to be affected osmotically in such an environment by the salience of technical criteria and analysis, even if used only to legitimate political positions. Relative to bureaucrats, congressmen are generalists, but compared with legislators elsewhere, the American legislative process has made them specialists.

In some countries the ranks of MPs are themselves populated with former civil servants.[16] Among countries in which there is a significant proportion of civil servants in parliament—Germany, the Netherlands, and to some extent Italy—we expect to see, as we do from Table 4-3, a greater tendency for MPs to adopt the technician role focus than in Britain, for example. Probing further, however, we have been able to test whether the MPs with civil service backgrounds are more technician-focused than their colleagues. In Germany the answer to this question is no, but in the Netherlands and in Italy the answer is yes.[17] A reasonable inference is that in a relatively nonspecialized and nontechnical environment the civil service background makes a difference in how members approach their jobs, but in a legislative environment in which committees assume significant powers in shaping legislation (as in the case of the German Bundestag) the technical thickets of legislative detail are likely to occupy the attention of highly involved members regardless of their occupational background.

The principal thrust of our findings, however, especially those shown in Figure 4-2, is to throw into bold relief the aberrant character of the worlds of American bureaucrats and politicians in comparison to those inhabited by European bureaucrats and politicians. American bureaucrats are clearly more political in their role focus than their European counterparts, and American congressional politicians are apt to be more technically oriented than are European parliamentary politicians. The fragile and uncertain nature of political authority in America makes for bureaucratic orientations that emphasize the building of political support. But the policy-shaping responsibilities given to the legislative body in the American system of government help to make legislators more sensitive to the technical details of policy. In this system of fragmented responsibilities each institutional actor plays a major role and each, to a degree unknown in Europe, has come to speak the other's language.

### "Political Government" in America

If politics is defined as the process by which interests and causes are articulated (the energy metaphor of Image III), and governing as the process by which public problems are authoritatively resolved through policy (the equilibrium metaphor of Image III), American bureaucrats are much more oriented to traditionally political roles such as advocacy, representation, and partisanship than are their European peers. Uncertain lines of authority encourage American bureaucrats to play political roles—to cut deals with congressmen who can protect their agencies from central executive control, to pursue the interests of clienteles who can help to protect their programs, and to act as advocates for interests inadequately represented through the ostensible channels of political representation.[18]

Interestingly, however, while American bureaucrats focus on facilitating interests to a far greater degree than bureaucrats in other systems, American politicians also focus upon representing specific interests to a far greater extent than legislative politicians in other systems. Among bureaucrats (Table 4–3) the Americans are highest on both the advocacy and the facilitator focus. Although congressmen rank low on the advocacy role focus, they are at the top on the facilitator focus, indicating that American politicians promote functionally specialized and localized claims more readily than broader appeals on behalf of social doctrines. Ironically, for a political system often celebrated for its ability to reconcile conflict in the midst of diversity and institutional fragmentation,[19] neither American elite seems especially oriented to brokering conflict. Both, relative to their European counterparts, are far more oriented to advancing claims than to settling them.

Thus, a distinctive attribute of elite culture in America lies precisely in its acute sensitivity to what David Truman terms "the specialized demands emerging from its pluralistic base."[20] This sensitivity guarantees a high degree of "segmented responsiveness"; American policymakers focus more readily on the "who gets what" question than on the "why are we doing this" question.[21]

"Directionless consensus"—the reconciliation and incremental adjustment of interests—reflects the spirit of "administered government." The spirit of "political government," however, may be one of "directionless conflict." The transmission lines of political government carry voltage from society to government, but the absence of a central grid dissipates energy needed for sustained productive purpose. Policy surges in the

United States often result from momentary energies, so that they typically remain unassimilated into a broader policy mosaic. A Swedish political scientist contrasting American and Swedish policy processes, argues that

> in times of a large upsurge in public opinion, the constitutionally built-in competitiveness of the American political system, coupled to the peculiarities of the electoral and party systems, provide policy-makers with tremendous incentives to embark on a course of policy escalation. So visible in the eyes of his constituents, but without responsibility for actual policy implementation, the American Congressman will see much merit in selecting radical alternatives.[22]

In Europe, political parties are the switching stations for transforming opinions, discontents, and demands into programmatic political current. Parties direct, but also redirect, energies toward broad programs and the development of organized will within parliament. In the absence of this capacity, politics becomes rudderless, personal, and entrepreneurial. Thus, the American "directionless conflict." It is particularly noteworthy that while American federal executives are (along with the Swedes) the most partisan among our bureaucrats (even when the political executives are set aside), American congressmen are by far the *least* partisan in their role focus of any of the legislative samples (Table 4–3). Indeed, only in America are the politicians less partisan in their role focus than the bureaucrats.[23] One consequence of feeble parties is that momentary surges of opinion or expressions of issue interest command immediate attention. Yet they remain disconnected from and unassimilated into party principles and programs of action.

All political systems must provide for both interest articulation and interest mediation. In general, our data suggest, politicians help to articulate competing interests, whereas bureaucrats help to manage their reconciliation. In the United States, however, both elites are unusually active on the "political" side of this equation. Ultimately in all systems the process of brokering and reconciling interests is given more attention at the pinnacle of political authority—among cabinet ministers, prime ministers, and presidents and their staffs. Nevertheless, the structure of politics and government in America is *sui generis*. The bread and butter of congressional politicians and high-level bureaucrats in America is earned by their responsiveness to what each sees as relevant local constituencies, whether these are composed of electorates and local interest groups or bureaucratic clients.

### Winner-Take-All Electoral Systems and Constituency Tending

One of the key roles of legislative politicians is that of representing their constituencies and facilitating the access of constituency interests. To a considerable extent, however, the way a legislator is elected structures his incentives for representing interests. As Table 4–3 illustrates, the two countries possessing clear-cut winner-take-all electoral systems, the United States and Britain, show the highest facilitator role focus among politicians. Despite differences in party organization between Britain and the United States that give British parties a firmer grip on nominations than American parties, the winner-take-all system means that candidates must stand alone before a local constituency. Each must be concerned with producing a favorable personal image among his constituents, although personal appeal remains a far more important ingredient of American congressional elections than of British parliamentary contests.[24] In the British case, local party committees are of special importance in the nomination process; therefore the British MP, unlike his American counterpart, is also an enthusiastic partisan. The British MP, then, must be both a partisan (to please those who control his nomination) *and* a facilitator of particular demands (to please those who control his election).

British MPs also focus heavily upon the ombudsman (or caseworker) function,[25] although judging from the Dutch MPs' tendencies in the same direction (Table 4–3) the ombudsman role focus, unlike that of the facilitator, may be influenced less by electoral systems than by cultural norms. The German data reinforce this interpretation. Approximately half of the Bundestag is elected by a specific constituency, whereas the other half is elected through proportional representation on the basis of party lists. In our German sample, 40 percent of those MPs elected directly by constituency emphasize the facilitator role, but only 23 percent of those elected on the basis of party lists do. On the other hand, the constituency and list MPs do not differ significantly with respect to the ombudsman role focus.

The nurturing of constituency interests, we have stressed, has long been the hallmark of American congressional politicians, above and beyond the faint call of partisan duty. Recently, "partisan dealignment" has apparently accentuated this norm, as short-run personal evaluations by the electorate become increasingly important. Although fewer incumbents may fail at the polls, more of them run scared.[26] Concomitantly, expanding federal assistance programs frequently have spawned institutional networks that represent a new set of localistic pressures on Congress. As

Thomas Anton persuasively argues, this trend has tended "to change the major 'face' of the political question from 'what is this program for?' to 'what organization in what districts, in what regions will get how much from formula X or formula Y?' "[27] As a general matter, the distribution of largesse from the center requires legislators who represent local districts to facilitate local interests. Surely, then, the pressures toward adoption of the facilitator role are stronger to the extent that the MP is visible, locally elected, and relatively detached from his party. Winner-take-all systems necessitate single-member districts and promote candidate visibility. Since dealignment tends further to detach the candidate's fate from that of his party, constituency tending is especially emphasized in the United States, where both winner-take-all rules and partisan dealignment prevail. Unlike Britain or Germany, the enfeeblement of party in America fails to counteract the localistic incentives generated by the winner-take-all system.

### Images and Mirror Images

By analyzing the ways in which bureaucrats and politicians focus on their roles, we see that each is drawn to the policymaking function, although in distinctive ways and filtered through distinctive constituencies. Because bureaucrats possess special resources of expertise and detailed knowledge, politicians may fear threats to their own authority in the policy process posed by bureaucrats' tactical advantages. We might expect politicians, therefore, to define a more passive and compliant role for bureaucrats than bureaucrats accept for themselves. On the other side of the coin, bureaucrats may view politicians as interfering irrationally with knowledgeable decisions, and they may define the roles of politicians in ways that limit their involvement in day-to-day policymaking.

DEFINING ROLE NORMS   To determine how bureaucrats and politicians define one another's roles, as well as their own, we asked each to describe the qualities they think an administrator should have and those they think a politician should possess. Open-ended coding rated twelve traits that bureaucrats and politicians thought desirable for an administrator. (Only eight traits were explored in the American case.) Ten traits were used to describe the characteristics that politicians should possess. (Again a smaller number were used in the American case.) Individuals varied in the number of traits cited: some respondents spoke at great length and cited several important traits, whereas others, less expansive, sometimes cited only a single trait as important.

The twelve summary traits employed to characterize the desirable features of an administrator's role are (1) organizational and managerial abilities; (2) mediating, bargaining, and conciliating skills; (3) sociability and personal relations; (4) intellectual ability; (5) charisma and leadership; (6) representation and responsiveness; (7) personal character and conscience; (8) policymaking interests; (9) ideological commitment and advocacy; (10) technical skills; (11) advising and counseling of superiors; and (12) neutral execution of laws. The first ten traits were also used to characterize desirable role attributes for MPs.

Traditional conceptions of the bureaucratic role, gleaned from Images I and II, emphasize organizational efficiency, neutral execution of laws, technical expertise, and intellectual ability. However, our analysis of the focus that bureaucrats give to their roles suggests that they emphasize policymaking and, to a lesser extent, mediating between various interests and the government. Even more activist role norms have been stressed by some, particularly in the United States, who believe that administrators should undertake advocacy and represent clienteles served by their programs.[28]

The classic conception of the role of parliamentary politicians embodied in Image I stresses policymaking, to which Images II and III add the representation of interests and the articulation of causes, despite the potential conflict between representation of interests and involvement in policymaking.

Unlike the role focus data employed earlier, our data on role norms are not intended to capture an individual's approach to his own role, but instead are meant to identify how respondents characterize each role prescriptively. Our attention now shifts from the personal *is* to the generic *ought*. Since enunciating role norms is more abstract than defining one's own role focus, these data should reinforce with greater vigor the classic distinctions between the two roles. Deviations from textbook notions about bureaucratic and political role norms, therefore, are worthy of special attention.

ROLE NORMS FOR BUREAUCRATS    In general, as Table 4–4 indicates, there is strong agreement between bureaucrats and politicians on the traits that are desirable for the bureaucratic role. (The Spearman's rho coefficient between bureaucrats' and politicians' rankings is .85.) Two

*Table 4-4*   Mentions and rank orders of traits accorded to the role of a senior civil servant.

| Traits | Bureaucrats | | | Politicians | | |
|---|---|---|---|---|---|---|
| | Percentage mentioning | Deviation from mean percentage across traits | Rank | Percentage mentioning | Deviation from mean percentage across traits | Rank |
| Organizational and managerial | 72 | +29 | 1 | 46 | + 9 | 5 |
| Intellectual | 69 | +26 | 2 | 70 | +33 | 1 |
| Policymaking | 59 | +16 | 3 | 45 | + 8 | 6 |
| Technical | 50 | + 7 | 4 | 47 | +10 | 4 |
| Neutral execution | 48 | + 5 | 5 | 62 | +25 | 2 |
| Character and con- science | 48 | + 5 | 5 | 55 | +18 | 3 |
| Advising and coun- seling | 44 | + 1 | 7 | 40 | + 3 | 7 |
| Sociability and per- sonal relations | 44 | + 1 | 7 | 28 | − 9 | 8 |
| Mediating, bargain- ing, and conciliat- ing | 32 | −11 | 9 | 13 | −24 | 10 |
| Representation and responsiveness | 17 | −26 | 10 | 27 | −10 | 9 |
| Ideological and ad- vocacy | 16 | −27 | 11 | 10 | −27 | 11 |
| Charisma and lead- ership | 14 | −29 | 12 | 6 | −31 | 12 |
| Mean percentage across traits | 43 | | | 37 | | |

Spearman's rho between ranks = .85

| | | |
|---|---|---|
| Traits one standard devia- tion above the mean (most emphasized): | Organizational and mana- gerial Intellectual | Intellectual Neutral execution |
| Traits one standard devia- tion below the mean (least emphasized): | Charisma and leadership Ideological and advocacy Representation and re- sponsiveness | Charisma and leadership Ideological and advocacy Mediation, bargaining, and conciliating |

things stand out from this general concordance of views. First, both bureaucrats and politicians believe that engaging in policymaking is an important part of the bureaucrat's role. Nearly 60 percent of the bureaucrats believe this and, surprisingly, so do 45 percent of the MPs. To a considerable extent, it appears, politicians have come to accept bureaucrats as policymakers—although, as we shall soon note, this acceptance is ambivalent. Thus, the second salient feature of Table 4–4 is that while both bureaucrats and politicians think that the former should be involved in aspects of policymaking, neither supports the idea that high-level administrators should undertake activities more traditionally associated with the politician's role. To put it another way, there is considerable support among both elite groups for the traditional norms of the bureaucrat's role. Politicians in particular, while accepting the idea that bureaucrats should be involved with policymaking, suggest even more strongly that bureaucrats should principally contribute intellectual skills to the process, but then carry out government decisions. In short, politicians are willing to concede a role for bureaucrats in policymaking under a set of ground rules that denies them discretion. Politicians apparently want bureaucrats to help them make decisions; at the same time, they want to limit bureaucratic latitude in administering those decisions. These desires generally accord with Image II.

The portrait that emerges from politicians' prescriptions for the role of bureaucrats is that fundamentally bureaucrats should be "smart tools" able to guide politicians past the rocky shoals of complex policy options and then to execute intelligently the politicians' decisions. While politicians accept a policymaking role for bureaucrats, they claim center-stage for themselves.

If politicians are skeptical about bureaucratic power and discretion, it is equally clear that bureaucrats hold a more activist conception of their own roles. Notwithstanding the politicians' acceptance that bureaucrats should be involved in making policy, bureaucrats are even more likely to think that policymaking is an important element of their role. And, although neither elite group emphasizes mediating, bargaining, and conciliating skills for bureaucrats, bureaucrats are more inclined than politicians to see these traits as important to the job of a high-level administrator. Since this issue is central to contemporary differences between bureaucrats and politicians (who deals with what interests?), it is understandable that politicians want such activities to be handled by those who are politically accountable. Among the more active prescriptions for the bureaucratic role, only representation and responsiveness are emphasized more by MPs than by the bureaucrats themselves. From the MPs' standpoint, however, this grants little to bureaucrats, for MPs are likely to define bureaucratic responsiveness as responsiveness toward politicians and the interests they represent.

Nonetheless, bureaucrats do not fundamentally dispute the politicians' prescriptions for the bureaucrats' role. Like MPs, bureaucrats value intellectual qualities in administrators, although they are less inclined to believe that intelligence alone is necessary to be an effective administrator. Bureaucrats live in a world of large and complex organization—a world usually foreign to parliamentary politicians. As bureaucrats see their own roles, the first order of business is to manage matters and get things done, tasks that demand organizational skills. Such considerations are not at the forefront of the politician's mind. MPs are apt to assume that administration ought to be self-executing. Indeed, politicians often mistakenly assume that making choices, which is the substance of the politician's task, is tantamount to managing choices, which in turn is the substance of government.

In sum, bureaucrats and politicians generally agree about the bureaucratic role, although politicians are skeptical about trends that increase the activist aspects of that role. While there is rough agreement that bureaucrats ought to be engaged in policymaking, politicians are more hesitant to grant bureaucrats powers of negotiation and discretion.

ROLE NORMS FOR POLITICIANS    Parliamentary politicians stress two of the classic, if frequently contradictory, elements of their roles—the policymaking function and the representational function (Table 4–5). According to Image I, we should recall, only politicians are policymakers, and according to Image II, only politicians represent interests. But according to Image III, bureaucrats share both these functions with politicians. In this image the chief difference between high-level civil servants and MPs lies in the breadth of the interests with which they deal and the manner in which they deal with them.

A comparison of Tables 4–4 and 4–5 affords further insights into the nature of this distinction. Politicians stress the representational aspect of both roles more than do bureaucrats. In turn, bureaucrats emphasize the mediating, bargaining, and conciliating aspects of both roles more than MPs do. This contrast seems to reflect a basic difference in the mental model of representation that bureaucrats and politicians hold. Bureaucrats

*Table 4-5*   Mentions and rank orders of traits accorded to the role of a parliamentary politician.

| Traits | Bureaucrats | | | Politicians | | |
|---|---|---|---|---|---|---|
| | Percentage mentioning | Deviation from mean percentage across traits | Rank | Percentage mentioning | Deviation 'from mean percentage across traits | Rank |
| Policymaking | 71 | +35 | 1 | 70 | +27 | 1 |
| Intellectual | 50 | +14 | 2 | 64 | +21 | 3 |
| Representation and responsiveness | 48 | +12 | 3 | 68 | +25 | 2 |
| Ideological and advocacy | 44 | + 8 | 4 | 40 | − 3 | 5 |
| Mediating, bargaining, and conciliating | 40 | + 4 | 5 | 29 | −14 | 8 |
| Charisma and leadership | 31 | − 5 | 6 | 37 | − 6 | 7 |
| Character and conscience | 28 | − 8 | 7 | 55 | +12 | 4 |
| Sociability and personal relations | 18 | −18 | 8 | 38 | − 5 | 6 |
| Organizational and managerial | 15 | −21 | 9 | 14 | −29 | 10 |
| Technical | 12 | −24 | 10 | 18 | −25 | 9 |
| Mean percentage across traits | 36 | | | 43 | | |

Spearman's rho between ranks = .83

| | | |
|---|---|---|
| Traits one standard deviation above the mean (most emphasized): | Policymaking | Policymaking
Representation and responsiveness
Intellectual |
| Traits one standard deviation below the mean (least emphasized): | Technical
Organizational and managerial
Sociability | Organizational and managerial
Technical |

typically deal with established and organized interests, and their relation with such interests involves bargaining and mediation. Politicians more often deal with broad currents of opinion, social classes, and large-scale interests, and thus they are likely to emphasize responsiveness to less organized or more vaguely defined elements of society. Each actor may well project his own model of linkage with nongovernmental actors onto the other. Politicians inhabit a world of diffuse political pressures, whereas bureaucrats live in an environment in which pressures are filtered through interest-group representatives. One requires broad and often symbolic responsiveness, the other mediation and negotiation.

Finally, we note in Tables 4-4 and 4-5 that both samples rate civil servants relatively high and MPs relatively low on technical and managerial traits. In other words, there is broad agreement that detailed policy design and implementation are the province of civil servants.

### Styles and Criteria of Policy Analysis

Bureaucrats and politicians are both intimately involved in making public policy—on this our data are strikingly convergent. *How* each group is involved cannot be summarized precisely, because neither role is monolithic and because systems differ in the opportunities they provide. Yet it seems likely that politicians and bureaucrats bring different criteria to bear in assessing policy and making decisions.

To explore this hypothesis, we asked most politicians to discuss at some length what they felt to be one of the most important problems facing their country at the time of the interview, and we asked civil servants to discuss the most important problem they saw confronting their department. We also asked each group about economic planning and the role of the state in the economy. We analyzed the responses to these questions, exploring not merely the substance of the replies, but (even more elaborately) the approaches and criteria applied in defining the problems and examining proposed solutions.

We were less interested in a policymaker's "bottom line" than in how he got there. Therefore our coders rated each respondent's discussion of each policy problem along a series of stylistic dimensions. Did the respondent moralize the issue, for example, by assigning blame for the problem? Did he discuss conflicting interests among different social groups or did he imply that the issue was a technical one that could be resolved in everyone's interest? Did he use political acceptability as a criterion for judging alternative policies? Did he use technical or administrative or financial practicality as criteria? Did he refer to particular ideologies or doctrines, such as socialism or free enterprise? Did he analyze the problem synoptically, deducing his solution from some general social theory, or did he forgo theory in favor of induction from practical experience?

Because the "most important problem" question typically varied between bureaucrats and politicians in a way that invited politicians to treat a wider arena, the stylistic characteristics of this discussion might have been biased so that bureaucrats would appear more focused, detailed, and narrow, and politicians more general, visionary, and societal in scope. Such a bias would falsely favor our underlying hypotheses about the distinctive policy styles of bureaucrats and politicians. To reduce this risk and to utilize fully the available data, we created composite indexes for the parallel style items across both the "most important problem" discussion and the "planning" discussion. Bias in the former should have been reduced by the more direct comparability of the latter. Even more compelling is the fact that the mean correlations between the two sets of parallel items are essentially the same among politicians and bureaucrats, suggesting that the differences in wording of the "most important problem" question had a negligible impact on the internal consistency of the responses.

To discern underlying patterns in the ways our respondents analyzed policy, we carried out a principal-factor analysis of the composite stylistic indexes. The primary factor (accounting for a third of the variance) identifies a set of items that capture key differences in the way bureaucrats and politicians assess policy. Results for these items appear in Table 4–6, together with two additional items that are less closely related to the primary factor, but that nevertheless reflect interesting differences in the policy styles of bureaucrats and politicians.

As Table 4–6 shows, the criteria of bureaucrats for evaluating policy are markedly different from the criteria of politicians. Politicians begin with an ideological and theoretical framework that is far less prevalent among bureaucrats. Politicians are more likely to think of policy in distributive or redistributive terms; they tend to believe that policy affects groups differently, that some win and others lose, and that conflicting interests are at the core of proposed solutions. Politicians formulate policy for particularistic purposes (that is, to help a group for its own sake),

*Table 4-6*  Approaches to policy analysis by bureaucrats and politicians.[a]

| | Percentages | | | |
| | Bureaucrats | Politicians | Factor loading | Yule's Q |
| Approach | | | | |
|---|---|---|---|---|
| Emphasizes general principles | 47 | 73 | .67 | −.50 |
| Moralizes issues by assigning blame | 32 | 63 | .69 | −.57 |
| Refers to an ideal future society as a goal | 3 | 20 | .75 | −.78 |
| Refers to a specific doctrine or ideology | 18 | 35 | .82 | −.42 |
| Reasons deductively from a political, social, or economic theory | 39 | 62 | .65 | −.44 |
| Refers to specific group benefits or losses as a relevant criterion | 33 | 57 | .61 | −.46 |
| Refers to political feasibility or acceptability as a relevant criterion | 49 | 66 | .29[b] | −.34 |
| Refers to financial practicality or cost as a relevant criterion | 45 | 32 | −.25[b] | .27 |
| Refers to technical or administrative practicality as a relevant criterion | 46 | 24 | −.60 | .46 |
| Refers to conflicting interests between different social groups | 40 | 67 | .69 | −.51 |

[a] Swedish and American samples are excluded.
[b] Items do not primarily load on this dimension.

rather than advocate collective solutions, as bureaucrats are likely to do. Politicians tend to attribute policy problems to personal or intentional action to a far greater extent than do bureaucrats, who seem to view impersonal forces as more important in explaining problems. To the limited extent that the future is a source of inspiration in thinking about contemporary problems and issues, politicians are more forward-looking. In contrast to heady visions of future utopias, bureaucrats are firmly planted in the here and now: "Will it work?" rather than "What is it for?" is the question they prefer to ask. While for bureaucrats "Will it work?" is equally likely to be asked from the standpoint of technical or administrative, cost, or political feasibilities, politicians are much more concerned about the politics of the proposed solution.

The politician is informed by a broad-gauged view of society, inclined to see conflict and group differences, and prone to formulate policy that distinguishes between groups in society. He is inclined to think that someone is to blame when things go wrong. He characteristically applies the criterion of political acceptability to policy proposals, though it should be noted that almost half of the bureaucrats employ this criterion as well.

Politicians—at least more than bureaucrats—look to the future. In sum, the key policy question that politicians are likely to ask is "What ends will be served and whose interests will be satisfied?" Politicians are generalists motivated by political ideals and broad interests, and the world view of the generalists is usually keyed to simple explanations. Thus, personal or social forces rather than technical capacities or complex intertwining forces are seen as the causes of social problems more frequently by politicians than by bureaucrats.

The bureaucrat has a more detailed view of policy and thus is constrained by practical considerations that often escape the consideration of politicians: "Is it do-able?" However, the bureaucratic mode of policymaking also is geared more toward problems of collective goods than toward problems of distribution and redistribution. The bureaucrat fails to see grievances, divisions in society, and imbalances in power as clearly as the politician does. The bureaucrat, therefore, may be blind to the distribution of costs and benefits in society. On the other hand, the politician may see all policy proposals from this standpoint and hence may be blind to the need for collective action.

In short, politicians and bureaucrats both perform policy analysis, but in important respects they do it quite differently. Our evidence from seven nations is quite consistent with the conclusions of one recent study of decision making in Germany:

> In fact one gets the impression that in the federal departments all hierarchical levels [both political and administrative decision makers] are doing qualitatively more or less the same thing with respect to policy making, except that they do it on the basis of different sets of information, with a different breadth of horizon, and with different decision criteria.[29]

## Conclusion

As public problems in advanced industrial democracies have grown increasingly complex, as the basis for grappling with these problems has become more technical, and as interest groups have taken root in the administrative structures of the modern state, it has been said that policymaking powers have shifted in a major way from the ostensible sphere of politics to the bureaucracy.[30] Early in this chapter we sidestepped the debate over the relative power of politicians and bureaucrats, principally because our data could not help clarify this controversy. What we could do, however, was illustrate how bureaucrats and politicians focus on their roles, demonstrate the principles they think are relevant in governing, show how they define the norms for their roles and those of their counterparts, and assess the criteria by which they analyze policy.

Our evidence highlights important similarities and differences between bureaucrats and politicians. In contrast to the austere simplicities of the policy/administration dichotomy (Image I), it is now clear that bureaucrats do engage in policy formulation. The Weberian distinction (Image II) between the bureaucrat's technical skills and the politician's responsiveness to broad social interests and advocacy of political principles continues to be relevant. But it is an incomplete portrayal of the contemporary roles of civil servants and parliamentary politicians. In many respects, technical and intellectual competence is an important source of the influence that civil servants are able to wield in structuring political choices. In addition to the classic distinctions for which we found much evidence (except, we must repeat, in the United States), we discovered simultaneously a convergence of functions between politicians and bureaucrats and some continuing dissimilarities of environment, approach, and outlook. To the extent that bureaucrats have come to be intimately involved with policymaking, they necessarily help shape decisions that are inherently political, and, in this limited sense, they cannot help but be political actors.[31]

Because they are policymakers, bureaucrats engage in politics. But their "political game" differs dramatically from the one played by parliamentary politicians. While the close involvement of interest groups with the administration of the state requires political skills on the part of administrators, these are the skills of mediation and bargaining—the ability to broker conflicting interests in specific terms. Incremental adjustments between established interests involve skills and temperamental characteristics fundamentally different from those that parliamentarians bring to their roles. The politics of bureaucrats is a politics that juggles carefully the interests of key groups; it does not typically advance broad claims upon government. That, at least in Europe, is largely the province of politicians. If contemporary agendas and the prevailing network of policy interests inevitably drive high-level bureaucrats into a political game, this does not mean, with allowances for the American exception, that bureaucrats are imbued with the spirit of politics.

In contrast to politicians, bureaucrats bring different criteria to decision making, and the interests they deal with are more clearly defined and established. The biases of bureaucrats lead them toward technically defined and administratively feasible solutions and toward negotiation with well-defined interests, whereas the characteristic biases of politicians lead them to definition of problems first in terms of political advantage and political principle.

Indeed, from this distinction we are able partially to account for the "American exception." The highly specialized committee and subcommittee system provides congressmen with opportunities to specialize in particular policy areas. As with bureaucrats, specialization and detail lead to a greater awareness of technical considerations in policymaking, which American congressional politicians possess to a far greater extent than their peers in Europe. At the same time, congressional committees and subcommittees provide forums for well-defined interests to seek to influence decisions. Thus, unlike most other parliamentarians, American congressmen are accustomed to working on legislative detail with highly specialized and established interests. This environment often leads American congressmen to see their political advantage as lying with the interests that are intimately connected with the legislative functions performed through their committees.

The different styles and approaches that bureaucrats and politicians bring to government have broad implications. Politicians are inspired by goals and the advancement of interests; bureaucrats are forced to consider sobering possibilities. Politicians trade in generalities that must be given concrete expression by bureaucrats. Each is concerned with feasibilities, but with very different ones. Politicians are more apt to be concerned with how a proposal will affect an important constituent group, whereas bureaucrats are more likely to be concerned with the technical and administrative aspects of implementing proposals. Politicians are more inclined to ask, "Whom will this benefit?" Bureaucrats, on the other hand, are more inclined to ask, "What is an efficient outcome?" From the questions they ask, politicians seem especially sensitized to issues involving the distribution and redistribution of benefits; bureaucrats, on the other hand, by their questions seem especially sensitized to issues involving collective goods.

In the decade since our interviews were undertaken, new issues have come to the fore in the West as unprecedented prosperity and abundance have waned. Prudent analysis and managerial competence—central strengths of the bureaucrat's orientation—are necessary to engage these issues. But at least equally essential to dealing with them is the broad-scale perspective that politicians bring to policy. Even if the times evoke the criteria of prudence and expertise (criteria that seemed less in vogue a decade ago), bureaucrats alone are unlikely to provide comprehensive direction, or to be sensitive to allocative costs. Their perspectives, reflecting both their relatively narrow functional responsibilities and their need to consider the views of affected interests, are often a mile deep and an inch wide. While focused on a broader landscape, politicians risk pushing agendas without attention to operative details. Their perspectives are often a mile wide and an inch deep. Against the politician's zeal, bureaucrats counter with facts and caution; and against the bureaucrat's preference for a consensual environment, politicians counter with the mobilization of broad-based interests. Whether the new issues will lead to more bureaucratic styles of decision making emphasizing management and analysis, to more political styles of decision making emphasizing advocacy and distributive considerations, or to a creative amalgam of these, is for the moment a matter of conjecture, one that we shall consider in somewhat different form in our concluding chapter.

# The Compass of Elite Ideology

## 5

The preceding chapters have discussed how politicians and bureaucrats are recruited and how they conceive their respective roles in the policy process. In this chapter we explore how they orient themselves to the substance of policy. How do the ideological commitments of politicians and bureaucrats differ?

The word *ideology* is traditionally one of the most controversial in social science, and while we have no wish to join this terminological fray, we must say a bit about the conception of ideology that underlies our analysis.[1] For our purposes, an ideology may be defined briefly as a coherent system of beliefs and values that guides policy choice. Ideology is of interest to students of politics primarily because it orders (and renders predictable) the choices of policymakers on a myriad of specific issues—from school busing to monetary policy, from air pollution to public housing.

To merit the name, however, an ideology must be more than a list of policy preferences. Those preferences must be embedded in a larger social philosophy, linking short-run choices to long-run trends and to basic moral values. Joseph LaPalombara, for example, has argued that ideology "involves a philosophy of history, a view of man's present place in it, some estimate of probable lines of future development, and a set of prescriptions regarding how to hasten, retard, and/or modify that developmental direction."[2] Similarly, for Robert Haber, "Ideology . . . has several elements: (1) a set of moral values, taken as absolute, (2) an outline of the 'good society' in which those values would be realized, (3) a systematic criticism (or, in the case of status quo ideology, affirmation) of the present social arrangements and an analysis of their dynamics, (4) a strategic plan of getting from the present to the future (or, in the case of status quo ideology, how continued progress is built into the existing system)."[3]

Individuals vary, of course, in the degree to which their political actions are consistently informed by a coherent ideology, and they vary still more in the degree to which they are able to articulate the basic tenets of their ideology. Political elites typically operate with more elaborate, coherent, well-articulated ideologies than most of their fellow citizens.[4] For this reason (and because of the diversity of national agendas), our interviews with bureaucrats and politicians attempted to move beyond a cataloguing of their positions on issues of the moment to elicit more fundamental social values and ideological orientations. Although our research was not specifically designed to "test" the conception of ideology outlined here, the evidence in this chapter is consistent with our expectation that national policymakers do indeed operate with an ideology in this sense.

What dimensions of ideology should be explored? A casual glance at history reveals how infinitely various are the themes around which men and women can integrate their social values and political choices. Great struggles have raged between ideologies centered on religion and theology, for example, and great empires have been undone by ideologies centered on national or ethnic identity. Indeed, in much of today's world such themes dominate ideological discourse, and even in Western polities faint echoes of religious and national ideologies still can be heard. But throughout this century the primary dimension of ideological controversy in the West has involved social change and, more specifically, the role of the state in promoting social and economic equality.

At one pole have been those who favor far-reaching changes in the established social order. Their goal has been a more equal distribution of power, wealth, and privilege, and for the most part, they have sought this goal through broad and vigorous state action. At the other pole have been those typically defending the existing social structure on both moral and expediential grounds. Primarily in the name of individualism, these conservatives have resisted proposals for expanding state control and collective provision.

So pervasive and familiar is this distinction that for generations political actors have used a simple spatial metaphor—a Left-Right dimension—to characterize ideological disputes and disputants. The terms *Left* and *Right* originated in France during the 1790s to distinguish, respectively, those who supported egalitarian changes and those who resisted them. Now, as then, attitudes toward egalitarian change are the essence of this ideological dimension. In British and especially in American politics, the words *liberal* and *conservative* have been used to label an equivalent dimension, although these terms have undergone a striking metamorphosis as ideas shifted on the question of the appropriate link between state action and social reform. Originally, the British liberals championed freedom from state intervention in the economy, then used primarily on behalf of the landed aristocracy. But by the end of the nineteenth century, government intervention had come to be seen as an essential tool of redistributive politics and opposition to state intervention became a conservative stance. Thus, during the twentieth century, support for state intervention and support for social reform have been strongly correlated.

To be sure, not all political actors have fit easily into this one-dimensional framework. "Conservative modernizers" from Alexander Hamilton to Charles de Gaulle have favored an activist state role for promoting economic development, while resisting more egalitarian forms of social change. Others, from turn-of-the-century anarchists to some contemporary "new Leftists," have sought radical social change, while opposing state expansion. As we enter the 1980s, some observers discern signs of an impending revision in the fundamentals of ideological debate in the West, visible in such disparate phenomena as conservatives' endorsement of "industrial policy" and progressives' concerns about unnecessary government regulations. Attitudes on such contemporary topics as nuclear power, terrorism, and abortion are not necessarily related to views on classic issues of socioeconomic reform. But the simple Left-Right ideological dimension has proved remarkably durable, parsimonious, and pervasive. Predictions of its early demise should be entertained only with great caution. Even in the reputedly non-ideological climate of American politics, knowing a politician's stance on government regulation of business or tax reform provides a remarkably accurate clue to his or her position on the Equal Rights Amendment or national health insurance.[5] Our own evidence will illustrate the continued centrality of this Left-Right ideological spectrum.

How should we expect the ideological stances of politicians and bureaucrats to differ? Apart from the special case of the United States (which, as our data show, is indeed quite special), we know of no systematic, empirical studies of this issue.[6] A plausible case might be made for any one of four alternatives:

(1) Bureaucrats have a vested interest in expanding the role of the state, and in claiming to offer cures for alleged social ills. Thus, as a group, bureaucrats should stand to the left of politicians, at least some of whom will defend conservative positions. (This hypothesis is often endorsed by rightist politicians, scenting bureaucratic interventionism.)

(2) By social background, by present status, and (at least in Europe) by tradition, bureaucrats have a major stake in the existing social order and an aversion to government policies designed to overturn that order. Thus, as a group, bureaucrats should stand to the right of politicians, at least some of whom will be social reformers. (This hypothesis is often endorsed by leftist politicians, scenting bureaucratic conservatism.)

(3) By temperament, bureaucrats are skeptical of the passions of politicians at both ideological extremes. Thus, as a group, bureaucrats will exert what Fritz Morstein Marx terms "a pull toward the center," seeing public policy in consistently pallid grays, rather than the starkly contrasting blacks and whites of politicians.[7]

(4) The division of labor between politicians and bureaucrats encourages politicians to incorporate their policy views within a relatively simplistic ideological framework, but the world of bureaucrats is one of technical expertise and operational detail, predisposing them to an agnostic outlook that encompasses "leftist" positions on some issues and "rightist" positions on others, and cumulates to no consistent ideological stance whatsoever.

We shall see that none of these four alternative expectations is wholly accurate, although the third hypothesis, that of "consistent centrism," is most nearly consistent with our evidence, at least in Europe.

In this chapter we shall first examine the distribution of our respondents on several measures designed to probe their basic stance on questions of social change and state intervention, as well as the consistency of their responses across these "core variables." Having established the reasonableness of classifying these policymakers along a Left-Right dimension, we shall turn to an exploration of the correlates of this dimension. We shall show that a decision maker's basic ideological stance predicts and helps explain his views on specific issues of policy, as well as his vision of the future of his society. (We shall also show that, with ideology held constant, significant differences persist in the ways politicians and bureaucrats approach contemporary policy issues.) Next, we shall show that a decision maker's ideology is linked, also, to his or her perspective on the process of policymaking itself; loosely speaking, Leftists stress politics, whereas Rightists stress governance. (Again, we shall see that, with ideology held constant, bureaucrats differ from politicians in their images of the policy process.) Finally, we shall explore the origins of ideological preferences, with special attention to the linkages between ideology and party identification. Throughout, our central concern is this: How do bureaucrats and politicians differ ideologically, and in what ways does the difference matter?

### The Contours of Ideology

In exploring the ideological outlooks of policymakers in our seven countries, we hypothesized that attitudes toward state intervention in the economy and in society would be correlated with attitudes toward social change. Five core variables—each available for most of our national subsamples, though none for all seven—were designed to tap these central ideological themes. Three of the variables elicited attitudes toward state interventionism, and two measured attitudes toward social change. (Responses on these five variables for our total sample, weighted to equalize national subsample sizes, are given in Table 5–1, along with an indication of which variables were available for each subsample.)

The first of the three variables tapping attitudes on state intervention summarizes respondents' answers to questions about the proper scope of *government economic planning*. Attitudes are arrayed along a six-point scale, ranging from a laissez-faire, free-enterprise view to one that espouses full state ownership and control of the economy. Table 5–1 shows that national elites in Western democracies are dispersed fairly widely along this dimension, with the average respondent favoring a mixed economy with government incentives and perhaps some government ownership of a few sectors.

A second variable measures attitudes along a five-point continuum related to *state involvement* generally. This indicator is especially sensitive to the social security side of government involvement and specifically measures whether the respondent's outlook throughout the open-ended interview reflects a preference for more state involvement and social provision, the present balance, or less reliance upon the state and more on individual initiative. Our results here show that, at least in the early

Table 5-1  Five core Left-Right ideological variables.[a]

I. What role does the respondent favor for the government in the national economy, especially in economic planning?

| Full, direct control | Large public sector | Limited investment | Incentives | Voluntary guidelines | None | Weighted N |
|---|---|---|---|---|---|---|
| 7 | 16 | 28 | 31 | 17 | 2 | (781) |

Data available for Britain, France, Germany, Italy, and the Netherlands, and for American bureaucrats.

II. In general, what is the respondent's preferred degree of state involvement in the economy and society?

| Much more state involvement and/or social provision | Some more state involvement and/or social provision | Present balance | Some more individual initiative | Much more individual initiative | Weighted N |
|---|---|---|---|---|---|
| 11 | 27 | 42 | 16 | 5 | (1108) |

Data available for Britain, France, Germany, Italy, the Netherlands, and the United States, and for Swedish bureaucrats.

III. Does the respondent agree or disagree that: "Many of the doubts and fears expressed about the growing intervention of the state in economic and social spheres are fully justified"?

| Disagree without reservations | Disagree with reservations | Agree with reservations | Agree without reservations | Weighted N |
|---|---|---|---|---|
| 20 | 31 | 32 | 17 | (776) |

Data available for Britain, Germany, Italy, and the Netherlands, and for Swedish bureaucrats.

IV. What is the respondent's preferred mode for social and political change?

| Revolutionary | Radical (major, directed change) | Moderately active (guided change) | Laissez-faire | No desired change | Weighted N |
|---|---|---|---|---|---|
| 0 | 13 | 64 | 19 | 3 | (836) |

Data available for Britain, France, Germany, Italy, and the Netherlands.

V. What is the respondent's attitude toward the existing socioeconomic order?

| Passionate, total rejection | Rejection, but ameliorative reforms proposed | Acceptance, but ameliorative reforms proposed | Acceptance; no important reform proposed | Passionate affirmation of existing order | Weighted N |
|---|---|---|---|---|---|
| 1 | 10 | 48 | 37 | 4 | (1028) |

Data available for Britain, France, Germany, Italy, the Netherlands, and Sweden.

[a] Entries are percentages based on equally weighted national samples from the indicated countries. The entries sum across the rows to 100 percent, within rounding error.

1970s, a plurality of leaders favored the current balance between individual and collective provision, with the rest mostly favoring a somewhat more interventionist view.

A third variable is based on a closed-ended item, asking for agreement or disagreement with the statement, "Many of the doubts and fears expressed about the growing intervention of the state in economic and social spheres are fully justified." Table 5–1 shows that our respondents were evenly divided on this question.

Two ordinal variables, both based on the open-ended interviews, were used to tap attitudes toward social change. The first measures the *mode of social and political change* that the respondent prefers, ranging along a five-point scale from a preference for revolutionary change to a preference for no change at all. The second taps the respondent's *attitude toward the existing socioeconomic order.* This five-point scale ranges from a passionate rejection of the existing order to a passionate affirmation of it. Both measures indicate that only small minorities of the leaders interviewed favor radical social transformation or reject all change. Most of these politicians and bureaucrats favor modest social reform.

Taken together, these five indicators show that the average Western policymaker in the 1970s was a cautious social reformer, committed to a modest degree of state intervention and a mixed economy, though chary of radical change and excessive state control. But our data also reveal considerable diversity of views on these issues, with significant numbers of respondents standing to the left and right of this modal figure. How is this diversity patterned across the roles of bureaucrat and politician in our several countries?

Of our five original core variables, the single most central one (in a matrix of intercorrelations among the five), and the one for which data are most widely available, is the measure of attitudes toward the balance between state involvement and individual initiative. As an introductory illustration of our findings, Figure 5–1 displays graphically the distribution of the scores of each of our subsamples on this variable.[8] The contrast between bureaucrats and politicians in the five European countries is striking. In each country civil servants are heavily concentrated in the center category, favoring the current balance between state involvement and individual initiative, whereas politicians' views are dispersed more widely, with some tendency to favor more state involvement. Across our British, French, German, Italian, and Dutch samples, an average of 60 percent of the bureaucrats fall into the center category, compared to only

*Figure 5-1*    Attitude toward state involvement, by role and country.

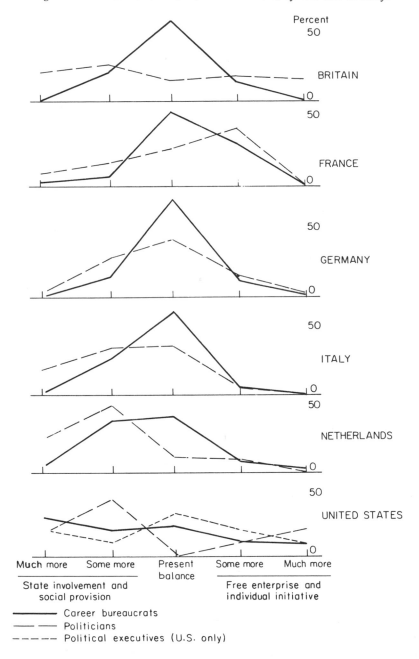

Career bureaucrats
Politicians
Political executives (U.S. only)

27 percent of the politicians. Of the remaining politicians, 50 percent favored greater state involvement and 23 percent favored more reliance on individual initiative. Among bureaucrats, the comparable figures were 25 percent for a bigger state and 15 percent for a smaller state. In each of the European countries, the variance or spread of the bureaucrats' scores was smaller than among politicians, usually by a substantial margin.

We have already indicated our methodological qualms about cross-national comparisons on such variables as this. Here, for example, the coding itself is anchored to the "present balance" between state involvement and individual initiative in the respondent's country, and there is no reason to assume that this balance had been struck at precisely the same point in all these countries. Nevertheless, certain of the cross-national differences are worthy of a cautious glance. The British parliamentary data clearly reflect the ideological polarization of the first year of the Heath government, as described in Chapter 2, a polarization that seemed to re-emerge in full vigor with the election of the Thatcher government at the end of the 1970s. The French data, by contrast, reveal the impact of the conservative landslide of 1968 (as well as our undersampling of French Communists), also described in Chapter 2; the results again hint that to some extent Leftists may have been excluded from the higher civil service under the Fifth Republic. The German results are quite consistent with the moderate social reformism that has characterized the Socialist-Liberal coalition over the last decade. The responses of the Italians reflect the widespread support among Italian officials, particularly those on the left of the political spectrum, for state-directed solutions to social problems. In the Netherlands, these data (as well as other evidence from our Dutch interviews) show a somewhat surprising degree of support for state intervention and social reform. In this context one must recall that a government dominated by the Left, including a fairly strong "new Left" component, had come to power in the Netherlands the year before our interviews. There are grounds for believing that the leftist sentiments expressed by our Dutch respondents were more than merely verbal. From 1972 through 1977, Dutch politicians took part in a program of social and cultural change that was little noticed outside their country but had a major impact on Dutch society.

Through this thicket of national peculiarities, two regularities are clearly visible in our European data: (1) bureaucratic elites are heavily concentrated at the center of the ideological continuum, and (2) politicians are more skewed toward the left. The second of the two patterns—

the more leftist orientation of the politicians—might possibly have been a phenomenon of the early 1970s, subject to reversal in the more conservative climate of the 1980s, although we note that of the five European countries depicted in Figure 5–1, three (Britain, France, and Italy) were ruled by conservative majorities at the time of our interviews. The first of the two patterns—the centrism of the bureaucrats—seems likely to be an enduring feature of these systems, although obviously only subsequent research can confirm that judgment. As we shall see shortly, these two regularities are found on all five of our core ideological measures in Europe.

The American pattern is different. Our congressional respondents were distributed bimodally, with a substantial number of liberals and a smaller band of firm conservatives, much as we would expect. On the bureaucratic side, Figure 5–1 makes the customary distinction between career civil servants and political appointees. Unlike their European counterparts, the American career officials are skewed substantially toward the left of this ideological dimension, with the modal category favoring much more state involvement and social provision. Well to their right stand the Nixon political appointees. Internally, each of the two American administrative samples is more heterogeneous than any of the European bureaucratic samples, and collectively the American respondents from the executive branch are a much more diverse lot ideologically than any European bureaucratic sample. Indeed, the American executive elite is more diverse ideologically, at least as measured by this variable, than any of the European parliamentary elites.

In short, whereas bureaucratic elites in Europe are ideologically much more homogeneous, and slightly more conservative, than their parliaments, bureaucratic elites in the United States are fully as heterogeneous as Congress, and U.S. career officials, at least, stand slightly to the left of the average congressman.[9] Under a Republican administration, our data suggest, the impact of these liberal career officials is to some extent blunted and masked by an influx of conservative political appointees. By contrast, the political appointments of a Democratic administration are apt to magnify the impact of the liberalism of the career civil service. The central point, however, is that in neither case is the American executive branch dominated, as are the European bureaucracies, by centrists. For reasons addressed at several points in this book, the American bureaucracy is much more reflective of the vivid hues of the full national ideological spectrum than are the rather pastel European bureaucracies, and the general tinge of the U.S. career civil service is slightly pinker than its European counterparts.

Figure 5–2 shows how European bureaucrats and politicians scored on our four other core ideological measures. (For economy of presentation, we have combined data from the several countries, since a more detailed nation-by-nation analysis reveals no substantial deviation from the common patterns.) On each measure bureaucrats are heavily clustered at the moderate, centrist position, while politicians are more widely distributed across the ideological spectrum, with a marked skew towards the left. In statistical terms, in each case the mean score for bureaucrats is to the right of that for politicians, and the variance of the bureaucratic distribution is lower than that for politicians. European bureaucrats favor a mixed economy rather like the one they now have; they express caution, but not passionate concern, about the dangers of an interventionist state; they prefer moderate social change; and they accept the existing social order, offering few major reforms. Parliamentary opinion, by contrast, is more polarized ideologically between a substantial block on the left, wanting a bigger state and major social reform, and a group on the right, smaller than the first (at least in the early 1970s), calling for less state intervention.

### The Coherence of Ideology

The simplest, most fundamental assumption of our analysis is that the ideological coherence of Western elites along the Left-Right dimension is sufficiently high that our five variables should all be closely correlated. Table 5–2 presents the intercorrelations among the five core variables, together with the results of a factor analysis of those intercorrelations. The data show that indeed the core variables are closely linked, with a mean intercorrelation of $r = .47$. As expected, a single dominant dimension emerges from the factor analysis; the mean correlation of the five variables with this underlying factor is .76, implying that 58 percent of the total variance in the average core variable is accounted for by a single ideological dimension.[10] By standards usual in survey research, these results argue quite strongly that our respondents' views on these basic issues are powerfully determined by their position on a single ideological dimension of support for, or opposition to, state intervention and social reform.

Correlational analysis of the sort illustrated in Table 5–2 has been used

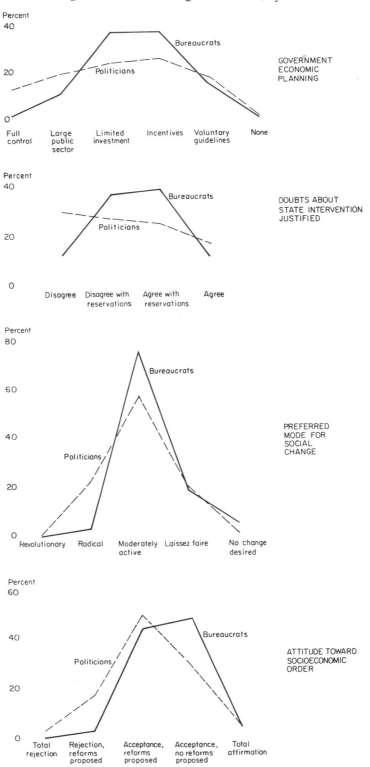

*Figure 5-2*  Core ideological measures, by role.

*Table 5-2*  Correlations among core ideological variables.

| Variable | I | II | III | IV | V | Loading on principal factor |
|---|---|---|---|---|---|---|
| I. Government economic planning | — | .64 | .44 | .56 | .49 | .84 |
| II. State involvement | .64 | — | .53 | .49 | .50 | .84 |
| III. Doubts about state intervention | .44 | .53 | — | .29 | .41 | .69 |
| IV. Mode of social change | .56 | .49 | .29 | — | .38 | .71 |
| V. Attitude toward socioeconomic order | .49 | .50 | .41 | .38 | — | .73 |

conventionally to assess the relative degree of coherence or "constraint" of belief systems in different populations. In a classic study, for example, Philip Converse showed that the intercorrelations among views of American voters on a number of policy issues were substantially lower than the comparable figures for congressional candidates; from this (and related) evidence, Converse concluded that voters' views were less coherently structured in ideological terms.[11] Following this strategy, one is tempted to assess the relative ideological coherence of politicians and bureaucrats by calculating the intercorrelations among the five core variables separately for the two groups. The results of such an analysis seem to demonstrate that bureaucrats are much less consistent ideologically than politicians, for the mean intercorrelation in the political sample is .58, while the comparable figure for the bureaucratic sample is .29. This methodological approach is, however, fatally flawed, and in order to understand the rest of this chapter, one must grasp the nature of the flaw.[12]

Mathematically, the correlation between two variables depends on the range of variation in each observed in a given sample. Other things being equal, reducing the variance in one (or both) of the two variables will inevitably reduce their correlation. To take an athletic example, we all know that the pugilistic ability of a boxer is closely related to his weight. Indeed, in order to reduce the predictability of boxing matches, it is necessary to constrain artificially the variance in the "independent variable" by arranging matches only between boxers whose weights are very similar. Thus, within a given weight class—say, among heavyweights—there is virtually no correlation between a fighter's weight and his pugilistic success. But obviously it would be wrong to draw from this statistical fact the conclusion that weight has no connection with fighting ability.

The implication for our analysis of ideological coherence among bureaucrats and politicians should be clear. On each of the five core ideological measures, bureaucrats are much more closely clustered at the center than politicians. This substantially lower variation among bureaucrats means that we must (mathematically "must") expect lower intercorrelations of the ideological measures among bureaucrats than among politicians, *whatever* the ideological consistency of individual politicians and bureaucrats. The unanswered question is this: Do the lower intercorrelations we have discovered for our bureaucratic samples mean that the average bureaucrat's views on the five core ideological measures are in fact internally inconsistent—mildly Leftist on some issues, mildly Rightist on others, for instance? Or instead, is the average bureaucrat just as consistent as the average politician, differing only in that the bureaucrat is typically a consistent centrist, whereas the politician is typically a consistent Leftist or a consistent Rightist?

One technique for answering this question involves a direct assessment of the consistency of each respondent's relative standing on each of the five core variables. A respondent who ranks, let us say, in the fourth decile from the left on each of the five variables is more consistent ideologically, by this measure, than a respondent who ranks in the second decile on two variables, in the sixth decile on two, and in the fourth decile on only one, even though the mean left-right rankings of the two respondents are virtually identical. Unlike correlational analysis, this technique enables us to calculate for each individual a measure of his internal ideological consistency.[13]

Figure 5–3 shows graphically how our two samples rank on this measure of ideological consistency. The two profiles are virtually identical. Although a few individuals in each group expressed quite inconsistent (or at least idiosyncratic) sets of views on our core ideological measures, the vast majority of both politicians and bureaucrats demonstrated a very high degree of consistency. In fact, the consistency score of the median bureaucrat is slightly higher than the score of his political counterpart.

To illustrate the consistency typical of actual respondents, consider, first of all, a slightly right-of-center British civil servant, who wanted the role of government in the economy limited to providing incentives for private enterprise; wished the present balance between state involvement and individual initiative to be tipped modestly toward the individual; agreed (but with reservations) that many fears about big government were justified; indicated a preference for moderate, guided social change; and accepted the existing social order without major reform. Also earning a consistency score at just about the median for our sample was a Dutch

*Figure 5-3* Ideological consistency, by role.

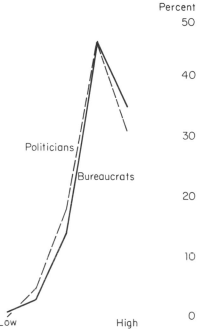

NOTE: Based on equally weighted samples from Britain, France, Germany, Italy, and the Netherlands.

left-wing politician who wanted full and direct government control of the economy; argued for much more state involvement and social provision; disagreed totally with the claim that growing government intervention is a cause for concern; preferred radical social change; and while accepting the fundamentals of the existing social order, proposed important ameliorative reforms. By any reasonable standard, the ideological stances expressed by both politicians and bureaucrats in our interviews must be considered quite coherent and internally consistent.[14]

Since responses to our five core variables are coherently intercorrelated, we can combine these replies into a single composite indicator of a policymaker's ideological stance. Figure 5-4 shows how our bureaucrats and politicians are distributed along this new continuum.[15] The ideological profiles of the two groups are by now familiar: the heavy concentration of bureaucrats in the center, coupled with a slight bureaucratic bias toward moderate conservatism; the more polarized distribution of politi-

*Figure 5-4*    Ideological stance, by role.

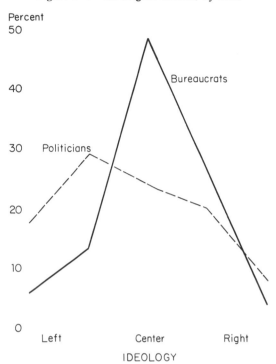

NOTE: Based on equally weighted samples for all seven nations.

cians, skewed toward the left. Among bureaucrats, 20 percent are Leftists, 49 percent are centrists, and 31 percent are Rightists; the equivalent figures for politicians are 47 percent Leftists, 24 percent centrists, and 29 percent Rightists.

We can now begin to glimpse some answers to our initial question about the ideological positions of politicians and bureaucrats. First, both types of policymaker typically express ideologically consistent points of view on the basic issues of social change and government activism that have structured politics in the West during this century. Bureaucrats may display a more inductive, less philosophical approach to public affairs than politicians—indeed, we will shortly examine some evidence to that effect—but this does not mean that their positions on fundamental ideological issues are any less coherent.

Second, bureaucrats in Europe appear to be more consistently centrist than politicians in several senses:

(1) On virtually all our ideological measures in almost all countries the average civil servant stands closer to the ideological center than does the average member of parliament. "Center" here is defined in terms of the total array of opinions expressed by all our respondents, but a glance back at Table 5–1 shows that this central position corresponds in all cases to a preference for the sort of mildly reformist policies actually being pursued by Western governments. The average civil servant is more likely than the average politician to prefer "doing it the way we do it now." At least in the early 1970s, holding this position was tantamount to standing to the right of the average politician, ideologically speaking, although we cannot be sure whether bureaucratic conservatism in this relative sense is an enduring feature of the relationship between bureaucrats and politicians.

(2) On virtually all our ideological measures in virtually all countries, the distribution of bureaucrats is much more tightly clustered than the distribution of politicians, who tend to be more polarized. That this cluster is located at the center of the ideological spectrum does not follow logically, but it is, of course, true empirically. (In statistical terms, the *mean* of the distribution of bureaucrats is closer to the center of the scale than is the mean of politicians, the *variance* of the distribution of bureaucrats is lower, and the *kurtosis* of the distribution—its "peakedness"—is higher.)

(3) The position of the median civil servant is slightly more consistent across different ideological measures than is that of the median politician. It is worth noting that this greater inter-item consistency does not follow logically from the bureaucrats' ideological centrism, since ideological extremists could also be highly consistent, as in fact many of them are. Nevertheless, consistent centrism is a distinctive feature of the ideological outlook of bureaucrats.

The United States, we must recall, is different. In terms of the measures used here, the pattern of ideological polarization among American politicians is not dramatically different from the European patterns, but American bureaucrats are quite distinctive. Consistent ideological centrism is not a characteristic of American bureaucratic thought, as it is in Europe. In part, this American peculiarity is due to the presence of political appointees in the bureaucratic elite, a factor highlighted in our Nixon-era interviews. But our evidence makes clear that ideological centrism in the several senses described above is also not characteristic of career civil servants in America. We shall, of course, have occasion to return subsequently to the implications of this American anomaly.

Beyond the centrism characteristic of European bureaucrats and the polarizing tendencies of politicians, there is another closely related distinction between bureaucratic and political thought, as reflected in our interviews—a deductivist-inductivist distinction. At least in Europe, politicians are much more inclined than bureaucrats to incorporate their discussions of public affairs within some sort of overarching conceptual framework. Among European politicians, 71 percent were rated "high" by our coders on a measure of their tendency to apply "a single, simplified, conceptual explanatory schema to all discussion of public policy," whereas only 40 percent of our European bureaucrats were similarly rated. (America, again, is different; the comparable figures are 56 percent for politicians and 53 percent for bureaucrats.)

As we have already suggested in Chapter 4, the bureaucrat's concern with "what works" disposes him to an inductive outlook on policy issues. This pragmatic style of policy analysis is quite compatible with political views that are incremental and centrist ideologically. Politicians, on the other hand, can be great simplifiers. Since the mechanics of policy engage their attention more rarely, they are driven more readily toward abstract, even utopian, thinking, and hence toward framing the policy agenda in more elaborate, deductive terms. More than bureaucrats, politicians are conceptualizers, in the sense that they have a well-articulated theory about society and politics that permeates their discussion of policy. The world of the bureaucrat is one of technical detail, interpretive nuance, and operational responsibility. To be sure, individuals in such an environment are rarely political neuters; nor are they immunized from the rigidities that affect politicians; nor, above all, are they necessarily uninspired by ideologies. Still, the immediacy and concreteness of the problems that bureaucrats typically address rarely require explicit reference to "first principles." Moreover, as one of us reports elsewhere, politicians typically enter politics because they are power seekers, champions of causes, and facilitators of interests. By contrast, civil servants are attracted to their calling for reasons having to do with the application of expertise to practical problems, as well as more mundane reasons of pay, status, and job security.[16] These motivational differences are reinforced by the divergent tasks that politicians and bureaucrats undertake. An absorption with "the big picture" is as congenial to the politician's vocation as it is alien to the bureaucrat's.

*Figure 5-5*    Left-Right ideology and levels of conceptualization.

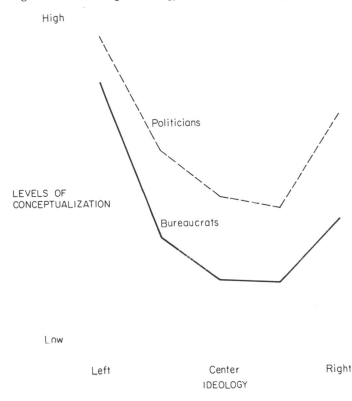

NOTE: Based on equally weighted samples from Britain, Germany, France, Italy, Sweden, and the Netherlands.

A leader's propensity for abstract, deductive conceptualization of public issues is related to both his role (political or bureaucratic) and his ideology (Left, center, Right) in a close, complex, and quite intelligible manner. Figure 5–5 displays this relationship graphically, with three features worthy of particular note:

(1) *Curvilinearity.* Ideological "extremists" are much more likely than centrists to frame their discussions of public affairs in abstract, highly conceptual terms.[17] Centrists, content with current practice, may have an ideology—our evidence suggests they do—but they are not "ideologues," prone to phrasing issues in theoretical terms.[18] Working toward distant goals requires a theory; "muddling through" does not.

(2) *Asymmetry.* Conceptualization tends to be lower among Rightists than among Leftists; indeed, moderate Rightists are no more inclined to abstract, deductive thinking than are centrists. The explanation seems to be that those who want change are more in need of a clear set of goals and an explicit social theory than those who resist change. Since Leftists generally have more substantial aspirations to remold society than do moderate Rightists, these aspirations are more apt to be expressed in doctrinal terms. (Extreme conservatives, of course, are apt to be discontent with social and political trends in their societies, and thus they too need a theory about how to reverse those trends.) The more distant one's objectives, the more necessary a road map; if one is content to stay in place, a map is unnecessary.

(3) *Role differences.* At each point on the ideological continuum, bureaucrats are less prone to abstract, deductive, conceptual schemes than politicians. Thus, the gross role differences in conceptualization we noted earlier have several roots. First, ideologically speaking, bureaucrats are much more heavily concentrated in the center (and, to some extent, the moderate right), which is precisely where conceptualization is least common. Second, controlling for ideology, the differences in task and motivation discussed earlier seem to incline bureaucrats to a more inductive, practical orientation to public issues. These findings are, of course, fully consistent with the role differences discussed in Chapter 4.

## The Consequences of Ideology

POLICIES AND THE FUTURE    We have seen thus far that bureaucrats and politicians have reasonably coherent and well-defined positions on the Left-Right ideological dimension that has structured most of the great political battles of this century in Western polities. We need to ask next, in part as a matter of validating our ideological measures, if a policymaker's position on these grand issues of state intervention and social change actually is related to his day-to-day decisions. At his desk or at a committee table, a bureaucrat or politician is asked to decide not whether the state should be expanded and society reformed, but rather whether Naples should get a new grant for public housing, or whether the national canal network should be phased out, or where the third London airport should be located, or how secondary schools should be reorganized, or whether pollution controls should be required on steel plants. It makes sense, then, to ask whether a policymaker's position on such practical

*Table 5-3*   Policy reformism, by ideology and role.[a]

| Role | Ideological stance | | | Left-Right difference |
|---|---|---|---|---|
| | Left | Center | Right | |
| Politicians | 87 | 74 | 63 | +24 |
| N = | (203) | (134) | (111) | |
| Bureaucrats | 57 | 45 | 36 | +21 |
| N = | (72) | (240) | (142) | |
| Role difference: | +30 | +29 | +27 | R = .46 |

[a] Entries are percentages of each category (for example, of leftist politicians) proposing important or major changes in policy. Analysis is based on equally weighted samples from Britain, France, Germany, Italy, and the Netherlands.

problems as these is related at all to his broad ideological stance, or for that matter, to his role as politician or bureaucrat.

Each respondent in Britain, France, Italy, Germany, and the Netherlands was asked to discuss in some detail "the most important problem facing the country in [his] area of special responsibility or interest."[19] In the course of these discussions, roughly three-fifths of the respondents proposed major or important changes in current policy, while the remaining two-fifths were content to recommend only minor changes or none at all. Table 5–3 shows how this measure of policy reformism in the respondent's specific field is related to his role, as well as to his general ideological stance.[20]

Since the same format will be used throughout this chapter to present findings about the correlates of role and ideology, we should pause a moment over Table 5–3. As aids to interpretation, we show the percentage differences between bureaucrats and politicians, controlling for ideology, and the percentage differences between Leftists and Rightists, controlling for role. These percentage differences indicate the relative importance of role and ideology in accounting for the dependent variable—policy reformism, in this case. Finally, as a summary measure of the joint importance of role and ideology, we give the multiple correlation coefficient (*R*).

In this instance, we can see that both role and ideology have a significant independent impact on the average respondent's approach to the practical policy problems on his desk. Among both bureaucrats and politicians, Leftists are considerably more likely than Rightists to propose substantial changes in current policy, and the effect of ideology is about equally strong on politicians and on bureaucrats.[21]

On the other hand, controlling for ideology, politicians are much less satisfied with current policy than bureaucrats are. Perhaps bureaucrats are more conscious of the intractable dilemmas that make far-reaching reform unrealistic, however desirable. Perhaps bureaucrats are so enmeshed in the details of muddling through that they have no time or energy to articulate large alternatives, whatever their ideological predispositions. It may be that bureaucrats and politicians have both adjusted intellectually to a division of labor in which the former administer existing policy, and only the latter worry about changing it, no matter how unrealistic this division of labor seems to outside observers. Or perhaps, with their longer tenure and greater specialization, bureaucrats have simply developed a stronger psychological identification with current practice, a sense not merely that "this is how it's always been done," but that "this is how *we* have always done it." Whatever the proper explanation, it is clear that where politicians see a need for major policy innovation, civil servants are typically content to propose marginal adjustments.

In the aggregate, of course, part of the explanation for the limited policy reformism of bureaucrats is their ideological centrism. But the evidence of Table 5–3 makes it clear that ideology is less than half the story. The one bureaucrat in six or seven who stands on the left ideologically is not so reformist on immediate policy issues as even the most conservative politician. The contrast is, of course, even greater if we compare the opposite corners of Table 5–3. Between the nearly half of all politicians who stand on the left ideologically and the one-third of all bureaucrats who are on the right yawns a gulf of 51 percentage points in terms of policy reformism. We shall have occasion repeatedly to return to the stark differences in outlook between these two sizable groups of policymakers—progressive politicians and conservative bureaucrats.

The evidence we have just examined provides some insight into how role and ideology affect the decisions policymakers must make about the problems on their agendas. Less important in the short run, but more important in the long run, is the question of how new problems make it onto those agendas. The process of agenda formation in modern polities is highly complex. Elites and their ideologies are by no means the sole determinants; grass-roots social movements, technological change, intellectual currents, and organized interest groups are among the factors that seem likely to be critical. But we believe that elite ideologies will also turn out to be important, for at least in part, policymakers can set their own agendas.

As one technique for exploring this issue, we asked our respondents in Britain, France, Germany, Italy, Sweden, and the United States to describe for us "the kind of society you would like to see for your children and grandchildren. How would that society differ from today's society?" Not surprisingly, the question evoked a profusion of disparate and often idiosyncratic nominations for the agenda of the future. Yet common themes emerged. Some respondents offered passionate pleas for greater social justice:

> It should be more democratic than it is today. It should show small differences in wealth and income. It should give everyone the same chance for education. These are the things that concern me, because I come from the real working class, and indeed from a time—even before the great world economic crisis—when there was still a proletariat in the genuine sense, with nothing more than its labor to sell and living constantly under the scourge of unemployment.

Others emphasized economic stability and growth, without particular reference to distributive issues:

> As a society, in terms of composition, I don't think there can be great innovations. There should be further improvements in the standard of living, which I hope we can achieve with a further thrust toward industrialization.

A number of respondents, particularly in Italy, but elsewhere as well, emphasized the desirability of political reforms:

> I would like an improved democracy, a democracy that had better instruments—parties, parliament, associations, unions—more efficient than ours, and that gave our children the opportunity for better choices and decisions than we have.

Some respondents were concerned about collectivist trends, and emphasized the importance of freedom, particularly free enterprise:

> The future society can be essentially that of today. Obviously, if we were to eliminate individual initiative, we would eliminate the element that brought us to our current position. If we regimented everything, leveled everything downward, we would badly serve society.

Some stressed the importance of security and social stability:

> I think one of the things that plagues the younger generation is uncertainty. I would like to see a society in which there is a little more

stability. I recognize that, though it is not meant to be, this could be interpreted in a rather reactionary way. The world in which I was born contained a great deal of poverty; it is easily represented as a dreadful world. But it had a structure in which people sort of fitted. It was jolly unfortunate if you fitted in one of the unpleasant holes, but you fitted into it. Now younger people hardly know whether they're destined to be a dustman or a prime minister, which produces almost a neurotic outlook on the world.

Some people found it difficult to lift their sights beyond the present national agenda:

The two outstanding problems we have today are both financial. One is the balance of payments in our changing position in the world, the other is the growing fear of runaway inflation in this country. Get those two put right, and there is nothing fundamentally so wrong today that it must be put right for the benefit of the next generation.

Some people seemed unwilling or unable to formulate even the most pallid dreams:

There are always changes, but on the whole I find the world in which we live at the moment really quite good. In ten years it won't be the same as it is today, for there will always be improvements. But already one can be quite satisfied.

And finally, a few pessimists were resigned to a future they thought would be ineluctably worse than the present:

I don't think about the society I'd like to see for my children, because I don't really expect it to materialize. I mean, I regard myself as out of place in the modern world. I see the future mainly in terms of a less tolerable existence. It's very difficult to see much ground for expecting anything more than a kind of bigger and bigger ant heap the longer the thing goes on.

As these comments suggest, this question was something of a Rorschach test, inviting these busy men and women of affairs to push their chairs back from the desk and spin out their more distant hopes and fears. As with any projective test, the inference from responses to behavior in a specific situation is hazardous. But listening closely to soliloquies evoked by this question, we are convinced that these reflections often embody the basic value priorities of these policymakers, priorities that may well influence their behavior in those rare, but important moments when the constraints of situation and role are relaxed, allowing new issues to be added to the national agenda. How are a policymaker's hopes and fears for the future related to his role and ideology?

Table 5–4 summarizes our findings on this question. As we would expect, ideology has an even more substantial impact on a person's images of the future than on his proposals for immediate policy problems. Among both politicians and bureaucrats, Leftists want substantially more change for the future than do Rightists.[22]

The content of these utopias also varies with ideology. Leftists are far more likely to emphasize social justice and equality; the egalitarian ideal seems to remain at the heart of the leftist vision of "the good society." And Leftists are also more likely to stress political or institutional reform. What Rightists want is, by contrast, more blurred, in part because more of them are content with the status quo. They give greater emphasis to the less visionary values of liberty and security, each representing a separate strand of conservative thought. The value of liberty, as expressed in these answers, represents the free-market ideology of a modern conservatism that grew out of nineteenth-century liberalism. On the other hand, the value of security belongs to an older tradition of conservatism that emphasizes the importance of authority. Perhaps nowhere are these two threads in the tapestry of conservatism as distinct as in France, where the libertarian *Giscardiens* frequently clash with the *étatist* Gaullists. In contrast to the sharp Left-Right division over the desirability of social equality, the weaker relationships between liberty and security, on the one hand, and the Left-Right cleavage, on the other, probably reflect the independence of these two strands of conservatism.

Turning to the comparison of politicians and bureaucrats, we notice first that the impact of ideology is essentially the same within each group. Although we know from our earlier findings that there are relatively few leftist and rightist bureaucrats, the differences between them with respect to images of the future are as sharp as those between leftist and rightist politicians.

Controlling for ideology, we find small but consistent differences in the images of the future expressed by bureaucrats and politicians. The sketches of a better society offered by politicians are richer in detail and more far-reaching in substance than is the marginal tinkering suggested by civil servants. Civil servants are a bit more likely to stress social stability and material progress, and a bit less likely than politicians to think in

*Table 5-4*  Desires for the future, by ideology and role.

| Role | Ideological stance | | | Left-Right difference |
|---|---|---|---|---|
| | Left | Center | Right | |
| **I. Percentage of each category who propose more than "minor" *changes for the society of the future*** | | | | |
| Politicians | 87 | 76 | 43 | +44 |
| $N =$ | (177) | (106) | (137) | |
| Bureaucrats | 87 | 56 | 36 | +51 |
| $N =$ | (73) | (231) | (141) | |
| Role difference: | 0 | +20 | +7 | $R = .39$ |
| **II. Percentage of each category who propose changes involving *social justice and equality*** | | | | |
| Politicians | 68 | 38 | 19 | +49 |
| $N =$ | (140) | (108) | (114) | |
| Bureaucrats | 55 | 29 | 13 | +42 |
| $N =$ | (48) | (213) | (126) | |
| Role difference: | +13 | +9 | +6 | $R = .40$ |
| **III. Percentage of each category who propose changes involving *freedom and free enterprise*** | | | | |
| Politicians | 11 | 22 | 30 | −19 |
| $N =$ | (140) | (108) | (114) | |
| Bureaucrats | 9 | 8 | 23 | −14 |
| $N =$ | (48) | (213) | (126) | |
| Role difference: | +2 | +14 | +7 | $R = .23$ |
| **IV. Percentage of each category who propose changes involving *political or institutional reform*** | | | | |
| Politicians | 30 | 28 | 14 | +16 |
| $N =$ | (140) | (108) | (114) | |
| Bureaucrats | 22 | 19 | 10 | +12 |
| $N =$ | (48) | (213) | (126) | |
| Role difference: | +8 | +9 | +4 | $R = .17$ |
| **V. Percentage of each category who propose changes involving *security or stability*** | | | | |
| Politicians | 9 | 20 | 29 | −20 |
| $N =$ | (140) | (108) | (114) | |
| Bureaucrats | 11 | 26 | 34 | −23 |
| $N =$ | (48) | (213) | (126) | |
| Role difference: | −2 | −6 | −5 | $R = .19$ |

NOTE: Data in I are based on equally weighted samples from Britain, France, Germany, Italy, Sweden, and the United States. Data in II to V are based on the same samples, minus the United States.

terms of distant ideals, whether of the Left (social justice) or of the Right (liberty). In the aggregate, these differences between bureaucrats and politicians are accentuated by the tendency for bureaucrats to be found at the center of the ideological spectrum, where abstract ideals are in any event less popular. Both by role and by ideology, bureaucrats dream somewhat drabber dreams.

Although consistent and intelligible, these role differences should not be overemphasized, for the impact of role on hopes for the future is much less than its impact on policy for the present. In contrast to the powerful effect of role on policy reformism, its effect fades as our respondents look to the future; ideological differences become more dominant. In short, to predict a policymaker's reactions to issues on his present agenda, it is helpful to know his ideological stance, but it is more important to know his role in government. On the other hand, to predict his agenda for the future, it is helpful to know his role, but it is a great deal more important to know his ideology. With their feet on the desk, politicians and bureaucrats think more similarly than with their feet on the floor. If role counts more in the short run, ideology points the way to the future.

POLITICS AND GOVERNANCE    Ideology and role influence a policymaker's views on the substance of policy—his notion of what government should (or should not) do to and for people. That much is clear from the evidence offered thus far. We now want to explore the consequences of ideology and of role in another domain—not the *what* of policy content, but the *how* of policymaking. Are there systematic differences between Leftists and Rightists, or between bureaucrats and politicians, in their images of the policy process and their ideas about how society ought to manage its affairs?

To explicate the patterns that emerge from our interviews, we need to contrast two venerable perspectives on society and public affairs. The first—we shall term it the Governance model—traces its intellectual ancestry from Plato to Hegel, while the lineage of the second, which we shall call the Politics model, runs from Aristotle to Madison.

The two models differ, first and fundamentally, in their conception of the public interest. Adherents to the Governance model postulate a monistic public interest, encompassing the real interests of all members of the community, or "the body politic" (organic metaphors abound in this school of thought). The object of leaders is, or ought to be, to understand and implement that public interest, drawing counsel from the wise, the expert, and the prudent, but giving no quarter to "self-interested" pleas from "partisans" or "special interests." Social and political conflict is, according to the Governance model, marginal, illusory, and often artificial. Public issues can be—and therefore should be—resolved in terms of some objective standard of justice, or of legality, or of technical practicality, rather than in terms of the clash of particularistic interests.

The Politics model, by contrast, endorses a pluralistic conception of the public interest and affirms the reality and legitimacy of conflict. This model assumes that different segments of society will have divergent perspectives and even divergent interests with respect to most public issues. The task of leaders is, first, to ensure the articulation of all relevant interests and, second, to seek to reconcile those interests wherever possible. They must recognize that policy choice is not value-free, and that policy is typically the resultant of the parallelogram of contending forces (metaphors from physics permeate the works of this school). The Politics model sees the clash of divergent groups and parties as inevitable and even healthy, and it is skeptical of the claims of expertise and "objectivity." If stability and efficiency are the prime objectives of Governance, progress and distributive justice are the goals of Politics.

These contrasting views of the public good have important implications for the institutions through which that public good is sought. The Governance model, in its more extreme versions, endorses an elitist and even authoritarian approach to policymaking—rule by the best and the brightest—for the ability to discern and implement truth is unequally distributed. Even in its milder versions, this model emphasizes the role of the executive branch of government and the permanent officers of state. A career civil service—expert and "above politics"—is said to be the mark of a mature and well-ordered state. The autonomy and political neutrality of this institution should be cherished, and its strength protected. Policymakers are, in this view, trustees for the permanent interests of the community and the state—"guardians," as Plato called them.

The Politics model takes a kinder view of the noisier institutions of pluralistic democracy—political parties, interest groups, parliaments, elected politicians. Their contentious hubbub represents the natural and proper functioning of a system in which a variety of interests must find expression and reconciliation. Experts, in the view of the Politics model, should be on tap, not on top—clarifying technical issues, but not cloaking their advice in a synthetic mantle of "objectivity." Administrative neutrality is a will-o'-the-wisp, and administrators should not hesitate to engage in policy advocacy, on the assumption that opposing interests also will find effective advocates. Deprecation of expertise and emphasis on the legitimacy of all interests gives this theory a distinctively egalitarian cast. Jacksonian democracy is a kind of apotheosis of the Politics model. The ideal leader in this perspective is not a guardian, but a tribune, defending a group or cause.

While conceding that this sketch of the two models is somewhat overdrawn, integrating ideas from a variety of theorists and activists, we believe that it does distinguish two broad approaches to public affairs that have contended throughout Western political and intellectual history. (We also concede that, as American social scientists, our appreciation for the subtle workings of the Politics model can hardly be hidden, although we hope we have indicated some appreciation, too, for the virtues of Governance.) The next question is this: How might allegiance to one or the other of these two models on the part of practical policymakers be linked to their ideologies and roles?

In Ralf Dahrendorf's view, "the fundamental inequality of social structure and the lasting determinant of social conflict is the inequality of power and authority which inevitably accompanies social organization." The value patterns of Leftists and Rightists and the ways they think about the process of policymaking accords with the priority each gives to redressing these inequalities. From the perspective of inequality of power and authority, Leftists think from the bottom up and Rightists think from the top down. As Dahrendorf puts it:

> The dominant groups of society express their comparative gratification with existing conditions *inter alia* by visualizing and describing these conditions as ordered and reasonable; subjected groups, on the other hand, tend to emphasize the cleavages that in their opinion account for the deprivations they feel ... The integration model, the hierarchical image, lends itself as an ideology of satisfaction and conservation; the coercion model, the dichotomous image, provides an expression for dissatisfaction and the wish to change the status quo.[23]

Leftists, in short, think in terms of Politics; Rightists, in terms of Governance. That is our hypothesis.

An analogous distinction, we surmise, applies to the thought patterns of politicians and bureaucrats. William Gamson has characterized two perspectives in the following terms:

> One view takes the vantage point of potential partisans and emphasizes the process by which such groups attempt to influence the choices of authorities or the structure within which decisions occur.

The second view takes the vantage point of the authorities and emphasizes the process by which they attempt to achieve collective goals and to maintain legitimacy and compliance with their decisions in a situation in which significant numbers of potential partisans are not being fully satisfied.[24]

Whereas the authorities are the agents of control, partisans are the targets of control; conversely, authorities are the targets of influence, and partisans are the agents of influence. Politicians, as "partisans," think in terms of Politics; bureaucrats, as "the authorities," think in terms of Governance.

We do not suppose that the link between ideology and role, on the one hand, and images of Politics and Governance, on the other, is immutable and universal. History provides ample illustrations of leftist politicians in power who acted on the tenets of Governance, while many conservative bureaucrats in pluralist democracies embrace the Politics creed. But the pairings we have hypothesized are worth exploring. How do politicians and bureaucrats of the Left and of the Right conceive the social and political process within which they play such central roles? In the term given currency by Alexander George, what are their "operational codes"?[25]

First, how salient is conflict for the two groups? Each of our interviews touched questions of social and political conflict several times. At one point we addressed the issue quite directly, if a bit philosophically, asking

> Some people say that in politics and society generally, there is always conflict among various groups, while others say that most groups have a great deal in common and share basically the same interests. How do you feel about this?

Roughly half of these experienced politicians and bureaucrats thought conflict the normal state of affairs, while the rest believed consensus and cooperation to be at least as common.

A second, more indirect indicator of the salience of conflict for each policymaker comes from an intensive analysis of his discussion of two policy issues, one that he had previously nominated as "the most important problem" in his area of interest, the other involving the role of the state in the economy. Each discussion was rated in terms of the prominence of conflicting interests, as the respondent saw the problem, and the ratings for his two discussions were then averaged together. Roughly half of these policy analyses referred, more or less explicitly, to the existence of divergent interests within the issue-area, while the rest implied that a single public interest was at stake, so that a policy good for one sector of society would be good for all.

A third probe of our respondents' perceptions of conflict is based on questions about "the most important differences between the political parties in this country." Again, roughly half described important inter-party differences, whereas the other half saw only marginal or insignificant differences between the parties. Naturally, a very wide array of party distinctions was cited, including such factors as ideology, stands on economic policy and social welfare, and differences in party leadership and style. One type of description that is particularly relevant to our discussion of social conflict attributed party differences to cleavages between social classes or other socioeconomic groups; 47 percent of our interlocutors spontaneously mentioned this sort of difference between parties. It is reasonable to infer that these people were particularly sensitive to the linkage between social and political conflict. Finally, in Britain, Germany, Italy, and the Netherlands, we also asked our bureaucrats whether they noticed differences between the parties in the work of their own department; slightly more than half said that they did.

On all these questions about social and political conflict, it would seem that those policymakers whose image of their environment is structured by the Politics model should find conflict more salient, whereas those operating with the Governance model should stress consensus and shared interests. On this assumption, Table 5–5 shows that both role and ideology are closely tied to the Politics-Governance dichotomy, just as expected.

On our philosophical question about social conflict, ideological differences are marked, while role differences are minimal; but on the measure of conflict salience in policy discussions, role differences are much more marked. In both cases, Leftists are sensitive to the reality of social conflict, while Rightists emphasize shared interests, and conflicting interests are much more salient to politicians than to bureaucrats, at least when the question is framed in terms of concrete policy issues. (Once again, policy analysis divides politicians and bureaucrats more than does philosophy.)

It is not surprising that role differences are very marked on the question about party relations, for these politicians are, after all, *party* politicians. However, it is striking that ideology is an important determinant of responses to this question among both bureaucrats and politicians. Leftists in each role are more inclined than Rightists to stress what divides the

*Table 5-5*  Salience of social and political conflict, by ideology and role.

| Role | Ideological stance | | | Left-Right difference |
|---|---|---|---|---|
| | Left | Center | Right | |
| **I. Percentage of each category who perceive conflict as more typical than consensus in politics and society** | | | | |
| Politicians | 70 | 54 | 46 | +24 |
| $N =$ | (240) | (126) | (157) | |
| Bureaucrats | 68 | 54 | 45 | +23 |
| $N =$ | (80) | (249) | (154) | |
| Role difference: | +2 | 0 | +1 | $R = .26$ |
| Based on equally weighted samples for all seven nations. | | | | |
| **II. Percentage of each category whose discussions of policy emphasize conflicting interests** | | | | |
| Politicians | 73 | 55 | 63 | +10 |
| $N =$ | (251) | (138) | (128) | |
| Bureaucrats | 46 | 36 | 35 | +11 |
| $N =$ | (115) | (289) | (179) | |
| Role difference: | +27 | +19 | +28 | $R = .29$ |
| Based on equally weighted samples from all seven nations, with the exception of Swedish politicians. | | | | |
| **III. Percentage of each category who perceive "important" or "very great" interparty differences** | | | | |
| Politicians | 76 | 63 | 61 | +15 |
| $N =$ | (206) | (121) | (150) | |
| Bureaucrats | 42 | 34 | 26 | +16 |
| $N =$ | (106) | (260) | (160) | |
| Role difference: | +34 | +29 | +35 | $R = .38$ |
| Based on equally weighted samples from all seven nations. | | | | |
| **IV. Percentage of each category who perceive interparty differences in the work of their own department** | | | | |
| Bureaucrats | 69 | 50 | 45 | +24 |
| $N =$ | (45) | (131) | (67) | |
| Based on equally weighted samples from Britain, Germany, Italy, and the Netherlands. | | | | |
| **V. Percentage of each category who discuss party differences in terms of social class and other socioeconomic groups** | | | | |
| Politicans | 54 | 42 | 22 | +32 |
| $N =$ | (232) | (99) | (140) | |
| Bureaucrats | 43 | 47 | 21 | +22 |
| $N =$ | (103) | (240) | (154) | |
| Role difference: | +11 | −5 | +1 | $R = .26$ |
| Based on equally weighted samples from Britain, Germany, Italy, the Netherlands, Sweden, and the United States. | | | | |

parties rather than what unites them. Leftist bureaucrats are also much more aware of party differences within the work of their own department than are their more conservative colleagues. Finally, both among bureaucrats and among politicians, Leftists are more likely than Rightists to attribute party differences to class and socioeconomic alignments.

In short, both role and ideology have a marked impact on a policymaker's operational code. Both are powerful predictors of the degree to which he sees his world as one of Politics or Governance. Take a single illustration: More than three-quarters of the leftist politicians see important differences among the parties in their respective countries. Yet among rightist bureaucrats, equally sophisticated and experienced in national affairs, observing exactly the same party systems, and deeply involved in managing the outputs of those party systems, only one in four judged the party differences to be important. For most Leftists and for most politicians, seeing the world in terms of diverse interests, conflict is the essence of public affairs. For more Rightists and for most bureaucrats, seeing the world in terms of shared interests, conflict is secondary, overshadowed by common interests, shared outlooks, and social consensus.

Against this background it is not surprising that other features of these policymakers' operational codes are also influenced by role and ideology. Three items designed to distinguish programmatic, goal-seeking policymakers from "muddlers-through" were included in the closed questionnaires filled out by our respondents in Britain, Germany, Italy, and the Netherlands. Respondents were asked to agree or disagree that:

(1) Generally speaking, in political controversies extreme positions should be avoided, since the right answer usually lies in the middle.

(2) Politics is the "art of the possible," and therefore the leaders of the country should worry more about what can be done in the short run than about ambitious ideals and long-term plans.

(3) The strength and efficiency of a government are more important than its specific program.

Responses to these three statements were correlated, as expected, and we combined them into a single Index of Programmatic Commitment (IPC).[26] Those who rank high on this index believe that policymakers should lift their eyes above the in-box and seek grander goals, even at the cost of increased controversy and reduced efficiency. Those who rank low are the practitioners of "directionless consensus," seeking lowest-common-denominator policies and skeptical that "thinking big" will lead to better governance.

*Table 5-6*  Programmatic commitment, by ideology and role.[a]

| Role | | Ideological stance | | | Left-Right difference |
|---|---|---|---|---|---|
| | | Left | Center | Right | |
| Politicians | | 66 | 24 | 35 | +31 |
| | N = | (188) | (93) | (82) | |
| Bureaucrats | | 44 | 32 | 16 | +28 |
| | N = | (59) | (191) | (81) | |
| Role difference: | | +22 | −8 | +19 | R = .45 |

[a] Entries are percentages of each category who rank high on the Index of Programmatic Commitment, an additive index combining three agree-disagree items:

(1) Generally speaking, in political controversies extreme positions should be avoided, since the right answer usually lies in the middle.
(2) Politics is the "art of the possible," and therefore the leaders of the country should worry more about what can be done in the short run than about ambitious ideals and long-term plans.
(3) The strength and efficiency of a government are more important than its specific program.

Analysis is based on equally weighted samples from Britain, Germany, Italy, and the Netherlands.

Table 5–6 shows that programmatic commitment in this sense is related to both role and ideology, though in a rather complex way. Among both politicians and bureaucrats, conservatives are more likely to be muddling incrementalists than are left-wingers. Moreover, in general, bureaucrats seem to prefer muddling more than politicians. All this is consistent with our thesis about the connections between role, ideology, and the Politics/Governance dimension. Leftists and politicians have their gaze fixed on the stars, while Rightists and bureaucrats keep their feet on the ground.

There is, however, a curvilinear anomaly in the parliamentary samples, for centrist politicians are quite *un*programmatic, even more incrementalist in this sense than the average bureaucrat. In retrospect, it is not surprising that middle-of-the-road politicians find muddling agreeable and are skeptical of ambitious programs. By definition, they are content with current policy trends, and they doubtless find the prudence of bureaucrats more congenial than the enthusiasms of fellow politicians. We shall shortly see other evidence of this affinity between centrist politicians and bureaucrats. However, this anomaly should not distract our attention from the importance of the fundamental Left-Right and politician-bureaucrat polarities. To revert to a familiar comparison, note that by this measure five out of every six conservative bureaucrats endorse muddling, as contrasted with only one in three among leftist politicians.

Other evidence from our closed questionnaire enables us to assess the attitudes of our respondents toward the characteristic institutions of pluralistic politics—pressure groups, parties, parliaments, and politicians— all esteemed by the Politics model and deplored by the Governance model. Respondents in Britain, Germany, Italy, and the Netherlands (and Swedish bureaucrats, as well) were asked to agree or disagree with statements that:

(1) The general welfare of the country is seriously endangered by the continual clash of particularistic interest groups.

(2) Although parties play an important role in a democracy, often they uselessly exacerbate political conflicts.

(3) Basically it is not the parties and parliament, but rather the civil service that guarantees reasonably satisfactory public policy in this country.

(4) Often those who enter politics think more about their own welfare or that of their party than about the welfare of the citizens.

(5) In contemporary social and economic affairs it is essential that technical considerations be given more weight than political factors.

Responses to these questions proved to be appropriately intercorrelated, that is, respondents critical of interest groups were also generally critical of parties, parliaments, politicians, and "political factors" in decision making. We therefore combined responses to these five items into a single Index of Support for Pluralist Politics.[27]

Table 5–7 shows, first, that both role and ideology are significantly related to a respondent's attitude toward the institutions of pluralism. Leftists and politicians—devotees of Politics—reject criticism of the channels through which political pressures flow. Rightists and bureaucrats, more concerned with Governance, are dismayed by what they see as the chaotic collision of selfish interests, obscuring and subverting the commonweal. The ideological differences are particularly noticeable among bureaucrats.

Among politicians, on the other hand, we see once again that the effect of ideology is not linear. Much more than their colleagues on either the Left or the Right, centrist politicians share the bureaucrats' skepticism of pluralist politics. An item-by-item analysis suggests that these middle-of-the-roaders are particularly fearful that bickering among parties and interest groups will undermine prospects for technically sound public policy.[28] Other evidence shows that they are also worried about demands for increased citizen control over governmental affairs and skeptical that

*Table 5-7*   Support for pluralist politics, by ideology and role.[a]

| Role | | Ideological stance | | | Left-Right difference |
|---|---|---|---|---|---|
| | | Left | Center | Right | |
| Politicians | | 74 | 44 | 65 | +9 |
| | $N =$ | (186) | (93) | (81) | |
| Bureaucrats | | 60 | 45 | 37 | +23 |
| | $N =$ | (70) | (216) | (133) | |
| Role difference: | | +14 | −1 | +28 | $R = .34$ |

[a] Entries are percentages of each category who rank high on the Index of Support for Pluralist Politics, an additive index combining five agree-disagree items:
(1) The general welfare of the country is seriously endangered by the continual clash of particularistic interest groups.
(2) Although parties play an important role in a democracy, often they uselessly exacerbate political conflicts.
(3) Basically it is not the parties and parliament, but rather the civil service that guarantees reasonably satisfactory public policy in this country.
(4) Often those who enter politics think more about their own welfare or that of their party than about the welfare of the citizens.
(5) In contemporary social and economic affairs it is essential that technical considerations be given more weight than political factors.
Analysis is based on equally weighted samples from Sweden (bureaucrats only), Britain, Germany, Italy, and the Netherlands.

most citizens know what is in their own best interest. They are especially dubious of the proposition that "it is social conflicts that bring about progress in modern society." A glance back at Table 5–5 shows, too, that their discussions of policy issues revealed less sensitivity to conflicting interests than did those of their colleagues to the left and right. Recall, as well, their hearty endorsement of the maxims that politics is the art of the possible and that extremes should be avoided.

Although these centrists have been in parliament somewhat longer than most of their colleagues, they express unusual dissatisfaction with the profession of politics. Many of them belong to the same conservative parties as those to their ideological right, but they do not share the Rightists' zest for political debate, nor their zeal for conservative ideals. Indeed, in many respects these reluctant warriors seem miscast as politicians. Their emphasis on practical competence, caution, and consensus is more appropriate to the quiet of the civil service than to the hurly-burly of a parliamentary caucus or a party rally. Governance is more nearly their game, and they disturb the otherwise neat symmetry of the relationships between role, ideology, and our respondents' images of the policy process.

*Table 5-8*    Commitment to bureaucratic convention, by ideology.

| | Ideological stance | | | Left-Right |
| Role | Left | Center | Right | difference |
|---|---|---|---|---|
| I. Percentage in each category who propose "important" or "major" *reforms in the civil service* | | | | |
| Bureaucrats | 67 | 58 | 27 | +40 |
| N = | (47) | (110) | (81) | |
| Based on equally weighted samples from Britain, Germany, Italy and the Netherlands. | | | | |
| II. Percentage in each category who stress the *neutrality of the role of the civil servant,* rather than political advocacy or ideological commitment | | | | |
| Bureaucrats | 45 | 59 | 76 | −31 |
| N = | (46) | (196) | (112) | |
| Based on equally weighted samples from Britain, Germany, Italy and Sweden. | | | | |
| III. Percentage in each category who like the *political side of their work* | | | | |
| Bureaucrats | 69 | 59 | 37 | +32 |
| N = | (70) | (217) | (128) | |
| Based on equally weighted samples from Britain, Germany, Italy, the Netherlands, and Sweden. | | | | |
| IV. Percentage in each category who express high satisfaction with *civil service career and colleagues*[a] | | | | |
| Bureaucrats | 54 | 64 | 78 | −24 |
| N = | (59) | (206) | (125) | |
| Based on equally weighted samples from Britain, Germany, Italy, the Netherlands, and Sweden. | | | | |

[a] Based on factor score combining:
(1) Overall assessment of satisfactions and dissatisfactions of career in administration.
(2) Overall assessment of attitude to civil service colleagues.
(3) Agree/disagree: "The disadvantages of a civil service career are more than outweighed by the personal satisfactions."
(4) Agree/disagree: "One of the positive aspects of a civil service career is the high intellectual and moral quality of one's colleagues."

One of the points of distinction between the Politics and Governance models, we hypothesized, is attitude toward the career civil service. Our evidence on this point is most complete for our bureaucratic respondents, and we shall confine our attention to them. Table 5-8 presents some relevant data and confirms that Leftists are considerably less content than Rightists with the orthodox canons of administration. In response to a question about the problems and prospects of the civil service, left-wing bureaucrats are much more likely than their conservative colleagues to propose important reforms. Some flavor of the sorts of changes they favor are captured by their responses to questions about the proper role of the civil servant in public affairs. The more change oriented a bureaucrat and the more state intervention he desires, the more likely he is to reject the classic notion of administrative neutrality.

Similarly, when we asked our bureaucratic respondents their personal reactions to involvement in the gray area between politics and administration in a strict sense, roughly two-thirds of the ideological conservatives expressed ambivalence or distaste. Explained one:

> I personally don't like it [politics] too much. Insofar as political aspects tend either to push the objective aspects [of the job] out, or to argue against them, and even on occasion require one to try to find reasons to back up a particular political thing, this doesn't make me very happy.

By contrast, more than two-thirds of his leftist colleagues expressed pleasure at the opportunity for political involvement. One said:

> Oh, I enjoy it. Because I'm interested in public affairs, and originally went into the job for that reason, I am as interested in the political side of it as I am in the nonpolitical side. For me, the two things go together. One of the rewards as you get up the tree is . . . the greater ability to work at the interface of administration and politics.

This enthusiasm for political involvement is the natural counterpart of the Leftists' rejection of the norm (or, as they would say, the "myth") of administrative neutrality. Most conservative bureaucrats find this *engagé* outlook quite alien.

One senses in many of these interviews that leftist bureaucrats are quite uncomfortable in the conventional role of the civil servant. This discomfort emerges in response to questions both about career satisfactions and about the congeniality of one's fellow civil servants. Included in Table 5–8 are the scores of our bureaucratic respondents on a composite measure of contentment with their career and colleagues. Although the general level of professional satisfaction among bureaucrats was quite high—higher, for example, than among politicians—it varied significantly with the bureaucrat's ideological position. Conservatives were very satisfied, but Leftists were more ambivalent. The point is not that leftist bureaucrats are unhappy people in general; indeed, most of them derive a great deal of satisfaction from public service and political decision making. But they are less enthusiastic than their conservative colleagues about the essential features of a classic administrative career—the anonymous application of apolitical expertise to technical or legal issues in the company of other apolitical experts. Exposure to "politics" is the bright side of the work for Leftists, and the dark side for Rightists.

What emerges from these successive arrays of data is a clear and consistent contrast between the images of the policy process held by Leftists and Rightists.[29] A policymaker on the Left sees the world through the lens of Politics. He is more sensitive than the Rightist to social and political conflict and more sympathetic to programmatic policymaking and pluralist politics. He is more critical of conventional notions about the role of the civil service, endorsing instead a more "political," *engagé* interpretation. We shall see in Chapter 6 that he is also more sympathetic to citizen involvement in politics and government, less elitist, more critical of existing patterns of political power, and more tolerant of political dissent.

The average Rightist, by contrast, sees the world and his job in terms of Governance. He is more supportive of civil service traditions and institutions, especially administrative neutrality. He shuns politics and disdains political institutions, including parties, pressure groups, politicians, and even involvement by ordinary citizens in the serious business of government. He finds consensus more congenial and normal than conflict, and he is skeptical of a programmatic approach to policymaking.

Virtually all these ideological correlations are echoed among politicians, although the Left-Right distinction is complicated by the peculiar affinity of centrist politicians for governance. This perturbation is highly significant and intelligible, as we have seen. But it should not obscure the important differences between Left and Right among politicians, as well as among bureaucrats, differences that transcend disagreements regarding the substance of policy. Indeed, it is these differences over substance that give shape to the images of the policy process held by Leftists and Rightists. The substantive priorities of the Left are expansionary—to push more demands onto the public agenda; to mobilize mass constituencies; to seek redistribution of wealth, status, and power. Such priorities demand a style that emphasizes advocacy and Politics.

The priorities of the Right, as our evidence has intimated, are less clearly sketched. It is easier to say what the Right opposes than what it supports, and what it opposes, typically, is any significant leveling of social, economic, and political differences. Whereas Leftists are inveterate politicizers, Rightists are inveterate managers, and each defines the policy process in such terms. Managers rarely seek out new problems, grievances, demands, or participants in the policy process, for new participants and new demands threaten the harmony essential for orderly Governance. These characteristic ideological differences will reappear in our discussion of attitudes toward democracy in Chapter 6.

Overlaid on these ideological patterns, of course, are the effects of role. One reason that politicians in the aggregate are less inclined to embrace Governance than bureaucrats is that politicians are somewhat farther to the left ideologically. However, even when we control for ideology, politicians are more sensitive to conflict, more programmatic in orientation, more sympathetic to pluralism, and so on. Although politicians and bureaucrats are partners of a sort in the national policymaking arena, our data make clear that they perceive that arena in quite different terms.

It is, of course, hardly surprising that politicians are more apt to see public affairs as politics rather than as management, because their role rarely requires them to manage. Conversely, administrators are more inclined to see public affairs as management, because their responsibilities are in fact heavily (though not exclusively) managerial. Whether these differences in outlook result from on-the-job experience, or whether instead they predate and indeed help explain policymakers' career choices, is an important theoretical issue that, sadly, lies beyond the reach of our data.

Many of these differences can be summarized in terms of the role focus of our respondents, as analyzed in Chapter 4. One focus emphasized by nearly half our respondents is the *advocate* role, a job conception that stresses defending the interests of a broad social group, class, or cause, or protesting injustice. Like Roman tribunes, policymakers emphasizing this approach have a bottom-up perspective on public affairs, whereas those rejecting it have a top-down view. More than any other single variable in our study, this one seems to capture the essence of the Politics/Governance distinction. Table 5–9 shows that it is very strongly correlated with both role and ideology. An average of 35 percentage points separates politicians from bureaucrats (controlling for ideology), and an average of 32 points separates Left from Right (controlling for role). Barely one rightist bureaucrat in seven sees himself as a tribune in this sense, whereas scarcely one leftist politician in five does *not*.

*Table 5-9*   Focus on advocate/tribune role, by ideology and role.[a]

| Role | | Ideological stance | | | Left-Right difference |
|---|---|---|---|---|---|
| | | Left | Center | Right | |
| Politicians | | 79 | 60 | 50 | +29 |
| | N = | (266) | (141) | (167) | |
| Bureaucrats | | 50 | 18 | 15 | +35 |
| | N = | (122) | (296) | (186) | |
| Role difference: | | +29 | +42 | +35 | R = .56 |

[a] Entries are percentages of each category who are judged, on the basis of the entire interview, to focus their role to some extent on defending a cause, class, or social group, or protesting injustice. Analysis is based on equally weighted samples from all seven nations.

### The Origins of Ideology

We have seen that, among both politicians and bureaucrats, a policy-maker's position on the Left-Right ideological dimension is a fundamentally important predictor of his beliefs and values across a wide range of topics. What, in turn, predicts his ideological stance? We shall seek an answer, first, by focusing closely on the link between ideology and party affiliation. Then we shall progressively widen our focus, taking into account the party preferences of our respondents' fathers and their social origins. Finally, we shall consider briefly the causes of our European civil servants' special proclivity for consistent ideological centrism.

Many previous studies have demonstrated a strong and ubiquitous link between political ideology and party identification. Regarding parliamentary elites, Allan Kornberg has said that "party affiliation constitutes a kind of 'conceptual net' for capturing, organizing, and evaluating incoming information which may be politically relevant."[30] Bureaucratic elites are politically sophisticated, and we would expect them too to display a reasonable consistency between ideology and party identification. But partisanship clearly plays a different role for politicians than for bureaucrats. As Max Weber noted in his famous lecture on "Politics as a Vocation," the politician in a democratic order is supposed "to take a stand, to be passionate"—and this passion is typically channeled through parties—whereas the primary task of the bureaucrat is impartial, dispassionate administration.[31] This, of course, does not mean that bureaucrats are necessarily apolitical; it suggests only that, for the most part, their political instincts are not fundamentally of a partisan character.

*Table 5-10*   Party and ideology, by role.[a]

| Role | Party affiliation | | |
|---|---|---|---|
| | Left | Center | Right |
| Politicians | 76 | 36 | 19 |
| N = | (268) | (96) | (259) |
| Bureaucrats | 48 | 20 | 11 |
| N = | (90) | (46) | (124) |

[a] Entries are percentages of each category whose ideological stance is leftist. Analysis is based on equally weighted samples from Britain, France, Germany, the Netherlands, and the United States.

Against this background it is not surprising that we find a strong tie between ideology and party, as illustrated in Table 5–10, a tie that is visibly stronger among politicians than among civil servants. Across those countries for which we have data on party preference for both politicians and bureaucrats, the mean correlation between party and ideology is .68 for politicians and .42 for bureaucrats, which implies that party accounts for more than two and a half times more ideological variance among politicians than among bureaucrats.[32]

In one sense, this simple contrast understates the difference between the roles; in another, it overstates the difference. In the first place, whereas virtually all of our politicians are party members, a third of our administrators are avowed independents. Our calculations of the correlation between party and ideology necessarily excluded these nonidentifiers, but in the aggregate they dampen still further the association between party and ideology among bureaucrats.

Given the moderate to conservative climate that we have observed in the world of bureaucracy, and given the fact that conservative governments were in power at the time of our interviews in Britain, France, Italy, and the United States, it might be thought that our category of independents contained a disproportionate number of Leftists, cautiously discreet about their party preferences. Alternatively, we might suppose that independents as a group would be quite heterogeneous, or middle-of-the-road, perhaps even inconsistent ideologically. In actuality, none of these expectations is accurate. Throughout Europe bureaucrats who refuse identification with a political party are ideologically conservative. Indeed, in Britain, France, and Germany, independents are as consistently conservative as those of their colleagues who explicitly identify with a right-wing party. The independents' refusal to identify with a party probably reflects their deep skepticism about party politics in general—a skepticism rooted, as we have seen, in their emphasis on Governance, not Politics. The United States, once again, is an exception, for the independents in the American sample are almost as liberal ideologically as avowed Democrats. This national peculiarity reemphasizes the ideological distinctiveness of the American civil service. (We also suspect in this instance that the category of independents contains a number of closet Democrats, prudent in the face of the Nixon administration's emphasis on rooting out "disloyalty.")

The loyalties of those bureaucrats who do identify with a political party vary somewhat from country to country. In the three countries with "turnover," two-party or two-and-a-half-party systems—Britain, Germany, and the United States—the division of party sentiment in the bureaucratic elite roughly mirrors that in the political elite. On the other hand, in France, the Netherlands, and (we strongly suspect, though our study lacks data on this point) Italy, the major conservative party is substantially overrepresented and the left half of the party spectrum underrepresented. Where smaller centrist parties exist  the Liberals in Britain, the Free Democrats in Germany, and so on—they attract a disproportionate share of the preferences of these senior bureaucrats. Generally speaking, the votes of civil servants faithfully reflect their center and center-right location on the ideological spectrum.

The heavy concentration of bureaucrats in the center of the ideological spectrum, as well as their tendency to disclaim party affiliation, weakens the correlation between party and ideology. However, if we look only at that minority of civil servants who (a) have a distinctive (noncentrist) ideological coloration and (b) identify with a political party, the linkage between party and ideology is virtually as firm and consistent as it is among politicians. In short, the looseness of this linkage in the aggregate is due, not to ideological inconsistency, but to consistent centrism and a predilection for nonpartisanship.

With only the evidence at hand, we cannot say which is cause and which effect in the relation of party to ideology. Past studies of political socialization suggest that most people acquire an affinity for a specific party fairly early in life, and that party loyalty structures one's policy views as they develop. Some evidence we shall present below is consistent with this view, and for convenience in presenting our findings we shall assume that party influences ideology. We emphasize, however, that in many cases the reverse may also be true, that ideological stances forged from reflection and experience provide the basis for party choice.

That the ideological positions of bureaucrats and politicians vary from party to party is clear from the evidence presented thus far. But *how* do they vary? Figure 5–6 displays the relationship graphically.[33] The horizontal axis represents our measure of Left-Right ideology, while the political parties are arrayed along the vertical axis. On the graph are shown the best-fitting regression lines for predicting ideology from party among our bureaucratic and political respondents. The differing slopes and heights of the two lines indicate that the link between party and ideology is significantly different in the two groups. Within moderately conservative parties, politicians and bureaucrats are ideologically quite similar; but within centrist and leftist parties, bureaucrats are typically more conservative than politicians. Moreover, the further left a party, the bigger the ideological discrepancy between its political and bureaucratic identifiers. Only within parties of the far Right, this analysis suggests, would bureaucrats stand ideologically to the left of the politicians.[34]

Beyond confirming that party affiliation has more impact on ideology among politicians than bureaucrats and that, when we control for party preference, bureaucrats are typically more conservative in outlook than politicians, this graph reveals a more subtle pattern. There is much more difference between the outlook of politicians and bureaucrats of the Left than between those of the Right. This finding is by no means obvious and seems to us quite significant. We interpret it as reflecting an inherent tendency for the bureaucratic role to encourage a moderately conservative outlook. The ideological atmosphere of bureaucracy is not hospitable to radical reformism, and even bureaucrats who identify with parties of the Left seem to be influenced by their professional environment. The professional arena of politicians, by contrast, encourages a more consistent ideological polarization along party lines. The result is a greater gap between bureaucrats and politicians on the Left, where party cues and professional climate work in opposite directions, than on the Right, where partisan influences are more compatible with those of the bureaucratic role. (On the far Right, this analysis implies, the discrepancy between party and role cues for bureaucrats begins to reemerge.) We shall soon see additional evidence that the ideology of civil servants is more influenced by the bureaucratic air they breathe, whereas the ideology of politicians is more determined by their sociopolitical roots.

In Chapter 3 we learned that although politicians and (especially) civil servants come disproportionately from upper-class and middle-class homes, the present distribution of party preferences among policymakers

*Figure 5-6*   Predicting ideology from party, by role.

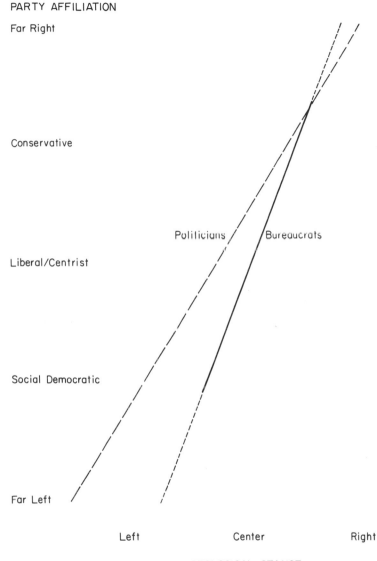

PARTY AFFILIATION

Far Right

Conservative

Politicians / Bureaucrats

Liberal/Centrist

Social Democratic

Far Left

Left                     Center                     Right

IDEOLOGICAL STANCE

NOTE: Based on equally weighted samples from Britain, Germany, France, the Netherlands, and the United States. The broken segments of the line for bureaucrats are linear extrapolations, since very few bureaucrats identified with extremist parties appear in our samples.

is not nearly so biased in a conservative direction as we would normally predict. The implication is that many of these politicians and civil servants have moved away from the conservative faiths of their fathers. On the other hand, we also noted in Chapter 3 that there remains a quite substantial correlation between fathers' party preferences and the party preferences of our respondents. Against such a background how are the ideologies of these elites related to their social and political origins? The answers to this question turn out to be quite different for bureaucrats and politicians.

First, one-third of the bureaucrats, as compared to one-quarter of the politicians, were unable (or unwilling) to tell us their father's party choice. The role difference vanishes if we control for the reported salience of politics in the home, suggesting that parental politics had a more intense impact on future politicians than on future civil servants. This interpretation is bolstered by the fact that among those whose father's partisanship we do know, there is a much closer correlation between paternal partisanship and the respondent's own ideological stance among politicians than among bureaucrats. The correlation between father's party and son's ideology is .44 for politicians and .09 for bureaucrats. As the evidence arrayed in Table 5–11 shows, civil servants from leftist families are more likely to be leftist in ideology than their bureaucratic colleagues from more conservative homes, but they are much less likely to be leftist than politicians from leftist backgrounds. The same pattern applies to those from rightist backgrounds. Only in the case of those from centrist backgrounds (roughly 25% of our total sample) are civil servants more likely than politicians to follow their father's faith.

*Table 5-11*    Ideology and father's party, by role.[a]

| | Father's party for— | | | | | |
| | Politicians | | | Bureaucrats | | |
| Son's ideology | Left | Center | Right | Left | Center | Right |
|---|---|---|---|---|---|---|
| Left | 71 | 41 | 26 | 36 | 19 | 17 |
| Center | 23 | 40 | 29 | 42 | 59 | 50 |
| Right | 6 | 19 | 46 | 22 | 22 | 33 |
| | 100 | 100 | 101 | 100 | 100 | 100 |
| *N* = | (110) | (88) | (124) | (102) | (97) | (137) |

[a] Entries are percentages; because of rounding, they do not always sum to 100. Analysis is based on equally weighted samples from the United States (bureaucrats only), Britain, France, Germany, Italy, and the Netherlands.

There seem to be two reasons for this stronger intergenerational transmission of political ideology among politicians than among bureaucrats. First, as we reported earlier, the direct link between father's party preference and son's party preference is significantly stronger among politicians than among bureaucrats. Second, even when we control for a politician's party affiliation, his father's party allegiance seems to have had an independent impact on the politician's own ideological position. In other words, among politicians those with leftist fathers are not only more likely to be in leftist parties, but are likely to stand on the left wings of those parties. Conversely, rightist fathers are likely to have sons in the right wings of rightist parties. Even when the son has moved away from his father's party, his ideological outlook continues to show the impact of his father's partisanship. Among civil servants, there is no comparable effect at all once we control for the simple transmission of party affiliation. Ideologically speaking, civil servants get one weak dose of parental influence, whereas politicians get a strong double dose.

This pattern of strong partisan inheritance among politicians and weak inheritance among bureaucrats is even more intelligible when put into social context. The party affiliation of politicians' fathers was much more firmly rooted in their social location than was true for the fathers of bureaucrats. Among politicians' fathers, as in the electorate at large, party preference was closely correlated with social class and with urbanism. Support for left-wing parties was much more common in the working class and in larger cities. Faintly similar patterns are detectable among the fathers of our bureaucratic respondents, but the linkages are much weaker. Statistically, the multiple correlation between party, on the one hand, and social class and urbanism, on the other, is $R = .44$ for politicians' fathers and $R = .18$ for bureaucrats' fathers.[35] In other words, in explaining differences in party preference, these social factors were at least six times more important for the fathers of politicians than for the fathers of bureaucrats.

These ties seem to have been faintly weaker in homes where politics was not a frequent topic of conversation, but controlling for the reported salience of politics in our respondents' homes does little to reduce this difference between politicians and bureaucrats. The explanation for the role difference is *not* simply that bureaucrats tend to come from relatively apolitical homes. Even when politics was salient, the nexus between social traits and partisanship was weaker in the homes of future bureaucrats than in the homes of future politicians. Phrased differently, civil servants were more likely than politicians to come from homes where the class-party tie was anomalous, that is, working-class conservative homes and upper-class leftist homes.

We noted earlier that a politician's ideology is more closely tied to his father's partisanship than is true for the typical bureaucrat, and now we have seen that the partisanship of the politician's father was, in turn, more closely tied to his social context than was true for the bureaucrat's father. Combining these two patterns, we find that the ideological stance of a politician can be traced much more precisely to his social and political origins than is true for bureaucrats. The multiple correlation between social class, urbanism, and paternal partisanship, on the one hand, and one's own ideology, on the other, is $R = .46$ for politicians and $R = .16$ for bureaucrats.[36] The three factors together are eight times more important in accounting for the politician's ideological stance than for the bureaucrat's.[37]

The fathers of our bureaucrats were apparently much more "independent" politically than the fathers of our politicians, or for that matter, than most voters of their generation. That is, the bureaucrats' fathers were more likely to choose a party that was unusual for someone in their social position. In turn, these uncommonly independent fathers had sons who were uncommonly independent, in at least two senses. Not only do more bureaucrats decline to state a party preference, but even those who do are less influenced by their father's party preferences. These contrasting patterns of political and social inheritance are laid out in Figure 5–7, using the technique of causal path analysis.[38]

To summarize: For politicians, party affiliation and ideology are firmly embedded in a sociopolitical context. A politician's party and his ideology are closely correlated, and both are relatively predictable from his father's ideology and social background. For bureaucrats, party and ideology are more loosely related, with ideology apparently influenced in addition by the bureaucratic climate of opinion, and both party and ideology are much less closely related to social and political background.

In fact, in at least two of our countries a civil servant's ideological stance is much more closely related to the department in which he works than to his sociopolitical origins. In the United States and Germany, bureaucrats in social welfare departments, broadly defined, are much more likely to be Leftists than their colleagues elsewhere in the bureaucracy.[39] To be sure, our data do not allow us to say whether department has in-

*Figure 5-7* Causal antecedents of ideology, by role.

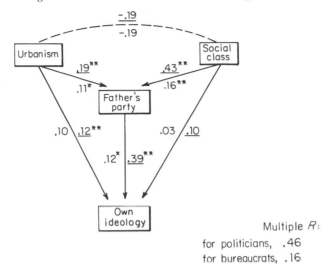

Multiple *R*:
for politicians, .46
for bureaucrats, .16

NOTE: Entries are path coefficients; those underlined are for politicians, those not underlined are for bureaucrats. * $p \leq .05$; ** $p \leq .01$.

fluenced ideology or whether ideology has affected placement. In either event, the pattern is consistent with our general theme: the ideologies of bureaucrats are closely tied to their bureaucratic environment, whereas the ideologies of politicians are anchored in a much wider sociopolitical setting.

All this is consistent with our distinction in Chapter 3 between "political" and "administrative" family backgrounds. Recall, for example, that bureaucrats are more likely to have family connections in government, whereas politicians are more likely to have family connections in politics. The distinction between Politics and Governance seems to reach deep into the backgrounds of our political and bureaucratic elites.

One reason (though only one) why our search for the antecedents of ideology has been more fruitful among politicians than among civil servants is the heavy concentration of European bureaucrats right in the center of the ideological spectrum. In the broadest sense, this consistent bureaucratic centrism must be traced to the institutional division of labor between bureaucrats and politicians. In the terms introduced in Chapter 1, whether one endorses Image I (policy versus administration), Image II (facts versus interests), or Image III (energy versus equilibrium), bureaucrats are supposed to concentrate on managing and adapting current policy, leaving broader objectives and more distant ideals to politicians. Within this general framework several specific factors are probably relevant to explaining the consistent centrism of bureaucrats.

First, self-selection probably guides consistent centrists toward the civil service and away from a political career. Politics puts a premium on articulating a distinctive view of a better world—a world of the future or, occasionally, a world of the past. By contrast, as one of our respondents explained, "If a man wants to change the world, he doesn't become a civil servant." Some evidence on the importance of motivation in this context emerges from our respondents' answers to a question about what attracted them to the civil service in the first place. Among the roughly one in three who entered the civil service *faute de mieux*—because no equally good jobs were available elsewhere—or because of family traditions, 63 percent are consistent centrists ideologically. On the other hand, among the one-third who were drawn primarily by an interest in politics or policymaking or by broader ideals, only 44 percent are consistent centrists. A "political vocation" seems somewhat inconsistent with ideological centrism, and that sort of motivation is much less common among bureaucrats than among politicians.

Recruitment criteria and role socialization probably also contribute to the consistent centrism of bureaucrats. Among our respondents, for example, centrism is to some extent a function of tenure; the longer a bureaucrat has served, the more likely he is to be a consistent centrist. Without data gathered over time, of course, we cannot decipher the exact import of this pattern, but it is consistent with the notion that moderation is fostered by service in the bureaucracy. In both politics and government, those who go along get along. In politics, going along usually means adhering to party doctrine, while in the bureaucracy (at least in Europe), going along means eschewing political passions. "A chap with ideals hasn't got balance," sniffed one of our bureaucratic respondents. By and large, at least in Europe, our politicians got where they are by being partisan enthusiasts, whereas our bureaucrats reached the top by being prudent and workmanlike. Each group seems to have learned its lessons well.

### Some Implications

The clearest ideological contrast that emerges from our findings is that between the polarized but leftward-leaning politicians and the consistently centrist bureaucrats. Whereas the typical politician is led by his political outlook—and by the political incentive structure—to articulate broad alternatives, the typical bureaucrat is more interested in making adjustments at the margins of current policy. The consistent centrist among our respondents sees a certain inevitability about the existing direction of policy. He is concerned with the world as it is, not as it might be. Richard Rose has described a climate of opinion in the British civil service that, our evidence suggests, is common throughout Europe:

> The civil servant develops, as part of his daily routine, skill in working the machinery of Whitehall and administering the existing policies of government. The compound result of knowledgeable skepticism and familiarity with routine is that civil servants, without regard to partisan implications, are likely to be biased against change *until it occurs.*[40]

We emphasize the final qualification in Rose's description, for it is important to distinguish between the outlook of consistent centrists and the more passionate resistance to social change and state intervention that is characteristic of conservative politicians (and bureaucrats). Indeed, the centrists' penchant for muddling and moderation may well lead them to resist radical innovations proposed by conservatives, as well as those offered by left-wingers. The Tory government of Edward Heath, for example, entered office in 1970 on a platform proposing a sharp right turn in national economic policy—the reinvigoration of British capitalism and the elimination of many government controls and subsidies. Over the next three years, however, this strident program was progressively muted, and many observers attributed the changes in part to the moderating influence of the British civil service. That interpretation is fully consistent with the evidence from our own interviews in London in 1971. (Whether a similar fate awaits the Thatcher government remains to be seen.)

Like a gyroscope, the consistent centrist who dominates the European bureaucracies resists temporary pressures for change in the preestablished route. Fritz Morstein Marx's description of "the administrative state" makes this point well:

> The merit bureaucracy, as a constant element, provides a stabilizing influence. It represents not only the continuing aspects of the ad-

ministrative process, crystallized in long experience, but also an unbroken general line in the evolution of government programs, marked by series of cherished precedents . . . In this fashion the merit bureaucracy operates like a brake; it favors a coherent evolution and discourages excessive swings of the pendulum.[41]

The same point was made more crisply by J. H. Thomas, a working-class Labour party cabinet member, "Every time I ask my Civil Servants 'ow to do something, they give me papers saying 'ow not."[42]

Bureaucratic centrists provide ballast and stability, but they cannot provide direction and innovation. Their approach is captured precisely by Rose's label for administrative policymaking in Britain: directionless consensus.[43]

In a world in flux, of course, some change is unavoidable, as most of our administrative respondents recognized. Perhaps timeservers in the bowels of the bureaucracy resist any alteration whatever in their routines; but the officials we interviewed, sitting atop major departments of state, know that adjustments in policy are needed constantly, just as a gyroscope signals minor corrections to the rudder in order to hold the preestablished course. It is not change per se but *directed* change, *substantial* change, change in the *framework* of policy, that centrist bureaucrats find uncongenial. For the most part, change of that sort can be generated only by politicians. Without their intervention the ship of state holds its fixed course.

It might be tempting to conclude that bureaucrats are "nonideological," immune to the ideological imperative. But our evidence speaks against this view. The very consistency and coherence of the bureaucrat's centrism suggests that it *is* an ideology. The bureaucrats we interviewed are not randomly centrist, flip-flopping from issue to issue. They are determinedly centrist. In fact, our data show that ideology, when it differs, makes almost as much difference for bureaucratic outlooks as for the outlooks of politicians. In most of the data arrays we have examined, the differences between leftist and rightist bureaucrats are as great as those between leftist and rightist politicians. But Rightists and (especially) Leftists are simply much rarer in the European bureaucracies and, as we have seen, by comparison with their ideological counterparts in politics even leftist bureaucrats are more inclined to preach caution and consensus, particularly when it comes to specific issues.

The impact of ideology on the outlooks of civil servants can be illuminated by looking more closely at that minority of one in six among the European bureaucrats who stand ideologically on the Left. By profession they are moderates, but by ideology they are more progressive. They practice Governance, but they are sensitive to Politics. A glance back at the tables in this chapter will reveal that on most of the questions we have explored, leftist bureaucrats have more in common with politicians than with their civil service colleagues.

Their hopes for the future, for example, are almost as radical as those expressed by left-wing politicians. They rank virtually as high as the average politician on our measures of sensitivity to social conflict, of commitment to programmatic policymaking, and of support for the institutions of pluralism. We shall see in Chapter 6 that they have an egalitarian, even populist perspective on the policy process that is more common among politicians than among other bureaucrats. They are even more critical of the bureaucracy than the average politician is, they reject the idea of apolitical administration, and they are more enthusiastic about the political side of their jobs than about the strictly administrative work. Compared to their moderate and conservative colleagues, they are more apt to avow a party preference, and if they do so, they are very likely to favor a left-wing political party. Only on those measures that reflect the policy issues currently on their desk do they appear conventionally bureaucratic in outlook.

In at least a few cases we can trace the existence of these leftist administrators to the efforts of left-wing governments to gain a measure of control over the activities of the permanent bureaucracy. In Germany, for example, our leftist bureaucrats for the most part are lateral entrants to the civil service, imported by the Social Democratic–Liberal coalition that took power in 1969—a practice criticized at the time as "politicization" by a number of conservative bureaucrats and their political allies. In Sweden, the Leftists in our bureaucratic samples were heavily concentrated in the ministries, serving directly the Social Democratic ministers then in power; Swedish bureaucrats in the boards and public corporations were much more conservative in outlook.

It is tempting to see these politicians-in-bureaucratic-garb as providing needed spice to the bland world of administration. But the division of labor between politicians and bureaucrats at the heart of modern polities is delicate. A general increase in ideological commitment among bureaucrats could easily erode the norms of impartiality and objectivity that observers from Weber to Morstein Marx have correctly praised as a fundamental element in effective administration. In statecraft, as in the culinary arts, excessive seasoning should be avoided. To revert to an earlier metaphor, these leftist bureaucrats can be helpful in charting new routes, but their contribution to gyroscopic stability is less certain.

In order to sort out theoretically the impact of role and ideology on policymakers, in this chapter we have controlled for each when examining the other. However, in practical terms controlling for ideology understates the aggregate differences between politicians and bureaucrats, for in the real world the ideological profiles of politicians and bureaucrats are far from identical. An example may illustrate this pervasive problem. We correctly reported in Table 5–4 that, controlling for ideology, bureaucrats are as likely as politicians to propose major changes in the society of the future. But in the real world, as reflected in our samples, barely half of all bureaucrats propose major changes, as compared to more than two-thirds of all politicians. Controlling statistically for ideology clarifies causal relations, but obscures political relations.

To counteract this artificial minimizing of real-world differences, we have also stressed the stark contrast in outlook between left-leaning politicians and conservative bureaucrats, two groups that together account for nearly two-fifths of all the policymakers interviewed in our study. The two groups obviously differ sharply on the substance of policy, with a difference, for example, of 51 percent in their support for important policy changes on the "most important problem." The potential for tension between the two groups is heightened by the disparity in their basic perspectives on public affairs. Nearly three-quarters of the leftist politicians discern conflicting interests at play in practical policy problems, as contrasted with barely one-third of the rightist bureaucrats. Two-thirds of the left-wing politicians embrace a programmatic approach to policy-making, as contrasted with one-sixth of the conservative bureaucrats. Three-quarters of these politicians endorse the institutions of pluralist politics, compared with barely one-third of these bureaucrats. We shall see in Chapter 6 that almost three-quarters of the rightist bureaucrats believe that the average citizen should leave government to the professionals, whereas only one leftist politician in five has such a constrained idea of mass political participation. Nearly nine in ten of the leftist politicians want major reforms in their political systems, whereas only one rightist bureaucrat in five does.

In short, left-wing politicians and conservative bureaucrats are likely to find it difficult to cooperate in the policy process because they differ not merely over what should be done but also over who should decide and how. Roughly speaking, three-quarters of the leftist politicians embrace Politics, whereas three-quarters of the rightist bureaucrats endorse Governance. Against this background it is hardly surprising that left-wing governments usually are very uneasy about relying on a conservative bureaucracy to carry out their programs and often seek to place sympathizers in administrative posts.

In our discussion of ideology, as elsewhere throughout this book, we have been forced frequently to distinguish between Europe and the United States. We need to be specific about the nature of this American anomaly. What is peculiar about American policymakers is basically *not* the nature of the difference between Leftists and Rightists, but rather the frequency of each, particularly in the bureaucracy. Just as in Europe, Leftists in America favor more far-reaching social reforms and see the world in terms of Politics, not Governance.[44]

However, the American bureaucracy is more ideologically polarized than the European bureaucracies. Consistent centrists are rarer in the American executive branch and Leftists are more common, particularly among career officials. Correlatively, American bureaucrats match congressmen on our measure of abstract conceptual thinking, and in Washington the link between party and ideology is slightly stronger among bureaucrats than among politicians. Nominal independents in the American bureaucracy lean to the left ideologically, whereas in Europe they lean to the right.

These cross-national differences have clear historical roots. As one commentator has noted:

> Among the many ways in which the American experience with bureaucracy differs from the European, none is more striking than the fact that executive agencies in the United States have so often been looked upon as major instruments of change in social and economic policy, while in Europe bureaucracy has historically been regarded as a chief source of institutional support for the status quo.[45]

As we have seen repeatedly in this volume—and as we shall note again in Chapter 7—American civil servants play a much more openly political role than their European counterparts. By tradition and by political culture, Americans are more skeptical of the idea that top-level executives can be party neuters. The successive Civil Service Acts have restrained the cruder forms of administrative partisanship, but both constitutional structure and informal usage make the distinction between politics and administration harder to sustain in this country. For better or for worse, bureaucrats in America are forced to be politicians as well. Their distinctive ideological profile reflects this enduring national idiosyncrasy.

# Democrats, Pluralists, Populists, and Others

## 6

How can the complex modern state be governed democratically? This question has long been of vital concern to political commentators. Elitist theorists, such as Robert Michels, have argued pessimistically that "every system of leadership is incompatible with the most essential postulates of democracy."[1] More hopeful philosophers and reformers have conceived a long list of ingenious institutional devices to ensure government responsiveness to public desires—constitutional checks and balances, parliamentary sovereignty, universal suffrage, party competition, "functional representation" of interest groups, "representative bureaucracy," "freedom of information" and "sunshine" laws, participatory administration—the inventory expands endlessly. But the still more rapid expansion of bureaucracy and its apparently increasing insulation from popular control seem to render the underlying dilemma ever more difficult.

Many thoughtful observers have come to the conclusion that a central piece of the puzzle involves the norms and values that guide decision makers. Speaking of political and governmental elites, V. O. Key urged that "any assessment of the vitality of a democratic system should rest on an examination of the outlook, the sense of purpose, and the beliefs of that sector of society."[2] More recently, J. Roland Pennock has argued that "a commitment of the elite [including important administrative officers] to democratic principles and procedures and a willingness to do all in their power to support the democratic regime is virtually a necessary condition for a stable democracy."[3] In short, the outlook for democracy depends on the commitment of bureaucrats and politicians to democratic principles. That, at least, is the premise of this chapter.

## Patterns of Democratic Ideals

That democratic ideals affect the development of democratic institutions is manifest in the history of Western constitutional democracy. Each important institutional development was preceded by philosophical exploration and elaboration of the underlying social and moral principles. These "operative ideals" then gradually spread from philosophers to men and women of affairs and were finally embodied in institutional form.[4] Of course, the institutions themselves have made a powerful independent contribution to government responsiveness, and democratic practice has influenced theory, as well as the other way around. Our point is simply that democratic ideals matter, or as Giovanni Sartori says, "in the final analysis, our political behavior depends on our idea of what democracy is, can be, and should be."[5]

Schematically, we can distinguish three broad phases in the evolution toward political democracy. The first epoch, spanning the seventeenth and eighteenth centuries, spawned constitutionalism, with its emphasis on due process and on certain fundamental political rights, particularly freedom of thought, of speech, and of the press. Speaking of the revolutionary upheavals of seventeenth-century England and of the central philosopher of that era, John Locke, George H. Sabine pointed out that "what the English Revolution contributed to the democratic tradition was the principles of freedom for minorities, together with a constitutional system both to protect and to regulate that freedom."[6]

During the eighteenth and nineteenth centuries, philosophers such as James Mill, John Stuart Mill, and Jeremy Bentham articulated the premises of liberal or representative democracy. Parliamentary sovereignty, cabinet responsibility, and the rights of organized opposition, including political parties and pressure groups, were the characteristic institutional innovations of the era. Victorian England, the Third Republic, and even Bismarck's Germany exemplify different species of this genus of incipient democracy. A special version of this approach—one attributing particular importance to limiting and even fragmenting governmental powers—was enshrined by James Madison and his colleagues in the American Constitution.

Some liberal democrats even as late as John Stuart Mill were not fully convinced of the desirability of universal and equal suffrage, but the third stage of the democratic revolution focused specifically on the question of mass participation. The philosophical roots of this development, of course, extended back several centuries to the radicals of seventeenth-century England and, more importantly, to Jean Jacques Rousseau. Extensions of suffrage were the institutional hallmark of the earlier decades of this third era, which spanned the nineteenth and twentieth centuries. But the egalitarian imperative by no means ended at the voting booth; indeed, Rousseau had been contemptuous of mere electoral equality. How to increase equality of influence in an increasingly intricate world has been, in a sense, the most important unresolved issue of applied political philosophy for the last hundred years. The clamor for participatory democracy that echoed in the background as we conducted our interviews in the early 1970s was merely the most recent reprise of this debate.

Observers have noted that much of the discussion about democracy in theory and practice can be cast in terms of two fundamental themes. From a philosophical perspective, Pennock notes that " 'liberty' and 'equality' comprise the basic elements of the democratic creed. Yet these twin ideals—slogans on the emblem of democracy—are not easily reconciled. Between them, at best, a considerable tension exists."[7] While both liberty and equality may be—often are—used as standards for judging the policies of government, our concern here is with standards for judging the process of government—with *political* liberty and *political* equality. In this sense liberty refers to those freedoms of political thought and action that had been broadly proclaimed in the West by the nineteenth century, though not universally implemented. Political equality, by contrast, refers to the distribution of access to these political freedoms, the sharing of political influence among all citizens. As we have seen, important steps toward equality in this sense have been taken over the last century, although the political systems studied here remain far from fully egalitarian except in the formalistic sense of voting rights.

From a more institutional perspective Robert A. Dahl has drawn an analogous distinction between "two somewhat different theoretical dimensions of democratization." The first, which he terms "contestation" or "liberalization," refers to the extent to which at least some members of the political system are guaranteed those political rights—the freedom of association, of expression, of organized competition for influence—that enable them to contest the conduct of the government. The second dimension, which Dahl labels "inclusiveness" or "participation," refers to "the proportion of the population entitled to participate on a more or less equal plane in controlling and contesting the conduct of the government." Using a familiar illustration, Dahl notes that "public contestation and inclusiveness vary somewhat independently. Britain had a highly developed system of public contestation by the end of the eighteenth century, but only a minuscule fraction of the population was fully included in it until after the expansion of the suffrage in 1867 and 1884."[8]

We shall organize our exploration of the democratic commitments of government leaders in terms of these two dimensions—liberty (or contestation) and equality (or participation). Initially a matter of rhetorical convenience, this broad distinction proves to be also a matter of considerable empirical significance. But what should be our expectations about bureaucrats' and politicians' commitments to political liberty and political equality?

In the first place, since all the countries in this study are representative democracies—"polyarchies," in Dahl's terminology—we anticipate that their leaders will, by and large, support both basic democratic values. By historical standards, however, even in the West, democracy is a recent and somewhat fragile innovation. Indeed, two of our countries, Germany and Italy, have so recently joined (or rejoined) the ranks of the democracies that a majority of our respondents there grew up under nondemocratic regimes, and a significant number began their careers under those regimes.[9] Moreover, even where democratic traditions have been more durably established, political liberty and political equality are matters of degree, not once-and-for-all acquisitions. Being matters of degree, they are likely to be accepted by our respondents with varying levels of enthusiasm.

We also expect support for political liberty and for political equality to be imperfectly correlated. These are, to be sure, two aspects of a single democratic ideal, but we have noted the historical tension between them, both philosophically and institutionally. More specifically, we expect equality to be somewhat more controversial than liberty, for liberty's longer lineage should have allowed it to spread more evenly across the political and bureaucratic elites. For the most part, Western regimes have recognized the rights of political contestation for a century and more, but debates still rage about equalizing influence and participation. We therefore expect political egalitarianism to be associated with support for more radical political reforms.

Democracy has long been the watchword of the Left and the bugbear of the Right. Historically, both sides have believed that increased democracy—and particularly, increased equality of participation—would redound to the political benefit of the Left. (A recent practical illustration may be found in the congressional debates about moves to facilitate voter registration, moves supported by liberal Democrats and opposed by conservative Republicans.) We therefore hypothesize that support for democratic norms, especially egalitarian norms, will be correlated with the Left-Right ideological spectrum discussed in Chapter 5.

What about role differences? Our expectations here are more conjectural. On the one hand, both politicians and bureaucrats serve the same democratic state, and both are heirs to the democratic evolution we have traced. Indeed, as we noted in Chapter 1, the growth of electoral democracy and the growth of professional bureaucracy are, broadly speaking, coeval processes. On the other hand, several factors lead us to expect politicians to be somewhat more enthusiastic supporters of democratic values.

Most fundamentally, there is the historically rooted division of labor between bureaucrats and politicians. Parliament was designed as the (or at least an) institutional embodiment of democracy; it was intended to exert the claims of the people against the permanent executive. Bureaucracy, by contrast, is supposed to make the state more efficient, not more democratic.

More immediately, we might anticipate that the career paths of the two groups of decision makers have imparted different degrees of respect for democratic values. Politicians seeking elective office may be more likely to appreciate the rights of contestation, and a subtle selective process may have pruned from their ranks the sternest skeptics of popular political participation. Bureaucrats, on the other hand, bear responsibility for carrying out the very policies that are being contested, and they may see less virtue in contestation and conflict. Moreover, bureaucrats, chosen for their technical competence rather than their popularity, may be more suspicious of the case for mass political equality. But all these speculations must be tested against the evidence, and that is the task to which we now turn.

## Measuring Support for Political Liberty and Contestation

A mutually reinforcing set of measures of support for political liberty and contestation is available for a majority of our national samples, although our coverage is narrower than usual. Since we lack comparable evidence on the libertarianism of our French and American samples, and of our Swedish politicians, our conclusions here rest primarily on evidence from Britain, Germany, Italy, and the Netherlands. The historical experience with democracy of these countries is sufficiently diverse, and their current political patterns sufficiently variegated, that we can be reasonably confident about the generalizability of our findings, at least throughout Western Europe. Yet given the importance that the transatlantic contrast has assumed in our research, we particularly regret the absence of comparable American evidence.

Freedom of political expression is the oldest strand in the skein of democratic values, and nominal commitment to the principle of free speech is so widespread among Western political elites that it is hardly a variable at all. An earlier study of British and Italian politicians found, for example, that 100 percent of the Englishmen surveyed, and 94 percent of the Italians agreed that "unless there is freedom for many points of view to be presented, there is little chance that the truth can ever be known," a paraphrase of John Stuart Mill's essay "On Liberty."[10] But as democrats have always recognized, the real test of freedom of political expression comes when the views in question are substantively repugnant or provocatively expressed. We therefore designed a pair of probes to test the tensile strength of our respondents' support for civic freedoms, to learn how firmly these elites defend the right to oppose, to criticize, to dissent.[11]

In the open-ended interviews we raised the possibility of "certain extremist organizations" engaging in "unfair or illegitimate tactics." The vast majority of our respondents accepted this premise, and we then asked, "Do you think there should be more controls over such activity?" This question was intentionally loaded, for in effect we were virtually asking whether subversives should be allowed free play. Our attempt, of course, was to press support for civic freedom to the breaking point. (Although the wave of political terrorism had not yet crested in Europe at the time of our interviews, a large number of our respondents noted the need to control physical violence, even if it were politically motivated. Our coding of these replies, however, disregarded such comments, on the ground that the democratic principle of freedom of expression is not infringed when violence is constrained.)

Analogously, in the closed questionnaire we asked respondents to agree or disagree with the proposition that "the freedom of political propaganda is not an absolute freedom, and the state should carefully regulate its use." Once again we tried to phrase a proposal for limits on political liberty as seductively as possible. In times of real tension, of course, the pressures to impose such limits are undoubtedly great—certainly greater in the real world than in the calm of a reflective interview.

Nonetheless, democrats would be comforted by the results depicted in Table 6–1. Substantial majorities rejected our invitation to express antiliberal sentiments. On the other hand, significant minorities (slightly larger among bureaucrats) did express some readiness to control freedom of political expression. (As we shall discuss shortly, these antilibertarians were heavily concentrated among Italian civil servants. If we set them aside, the general level of support for political liberty is even higher, and the role differences are correspondingly more marginal.) Overall, by these measures, roughly three-quarters of these European leaders are reluctant to limit the right of dissent, even for "extremists."

A second measure of support for political contestation, this time focused on the characteristic institutions of pluralist democracy, is provided by the Index of Support for Pluralist Politics, introduced in Chapter 5. This index, it will be recalled, is based on five questionnaire items, eliciting our respondents' feelings about political parties, pressure groups, parliaments, politicians, and "political" (as opposed to technical) considerations in policymaking. Those who rank low on this index express particular concern that these institutions and practices introduce needless, inefficient, and even dangerous disruption into the management of public affairs. Those who rank high discount these risks as unimportant compared to the right of institutionalized contestation in pluralist democracy.[12]

In absolute terms, these measures too reveal considerable support for democratic institutions. For example, three-fifths of our respondents rejected the view that "the general welfare of the country is seriously endangered by the continual clash of particularistic interest groups"; nearly half rejected the even milder claim that political parties "often . . . uselessly exacerbate political conflicts"; and more than five in six objected to the dismissive view that "basically, it is not the parties and parliament, but rather the civil service that guarantees reasonably satisfactory public policy in this country."[13] Evidence in Table 6–1 recapitulates the relative standing of our respondents on the summary index, showing that, not surprisingly, politicians are somewhat more sympathetic to pluralistic politics than are bureaucrats. (Once again, by far the lowest level of support for democratic contestation was expressed by Italian bureaucrats, but the role contrast shown in Table 6–1 was also visible within each of the other national samples.)

Our exploration of support for contestation has moved from the vener-

*Table 6-1*    Support for political liberty and pluralism.

| Measure | Percentage response of— | |
| --- | --- | --- |
| | Bureaucrats | Politicians |
| **(1) Support for political liberties** | | |
| "Some people say that certain extremist organizations engage in unfair or illegitimate tactics. Do you think there should be more controls over such activity?" (References to the need to control physical violence were disregarded in assessing respondents' attitudes.) | | |
| Yes, willing to impose controls | 26 | 23 |
| Yes, but only reluctantly | 43 | 41 |
| No, unwilling to impose controls | 31 | 36 |
| | 100 | 100 |
| $N =$ | (242) | (249) |

Based on equally weighted samples from Britain, Germany, and Italy.

| Measure | Percentage response of— | |
| --- | --- | --- |
| **(2) State control of political propaganda** | | |
| "The freedom of political propaganda is not an absolute freedom, and the state should carefully regulate its use." | | |
| Agree | 40 | 27 |
| Disagree | 60 | 73 |
| | 100 | 100 |
| $N =$ | (254) | (277) |

Based on equally weighted samples from Britain, Germany, and Italy.

| Measure | Percentage response of— | |
| --- | --- | --- |
| **(3) Index of Support for Pluralist Politics[a]** | | |
| High | 24 | 45 |
| Medium | 32 | 36 |
| Low | 44 | 19 |
| | 100 | 100 |
| $N =$ | (330) | (361) |

Based on equally weighted samples from Britain, Germany, Italy, and the Netherlands.

| Measure | Percentage response of— | |
| --- | --- | --- |
| **(4) Evaluation of social conflict** | | |
| How does the respondent evaluate conflict in society and politics, considering his entire discussion of conflict and cooperation, including his answer to the question, "Do you consider social conflict healthy or harmful?" | | |
| Positive | 44 | 50 |
| Ambivalent | 32 | 31 |
| Negative | 24 | 19 |
| | 100 | 100 |
| $N =$ | (373) | (388) |

Based on equally weighted samples from Britain, Germany, Italy, and the Netherlands.

(*continued*)

*Table 6-1    (continued)*

| Measure | Percentage response of— | |
|---|---|---|
| | Bureaucrats | Politicians |
| (5) Conflicts and progress | | |
| "It is social conflicts that bring about progress in modern society." | | |
| Agree | 55 | 64 |
| Disagree | 45 | 36 |
| | 100 | 100 |
| N = | (256) | (263) |

Based on equally weighted samples from Britain, Germany, and the Netherlands.

[a] An additive index combining five agree-disagree items:
(1) The general welfare of the country is seriously endangered by the continual clash of particularistic interest groups.
(2) Although parties play an important role in a democracy, often they uselessly exacerbate political conflicts.
(3) Basically, it is not the parties and parliament, but rather the civil service that guarantees reasonably satisfactory public policy in this country.
(4) Often those who enter politics think more about their own welfare or that of their party than about the welfare of the citizens.
(5) In contemporary social and economic affairs it is essential that technical considerations be given more weight than political factors.

able, fairly focused issue of freedom of expression to the more diffuse topic of institutionalized pluralism. In the background, as most democratic theorists have realized, stands the still broader question of the legitimacy of social and political conflict. Ralf Dahrendorf has well articulated the important theoretical link between attitudes toward conflict and toward political liberty:

> Wherever there is human life in society, there is conflict . . . Different attitudes toward conflict have ramifications for views and policies of liberty . . . Conflict is liberty, because by conflict alone the multitude and incompatibility of human interests and desires find adequate expression in a world of notorious uncertainty.[14]

To be sure, attitudes toward conflict are less central to democratic theory than, for example, commitment to free speech. We can imagine a fully committed democrat deploring social conflict, but it would be hard to classify an opponent of free speech as a democrat at all. We expect—and we shall find—that attitudes to social conflict are not so closely correlated with the rest of the liberty-contestation syndrome as the other items we have discussed. Nevertheless, an acceptance of the legitimacy of conflict is an important tonic note in the democratic chord.

Therefore, another element in our assessment of support for political liberty and contestation was a pair of questions on the desirability or harmfulness of social conflict. The closed-ended question asked simply for agreement or disagreement with the view that "it is social conflicts that bring about progress in modern society." The open-ended question came as part of a longer discussion of conflict in politics and society; "Do you consider social conflict healthy or harmful?" we asked.[15] Table 6–1 shows that roughly half of our respondents judged social conflict to be a sign of health and progress, while the balance expressed more ambivalent or negative feelings. Once again, we see that politicians expressed slightly more support than bureaucrats for this pluralist strand of democratic theory.

The five variables presented in Table 6–1 tap different facets of what we assume to be a single underlying dimension of support for, or skepticism about, political liberty, contestation, and pluralism. We do not imagine that the relatively modest variance in outlook measured by our questions will be perfectly correlated across the five items, since each facet raises specific issues in democratic theory and practice, and since our results suggest the existence of a widely shared consensus on these values within the West. But if we are to speak sensibly of a dimension of support for political liberty, there should be some significant correlation among these various measures.

Evidence presented in Table 6–2 sustains this presumption. Although the measures of attitudes toward conflict are, as we expected, not central to the syndrome, there is a single dominant dimension to this array of data. We therefore created for each respondent a summary index, based on these five items, which we have labeled the Pluralism Index.[16] Table 6–2 also gives the correlation between each item and the overall index. Those who rank high on pluralism reject limits on freedom of expression; defend the characteristic institutions of pluralist politics, such as parties and interest groups; and approve social conflict. Low scorers, by contrast, are more willing to infringe civic liberties; readier to criticize parties, pressure groups, parliaments, and politicians; and more worried about conflict and controversy. They are visibly less sympathetic to political liberty and contestation.

Figure 6–1 displays the distribution of our samples of politicians and bureaucrats along this dimension.[17] In interpreting this figure and our subsequent discussion, the reader must keep in mind that in absolute terms, support for pluralism is rather high among European elites. Even respondents at the center of this distribution are not "antidemocrats" by

*Table 6-2*  The Pluralism Index.[a]

| Measure | I | II | III | IV | V |
|---|---|---|---|---|---|
| I. Support for pluralist politics | — | .32 | .39 | .25 | .14 |
| II. Support for political liberties | .32 | — | .30 | .17 | .08 |
| III. Control of propaganda | .39 | .30 | — | .05 | −.15 |
| IV. Evaluation of social conflict | .25 | .17 | .05 | — | .36 |
| V. Conflicts and progress | .14 | .08 | −.15 | .36 | — |
| Correlation with Pluralism Index (factor loadings) | .77 | .67 | .58 | .56 | .34 |

[a] Entries are correlations among measures of support for political liberty and pluralism. Variables are scored so that a positive coefficient indicates an appropriate correlation between two measures of support for pluralism. Analysis is based on equally weighted samples from Britain, Germany, Italy, and the Netherlands, and Swedish bureaucrats.

any means, although they are not the most enthusiastic defenders of liberty, pluralism, and conflict. On the other hand, both graphs depict a knot of people at the antipluralist end of the spectrum who are at best deeply skeptical about the principles and practices of pluralist democracy. Like a radiograph of the body politic, our surveys seem to have detected a suspicious, possibly malignant, lump.

Figure 6–1 portrays a significant difference in the profiles of pluralism between politicians and bureaucrats. By an arbitrary but useful threefold classification, 46 percent of the politicians, compared to 28 percent of the bureaucrats, are enthusiastic pluralists; 33 percent of each group are lukewarm pluralists; and 21 percent of the politicians, as contrasted with 39 percent of the bureaucrats, are more skeptical about political liberty and contestation and are in this sense antipluralists.[18]

We have indicated repeatedly our caution about drawing cross-national comparisons from our data, but in this case an important bit of information emerges from a country-by-country analysis. As we might expect, British respondents rank highest overall on our Index of Pluralism, and differences between bureaucrats and politicians are slightest in Britain. The British are followed closely by the Germans, and at some distance by the Dutch, who express special concern about the conflict that seems engendered by pluralist politics in their divided society.[19] (Recall that we have no Dutch data on the issue of free speech.) But by far the most striking feature of the national analyses, already adumbrated in our

*Figure 6-1* Pluralism, by role.

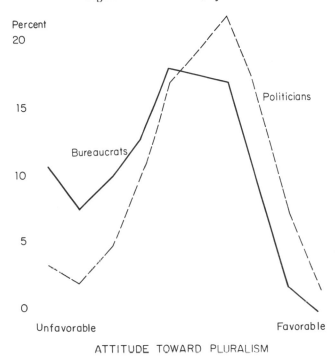

ATTITUDE TOWARD PLURALISM

earlier discussion, is the remarkably illiberal profile of the Italian respondents, most especially the Italian civil servants. Among the bureaucrats we interviewed in Rome, 77 percent ranked low on the Pluralism Index, as compared to 35 percent of Italian politicians, 30 percent of bureaucrats in Britain, Germany, and the Netherlands, and 16 percent of politicians in these other three countries. In short, Italian elites, particularly bureaucrats, are very much more alienated from the values and institutions of pluralism than their counterparts elsewhere in Europe.

As noted in an earlier report of this research, "any visitor to the Roman ministries soon senses the deep and bitter alienation of the bureaucratic elite from the country's political institutions, the utter despair of finding satisfaction in public service . . . The typical member of the Italian administrative elite appears here as the very essence of a classical bureaucrat—legalist, illiberal, elitist, hostile to the usages and practices of pluralist politics, fundamentally undemocratic."[20] The present relevance of this phenomenon is that Italian bureaucrats constitute almost half (44 percent) of all the antipluralist bureaucrats in the four samples for which we have comparable data. In subsequent descriptions of the characteristics of antipluralists, we shall have to take special precautions to be certain we are not simply describing the characteristics of Italian bureaucrats; with few exceptions, the findings we report below are, in fact, generalizable beyond the Italian case. But before exploring some of the intriguing ways in which pluralists differ from antipluralists, let us introduce the other primary theme in our democratic fugue—political equality and participation.

### Measuring Support for Political Equality and Participation

Several measures of support for political equality were gathered for each of our European samples. Our American cupboard is effectively bare, however, since we have no comparable evidence from the congressional interviews. Our most straightforward measure of attitudes toward equality and participation was a question we posed as part of a general discussion of who had political power and who ought to: "What should be the role of the public generally in politics and government?" This open-ended question often stimulated wide-ranging discussions of the merits and demerits of citizen involvement in public affairs, as well as occasional disquisitions on democracy and its ills. Our coders were able to align these discussions along a simple three-point scale, and the results are reported in Table 6–3.

*Table 6-3*   Support for political equality and populism.

| Measure | Percentage response of— | |
|---|---|---|
| | Bureaucrats | Politicians |
| (1)  Role of the public in politics<br>   "What should be the role of the public generally in politics and government?" | | |
|     Voting or less | 16 | 9 |
|     Interest in politics and/or communication to<br>      representatives | 45 | 30 |
|     More direct activity in parties, associations,<br>      local government, etc. | 39 | 61 |
| | 100 | 100 |
| $N =$ | (388) | (434) |

Based on equally weighted samples from Britain, Germany, Italy, Sweden, and France.

*Table 6-3    (continued)*

| Measure | Percentage response of— | |
|---|---|---|
| | Bureaucrats | Politicians |

(2)  More participation

"There has been a good deal of discussion in some countries about increasing popular control over the activities of government and increasing citizen participation in governmental affairs. How do you feel about this?"

| | | |
|---|---|---|
| Very favorable | 11 ⎫ 44 | 30 ⎫ 66 |
| Rather favorable | 33 ⎭ | 36 ⎭ |
| Ambivalent | 26 | 18 |
| Unfavorable | 30 | 16 |
| | 100 | 100 |
| $N =$ | (478) | (532) |

Based on equally weighted samples from Britain, Germany, Italy, France, Sweden, and the Netherlands.

(3)  Elitism Index[a]

| | | |
|---|---|---|
| High | 15 | 6 |
| Medium | 46 | 36 |
| Low | 39 | 58 |
| | 100 | 100 |
| $N =$ | (330) | (361) |

Based on equally weighted samples from Britain, Germany, Italy, and the Netherlands.

(4)  Sense of superiority

Based on the entire interview, to what extent does the respondent seem to feel that he and his colleagues are superior to the general public, in terms of knowledge, intelligence, sophistication, ability, and sense of responsibility?

| | | |
|---|---|---|
| Much superior | 20 | 8 |
| Somewhat superior | 58 | 42 |
| Not superior | 22 | 50 |
| | 100 | 100 |
| $N =$ | (481) | (539) |

Based on equally weighted samples from Britain, Germany, Italy, France, Sweden, and the Netherlands.

[a] An additive index combining six agree-disagree items:
(1)  In a world as complicated as the modern one, it doesn't make sense to speak of increased control by ordinary citizens over governmental affairs.
(2)  It will always be necessary to have a few strong, able individuals who know how to take charge.
(3)  Certain people are better qualified to lead this country because of their traditions and family background.
(4)  Few people know what is in their real interest in the long run.
(5)  All citizens should have the same chance of influencing government policy.
(6)  People should be allowed to vote even if they cannot do so intelligently.
Scoring for the last two items was reversed for inclusion in the index.

Some respondents thought mass political participation should be limited to choosing wise leaders in the solitude of the voting booth. (Included in this category were a few respondents who indicated some skepticism about the very notion of universal suffrage.) This first category, those least enthusiastic about political equality, included roughly one in eight among our respondents, but about twice as many bureaucrats as politicians. Next came those who thought politics should be primarily a spectator sport; the public should pay attention and perhaps occasionally call out advice to the players, but not run onto the playing field. "Write your member of parliament" was the typical advice from this category, which included nearly half the bureaucrats and just under a third of the politicians. Finally, a substantial number of leaders argued that politics ought to be a participant sport, that citizens should become actively involved in political parties and other organizations seeking to affect public affairs. A number of respondents in this category endorsed the search for more effective techniques of "participatory democracy," from referenda to advisory councils attached to the public administration. Three-fifths of the politicians and just under two-fifths of the bureaucrats expressed this most expansive view of participation.

These answers may somewhat exaggerate our respondents' commitment to political equality, since the question sometimes seemed to evoke memories of school civics texts. Nevertheless, the answers suggest that at least the public mores of European elites are rather sympathetic to fairly active citizen involvement. As we had expected, politicians are notably more enthusiastic in this regard than bureaucrats.

A second probe of attitudes to political equality posed the question in a less philosophical form, asking the respondents' views on the debates about more participatory democracy, which were then raging throughout the West. In fact, most respondents were familiar with the issue (which they could hardly avoid, since its outcome might have practical implications for their professional activities and careers) and most had definite views. Once again, more than three-fifths of the politicians and two-fifths of the bureaucrats expressed general approval of increased citizen participation and control; within this group, the politicians were notably more enthusiastic, the bureaucrats more nuanced. At the other extreme, roughly a third of the bureaucrats and half that many politicians expressed outright opposition to any increase in mass participation. Once again, the results show general support for political equality, although this more practical question did uncover more reservations, particularly among bureaucrats, than did our first, more philosophical query.

A third measure of attitudes to equality, called the Elitism Index, was composed of six items from our closed questionnaire. Some of these individual items tended to confirm our impression of broad support for the principle of political equality. For example, 90 percent of our respondents agreed that "all citizens should have the same chance of influencing government policy," and 91 percent agreed that "people should be allowed to vote even if they cannot do so intelligently." (However, it is also true that slightly more than one-quarter of our respondents expressed at least some reservation about this simple statement of the principle of universal suffrage, a figure that rose to 46 percent among Italian bureaucrats.)

Responses to some other items conveyed more skepticism about the practicality and even the desirability of political equality beyond the ballot box. For example, 74 percent of the bureaucrats and 59 percent of the politicians agreed with the rather paternalistic proposition that "few people know what is in their real interest in the long run." Thirty percent of the bureaucrats and 22 percent of the politicians agreed with the traditional aristocratic view that "certain people are better qualified to lead this country because of their traditions and family background." Responding to a rather vague, but somewhat authoritarian assertion that "it will always be necessary to have a few strong, able individuals who know how to take charge," 79 percent of the bureaucrats agreed, as did 62 percent of the politicians. Finally, 46 percent of the bureaucrats and 33 percent of the politicians agreed that "in a world as complicated as the modern one, it doesn't make sense to speak of increased control by ordinary citizens over governmental affairs."

Full political equality is a commendable ideal, most of these leaders seem to be saying, but let's be realistic. People are not equally competent to deal with the complexities of public issues. Modest efforts to increase public access to government may be useful, but firm leadership from the top will always be necessary. In stating this modal view, bureaucrats emphasized the "realistic" need for competence and leadership, whereas politicians accented the "idealistic" goal of ever greater political equality.

Responses to these six items were, as expected, intelligibly intercorrelated, so for convenience we combined them into a single index.[21] Table 6–3 shows that, quite consistently with the results from our open-ended probes, two-fifths of the bureaucrats and three-fifths of the politicians were ranked relatively low on this measure of elitism.

A final assessment of each respondent's orientation to political equality represents a summary judgment by our coders of the entire interview. Based on the respondent's comments on such widely disparate topics as the roles of politicians and civil servants, economic planning, the party system, social conflict, and the kind of society he would like to see for his children and grandchildren, we asked the coders to judge whether or not the respondent conveyed a sense of intellectual and moral superiority to the general public. Although clearly a much more subjective measure than those described above, this assessment turns out to be quite consistent with them, both collectively and individually. Collectively, bureaucrats were judged substantially more self-superior than politicians. Individually, respondents who ranked high, for example, on the Elitism Index were also judged by the coders (who were unaware of the questionnaire results) to display throughout the interview an uncommon sense of superiority to the common man. Beyond providing a comforting indication of convergent validity for our measures, this finding suggests that a decision maker's orientation to political equality is a rather basic orientation that pervades his approach to public issues, rather than a mere slogan mouthed to impress a visitor.

Indeed, all four of our basic measures of political equality and popular participation are strongly intercorrelated, as displayed in Table 6-4. We have, therefore, combined these four measures into a single Populism Index.[22] Those who rank high on populism want the public to take an active part in politics and government, express enthusiasm for measures to increase political participation, reject the elitist notion that only a minority are really qualified for public leadership, and convey a sense of personal humility. By contrast, those who rank low on populism think that the average citizen is at best competent only to choose wise leaders from among his betters; these antipopulists are scornful of the notion of partici-

*Table 6-4*   The Populism Index.[a]

| Measure | I | II | III | IV |
|---|---|---|---|---|
| I. Role of public | — | .57 | .30 | .32 |
| II. More participation | .57 | — | .31 | .36 |
| III. Elitism Index | .30 | .31 | — | .32 |
| IV. Sense of superiority | .32 | .36 | .32 | — |
| Correlation with Populism Index (factor loadings) | .78 | .80 | .63 | .67 |

[a] Entries are correlations among measures of support for political equality and populism. Variables are scored so that a positive coefficient indicates an appropriate correlation between two measures of support for populism. Analysis is based on equally weighted samples from Britain, Germany, Italy, France, the Netherlands, and Sweden.

*Figure 6-2* Populism, by role.

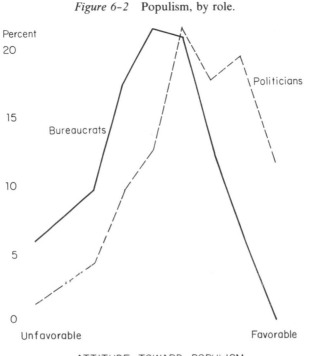

Percent

ATTITUDE TOWARD POPULISM

patory democracy, and occasionally reveal more than a little disdain for democracy itself.

Figure 6-2 shows how our bureaucrats and politicians distribute themselves along this dimension of populism. Role differences are even stronger here than on the Pluralism Index. Again employing a somewhat arbitrary threefold division, we find that 46 percent of the politicians, compared to only 20 percent of the bureaucrats, rank at the populist end of this continuum. Thirty-four percent of the politicians and 40 percent of the bureaucrats are moderates on this dimension, and 20 percent of the politicians, as contrasted with 40 percent of the bureaucrats, stand in the antipopulist category.

The absolute differences across these categories should not be exaggerated, of course, for our respondents are practical men of affairs, not ideologues or philosophers. Virtually none would seriously propose the repeal of universal suffrage, and only a handful seem even to yearn secretly for something of the sort. Conversely, very few advocate the Rousseauian ideal of direct democracy, and only a handful would subject all major issues to national referendum. In the aggregate, these leaders are democrats—but it is the institutions of representative democracy, not the ideals of direct democracy, to which they are allegiant.

The consistency with which politicians' enthusiasm for political equality and participation exceeds that of bureaucrats is quite remarkable. On virtually every measure in every one of the six countries for which we have comparable data, politicians are more populist than bureaucrats. The cross-national differences too are generally consistent with our expectations. Swedes rank relatively high on political egalitarianism; the British and the French (recall the Gaullist dominance of our samples) rank relatively low.[23] Once again, as with the Pluralism Index, the biggest role differences are found in Italy, and for the same reason—namely, the almost unrelieved elitism of Italian bureaucrats. The only faint surprise in the national analyses is that German civil servants seem surprisingly populist. (We shall see later that a major part of the explanation for this pattern was the recruitment into top administrative posts, shortly before our interviews, of a substantial number of younger, politically oriented Social Democrats, fired with egalitarian ideals.) Despite the uncertain validity of such direct cross-national comparisons, these differences are marked and consistent across each of our several measures of populism.

### Two Types of Democrats

POPULISM AND PLURALISM   Our investigations thus far have confirmed the significance of two dimensions of the democratic mentality among European policymakers—one involving support for pluralism, political liberty, and contestation; the second stressing populism, political equality, and participation. But are these *distinct* dimensions, or are they highly correlated? And if they are linked, is the correlation positive, so that pluralists are also populists and antipluralists also antipopulists? Or is the correlation instead negative, so that the more favorable a leader is to liberty, the more he opposes equality?

An initial answer to these questions is provided by Table 6–5, which charts how our samples of politicians and bureaucrats in Britain, Germany, Italy, and the Netherlands are arrayed across both dimensions considered simultaneously. Among both politicians and bureaucrats, these charts show, populism and pluralism are positively associated. The more strongly a leader favors political contestation, the greater his enthu-

*Table 6-5*  Pluralism and populism, by role.[a]

| Role | Pluralism | Populism Low | Populism Medium | Populism High | | | |
|------|-----------|-----|--------|------|---|---|---|
| Politicians | Low | 6 | 10 | 5 | = | 21 | |
| | Medium | 7 | 14 | 12 | = | 33 | |
| | High | 4 | 14 | 27 | = | 45 | |
| | | 17 | 38 | 44 | | 99 | $r = .36$ |
| | | | | N | = | (365) | |
| Bureaucrats | Low | 21 | 14 | 4 | = | 39 | |
| | Medium | 13 | 14 | 6 | = | 33 | |
| | High | 8 | 12 | 7 | = | 27 | |
| | | 42 | 40 | 17 | | 99 | $r = .28$ |
| | | | | N | = | (335) | |

[a] Entries are percentages of total sample falling into a given cell; rows and columns do not sum precisely because of rounding. Analysis is based on equally weighted samples from Britain, Germany, Italy, and the Netherlands.

siasm for popular participation as well. In the minds of European policy-makers political equality and political liberty are basically complementary values, not conflicting ones.

In counterpoint to this common feature of both charts, we want to stress three important differences between politicians and bureaucrats. The first point, obvious in Table 6–5 and implicit in our earlier discussion, is that politicians are more heavily concentrated than bureaucrats at the fully democratic corner of the chart. More than one politician in four scores high on both populism and pluralism, as compared to one in fourteen among bureaucrats. Since (as we have seen) even the more moderate supporters of pluralism and populism within our samples are basically sympathetic to democracy, it is also fair to combine the medium and high categories on each variable. On this basis, two-thirds of the politicians are reasonably prodemocratic in their respect for both contestation and participation, as compared to somewhat over one-third of the bureaucrats. At the far corner of the charts, more than one bureaucrat in five is unsympathetic to both liberty and equality, whereas only one in seventeen among the politicians is in this sense antidemocratic. In short, politicians are more wholehearted democrats than bureaucrats.

A second, more subtle contrast also appears in Table 6–5. The data show, once again, that politicians are more likely to outrank bureaucrats in terms of populism than in terms of pluralism. As a consequence, more bureaucrats than politicians fall into the lower left-hand section of the

chart, which contains those leaders who are at least moderately proplu-
ralist but quite antipopulist. These respondents, whom we might think of
as the modern descendants of nineteenth-century liberals, are defenders
of free speech and political competition, yet are skeptical about mass political participation; their ranks include 21 percent of the bureaucrats, but
only 11 percent of the politicians.

A third important contrast between bureaucrats and politicians, somewhat obscured in Table 6–5, is that the two democratic dimensions are
more closely correlated among politicians than among bureaucrats. The
distribution of politicians across this populism-pluralism matrix does not
vary substantially from country to country, whereas the distribution of
bureaucrats does. In particular, Italian bureaucrats are much more heavily concentrated in the antidemocratic (upper left-hand) corner of the
diagram than their administrative counterparts elsewhere. (Forty-seven
percent of the Italian bureaucrats fall into the antidemocratic portion,
compared to 15 percent of British, German, and Dutch civil servants.)[24]
The statistical result of this anomaly is that the multinational data for bureaucrats in Table 6–5 tend to exaggerate the overall correlation between
populism and pluralism. Averaged across the country-by-country arrays,
the correlation between populism and pluralism for bureaucrats is .23, as
compared to a correlation of .45 for politicians. In other words, when
considered country by country, politicians are more likely to be consistent in their attitudes toward liberty and equality than are bureaucrats.
Politicians more often tend to be full-fledged supporters of democracy or
(more rarely) full-fledged opponents. Bureaucrats, by contrast, are more
often idiosyncratic, favoring liberty but not equality, or (more rarely)
equality but not liberty. We shall return later to this intriguing distinction, as well as to the other cross-role contrasts we have noted. The main
point for the moment is that populism and pluralism constitute distinct,
though somewhat overlapping, orientations to democracy.

PLURALISTS: THE HAPPY WARRIORS    One pattern that emerges with
unexpected clarity from our interviews is that policymakers who are
strongly committed to political liberty are systematically different in their
approach to politics and government from their less pluralist colleagues.
There is, we have discovered a "pluralist syndrome" involving much
more than the simple, though fundamental, issue of political liberty.
Across both roles and all of the countries for which we have evidence,
pluralists appear disproportionately to be the "happy warriors" of demo-

cratic politics. They take their politics seriously and they enjoy a good fight, but they are also readier than most to seek accommodation when necessary. Let us look at the evidence.[25]

To begin with, these pluralists are not muddlers. In fact, they display considerably more programmatic commitment than their antipluralist compatriots. In the preceding chapter we introduced the Index of Programmatic Commitment, which measures the degree to which policy-makers endorse or reject the view that the right answer to political controversies usually lies in the middle, that politics is merely "the art of the possible" and ambitious ideals should be shunned, that a government's strength and efficiency are more important than its program. Table 6–6 shows that pluralists are disproportionately likely to *reject* this "directionless consensus" approach. Pluralists are more than two-and-a-half times more likely than antipluralists to rank high on our Index of Programmatic Commitment.

Second, these pluralists are not shy about political combat, for they believe that conflict is healthy. Whereas nearly three-quarters of the antipluralists say that political parties exaggerate or distort social cleavages for their own purposes, most pluralists told us that party conflict simply mirrors real differences of interest within a society. And pluralists reject the Rousseauian idea that individuals should sublimate their own interests in deference to "the General Will." Only one-third as many pluralists

*Table 6-6*　Programmatic commitment, by role and pluralism.[a]

| Role | Support for pluralism | | | Pluralist-antipluralist difference |
| --- | --- | --- | --- | --- |
| | High | Medium | Low | |
| Politicians | 65 | 39 | 26 | +39 |
| $N =$ | (164) | (124) | (74) | |
| Bureaucrats | 45 | 39 | 14 | +31 |
| $N =$ | (89) | (109) | (131) | |

[a] Entries are percentages of each category ranking high on the Index of Programmatic Commitment, an additive index combining three agree-disagree items:
(1) Generally speaking, in political controversies extreme positions should be avoided, since the right answer usually lies in the middle.
(2) Politics is the "art of the possible," and therefore the leaders of the country should worry more about what can be done in the short run than about ambitious ideals and long-term plans.
(3) The strength and efficiency of a government are more important than its specific program.
Analysis is based on equally weighted samples from Britain, Germany, Italy, and the Netherlands.

as antipluralists (9 percent versus 28 percent) denied that "citizens have a perfect right to exert pressure for legislation which would benefit them personally."

If they are politicians, pluralists are much more likely to welcome controversy within their own party. When we asked politicians in Germany, Italy, and the Netherlands whether they thought strong differences within a party were helpful or harmful, only 10 percent of the pluralists, as compared to 47 percent of the antipluralists, said that intraparty debates were harmful.

If they are bureaucrats, pluralists are more enthusiastic about the political side of the job and reject the traditional idea of the bureaucrat as a political neuter. On a summary measure of the bureaucrats' general disposition toward the world of politics, 74 percent of the antipluralists were rated ambivalent or hostile, compared to 42 percent of the pluralists. In their discussions of the proper role of a senior civil servant, 70 percent of the antipluralists stressed neutrality rather than advocacy, a position held by only 42 percent of the pluralists. In Britain, among both MPs and civil servants, pluralists were more likely than their colleagues to favor relaxation of the traditional civil service rule of anonymity and public reticence.

Support for political liberty and the institutions of pluralist democracy is not an isolated and ritualistic feature of a policymaker's outlook. Rather, it appears to be part and parcel of his basic approach to his job. One good measure of this pattern derives from the first dimension of the "role focus" factor analysis reported in Chapter 4. The panoply of roles open to a policymaker, it will be recalled, can be reduced initially to a broad distinction between the "politico," who stresses advocacy, partisanship, and the protection of constituency interests, and the "technocrat," who emphasizes technical solutions for policy problems. As we noted in Chapter 4, a respondent's position on this continuum depends very heavily upon whether he is a politician or a bureaucrat. But *among* politicians and *among* bureaucrats, it turns out, emphasis on the "politico" end of the continuum is closely related to attitude to pluralism. Among civil servants, barely half of the pluralists are what we might term "pure technocrats," compared to more than three-quarters of the antipluralists. Among politicians, nearly two-thirds (65 percent) of the pluralists are "pure politicos," as contrasted with less than half (41 percent) of the antipluralists. Whatever the constraints of his job description, a pluralist emphasizes the "political" aspects of his role and deemphasizes the "technocratic" aspects.

Wherever he operates, whether on the floor of Parliament or in a quiet bureau, the typical pluralist accents the adversarial, seeking a fight where the antipluralist seeks to avoid one, defending a particular interest where the antipluralist seeks to submerge it, sharpening an issue when the antipluralist is smudging it—or huddling behind self-proclaimed neutrality. All this makes the pluralist appear, as one of our British respondents might say, "a bit bloody-minded." However, this impression is quite misleading.

In fact, some evidence suggests that pluralists are actually more open-minded in dealing with adversaries than antipluralists. For example, more than half (53 percent) of the antipluralists agreed with the proposition that "when one group or individual gains something, it usually means that another group or individual loses." But barely one-third (35 percent) of the pluralists endorsed this zero-sum view of the world. Pluralists may fight hard, but they do not fear compromise. Roughly half as many pluralists as antipluralists (21 percent compared to 38 percent) agreed with the wary view that "to compromise with political adversaries is dangerous because it normally leads to the betrayal of one's own side." Pluralists seem to have a more benign interpretation overall of human nature than antipluralists. Two-thirds (67 percent) of the antipluralists agreed that "basically no one cares much what happens to the next fellow," but only a little over one-third (36 percent) of the pluralists endorsed this misanthropic view. Perhaps it is the pluralists' very optimism about human nature and social relations that encourages them to engage in vigorous political controversy, while at the same time remaining open to compromise.

Our exploration of liberal democratic attitudes began with a simple assessment of who favored free speech and pluralist politics and who did not. We have learned, however, that this commitment to democratic liberties is part of a broader constellation of attitudes toward politics and government. Pluralists—those most enthusiastic supporters of political liberty—are unusually relaxed and comfortable in the give-and-take of democratic politics. They are ebullient movers and shakers, not antiseptic social engineers and not cold-eyed true believers. Their motto is neither "Consensus at all costs" nor "Victory or death." It is "Here's where I stand. Now let's talk." The liberties of pluralism are essential to their operation. Antipluralists, perhaps because they see the world around them as more threatening, have adopted a strategy of resolute conflict avoidance. In their own job they stress the noncontroversial and the technical, and they decry the tendency of pluralist politics to exalt self-interest and foment discord. Muddling at the margins is more their style than agitating for "Action!" It is not surprising that they see less need for protecting the right of others to agitate.

POPULISTS AND POLITICAL REFORM    In virtually any political system some participants are wholly content with the existing rules of the game and others would like to see changes. There is more agreement on procedural principles in the Western democracies than in many other countries, but in the 1960s and 1970s many voices were raised in criticism of "the system." We anticipated that the vast majority of our bureaucrats and politicians would fundamentally accept the existing political order, but we wished to probe their attitudes toward political reform (a concept that, despite its connotations to some, need not mean change inspired by the Left). So we asked a series of questions about the current distribution of power, as they saw it, eliciting assessments of such actors as trade unions, businesses, members of parliament, party leaders, the press, senior civil servants, and so on. We then asked, "Thinking over this distribution of power, do you think this is all as it should be, or should there be some important changes?" The ensuing discussion often stimulated a number of additional probes, exploring the respondent's propensity for political reform.[26]

On the basis of this discussion our coders rated the respondents' overall attitudes to the existing political order, using a five-point scale that ran from "passionate, total rejection; destruction proposed" to "passionate affirmation of existing system; strong resistance to change."[27] Table 6–7 shows how our bureaucrats and politicians scored on this measure. As we anticipated, only a small minority—concentrated among French politicians and Italian politicians and bureaucrats—were judged to reject the existing system, and most of them were able to formulate reforms that would make it acceptable to them. At the other extreme, only a handful of respondents exhibited total resistance to the possibility of institutional change. The vast majority split almost evenly between moderate reformers and moderate conservatives.

The most powerful predictors of political reformism in this sense turn out to be the two variables analyzed at length in the preceding chapter: role and ideology. Table 6–8 shows that, controlling for role, ideology is an extremely important determinant of a leader's eagerness for changes in the existing political system. Whether politicians or bureaucrats, Left-

*Table 6-7* Political reformism.[a]

| Attitude toward existing political order | Percentage response of— | |
| --- | --- | --- |
| | Politicians | Bureaucrats |
| Passionate, total rejection; destruction proposed | 2 | — |
| Rejection of system, but ameliorative reforms proposed | 8 | 3 |
| Acceptance of system, but ameliorative reforms proposed | 54 | 37 |
| Acceptance with little inclination for change | 32 | 57 |
| Passionate affirmation of existing system; strong resistance to change | 4 | 3 |
| | 100 | 100 |
| $N =$ | (456) | (420) |

[a] Analysis is based on equally weighted samples from Britain, France, Germany, Italy, and Sweden.

ists (defined in terms of their attitude toward social change and state intervention) are much more likely than Rightists to seek changes in current procedures and patterns of power. On the other hand, controlling for ideology, role also has an important impact on political reformism. At each point along the ideological spectrum, bureaucrats are more content with the existing system. The effects of role and ideology are essentially cumulative, so that, to revert to a familiar comparison, 80 percent of the rightist bureaucrats expressed satisfaction with the political status quo, as compared to only 12 percent of the leftist bureaucrats. All this is quite consistent with our conclusions in Chapter 5.

Against this backdrop we now want to ask whether there is any connection between a policymaker's commitment to democracy and his support for political reform. In a simple bivariate sense populism is strongly associated with political reformism, as shown in Table 6–9. Defenders of

*Table 6-8* Political reformism, by role and ideology.[a]

| Role | Ideological stance | | | Left-Right difference |
| --- | --- | --- | --- | --- |
| | Left | Center | Right | |
| Politicians | 12 | 30 | 61 | −49 |
| Bureaucrats | 28 | 57 | 80 | −52 |
| Role difference | −16 | −27 | −19 | Multiple $R = .54$ |

[a] Entries are percentages of each category accepting existing political order *without* significant reforms. Analysis is based on equally weighted samples from Britain, France, Germany, Italy, and Sweden.

*Table 6-9*    Political reformism, by role and populism.[a]

| Role | Support for populism | | | Populist-antipopulist difference |
|---|---|---|---|---|
| | High | Medium | Low | |
| Politicians | 18 | 47 | 62 | 44 |
| N = | (217) | (139) | (100) | |
| Bureaucrats | 42 | 60 | 70 | 28 |
| N = | (86) | (159) | (175) | |

[a] Entries are percentages of each category accepting existing political order *without* significant reforms. Analysis is based on equally weighted samples from Britain, France, Germany, Italy, and Sweden.

political equality are much more likely to want changes in the existing political system than are critics of equality. This difference is particularly striking among politicians, but it is also marked among bureaucrats. Populists are political reformers.

To understand the causal dynamics underlying this pattern requires multivariate analysis. Populists, as we shall see later, are heavily concentrated on the left of the ideological spectrum. As we already know, they are more likely to be politicians than bureaucrats, and they are disproportionately pluralists. Is it their populism, their ideology, their role, or perhaps even their pluralism, that accounts for their enthusiasm for political reform? The technique of multiple regression allows us to solve this conundrum, assessing the impact of each of these variables separately while holding all the others constant. The results of this analysis are presented in Table 6–10.

Each of our key variables has a statistically significant independent impact on political reformism; collectively their predictive power is impressive.

The single most important determinant of a policymaker's eagerness for political reform is his substantive ideological position. Controlling for role and democratic attitudes, Leftists are much less content with the existing political order in the West than Rightists—no end of ideology here.

Thus, the bivariate data in Table 6–9 did to some extent overestimate

*Table 6-10*    Predicting political reformism.[a]

| Ideology (Left-Right) | Role (politician-bureaucrat) | Populism (high-low) | Pluralism (high-low) |
|---|---|---|---|
| .50 | .14 | .23 | −.30 |
| Multiple $R$ = .62 | | | |

[a] Entries are standardized regression coefficients. All coefficients are significant at .01 or better.

the direct causal link between populism and political reformism, since part of the correlation was created by the indirect effect of ideology. Empirically, populists are reformers partly because they also tend to be Leftists. Nevertheless, the results of our multiple regression indicate that, even with ideology held constant, populists tend to be more reformist politically than nonpopulists. Those Rightists who (despite their conservatism) support political equality are more likely to want political reforms than their less egalitarian colleagues, and those Leftists who (despite their progressive socioeconomic views) are skeptical of popular political participation are more apt to be content with the political status quo.

Perhaps the most intriguing finding reported in Table 6–10 is that the net effect of pluralism on political reformism is strongly *negative*. That is, with ideology, role, and populism held constant, the more committed a policymaker is to political liberty, the more likely he is to defend the political status quo. We are *not* saying that pluralists are conservative in terms of substantive policy; in fact, we shall see in the next section that pluralists tend to be somewhat left of center ideologically. Instead, the point is that whether Leftist or Rightist, populist or antipopulist, civil servant or bureaucrat, the more a policymaker appreciates the pluralist freedoms, the stronger is his defense of the existing political order. Conversely, the more disparaging a leader is of liberty and its political exercise, the readier he is to seek political change.

Let us make one final observation about the data in Table 6–10. After controlling for the powerful effects of ideology, populism, and pluralism, there remains a significant residual effect of role on political reformism. Whatever their political and social ideals, whatever their commitment to liberty and equality, bureaucrats are less eager for important shifts in power and influence than politicians, less willing to tamper with the political process. No matter how progressive their views on social issues and political equality, bureaucrats are ex officio conservatives, constitutionally speaking. Conversely, no matter how conservative a politician's ideological stance, and no matter what his views on democracy, he remains more willing than his bureaucratic counterpart to entertain thoughts of political reform.

Political equality and political liberty are in one sense complementary values, since the strongest supporters of one are likely to be strong supporters of the other. Still, in another sense, we have now learned, they are quite contradictory values. In the representative democracies of the West, support for pluralism and democratic liberties has come to have conservative implications in a constitutional sense. The crucial freedoms have been won, and leaders skeptical of or hostile to those freedoms favor political change. As democrats, pluralists are content.

Equality, on the other hand, retains radical implications. One man, one vote—even one person, one vote—is only a pale reflection of the egalitarian democrat's ideal of government of, by, and for the people. Realistic or not, participatory democracy is a dream that fuels reformism. Historically, democratic ideals have stimulated criticism of the established order. Liberty, it seems, has lost this role; equality has not. Populists remain discontent democrats.

### Explaining Pluralism and Populism

Although policymakers in the West generally support the central democratic principles of political liberty and political equality, we have seen that they vary in their enthusiasm for these principles. And the intensity of their support for liberty and equality, for pluralism and populism, makes a difference in the way they conduct themselves politically and in their commitment to the existing political order. We now turn to the question of why their enthusiasm for democracy varies as it does. In all the countries for which data are available, four explanatory factors are linked systematically to populism and pluralism. Two of these factors are familiar, but two are somewhat unexpected. Let us begin with the familiar.

IDEOLOGY AND ROLE    We indicated at the outset of this chapter our expectation that support for democratic values would vary with ideology and probably also with role. We have now seen repeatedly that bureaucrats are in fact somewhat less enthusiastic than politicians about political liberty, and considerably less enthusiastic about political equality. Table 6–11 shows that this distinction generally persists when we control for ideology, but the table also shows that the impact of ideology itself is even more powerful. Several interesting patterns emerge upon closer examination.

First, the sharpest ideological distinction is that between Leftists (whether politicians or bureaucrats) and the rest of the sample. Policymakers who favor social change and state intervention are very strongly committed to democratic values, whereas the difference between centrists and Rightists is more muted. For example, on populism 54 percentage points separate centrist politicians from those on their left, but only

*Table 6-11*  Populism and pluralism, by ideology and role.

| Role | Ideological stance | | | Left-Right difference |
|---|---|---|---|---|
| | Left | Center | Right | |
| (1) Pluralist margin (percentage ranking high minus percentage ranking low on Pluralism Index) | | | | |
| Politicians | +47 | −12 | +15 | +32 |
| N = | (194) | (95) | (83) | |
| Bureaucrats | 0 | −9 | −27 | +27 |
| N = | (62) | (198) | (82) | |
| Role difference | +47 | −3 | +42 | Multiple R = .36 |

Based on equally weighted samples from Britain, Germany, Italy, and the Netherlands.

| Role | Left | Center | Right | Left-Right difference |
|---|---|---|---|---|
| (2) Populist margin (percentage ranking high minus percentage ranking low on Populism Index) | | | | |
| Politicians | +63 | +9 | −7 | +70 |
| N = | (228) | (138) | (173) | |
| Bureaucrats | +13 | 23 | −35 | +48 |
| N = | (85) | (261) | (164) | |
| Role difference | +50 | +32 | +28 | Multiple R = .47 |

Based on equally weighted samples from Britain, France, Germany, Italy, Sweden, and the Netherlands.

16 points from those on their right. This special affinity between democracy and the Left of course has deep roots in European history. In fact, the very notion of Left and Right first emerged during what the historian R. R. Palmer has called "the age of democratic revolutions." Our evidence demonstrates that this affinity has not weakened, despite much talk about the supposed fading of ideological divisions.[28]

Second, there is one familiar exception to the basically monotonic relationship between ideology and attitudes toward democracy. Recall from Chapter 5 that centrist politicians show a special affinity for Governance rather than Politics. The same anomaly now appears in the case of pluralism. Unlike their colleagues to either the Left or the Right, centrist politicians are rather antipluralist in outlook. In fact, their distaste for dissent and contestation is no less than the average bureaucrat's. In the case of populism, the centrist anomaly is less marked, but here too an extraordinary gap separates them from their Leftist colleagues. Centrist politicians are far from the quintessential democrats that some theories imagine them to be, for they are unusually skeptical about both liberty and equality.

A third important fact is that ideological differences are twice as great on populism as on pluralism. Political liberty is more a matter of common agreement all along the political spectrum, whereas equality remains highly controversial, particularly in ideological terms. We noted in Chapter 5 that the issue of social justice is still at the heart of the ideological debate in the West, and we see now that this pattern includes political equality as well. While pluralism has come to be part of the common heritage of most Western policymakers, populism remains in dispute between Left and Right.

AGE    If role and ideology are predictable correlates of democratic attitudes, the finding that age makes a difference is more surprising, for age is a constrained variable in our samples. Seventy-seven percent of our European bureaucrats and 60 percent of our European politicians were born in the two decades between 1910 and 1930. Yet in virtually every one of our countries, for both politicians and civil servants, younger policymakers are significantly more favorable to populism and pluralism than their colleagues.

Students of socialization generally agree that the years of early adulthood—say, between seventeen and twenty-five—constitute a critical period during which a kind of "imprinting" often takes place. Dahl summarizes this argument in very stark terms: "Most people acquire their beliefs during a period when they are particularly receptive. Typically, a person is highly receptive during, and only during, the first two decades of his life. At the end of this period, one's outlook becomes fixed or crystalized."[29]

This pattern suggests the utility of dividing our European elites into two groups, those who reached the age of twenty before World War II and those who came of age, politically speaking, during or after the war. Table 6–12 shows how these historically defined generations differ in their attitudes toward democracy. Among both politicians and bureaucrats, the prewar generation is significantly more skeptical about political liberty and political equality than the postwar generation.

Why are older policymakers less prodemocratic? Age-related differences in outlook are notoriously difficult to interpret. The fact that we have presented these data in generational terms by no means proves that the differences are in fact generational in origin, that is, that the differences were formed by some major event or set of events while a generation came to maturity. One prominent alternative would be a life-cycle

*Table 6-12*   Populism and pluralism, by age and role.[a]

| | | Bureaucrats | | Politicians | |
|---|---|---|---|---|---|
| Democratic attitude | | Younger (50 and under) | Older (51 and over) | Younger (50 and under) | Older (51 and over) |
| | Low | 23 | 44 | 20 | 23 |
| Pluralism: | Medium | 37 | 34 | 28 | 46 |
| | High | 40 | 22 | 52 | 31 |
| | | 100 | 100 | 100 | 100 |
| | N = | (173) | (263) | (268) | (106) |
| Pluralist margin (% high − % low) | | +17 | −22 | +32 | +8 |
| | | | $r = .31$ | | $r = .25$ |

Based on equally weighted samples from Britain, Germany, Italy, the Netherlands, and Swedish bureaucrats.

| | | | | | |
|---|---|---|---|---|---|
| | Low | 32 | 46 | 18 | 27 |
| Populism: | Medium | 43 | 38 | 34 | 38 |
| | High | 25 | 16 | 48 | 34 |
| | | 100 | 100 | 100 | 100 |
| | N = | (204) | (301) | (314) | (143) |
| Populist margin (% High − % Low) | | −7 | −30 | +30 | +7 |
| | | | $r = .15$ | | $r = .16$ |

Based on equally weighted samples from Britain, France, Germany, Italy, the Netherlands, and Swedish bureaucrats.

[a] Entries are percentages.

interpretation. Perhaps as leaders grow older and wiser, they become wearier of contestation and mass participation. Maybe when our younger respondents have a bit more gray around the temples, they too will be less enthusiastic democrats.

Although this alternative cannot be excluded without data gathered at more than one point in time, on balance we find it implausible. The average respondent in our "younger" group was about forty-two years old at the time of our interviews, while the average "older" respondent was about fifty-six. It is difficult to imagine a theory of the life cycle that would account for a strong and relatively uniform movement in an anti-democratic direction during one's late forties and early fifties, across different nations and political roles.

A related interpretation would emphasize not biological age, but what we might call "professional age," that is, tenure in national government. Perhaps experience in democratic government diminishes its charms.

Among bureaucrats, who (as we saw in Chapter 3) tend to ride a single-speed escalator to the top, age and seniority are so closely correlated that it is statistically impossible to distinguish between them. Among politicians, on the other hand, age and parliamentary seniority are less closely correlated; in this case the more important variable seems to be age, not seniority.

Another sort of interpretation of the consistent age differences would emphasize period effects. Perhaps our younger respondents were simply more "trendy," that is, more open to the opinion fads of the late 1960s and early 1970s. If the climate of opinion in the West was unusually favorable to democratic values during the years of our interviewing, perhaps the effects of that temporary climate were exaggerated among our younger cohorts. Again, in the absence of time-series evidence, we cannot conclusively eliminate this possibility, but one feature of the data speaks against it. A fair description of the Western intellectual climate at the time of our interviews would probably say that concern about "participation" was much more fashionable than concern about the issues we have grouped under the rubric of pluralism. Yet the age differences in our data are, if anything, even greater on our measures of pluralism than on our measures of populism. We find the climate-of-opinion explanation intriguing, but not completely persuasive.

We therefore return to the generational alternative. It is, we think, quite plausible that politically aware and involved young men and women coming of age in postwar Europe should have acquired enduringly different perspectives on democracy from their colleagues who came to maturity before the war. The atmosphere throughout Europe, particularly in regard to issues of political liberty and political equality, was clearly quite different in the two epochs. In some countries, of course, a change of regime symbolized and amplified this difference. Yet we find age-related differences in outlook not merely among our German and Italian respondents, but also in countries like Sweden and the Netherlands. This suggests that if indeed a generational watershed did occur in the Europe of the mid-1940s, it was related to broader social changes, not merely to constitutional transformations. "I grew up in a settled world," one of our older respondents told us, "but the war changed all that." The lessons of the prewar period, and of the war itself, were read by the postwar generation as requiring a freer, more open, less elitist, more egalitarian society and polity—in short, more democracy. Our evidence suggests that this lesson has stuck.

SYSTEM INVOLVEMENT   The fourth consistent correlate of democratic attitudes in our surveys measures the degree of our respondents' involvement in policymaking at the highest levels. We gathered information on the frequency of our respondents' contacts with a wide range of other political and governmental actors, from cabinet to local officials and from interest-group representatives to ordinary citizens. As we shall discuss in Chapter 7, some of the most powerful influences on these linkage patterns are structural. Whom you see, and how often, depends on where you sit. Higher-ranking bureaucrats and senior politicians, for example, have more frequent contacts with cabinet officials than do junior politicians and bureaucrats. These structural determinants of contact patterns are so obviously significant that it might seem that relatively little room is left for any systematic impact from attitudinal variables.

We were, therefore, surprised and intrigued to discover that by most measures in most countries, respondents with less democratic attitudes are unusually isolated from the rest of the political system. To phrase the same finding differently, pluralists and populists seem to be exceptionally involved in the network of political and governmental interaction. Isolation, it seems, breeds—or is bred by—authoritarian attitudes.

On closer examination, a particular pattern of contact seems especially correlated with attitudes toward democracy. In Chapter 7 we shall discover that one important and distinctive network within which some, but not all, bureaucrats are involved is what we term the "policy net." These officials do business frequently with the cabinet office, ministers, civil servants in other departments, and party leaders. A roughly comparable dimension exists in our parliamentary data. Politicians involved in the "national policy net" have frequent contacts with national leaders of their own and other parties, with ministers, and with senior civil servants.

Table 6–13 shows that among both politicians and bureaucrats, the greater one's involvement in the national policy network, the greater one's commitment to pluralism and to populism. (The correlation between populism and "policy contacts" does not reach statistical significance among politicians. Populist politicians do report unusually intense contacts, but these are focused primarily on what Chapter 7 terms the "grass-roots" network of local party leaders and other local officials.)

In short, support for pluralism and (at least among civil servants) for populism is unusually high among those leaders who are closest to the centers of power. This effect is particularly strong among bureaucrats. It is as if contacts upward and outward from the bureaucracy remove them

*Table 6-13*  Populism, pluralism, and policy contacts.

| Contacts | | Pluralist margin (% high − % low) | Populist margin (% high − % low) |
|---|---|---|---|
| **Bureaucrats** | | | |
| Frequency of contact with | Low | −40 | −43 |
| "policy network": | Medium | −12 | −23 |
| | High | 20 | − 8 |
| | | *r* = .32 | *r* = .22 |
| **Politicians** | | | |
| Frequency of contact with | Low | 1 | 16 |
| "national policy net- | Medium | 32 | 36 |
| work": | High | 34 | 27 |
| | | *r* = .16 | *r* = .08 |

from a climate that is less hospitable to democratic ideals and expose them to an atmosphere more like that ordinarily breathed by politicians. This conjecture does not, however, account for the broadly similar pattern among politicians themselves.

This pattern is no less puzzling if it is described from the opposite pole. Why should isolates be antipluralist—or antipluralists isolated? Several contrasting interpretations suggest themselves:

(1) *Socialization.* Perhaps enthusiastic support for the principles of political liberty is diffused within the elite primarily via the policy network, so that those exposed to that network are more likely to catch the "pluralist infection." This hypothesis implies that involvement in matters of high policy increases one's sensitivity to the importance of the institutions of liberal democracy.

(2) *Selection/recruitment.* Perhaps top policymakers tend to include in their circle of closest collaborators those who find contestation congenial, and to exclude those who do not. This mechanism would not require explicit attention to an aspirant's views on political liberty. The effect could be indirect, with the central policymaker looking for an ebullient mover and shaker, who is likely (as we saw earlier) to have a special appreciation for the virtues of pluralism.

(3) *Self-selection.* Perhaps pluralists, who find political controversy appealing, seek involvement in central policymaking, while antipluralists, who resent political interference and see themselves as technicians, shun contact with political leaders.[30]

We cannot be sure which of these alternatives is most accurate. Indeed, we entertain the possibility that each of them is part of the story. Whatever the cause, the effect is striking. As we walk the corridors of power, the closer we get to what Italians call *la stanza dei bottoni*—the room with the push buttons of power—the more favorable the atmosphere for democracy, at least in its liberal versions. The most authoritarian policymakers rarely enter the charmed circle, at least in these Western democracies.

## Conclusions

Before delineating some of the broader implications of our findings about attitudes toward democracy among bureaucratic and political elites, we may find it useful to summarize those findings briefly. Most Western policymakers, we have found, are fundamentally sympathetic to the principles of liberty and equality that comprise the democratic ideal, although significant minorities among both politicians and bureaucrats are more skeptical. On balance, politicians are somewhat more committed to liberty than bureaucrats are, and politicians are much more enthusiastic about equality. Liberty and equality—or pluralism and populism—are complementary, yet distinctive, values. They are complementary in the sense that enthusiastic supporters of one tend to be enthusiastic supporters of the other, although the correlation is far from perfect. They are distinctive in the sense that, ceteris paribus, support for liberty and pluralism is associated with commitment to the political status quo, whereas support for equality and populism is associated with political reformism. All of this is as we anticipated. More unexpected is our discovery that pluralists have a quite distinctive political style. Undaunted by conflict, they stand up firmly for their beliefs; but they also defend the rights of their opponents and remain open to accommodation.

Seeking the antecedents of democratic attitudes, we found that support for both populism and pluralism is higher among Leftists than among Rightists, higher among younger elite members than among their older colleagues, higher among well-connected policymakers than among isolates, and higher among politicians than among bureaucrats. It is, of course, this last point that is most central to our concerns in this volume, and it merits a bit of reflection.

As one way of synthesizing the patterns we have found, Table 6–14 summarizes in reduced form the evidence reported earlier in Table 6–5.

*Table 6-14*   Matrix of democratic attitudes.[a]

| Pluralism | Populism | |
| --- | --- | --- |
| | Low | Moderate or high |
| Low | "Authoritarians" | "Totalitarian democrats" |
| | Bureaucrats: 21 | Bureaucrats: 18 |
| | Politicians:  6 | Politicians:  15 |
| Moderate or high | "Nineteenth-century liberals" | "Wholehearted democrats" |
| | Bureaucrats: 21 | Bureaucrats: 39 |
| | Politicians:  11 | Politicians:  67 |

[a] Entries are percentages.

Recalling that even the moderate scorers on our two dimensions are fairly prodemocratic in absolute terms, we have here grouped them together with the more enthusiastic partisans of liberty and equality. The resulting two-by-two typology—labeled with some poetic license—integrates our discoveries.

Those we call authoritarians express deep doubt about both political liberty and political equality. In historical terms they represent the survivors of the predemocratic era in European politics. To be sure, despite the name we have given them, these people do not constitute a cabal, ready to spring from hiding, stage a coup, and restore the ancien regime. But they do prefer a closed, hierarchical system of policymaking. They want decisions left in the hands of an elite, and they want as little dissension as possible. They object to political reforms of an egalitarian sort, but their very distaste for parties, pressure groups, and "propaganda" curbs their allegiance to the pluralist democracies within which they operate.

A minority everywhere, these authoritarians are more common among bureaucrats than among politicians. To be sure, if we set aside the Italian case, the role difference is more modest. Forty-seven percent of the Italian bureaucrats fall into this cell, compared to only 15 percent of bureaucrats elsewhere. This national peculiarity is probably best explained by the fact that 92 percent of these Italian bureaucrats first entered government under the Fascist regime; they appear not to have been convinced of the superior merits of a democratic regime despite more than a quarter-century's experience. This exception apart, few European administrators, and even fewer members of parliament, are wholehearted critics of democracy.

The historical antecedent of our second category is manifest in our label for its members—"nineteenth-century liberals." These policymakers are strong defenders of the free play of ideas; they welcome a good debate, but they are skeptical that the debate should be thrown open to the populace as a whole. Interestingly, of our four groups they are most at ease in the imperfect and inegalitarian contemporary democracies of the West. In their view representative regimes as now structured provide just the right balance between responsiveness and leadership, and they would be very reluctant to see any less liberty—or any more equality. This outlook is particularly congenial to many European administrators, and in fact our nineteenth-century liberals are roughly twice as common among bureaucrats as among politicians.

Our third category is somewhat harder to place in historical terms, and we have borrowed our label for it from J. L. Talmon's study of "totalitarian democracy,"[31] recognizing that this rubric overdramatizes the distinctive outlook of the respondents. What they share with the political theorists analyzed by Talmon is a strong commitment to the ideal of equality and a much weaker appreciation for the virtues of liberty. About equally represented among bureaucrats and politicians, they are wary of conflict and worried by dissent. They would like to widen participation, but they also long for political harmony and social peace. These policy-makers are doubly alienated from the noisy, but rather elitist political systems of the West. There is too much arguing among leaders, they feel, and too little listening to the chorus of the people.

The final category—the "wholehearted democrats"—contains most of our politicians, although only a plurality of our bureaucrats. Principal bearers of the complex heritage of three centuries of democratic theory, these individuals are peculiarly sensitive to the conflicting imperatives of liberty and equality, to what Pennock calls the "democratic tension."[32] They share with the nineteenth-century liberals a keen appreciation for the value of open dissent and for the institutions that express social conflict. But they also stress the need to involve ordinary citizens more deeply in public affairs and to make governments more responsive. Their notion of democracy at once legitimates the present system and calls it into question.

The contrast between politicians and civil servants discussed in this chapter reflects the historic institutional differences between parliament and the bureaucracy. European parliaments are today, as they have been historically, the primary source of support for progressive democratization of the polity. Most European bureaucrats accept "democracy acquired," but they are much more skeptical about "democracy yet to come." The classic administrative values—efficiency, expertise, neutrality, rationality—are more easily reconcilable with political liberty than with political equality. Defenders of pluralist freedoms will find nearly as staunch support among bureaucrats as among politicians, but reformers seeking to increase popular control over what they see as an ever more distant leviathan will find considerably more sympathy in parliament than in the bureaucracy. If democratic ideals are to retain their traditional role as goads to political change, it is primarily to politicians that we must look. If governments are to be made more responsive to the wants and needs of ordinary citizens, it is primarily to politicians that we must look. If technically expert bureaucrats are essential to modern government, politicians are essential to modern *democratic* government.

# Interactions at the Top

## 7

Theoretically, at least, one important difference between bureaucrats and politicians concerns whom they meet and how often. Bureaucrats, it is frequently claimed, live in a world of structured relationships. In words that reflect the spirit of classic bureaucratic theory, Lloyd Warner and his associates write that "the large bureaucratic systems of government and business formally express relationships with exactness" and therefore a bureaucrat "must always act with correct superordinate, subordinate, and associational behavior."[1] Defined in these terms, reminiscent of the administrative role of Image I, the world of the bureaucrat is largely one of insular hierarchical relationships. The bureaucrat's principal reference points are upward and downward in his organization, and occasionally lateral to other sectors of the government bureaucracy. In this view he rarely needs to deal directly with politicians, interest groups, or citizens.

Conversely, politicians are thought to mediate the links connecting government, parties, and society. If the world of the bureaucrat is largely confined to the formal administrative apparatus of the government and if his network of contacts runs mostly upward and downward, the politician reaches outward to his society. His world, in contrast to the reputed precision of the bureaucrat's, is governed by multiple demands from party leaders, interest groups, local interests, and most of all the citizens who cast ballots.

The increased complexity of public agendas makes it difficult to maintain this stark distinction between the linkage patterns of bureaucrats and politicians, if ever it was a reality. Massive growth in the public agenda shifts some of the traditional burdens of politicians—the search for public support and legitimation of policies—onto bureaucrats and forces them willy-nilly into the performance of political functions.[2] The net impact of such a trend, if accurately described, would be to lead bureaucrats to look outward for political support. On the other hand, the increasingly thorny problems that face advanced industrial societies also demand that political decision makers be technically informed. The intricacy of contemporary policy agendas may compel politicians to direct their attention toward the bureaucratic apparatus in order to absorb specialized knowledge relevant to policymaking.

Aside from the basic comparison between bureaucrats and politicians, we are also interested in exploring the varying contact patterns of individual bureaucrats and politicians. For example, one might look to the role conceptions and basic political attitudes of bureaucrats and politicians for factors stimulating particular patterns of interaction. There may, for example, be a polar syndrome of attitudes toward politics and politicians that broadly distinguishes "classical bureaucrats," who see themselves as being above politics, from "political bureaucrats," who view themselves as one of several important actors in a common pluralistic game.[3] Perhaps bureaucrats who are tolerant of a pluralistic political process, who enjoy the political side of administration, and who think that their roles take them beyond the mere neutral implementation of law, are apt to be more involved with political actors, with interest groups, and with citizens than those whose views more closely fit the classical bureaucrat syndrome. In other words, these so-called political bureaucrats should be less likely to have their network of contacts defined exclusively by formal organizational channels.

However, attitudes probably cannot fully predict the types of contacts that bureaucrats will have. Different tasks and different levels of responsibility may structure interactive opportunities differently and thus produce diverse patterns of contact.[4] The higher an official's status, for example, the more frequent may be his interaction with central policymakers, and the more he may be responsible for presenting his organization's perspectives to the outside. Similarly, civil servants in coordinating ministries such as finance seemingly should have many contacts with other executive actors but relatively few outside the executive milieu. In contrast, the programmatic emphases of social service ministries frequently require the nourishing of key political and interest-group constituencies.

Politicians too can be expected to vary in their patterns of interaction. The more junior an MP's status, the more he might emphasize local contacts in order to shore up constituency support among local party leaders, local interest-group leaders, and local officials. Conversely, the more senior an MP, the more likely it is that his contacts will be oriented to national elites, especially to actors in the bureaucracy—ministers and senior civil servants. In a similar vein, we might expect parliamentary politicians of governing parties to be linked more regularly than members of the "out" parties to ministers and senior civil servants.

We also have reason to anticipate important variations in the character of elite interactions across political systems. The clarity with which institutional authority is defined, we believe, will have an important bearing on bureaucrats' incentives to deal directly with actors outside the administrative arena. Specifically, fragmented authority structures are likely to increase incentives for cross-sectoral contacts. According to this hypothesis, the distinctiveness and insularity of elite sectors is heightened by centripetal authority structures.

To tame these speculations, we need to examine the patterns of contact reported by the high-level civil servants and parliamentary politicians in our samples. This chapter is developed along three lines: the first emphasizes differences between bureaucrats and politicians; the second, differences within each role; the third, differences across political systems. We begin by comparing the contact patterns reported by senior civil servants and by parliamentary politicians. The structure of these contacts also is explored for evidence of internal specialization in the contact patterns of bureaucrats and politicians. We then look at the impact of individual-level variables on contact patterns within roles, disregarding the impact of national setting. Finally, we examine the impact of institutional authority patterns on the interactions of bureaucrats with parliamentary politicians.

In the course of our interviews with senior bureaucrats and parliamentary politicians, we asked them to indicate the frequency of contact that they typically had with other actors. Only in one country—France—did we fail to elicit any information about the character of elite contacts.[5] In all cases but one, respondents were asked to position themselves on a six-point scale ranging from very frequent (more than weekly) contacts to no reported contacts at all.[6] We asked the members of each sample in most of the countries about their contacts with the actors listed below.[7]

**Bureaucrats**

*Contacts with —*
One's minister
Highest civil servant in department
Departmental peers (other senior civil servants)
Ministers of other departments
Peers in other departments
Central cabinet or presidential office
Parliamentary politicians (MPs)
Leading political party members
Representatives of clientele groups
Ordinary citizens

**Parliamentary politicians (MPs)**

*Contacts with —*
Own national party leaders
Own local party leaders
National leaders of other parties
Local leaders of other parties
Ministers (cabinet officials)
Senior civil servants (national)
Local government officials
Representatives of national interest groups
Representatives of local interest groups
Ordinary citizens

Rates of contact between actors in a political system provide important information, although they do not tell us about the substance of these contacts. While the sheer quantity of interaction is not necessarily equivalent to its importance, rates of contact provide the outline of interactive networks through which cues are given and taken. Our first task is to map out the basic contact patterns of senior bureaucrats and those of parliamentary politicians, in order to understand to whom each is especially attentive.

## Contact Patterns

It is scarcely surprising that bureaucrats are linked most closely to their own departmental apparatus. Dealing with departmental peers and superior officials on a continual basis is at the core of bureaucratic life. As we can see from Table 7–1, bureaucrats interact most frequently with other actors in their departments and least frequently with political actors. Contacts are rather limited with actors who are within the administrative system but outside one's own department. Thus, the key referent for bureaucrats is their department rather than "the bureaucracy." Bureaucratic integration obviously is severely limited by the complex division of labor that bureaucratic organization itself engenders.[8]

Parliamentary politicians, in general, have rather extensive contacts

*Table 7-1*   Contacts with various types of actors reported by senior bureaucrats and politicians.[a]

| | |
|---|---|
| A.  Contacts reported by senior bureaucrats with:[b] | |
| Departmental actors | 76 |
| Societal actors | 59 |
| Executive sector actors | 43 |
| Political actors | 25 |
| | |
| B.  Contacts reported by politicians with:[c] | |
| Local or national actors | |
| Local | 64[d] |
| National | 56 |
| Intraparty or interparty actors | |
| Own party leaders | 90 |
| Other party leaders | 28 |
| Societal actors | 72 |
| Bureaucratic-government actors | 60 |

[a] Entries are average percentages of respondents reporting at least "regular" contacts with each group. See notes b and c for details of group composition.

[b] Departmental actors include one's own minister, the top civil servant in one's department, and (other) senior civil servants; societal actors include representatives of clientele groups and ordinary citizens; the executive sector includes other ministers, senior officials in other departments, and a central cabinet or executive office; the political sector includes MPs and political party leaders.

[c] The actor types as defined here are not wholly independent of one another: some items overlap and are entered into more than a single mean. Local actors include local government officials, local party leaders, local leaders of other parties, and local interest-group representatives. National actors include governmental, party, and interest-group actors at the national level. Intraparty actors include local and national leaders of the MP's party, and interparty contacts involve leaders of other parties at the local level and the national level. Societal actors include interest-group representatives at the local and national levels, and ordinary citizens. Bureaucratic-government actors include ministers, senior bureaucratic officials at the national level, and local government officials.

[d] The mean percentage of politicians reporting at least regular contact with local sources rises to 70 percent if contacts with citizens are included.

with their own party leaders and rather few with leaders of other parties. Negotiation and bargaining across party lines is a matter left mostly to party leaders. As anticipated, MPs also have more extensive linkages with societal actors than do bureaucrats, although we shall soon see that this is because MPs report much more contact with nonorganized citizens than do bureaucrats. Bureaucrats, in fact, have more contact with organized interests than do politicians. These facts are wholly consonant with the idea that the element that most definitively separates bureaucrats from politicians today is the nature of the "constituencies" they deal with.

A significant final observation from Table 7–1 is that national political elites—at least, members of parliament—are linked to local actors as much as to national ones. Bureaucrats are national actors; the same cannot be said unequivocally for MPs. As we have already seen, for example, politicians in parliamentary bodies are attentive to local matters. Unlike bureaucrats, they spring from local soil and are nurtured through local organizations. Whether in Washington or Rome or Stockholm, they provide a voice for the airing of local needs, however parochial these may seem to the bureaucratic elites of the metropolis.

The evidence thus far examined, as well as that presented in more detail in Figure 7–1, supports the notion that bureaucrats and politicians each have a specialized system of linkages. This specialization suggests, as Image III does, that each receives cues from very different sources. Bureaucrats' networks, fundamentally intrabureaucratic, are concentrated within their own departments. External linkages are more sparse, particularly if contacts with clientele-group representatives are disregarded. The world of partisan politics, as judged by the infrequency of bureaucrats' contacts with party leaders, is clearly at the periphery of the bureaucrats' network of linkages. The "politics" in which bureaucrats engage in the conduct of their jobs has little to do with partisanship. And, as Figure 7–1 further illustrates, bureaucrats and politicians have different types of links with societal actors. Those of bureaucrats are developed largely through the organized interest groups that permeate the activities of their departments. Thus, their interactions with societal actors are conducted mainly through organized interest groups, a fact that may predispose bureaucrats to ignore, in James Q. Wilson's words, "broader, harder to organize constituencies."[9]

Politicians, on the other hand, are linked more closely to those whom they perceive to be ordinary citizens than to interest groups, as Figure 7–1 shows. The ballot box undoubtedly compels parliamentary politicians to keep nonorganized publics more directly in mind. Moreover, MPs increasingly serve as intermediaries between their constituents and the national government. Service and casework activities, well-known functions of congressmen in the United States, may well become more important for legislators everywhere.[10] In describing the activities of congressmen in the United States, Samuel Huntington observes that they have "come to play a more and more significant role as spokesmen for the interest of unorganized individuals."[11] If Huntington is correct—and our data fit his

*Figure 7-1* Contacts reported by bureaucrats and politicians.

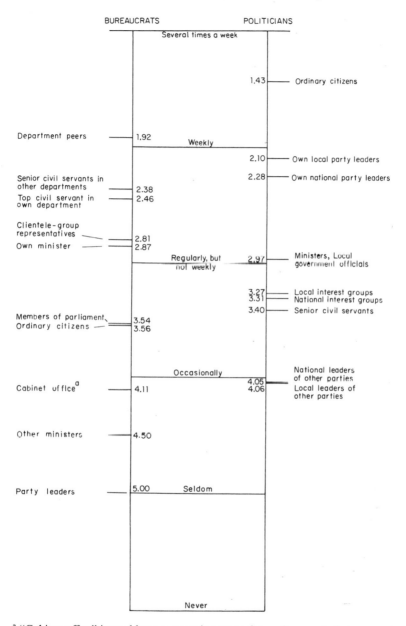

ᵃ "Cabinet office" is used here as generic nomenclature for a central clearance institution. The cabinet office in Britain, the Bundeskanzleramt in Germany, the Presidenza del Consiglio in Italy, and the Executive Office of the President in the United States are the pertinent organs.

view—the claims of organized interests are likely to be aimed increasingly at the administrative apparatus of the state simply because the general and abstract directives provided by representative assemblies will be less clearly relevant to particular interests than the specific and concrete meanings provided by administrative interpretations.[12] Our finding here that administrators interact with interest groups more than do parliamentarians is quite consistent with our finding in Chapter 4 that interest brokerage is more salient for bureaucrats than for politicians.

Fundamentally, the data in Table 7–1 and Figure 7–1 confirm the concepts of the bureaucrat as an actor sensitized to hierarchical flows of information within the organization world and the politician as a figure linked more broadly to nongovernmental actors. Each actor has a highly relevant referent. For the politician it is his party; for the bureaucrat it is his department. But politicians not only interact more frequently with other actors, they also interact with a broader array of actors. In this regard, our data are consistent with the energy/equilibrium distinction set forth in Image III; the world of the politician is one of popular constituencies and party organization, whereas the world of the bureaucrat is one of small groups and organized interests.

## The Structure of Contacts

While we have discussed the frequency of contacts that bureaucrats and politicians have with other actors in the system, we have said little about the way these contacts are structured. In his study of influentials in an American community, sociologist Robert Merton discerned two types— the "cosmopolitan" and the "local"—distinguished by the nature of their patterns of communication, their interpersonal relationships, their organizational activities, and their commitments to the local community. Other studies subsequently have drawn on this distinction to characterize differences across elite sectors, stressing that politicians have strong local roots and bureaucrats have cosmopolitan or national links.[13]

There is much in our data on background and career patterns to validate this proposition. Unfortunately, a direct test by comparison of contact networks is not possible, since bureaucrats were not asked about their contacts with local actors. However, a variant of the cosmopolitan-local distinction for bureaucrats involves an "inside" versus "outside" pattern of contacts. In other words, it is reasonable to expect some politicians to specialize in local contacts and others in national ones. Similarly, some bureaucrats might specialize in contacts within the administrative system, whereas others might specialize in developing contacts elsewhere.

In fact, the evidence in Table 7–2 reveals, first, that bureaucrats and politicians tend to have either a high rate of contacts across the board or a very low one. A factor analysis employing a principal-factor solution shows a tendency for the contact patterns of both bureaucrats and politicians to load along a single dimension, which alone explains 33 percent of the variance for politicians and 36 percent for bureaucrats. Since the most compelling dimensional structure distinguishes between respondents with a high rate of contact with most actors on the list and those who generally have little interaction across the list of actors, we then employed a varimax solution which preserves orthogonality across the factors and maximizes distinctiveness between them. The varimax results produced a three-factor solution for bureaucrats and a three-factor solution for politicians.

Among bureaucrats, the first factor revealed by the varimax solution is an executive-centered network not merely confined to departmental channels. Bureaucrats who rank high on this factor have access to the policymaking and coordinating centers of the executive, including executive actors outside their own departments. Metaphorically, these policy-centered officials appear to be connected to "the brain" of the political system. Or, to borrow an analogy from economics, they may be thought to be on the supply side of the governing equation. They represent the senior civil servant as a policymaker, but removed from unfiltered contact with popular political currents. On the other hand, those who rank low on this factor are more distant from the centers of policymaking.

The second factor suggests that some bureaucrats metaphorically serve as the "sensory organs" of the system. They appear to be closer to the demand elements of the governing equation—ordinary citizens, clientele-group representatives, and parliamentary politicians. On the surface at least, such officials seem to connect the traditional functions of large-arena politics with the specialized arenas of administrative government. The third factor, on the other hand, seems to highlight the traditional department-oriented contacts of bureaucrats.

The varimax solution generates an equally intriguing three-dimensional breakdown for the politicians. The loadings on the first factor clearly indicate a cosmopolitan network connecting MPs to policy leadership at the highest national levels: to party leaders, ministers, and senior bureaucrats. The second factor accords well with Merton's "localist" role

*Table 7-2*　Patterns for reported contacts of senior bureaucrats and politicians.

| Contacts | Principal-factor solution Factor loadings | | | Varimax solution Factor loadings | | |
|---|---|---|---|---|---|---|
| | $F_1$ | $F_2$ | $F_3$ | $F_1$ | $F_2$ | $F_3$ |
| | | | | Policy-centered network | Responsiveness/ facilitating network | Department-centered network |
| A. Bureaucrats with— | | | | | | |
| Own minister | .57 | −.27 | −.03 | **.56**[a] | .06 | .26 |
| Top civil servant in department | .71 | .16 | −.63 | .21 | .25 | **.91** |
| Department peers | .46 | −.01 | −.31 | .24 | .11 | **.48** |
| Other ministers | .60 | −.25 | .07 | **.61** | .13 | .19 |
| Civil servants in other departments | .54 | −.20 | .13 | **.55** | .16 | .12 |
| Cabinet office | .66 | −.43 | .14 | **.79** | .05 | .15 |
| Party leaders | .68 | .09 | .22 | .51 | .50 | .14 |
| Clientele-group representatives | .45 | .20 | .13 | .24 | **.43** | .12 |
| Members of parliament | .65 | .42 | .25 | .29 | **.75** | .13 |
| Citizens | .27 | .57 | .08 | −.13 | **.61** | .12 |

| | | | | National policy network | Grass-roots network | Interest-facilitating network |
|---|---|---|---|---|---|---|
| B. Politicians with— | | | | | | |
| Own national party leaders | .56 | −.57 | −.02 | **.78** | −.09 | .13 |
| National leaders of other parties | .65 | −.40 | −.27 | **.79** | .20 | .01 |
| Own local party leaders | .54 | .51 | −.38 | .09 | **.77** | .16 |
| Local leaders of other parties | .56 | .44 | −.49 | .19 | **.85** | −.01 |
| Local officials | .57 | .53 | .00 | .02 | **.65** | .42 |
| Citizens | .44 | .29 | .26 | .05 | .29 | **.51** |
| National interest-group representatives | .61 | −.18 | .56 | .42 | −.09 | **.73** |

*Table 7-2* (*continued*)

| Contacts | Principal-factor solution Factor loadings | | | Varimax solution Factor loadings | | |
|---|---|---|---|---|---|---|
| | $F_1$ | $F_2$ | $F_3$ | $F_1$ | $F_2$ | $F_3$ |
| | | | | National policy network | Grass-roots network | Interest-facilitating network |
| Local interest-group represen-tatives | .54 | .30 | .60 | .03 | .17 | **.84** |
| Ministers | .60 | −.43 | −.08 | **.73** | .05 | .13 |
| Senior civil ser-vants | .63 | −.25 | −.19 | **.65** | .25 | .10 |

[a] Highest-loading items distinctive to each factor in the varimax solution are in bold face for emphasis.

type, stressing grass-roots contacts. The third factor suggests a somewhat different form of facilitation, singling out politicians who are particularly attuned to interest groups, local and national, and to ordinary citizens. To use the anatomical metaphor by which we described the bureaucrats' contact structures, politicians too seem to specialize in being either parts of the brain of the system ($F_1$) or parts of its sensory apparatus ($F_2$ and $F_3$).

Two things need to be reiterated. One is that regardless of the internal differentiation of bureaucrats and politicians, the latter are far more involved with the sensory functions of the political system than are bureaucrats. But both are closely involved with the functions of the brain. Secondly, returning from the metaphorical to the statistical, we recall that all contacts for both bureaucrats and politicians are positively intercorrelated, indicating that the single most important distinction is between individuals who report fairly high levels of contact and those who report low levels of contact across the full array of actors.

Nevertheless, the internal distinctions raise a number of interesting hypotheses—alluded to earlier—regarding correlates of contact patterns. We turn now to a fuller explication of these hypotheses and an examination of the data relevant to them.

## Bureaucrats' Contact Patterns and Political Attitudes

Are the contact patterns of bureaucrats related to their orientations toward politics? The "classical" bureaucrat, as one of us originally described him, views politics derisively, thinks of politicians as mischievous, and emphasizes his own role as a neutral executor of laws (Image I).[14] Such a person might well dichotomize his environment into "us" (the administration) and "them" (the particular interests represented by politicians, interest groups, and citizens) and limit his interactions to a narrow set of actors within the administrative system. By contrast, the "political" bureaucrat believes that advocacy may be a proper function of his role and recognizes the need to develop support for his initiatives. Therefore, he probably sees himself as enmeshed with a multiplicity of actors who have diverse but adjustable interests. It is a hypothesis worth testing that attitudes favorable toward politics should lead to (or come from) more extensive contact networks.

We have set out in Table 7–3 the three variables used here to operationalize this complex distinction between "political" and "classical" bureaucrats. The first measure, based on a set of six agree-disagree items, taps the respondent's acceptance and understanding of representative political institutions. The differences by country in Table 7–3 suggest that tolerance for politics in this sense is partly a form of reality testing—of reactions to actual system performance—for it appears to vary at least as much across political systems as across individual bureaucrats. The second and third variables measure individual predispositions more directly;

*Table 7–3*  Bureaucrats' attitudes toward politics and advocacy across political systems.[a]

| Country | (ITP)<br>Tolerant of<br>politics[b] | (Gray Area)<br>Likes political<br>aspects of job[c] | (Advocacy-Neutrality Scale)<br>Emphasizes<br>advocacy[d] |
|---|---|---|---|
| Britain | 77 | 51 | 13 |
| Germany | 66 | 68 | 24 |
| Italy | 8 | 34 | 7 |
| Netherlands | 49 | 50 | No data |
| Sweden | No data | 38 | 15 |
| United States | No data | 37 | No data |

[a] Entries are percentages of respondents favoring politics and political advocacy.

[b] The Index of Tolerance for Politics is based on six closed-ended questions. See Robert D. Putnam, "The Political Attitudes of Senior Civil Servants in Western Europe: A Preliminary Report," *British Journal of Political Science*, 3(July 1973): 269–271. Entries are percentages of respondents above the pooled mean.

[c] The Gray Area is based on an open-ended interview question asking administrators whether they like the political aspects of their jobs that fall in the gray area between administration and politics.

[d] The Advocacy-Neutrality Scale is based on the coders' judgments of respondents' emphasis on commitment to a political philosophy or ideology, or on the neutral "tool" role of the civil servant, as indicated in responses throughout the interview.

the second taps the respondent's orientation to the political side of his work, and the third, his relative commitment to advocacy or neutrality as an administrator. These latter two measures are fairly closely correlated ($r$ = .43) but tolerance of representative political institutions is only modestly related to liking "politics" ($r$ = .21) and is even more weakly related to the advocacy-neutrality scale ($r$ = .13).[15]

The correlations arrayed in Table 7-4 show that the various measures of attitudes to politics are *not* consistently related to contacts with external actors. The strongest and most consistent correlations involve contacts with the cabinet office and party leaders. Bureaucrats who are favorable to politics appear to be well-connected to the centers of political power in their systems. On the other hand, politicalness as defined by

*Table 7-4*  Political attitudes and contact patterns among bureaucrats.[a]

| Contacts | Index of Tolerance for Politics | Gray Area | Advocacy-neutrality | Average coefficients across "political" variables |
|---|---|---|---|---|
| A. Contacts with— | | | | |
| Cabinet office | .28*** | .33*** | .15 | .25 |
| Own minister | .25*** | .09* | .03 | .12 |
| Other ministers | .10* | .07 | .13* | .10 |
| Civil servants in other departments | .24*** | .18*** | .09 | .17 |
| Party leaders | .16** | .32*** | .38*** | .29 |
| Top civil servant in department | .01 | .11* | .06 | .06 |
| Citizens | −.32*** | .06 | .07 | −.11 |
| Members of parliament | −.07 | .13*** | .30*** | .12 |
| Clientele-group representatives | .10* | .02 | −.03 | .03 |
| Departmental peers | .19*** | .00 | .01 | .07 |
| B. Contact factor scores:[b] | | | | |
| Index of Policy Centeredness | .34*** | .27*** | .12* | .24 |
| Index of Responsiveness/Facilitation | −.15** | .12* | −.04 | −.04 |

[a] Entries are Pearsonian $r$'s. Levels of statistical significance: *** $P < .001$; ** $P < .01$; * $P < .05$. All entries in this table include samples from Britain, Italy, and Germany. The Dutch sample is often included, and the American and Swedish samples are occasionally included.

[b] The indexes are normalized factor scores based on the first two factors extracted from the varimax rotation reported in Table 7-2.

these attitudinal measures is only mildly related to contacts with parliamentary politicians, virtually unrelated to contacts with clientele groups, and even inversely related to contacts with ordinary citizens. Interest groups appear to be a constant of bureaucratic life; they are necessary to deal with whether or not an official is politically oriented. At the same time, citizen contacts may seem less important for the politically oriented precisely because bureaucrats do not play their political game in broad arenas. That is the terrain of the politician. To judge from the composite pattern that emerges from Table 7–4, civil servants with positive orientations toward politics, compared to those with less favorable orientations, are close to the policy-coordinating mechanisms of the executive system and to party elites.

Moreover, as Table 7–5 shows, compared to bureaucrats who are isolated from the policy centers of the system, these well-connected bureaucrats are less likely to adopt a technical role focus and are more attuned to role styles that are policy oriented, partisan, and conflict adjusting (broker). On the other hand, Table 7–5 also shows that bureaucrats possessing especially strong links to outside actors, such as interest-group representatives and ordinary citizens, are significantly more likely to have adopted a facilitator (or representing) role focus than those lacking these links. (They also tend not to be brokers and, for reasons not immmediately obvious, they seem more oriented to the legalistic aspects of their job.) To be sure, the magnitude of these correlations is hardly staggering. But the patterns in general appear consistent with what we already know about the connection between bureaucrats' attitudes toward politics and their patterns of contact.

In sum, attitudes toward politics and contact patterns are indeed related, but the correlation is not entirely the one we expected. Instead of being connected mainly to the outside, bureaucrats whose attitudes toward representative political institutions are favorable and who are themselves more politically oriented are well connected with the power centers of the executive. These policy-connected bureaucrats are more likely to see themselves as partisans and policymakers and less likely to see themselves as technocrats. Recall, too, from the previous chapter that they are especially strongly committed to pluralism and populism. In other words, political attitudes are more decisively associated with the Index of Policy Centeredness (based on Factor 1 from Table 7–2) than with the Index of Responsiveness/Facilitation (based on Factor 2 from Table 7–2).

*Table 7-5* Role orientations and contact patterns among bureaucrats.[a]

| | | | | | Role focus | | | | |
|---|---|---|---|---|---|---|---|---|---|
| Contact pattern | Technician | Advocate | Legalist | Broker | Trustee | Facilitator | Partisan | Policymaker | Ombudsman |
| Index of Policy Centeredness | -.12* | .09 | .03 | .12* | .06 | .02 | .17*** | .17** | -.07 |
| Index of Responsiveness/Facilitation | .05 | .09* | .19*** | -.10* | -.06 | .20*** | -.04 | -.09 | -.01 |

[a] Entries are Pearsonian *r*'s. Levels of statistical significance: *** $P < .001$; ** $P < .01$; * $P < .05$. A sweep of the individual item correlations indicates that contact with party leaders (a contact that loads on both factors and also is the least frequent) is especially correlated with the partisan role focus ($r = .29$), the policymaker focus ($r = .28$), and the advocate focus ($r = .21$). For sample coverage see note 7, pp. 289–290. The contact pattern indexes are normalized factor scores based on the first two factors extracted from the varimax rotation reported in Table 7-2.

What this suggests is that bureaucrats, as well as politicians, can be energizers, but that activist bureaucrats differ from politicians in their energy sources and in their channels of transmission. Politicians are propelled by principles, doctrines, and particularistic pressures. For the most part, they seek support in public arenas. The "movers and shakers" among bureaucrats, however, push ideas and policy proposals in more private settings. The opportunities they discern and the support they seek comes from within—at the top and across the "joints" of the executive system and from strategic party elites. Bureaucrats who are "political" therefore are not "political" in precisely the same ways that politicians are.[16]

The political arena that bureaucrats are sensitized to, as we have noted earlier, is the arena of small groups and of leaders, not the arena of mass pressures. This much accords with Image III. Against this background, those bureaucrats who are well-connected to the policy networks— movers and shakers, as we have labeled them, or "super-bureaucrats" in the terminology of Campbell and Szablowski—seem to possess many of the characteristics that we would associate with the Image IV hybrid bureaucrats.[17] Rather than being the equilibrators suggested by Image III, these bureaucrats energize the policy process and are strongly linked to centers of policymaking, if not to representational forums. Our study was not designed to pinpoint such hybrids, but the data that we have examined in this section suggest that we may have found some.

### Bureaucrats' Contact Patterns and Structural Location

Attitudes and motivations by themselves are insufficient to account for contact patterns, for where one sits surely helps determine whom one sees. A bureaucrat's propensity to behave politically is undoubtedly conditioned by his opportunities, that is, by his strategic position in the structure of the government. Figure 7–2 diagrams the possible relations among these three variables—locations, attitudes, and contacts. While we treat contact patterns as the dependent variables here, we recognize that the relationship among the three could well be an interactive one.

We have selected three aspects of a bureaucrat's strategic location for specific examination:

(1) Is he employed in a social service department or not?
(2) Is he employed in a state maintenance department (for example, finance, internal affairs) or not?

*Figure 7-2* Attitudinal and structural factors as determinants of bureaucrats' contact patterns.

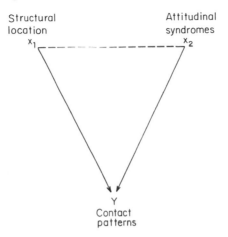

(3) Within the rather rarefied stratum of our samples, is he higher ranking or not?[18]

These features of a bureaucrat's position are *not* strongly or consistently related to his political attitudes. As Table 7–6 shows, service in a state maintenance department is unrelated to any of the attitudinal variables. Membership in a social service department is modestly related to all three, but the direction of the relationship involving tolerance for political institutions is unexpected. Rank is related only to an administrator's enjoyment of the political aspects of his job. There is, in short, some faint connection at the top of the triangle between attitudes and location (Figure 7–2), but no strong generic claim can be made that political attitudes are linked to particular functional or hierarchical sectors in Western bureaucracies.

*Table 7-6* Structural location and attitudes to politics among bureaucrats.[a]

| | Attitudinal variables | | |
| --- | --- | --- | --- |
| Structural variables | Tolerance for politics | Gray Area | Advocacy/ neutrality |
| Social service department | −.10* | .10** | .15*** |
| State maintenance department | .03 | .02 | −.07 |
| Rank | .02 | .15*** | −.01 |

[a] Entries are Pearsonian $r$'s. Levels of statistical significance: *** $P < .001$; ** $P < .01$; * $P < .05$.

*Table 7-7*  Structural location and contact patterns among bureaucrats.[a]

| Contacts | Department Social service | Department State maintenance | Rank |
|---|---|---|---|
| A. Contacts with— | | | |
| Cabinet office | −.08 | .11* | .18*** |
| Own minister | −.02 | −.03 | .35*** |
| Other ministers | −.07 | −.04 | .11* |
| Other civil servants | −.03 | .04 | .02 |
| Party leaders | .13*** | −.06 | .04* |
| Top civil servant in department | −.08 | .00 | .00 |
| Citizens | .03 | −.05 | −.14* |
| Members of parliament | .03 | −.05 | −.18*** |
| Clientele-group representatives | .07 | −.26*** | −.16*** |
| Departmental peers | −.07 | −.03 | −.27*** |
| B. Contact factor scores: | | | |
| Index of Policy Centeredness | −.04 | .03 | .25*** |
| Index of Responsiveness/Facilitation | −.04 | −.06 | −.08 |

[a] Entries are Pearsonian *r*'s. Levels of statistical significance: *** $P < .001$; * $P < .05$. See note a to Table 7–5 for an explanation of the samples and contact factor scores analyzed here.

What about the direct arrow between structural location and contact patterns? With a single significant exception, Table 7–7 shows that one's department has little bearing on patterns of interaction. (The exception is this: the state maintenance ministries, as "insider" departments with important clearinghouse functions,[19] are less involved with clientele groups.) Rank, on the other hand, is relevant. As Table 7–7 shows, higher-ranking bureaucrats are better connected to the centers of power and somewhat less closely linked to outsiders.[20] This conclusion is entirely expected; indeed, one might have anticipated the relationship between rank and contact with the policy center to be stronger than it is. What is more pertinent to ask is whether the relationship between political attitudes and contact patterns persists when rank is controlled.

A look at Table 7–8 tells us that attitudes make a major, generally consistent difference with respect to policy-centered contacts, especially among officials of lower rank. (It is important to keep in mind throughout that "lower" here is a relative term; even our lowest-ranking respondents are quite senior officials.) In terms of Figure 7–2, contact patterns (Y) are independently related to both attitudes ($X_2$) and structural rank ($X_1$). Where one is organizationally helps determine whom one sees, but appetite for politics apparently has self-propelling effects as well, particularly

*Table 7-8*    Political attitudes and contact patterns among bureaucrats, controlling for rank.[a]

| | Rank | | | | | |
| | High | | | Low | | |
| Contact pattern | Tolerance for politics | Gray Area | Advocacy/ neutrality | Tolerance for politics | Gray Area | Advocacy/ neutrality |
|---|---|---|---|---|---|---|
| Index of Policy Centeredness | .23** | .26*** | .00 | .45*** | .21** | .37** |
| Index of Responsiveness/Facilitation | −.24** | .05 | .00 | −.01 | .25 | .11 |

[a] Entries are Pearsonian $r$'s. Levels of statistical significance: *** $P < .001$; ** $P < .01$. A sweep of the individual item correlations indicates a strongly similar pattern. Contacts with party leaders, which are of course rare, show only modest or no correlation with political attitudes among higher-ranking bureaucrats, but are strongly and consistently correlated with political attitudes among lower-ranking bureaucrats. For sample coverage see Table 7-3. The contact pattern indexes are normalized factor scores based on the first two factors extracted from the varimax rotation reported in Table 7-2.

among those whose relatively modest rank would not itself require or assure contacts with the centers of policymaking.

**Politicians' Contact Patterns**

Our report on the individual differences among politicians in terms of their contact patterns can be quite brief. We explored in detail the possible impact of parliamentary seniority and of party membership, especially membership in governing versus opposition parties. Except for the unsurprising fact that legislators from governing parties have more frequent contacts with ministers ($r = .25$), we found no systematic difference in contact profiles between legislators from "in" and "out" parties.[21] Seniority, on the other hand, does make a difference. Junior MPs have significantly more frequent contacts ($r = .27$) with the grass-roots network, including local party leaders and local officials, and they have slightly more contacts ($r = .11$) with interest-group representatives and ordinary citizens. In most parliamentary systems, especially where there is some measure of district representation, junior members are likely to specialize in local and facilitative contacts in order to shore up bases of support within their constituencies. More senior politicians seem to devote less time to such contacts, although even they have more grass-roots contacts than do bureaucrats.

### Cross-National Comparisons of Bureaucrats' Contact Patterns

Bureaucrats' contact patterns within the administrative system itself vary little from country to country. Table 7–9 shows relatively small cross-national variation in average levels of contact with one's own minister, with other civil servants, or with clientele groups. Such differences as there are from bureaucrat to bureaucrat with respect to these contacts within the administrative system are affected more by individual characteristics, such as the official's specific role and possibly his political outlook. Connections to the outside, on the other hand, appear to be determined more by systemic factors, since contacts with such actors as party leaders, members of parliament, citizens, other ministers, and the cabinet office show great cross-national differences. Put slightly differently, intradepartmental contacts and interest-group contacts are basically similar in all national settings, whereas extradepartmental contacts are much more influenced by differing institutional structures and traditions.

Our guiding assumption about what links bureaucrats to forces outside the administrative system is quite simple: extensive involvement with outside actors is a function of institutional fragmentation. Taken together, traditions of collective cabinet responsibility, cohesive and disciplined parties, a relatively integrated executive, party government, and especially a party-centered parliament, reduce the propensity for bureaucrats to develop intense contacts outside the administrative system. This is so because in such circumstances external actors can bring little inde-

*Table 7-9*   Cross-national variability of bureaucrats' contact patterns.

| Types of contacts | Coefficients of variability[a] of contacts across national samples |
|---|---|
| Party leaders | .727 |
| Members of parliament | .622 |
| Citizens | .511 |
| Other ministers | .448 |
| Cabinet office | .350 |
| Top civil servant in department | .198 |
| Clientele-group representatives | .166 |
| Departmental peers | .120 |
| Other civil servants | .118 |
| Own minister | .101 |

[a] The coefficient of variability is a standardized measure of variation expressed as a ratio of the standard deviation of a distribution to its mean, that is, $V = SD/\bar{X}$. The higher its value, the greater the dispersion across national samples.

pendent leverage to bear in bargaining relations. By contrast, structural fragmentation disperses power to a wider array of actors and increases the interdependence of bureaucrats and parliamentary politicians.

Bureaucratic fragmentation exists in some degree everywhere. We have already seen that senior civil servants are linked more distinctly with a network of departmental contacts than with the bureaucracy as a whole. Departmental perspectives are arrived at sooner and more durably than "government" ones. Moreover, cabinet responsibility and party government do not always operate as the folklore claims. Indeed, the closer one looks at any system, the more pluralistic decisionmaking appears and the weaker the pull of centralizing forces.[22]

Nevertheless, some bureaucratic systems are more fragmented than others. For example, the American system of government with its independent legislature, its absence of a tradition of cabinet responsibility, its strong tendencies toward bureau autonomy, its relatively decentralized personnel system, its weakly organized political parties, and its specialized legislative committees most strikingly represents the centrifugal pole on a scale of fragmentation. As one writer has said about the American bureaucracy, "About the only thing that some Federal employees have in common is that they are paid by the U.S. Treasury."[23] These centrifugal forces encourage a mutual dependence between bureaucrats and politicians and foster the well-known "iron triangles" of bureaucrats, congressmen, and interest groups.[24]

In contrast, the British system more than most tends to concentrate governmental power. Departmental parochialism is softened by a rather high degree of lateral mobility across departments.[25] Ministerial responsibility and civil service anonymity reduce the dependence of bureaucrats on MPs. The tradition of collective cabinet responsibility, though sometimes exaggerated, does provide a centripetal coordinating force to the bureaucracy and tends to concentrate the power to establish agendas in the hands of the cabinet.[26] Majority-party government weakens the leverage that back benchers can apply in relation to the bureaucracy, for they must channel their claims through ministers who are, like themselves, parliamentary politicians. We expect that in such a system bureaucrats and members of parliament should have little incentive or opportunity for regular, direct contact with each other.

Table 7–10 displays the external contacts of bureaucrats across several political systems. As expected, bureaucrats in countries with centripetal authority patterns exhibit weaker linkage with actors outside the execu-

*Table 7-10*    External contacts of bureaucrats, by country.

| | Percentage of bureaucrats reporting "regular" contacts with— | | |
|---|---|---|---|
| Country | Members of parliament | Leading members of political parties | Representatives of clientele groups |
| Britain | 5 | 5 | 67 |
| Netherlands | 16 | 4 | 64 |
| Sweden | 31 | 7 | No data[a] |
|    Ministries | 86 | 26 | No data |
|    Boards and authorities | 17 | 3 | No data |
| Italy | 50 | 3 | 59 |
| Germany | 74 | 24 | 74 |
| United States | 64 | 14 | 93 |
|    Political executives | 65 | 26 | 92 |
|    Civil servants | 62 | 3 | 94 |

[a] Swedish respondents were asked about five interest groups; those data are excluded from this analysis as noncomparable.

tive system than do bureaucrats where authority is more diffused. (A partial exception to this generalization—but one quite understandable in light of Image III—involves contacts with interest groups, which are quite frequent in all these bureaucracies.)

Britain and the Netherlands fit our expectations about centripetal systems quite well. In both countries traditions of cabinet responsibility and bureaucratic neutrality inhibit civil servant linkages outside the administration. Similarly, Swedish administrators in the boards and public authorities are expected to be neutral policy implementers, and they have relatively few external contacts.

By contrast, civil servants in the Swedish ministries are intimately involved in program development and legislative liaison, a role similar in important respects to that of American political executives, and they display an active pattern of external contacts remarkably parallel to that of their American counterparts. Both groups report frequent contacts with members of parliament, and although party affairs are mainly the responsibility of their political superiors, both groups interact much more with party leaders than do civil servants elsewhere except for Germany, and certainly far more than either career officials in the United States or civil servants in the Swedish boards and authorities. The institutional separation of policy development from policy implementation in Sweden is clearly reflected in these contact profiles.

American career officials are as actively involved with members of

Congress as are the political executives. Because of the in-and-out career patterns of the latter, American career civil servants are in a prime position to build durable relations with congressional committee staffs and members. This enables them both to protect their superiors and, when the need arises, to protect themselves from their superiors. American bureaucrats are also superactive in their involvement with interest groups. Such groups swarm around bureaucracies everywhere, but the independence of Congress from the executive induces American bureaucrats to build support for their own interests from clientele groups who can wield influence on Capitol Hill. As one of our American respondents told us,

> You've got to work with interest groups and have a close relationship with them. You get involved with congressmen and vested interest groups, and they try to pressure you. But in my experience and my judgment you've got to work with them ... because if you haven't got a constituency, you're never going to get anything through Congress. Democracy is a case of vested interest groups, and at least the [proposed] legislation that I watch reflects that. [Your proposal] may be excellent in concept and excellent in form, but without interest-group support, it never gets passed.

It is hardly surprising, then, that American bureaucrats—career civil servants as well as political executives—have a high level of contact both with members of Congress and with clientele-group representatives, for this triangular relationship is bred from mutual dependency in a system notable for institutional disaggregation. Institutional incentives generate entrepreneurial instincts in American bureaucrats.

Civil servants in Germany, too, have very frequent contacts with interest groups and parliament. One reason for this may be that the Federal Republic seems to be evolving in directions similar to (but not coincident with) American institutional patterns. Perhaps the most powerful legislative chamber in Europe, the Bundestag has an elaborate committee structure akin to that of the American Congress, although it lacks the independent staffing that U.S. congressional committees have. German civil servants frequently advise Bundestag committees, especially in connection with legislation that involves much technical detail. A community of interest between German civil servants and parliamentarians is nourished in these committees and fostered by the large number of former civil servants in parliament.[27]

Important differences between German and American political institutions remain, of course. The Bundestag is still neither so independent nor so powerful as the U.S. Congress, and politicians are more dependent on bureaucrats in Germany than in the United States. However, power is fragmented in both polities—in one case by design and in the other more by institutional evolution—and in both, this fragmentation creates mutual dependence among civil servants, parliamentary politicians, and clientele groups.

In view of the traditional *Rechtstaat* ideology that exalts the role of the bureaucracy as superior to the particularistic divisions of politics, the relatively high level of German civil servant contact with party leaders seems curious. Part of the explanation is structural: ministries in Bonn concentrate on policy development, leaving implementation mostly to the Länder, so that our German bureaucratic respondents are functionally somewhat analogous to the Swedish ministerial civil servants and the American political executives. Moreover, as Nevil Johnson contends, a high proportion of federal political leaders have roots in Länder politics, and "often bring to Bonn officials whom they had known in earlier stages of their careers." Such recruitment practices create special ties between civil servants and party leaders. In addition, the involvement of civil servants in the legislative process requires them to be sensitive to "political undercurrents in the parties."[28] Closely tied to these structural features of the contemporary German administration is the gradual erosion in recent years of the traditional bureaucratic ideology of *Überparteilichkeit* (above parties). Our evidence indicates that German civil servants are more favorably inclined to politics and political advocacy than any other sample where comparable data exist.[29] In short, institutional similarities have induced both German and American bureaucrats to develop extensive linkages outside the bureaucracy and in some ways to think and act more like politicians than bureaucrats are accustomed to doing.[30]

The pattern of contacts exhibited by senior Italian civil servants is rather bewildering at first glance. Other evidence from our interviews makes clear that Italian bureaucrats are, for the most part, hostile to pluralistic politics and seem to see themselves as standing apart from it. On virtually every measure of background and attitude in our study, the distance between bureaucrats and politicians is greater in Rome than in any other capital, and other scholars too have observed that there is a great cleavage between the political class and the administrative class in Italy.[31] Nevertheless, the data in Table 7–10 suggest that Italian bureaucrats have a fair amount of contact with parliamentarians.

The explanation for this paradox seems to be that the Italian administrative system combines authoritarian traits with clientelistic penetration and political favoritism, so that the higher civil service is, at one and the same time, politicized and antipolitical. Sabino Cassese describes the outlook of Italian bureaucrats as "schizophrenic, the attitude of those who despise politics, but make use of it."[32] The Italian state, ruled by the Christian Democratic party for more than three decades, is riven by factionalism. The right party credentials provide the calling card for parliamentary entree into the bureaucratic labyrinth. This linkage process "can involve a bargaining relationship where favors are exchanged between MPs, offering their support for certain measures in Parliament, and bureaucrats, providing particular services for the parliamentarian or his constituents."[33] Factionalized politics and fragmented authority preclude government responsiveness on major issues, but on particularized issues the bureaucracy is often responsive to requests of deputies from the ruling party.[34] Senior civil servants are unsympathetic to the tugs and pulls of democratic politics, but in a cruder sense they are thoroughly politicized.

Turning to a fuller examination of linkages between politicians and bureaucrats (Figure 7–3), we discern a very clear pattern. In Britain, the Netherlands, and (subject to a later qualification) Sweden, linkages between senior civil servants and MPs are apparently mediated through the minister, for civil servants report quite infrequent contacts with parliamentarians and quite high levels of contact with ministers. (This pattern is particularly clear in Britain.) These are precisely the systems in which administrators are institutionally most insulated from the world of overt politics, where civil servants generally operate under the veil of anonymity, and where ministerial responsibility, collective cabinet government, and a party-centered parliament are most fully developed. This pattern of mediated linkage does not necessarily depend on the ministers themselves being MPs, as the Dutch case makes clear.

The dualism of the Swedish administrative system is evident in the data on civil service contact with MPs. The vast corps of civil servants in the boards and authorities have little direct linkage with politicians, reporting a level of contact with MPs (17 percent) that is about as low as the Dutch figure. Civil servants in the ministries, however, are very actively involved with parliament; 86 percent report regular contacts with MPs. This latter figure reflects the well-known pattern in Sweden of inducting diverse actors into the formative stages of policy planning.[35]

In each of these three countries, MPs report more contact with bureau-

*Figure 7-3*    Models of linkage: mediated, simultaneous, and end-run.

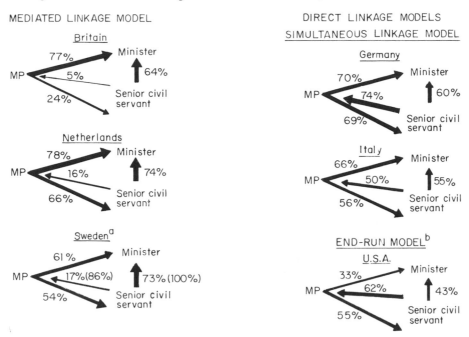

NOTE: Percentages are of "regular" contacts reported by MPs and civil servants.

[a] Figures not in parentheses are for nonministerial civil servants; figures in parentheses are for ministerial civil servants.

[b] The American figures are for career officials only. While the political executives report no more contact with members of Congress than do the career officials, they report almost twice as much contact (80 percent) with their department secretaries.

crats than vice versa. This asymmetry probably reflects a tendency for parliamentary contacts to be funneled to a single source within a ministry. Probably because of this concentration, senior civil servants as a group report relatively infrequent contacts with MPs.

By contrast with these three cases of mediated linkage, Germany, Italy, and especially the United States represent instances of direct linkage. Here parliamentary institutionalization is more advanced, and the system of governance more fragmented. In these countries, especially the United States, the path between senior civil servant and minister is often less trod than that between senior civil servant and parliament.

The American linkage pattern, more than any other, contravenes the mediated linkage model. First, contacts between civil servants and Congress are unusually intense, whereas both legislators and civil servants report less contact with department heads than in any other country. The direct link between two of the more durable forces in Washington—congressmen and civil servants—often comes at the expense of the temporary department secretaries, who frequently are "outsiders." The fact that U.S. civil servants report slightly more contact with congressmen than the reverse reflects in part the independent strength of Congress and the consequent need for civil servants to maintain good relations with its members. It may also reflect the strength of personal staffs in this most munificently equipped of all national legislatures, for much of a congressman's business with the executive branch is actually handled by his office. Indeed, while congressmen and bureaucrats are mutually dependent, Congress's constitutional powers and independent staffing make bureaucrats somewhat more dependent on congressmen than the reverse. This extreme case of direct linkage is called the end-run model in Figure 7–3, since both congressmen and civil servants are more likely to have contacts with one another than with the cabinet secretaries.

The German and Italian cases are referred to in Figure 7–3 as simultaneous linkage models, for in those countries MPs and civil servants report a high level of contact both with each other and with the minister. We have already discussed the peculiar Italian case in some detail. Some fundamental similarities between the German and American political systems are reflected in the extensive direct linkages between legislative politicians and senior bureaucrats in each country. Both systems tend to institutionalize competing centers of power, both lack strong central coordination, and both have legislative systems that tend to reinforce administrative fiefdoms.[36] Both systems have made the bureaucrat and the legislative politician dependent on one another, although the balance in this relationship tends to favor bureaucrats in Germany and congressmen in the United States. German bureaucrats play a more active and direct policy-shaping role in connection with legislative committees, although American bureaucrats trade favors and mutual support with congressional allies, often in the face of threats from elsewhere in the executive branch.

To sum up, the Americans, Germans, and Italians illustrate slightly different varieties of direct linkage between civil servants and MPs. In the American case, cabinet officials often are obstacles to be circumvented in accord with long-standing informal treaties among more durable actors. In Germany and Italy, contacts between MPs and senior civil servants are direct, but are accompanied by a high level of MP-ministerial contact. Although different in many other ways, these two systems have in common a fragmentation manifested in the weakness of cabinet responsibility and a growing institutionalization of parliament.

## Conclusion

Contrasting the contact patterns of bureaucrats and politicians, we have discovered that (quite consistently with our earlier findings) most politicians are better connected to broader social forces, whereas most bureaucrats are enmeshed in networks bounded by the departmental hierarchy, together with the associated interest groups. Looking more closely at those bureaucrats whose interactions do extend beyond their immediate niche, we have been able to distinguish basically two syndromes of politically oriented interaction. One syndrome is linked to what we metaphorically call the brain of the political system—the policymaking centers within the executive. The other is linked to what we term the sensory apparatus of the system—the demand-articulating sectors outside the executive. Contacts with the top sectors of the executive system are associated with an acceptance of pluralistic politics and with positive affect toward the political side of administration. Contacts with the demand-articulating sectors on the outside are fundamentally unaffected by individual attitudes. Similarly, the higher a bureaucrat's position in the hierarchy, the more frequent his contacts with the policymaking sectors and the less frequent his contacts with the demand-articulating sectors.

Just like elected politicians, bureaucrats *must* do some things and *may* do other things. Attitudes affect what individuals choose to do among the repertoire of those things they *may* do, but what *must* be done is greatly influenced by institutional arrangements. Institutional arrangements that fragment power create conditions of mutual dependence, and mutual dependence in turn encourages interaction between politicians and bureaucrats, because each holds resources valued by the other. By contrast, cabinet solidarity, ministerial responsibility, and a party-centered parliament lessen the proliferation of power centers and thus reduce the mutual dependence of bureaucrats and parliamentary politicians. Bureaucrats in systems with these institutional arrangements have far less need to be involved in overt politics than do those bureaucrats whose imperatives are defined by institutions that diffuse the source of authority. Civil servants in Britain, the Netherlands, and Sweden (except for the ministerial policy planners) rarely need move beyond the executive arena in their practice of politics, whereas civil servants in the United States, Germany, and Italy are more or less compelled to do so.[37]

Civil servants who operate in systems that do not shelter them from parliamentary politicians will necessarily act in more overtly political ways, whatever their predispositions about politics, because in large part they must create the political alliances to serve their interests. The involvement of civil servants with parliamentary politicians in such systems need not require or predispose the civil servants to like politics or appreciate pluralism or trust politicians. Conversely, insulation of bureaucrats from the tugs and pulls of parliamentary politics need not mean that such bureaucrats are apolitical or unsympathetic to pluralistic politics. It means simply that bureaucrats practice politics exclusively in the executive arena. Institutions as well as attitudes and roles are of critical importance for understanding links between bureaucrats and the world of politics.[38]

# Energy and Equilibrium in the Policy Process

## 8

The last hundred years have witnessed two remarkable social trends—the mobilization of new groups into the political system, bringing with them new issues and new demands, and the expansion of state authority to address these novel and complex problems. Each trend has affected the way public policy is made, and each has reshaped the decision-making elite. Mass enfranchisement has evoked political organizations focused on the attainment of power and the articulation of ideals—organizations led by professional party politicians contesting for control of parliament. The growth of state responsibilities has generated government organizations centered around technical knowledge and mastery of detail—organizations managed by a vastly expanded corps of professional civil servants.

Many observers have seen in the clash of these two trends the "axial problem" of modern society: Daniel Bell refers to the conflict between popular participation and bureaucracy; Christopher Lasch to meritocracy and populism; Peter Blau and Henry Jacoby to bureaucracy and democracy; Guy Benveniste and Jeffrey Straussman to expertise and politics; Jean Meynaud, Ezra Suleiman, and Alain Touraine to technocracy and democracy.[1] However phrased, this tension appears most vividly in the uncertain borderland between the province of top-level bureaucrats and the turf of professional politicians. This book has surveyed that cloud-shrouded terrain.

In Chapter 1 we outlined four images of the relationship between bureaucrats and politicians, four possible interpretations of the division of labor between them. Figure 8-1 recapitulates that discussion, showing

*Figure 8-1*  Bureaucrats and politicians: evolving roles.

| | Image I | Image II | Image III | Image IV |
|---|---|---|---|---|
| Implementing policy | B | B | B | B |
| Formulating policy | P | S | S | S |
| Brokering interests | P | P | S | S |
| Articulating ideals | P | P | P | S |

B=Bureaucrats' responsibility;  P=Politicians' responsibility;
S=Shared responsibility.

how each image allocates key policy functions between bureaucratic and political actors. The four successive images represent a progressive expansion of the role of bureaucrats to encompass functions once thought to be solely in the sphere of politicians. We have conjectured that this theoretical progression may mirror changes in the real-world roles of bureaucrats and politicians, perhaps to culminate in the virtual merger of those roles, as represented in Image IV. We recognize, of course, that our evidence itself cannot substantiate this conjecture, and later in this chapter we shall note some reasons for doubting any simple theory of inexorable bureaucratic aggrandizement, whether by merger or by takeover. On the other hand, it is clear—both from our own evidence and from case studies by other observers of the policy process   that the classic theories that excluded bureaucrats from any role in creating policy no longer fit reality, if ever they did.

What then is the most appropriate image of this division of labor? We now address that question, integrating our own findings with the results of more conventional studies of policymaking in Western democracies. On the basis of both sorts of evidence, we shall conclude by evaluating the strengths and weaknesses of bureaucrats and politicians as policy-makers.

## Paired Portraits

It could be a committee room in the modernistic Bundestag, or the prime minister's functional central Stockholm office, or a Renaissance chamber in a Roman ministry. Around the table are gathered a few members of parliament and several senior civil servants, discussing what to do about petroleum supplies, or housing subsidies, or university reform. In the shorthand of political science, they are "making policy." Each participant is unique, of course, with distinctive experiences, distinctive views, and distinctive interests. Yet the evidence of our research suggests that in important respects the two groups in the room—politicians and bureaucrats—differ systematically.

To begin with the past, their biographies and careers are different. Almost everyone in the room has a university degree, which distinguishes them sharply from most of their fellow countrymen, but if one of those present has had less formal education, he is virtually certain to be among the politicians. Most of the bureaucrats have come from rather comfortable and cosmopolitan family backgrounds, but a number of the politicians have risen from more humble and more parochial origins. Compared to conversations on the street outside, the accents in this room are predominantly upper middle class, but one can detect the slightly rougher tones of the working class from the politicians sitting at the left corner of the table.

Public affairs were unusually important in the homes of virtually everyone here, but more of the bureaucrats have come from families with a tradition of government service, whereas the families of the politicians were active in politics. Perhaps these backgrounds helped to stimulate the career choices of each, predisposing the politicians to a life involving personal and political entrepreneurship, and the civil servants to a quieter life of problem solving. Stated oversimply, the civil servants are in the room because they are clever and have impressed their superiors, whereas the politicians got there by being popular and impressing their peers and constituents. Explaining their career choices, many of the bureaucrats might echo one of our respondents who said, "I thought it was rather nice to find a good job one could get by simply passing a test." Most of the politicians, on the other hand, would recall their fascination with the world of high politics or their passion for some social cause.

The bureaucrats are slightly older and have sat around similar tables for many more years than the politicians, almost all of whom have had careers outside national government (though not necessarily outside politics). The bureaucrats have risen to the top through a rather closed world where long apprenticeship, prudent judgment, technical expertise, and ability to get things done inside a complex organization are greatly valued. The politicians live in a world where "selectorates" are more diverse, competition makes the job riskier, and ability to appeal to outside interests and to articulate broader ideals is the key to success. The bureaucrats are steady endurance runners, whereas the politicians are flashier sprinters, and the two groups have followed different training routines. For all these reasons the bureaucrats are likely to be better informed when the conversation turns to technical matters, although the politicians may be quite eloquent on matters of principle.

All these men (and they are almost surely all men) are here as policymakers, and all accept that civil servants are legitimate participants in the policy process. They implicitly reject the traditional notion (Image I) that bureaucrats merely carry out the decisions of politicians. Yet most see important differences between the appropriate responsibilities of bureaucrats and those of politicians, thereby rejecting the idea (Image IV) that these roles have fully converged. Asked to state the formal norms, most would endorse something like Image II, according to which bureaucrats worry about facts but leave values and interests to the politicians.

In practice, however, they do not seem to interpret their own jobs in quite this way. The civil servants, it is true, are especially concerned with technical matters, and in the discussion they emphasize questions of technical feasibility and administrative practicality. But they are also concerned about mediating among those organized interests that have expressed concern about the problem at hand. The politicians, by contrast, emphasize their own roles as partisans and advocates for broader causes and for less organized or more individual interests. Contrary to Image II, but consistent with Image III, brokerage among interests is less central to the role conception of politicians than of bureaucrats.

As policymakers both groups are engaged in politics, broadly defined, but they approach the game of policymaking quite differently. The skills and experiences of the bureaucrats lead them to seek technically appropriate solutions to more precisely defined problems, nudging well-established interests toward practical agreement. The politicians define problems chiefly in terms of political principle and political advantage. Strong commitments, even at the risk of intense conflict, mark the contributions of most politicians to the discussion. Competence, prudence, and, above all, balance are the characteristics of the bureaucrats; few convey the passion, conviction, and even occasional vision of the typical politician. The bureaucrats stress the specifics of the issue at hand, while the politicians emphasize "the big picture." Underscoring shared interests, the bureaucrats seek a consensual solution. (Critical observers, claiming that bureaucrats lack a sense of direction, would term them *muddlers.*) The politicians acknowledge divergent interests and, forswearing feigned impartiality, articulate a more programmatic approach. (Critics would label them *dreamers* or *dogmatists.*)

These differences of style extend to matters of substance as well. The politicians are rather polarized ideologically, holding strong and coherent views about the proper role of the state in social reform and applying those views to specific issues before them. The civil servants are no less consistent ideologically, but their consistency is centrist, seeing a certain inevitability about the existing direction of policy. They are willing to concede that problems exist in the status quo, but they see even greater difficulties in proposals for radical change. (No doubt their incrementalism derives too from the difficulties they anticipate in winning agreement to radical change from the organized interests.) Conversely, politicians— from whatever ideological wing they come—are more eager for innovation. These differences in style and substance are most consonant with the distinctions of Image III: the politicians energize the political system, the bureaucrats provide ballast and equilibrium.

Probably one reason for the more sharply defined ideologies of the politicians is that those ideologies are more firmly rooted in the politicians' social origins and political identities than is true for civil servants. The civil servants' ideologies are more closely tied to their bureaucratic environment, which is generally moderate. Compared to their parliamentary counterparts, civil servants are less consistent partisans from less consistently partisan homes. One interesting consequence is that they are not so conservative ideologically as one would expect of the products of such comfortable homes.

Both bureaucrats and politicians around the table are fundamentally sympathetic to the principles of liberty and equality that comprise the ideal of representative democracy. (Bureaucrats in Rome, it will be recalled, are an important exception to this generalization.) However, the bureaucrats are much more skeptical than most of the politicians that the ideal of political equality should be pushed very far. In the eyes of the bureaucrats "participatory democracy" is a simplistic and even dangerous slogan, for effective policymaking can best be conducted in the quiet privacy of rooms like this one. They are relatively content with the existing political system and its distribution of power. The politicians (particularly, but not only, the Leftists) are more attuned to demands from outsiders that their voices too be heard, and the politicians are more willing to entertain suggestions for political reform. In matters of procedure, as in matters of substance, they are the advocates of change; bureaucrats are wary of forces that might unsettle the machinery of government.

The contact patterns of bureaucrats and politicians also fit our theme of bureaucrats as equilibrators and politicians as energizers. Before coming to the meeting, the bureaucrats will have spoken most frequently with other colleagues in their ministries and with the representatives of the organized clienteles of those ministries—those actors most interested in fine-tuning the existing system. By contrast, the legislators have much closer ties to broader forces in society, as represented by their parties and the general public. Except for the most senior among them, the politicians are less well connected to the cosmopolitan policy community of the capital city, but they have more continuous contact with the grass roots. As their contrasting approaches to policymaking imply, the bureaucrats are more at home in the intimate and orderly world of organized interests and departmental hierarchies, whereas the ambience of the politicians is one of popular constituencies and party organization.

In sum, these paired portraits of bureaucrats and politicians, sustained by the serried arrays of data in the preceding chapters, are generally most consistent with the energy/equilibrium distinction of Image III, although some features of the evidence fit Image II rather neatly. However, as we have emphasized throughout, the United States is exceptional; the worlds of the two elites overlap much more than in Europe. Ironically, the American separation of powers means that face-to-face encounters like those we have been imagining are actually more frequent in Washington than in European capitals, and the bureaucrats and politicians across the hearing-room tables of Washington have much more in common than would be true in Paris, or Rome, or London, or even Bonn.

Institutions and history have pushed American bureaucrats toward more traditionally political roles as advocates, policy entrepreneurs, and even partisans, and have led congressmen to adopt a more technical role. American bureaucrats are much more polarized ideologically than their counterparts in Europe, and therein they resemble politicians more. They are much like congressmen in their conceptualization of policy matters and in the consistency of their partisanship and ideology. The pattern of bureaucratic-legislative contacts is also very special in the United States. We have referred to it as the end-run model, because senior civil servants report more contacts with congressmen than with the heads of their own departments, a sign of the very intimate role bureaucrats play in the

American legislative process, and another indicator of their unique role as policy energizers. Even in their respective social origins, bureaucrats and politicians are less distinct in the United States than in Europe. Differences exist, but they are much more muted and subtle.

While bureaucrats and politicians differ from one another, they differ also among themselves. As one commentator has noted, for example, with regard to the much heralded unity of French administration, "most of the evidence suggests that the French civil service is particularly prone to internal tensions and dissensions. It is characterized not by uniformity, but by diversity and fragmentation."[2] Bureaucrats with programs to administer, and thus funds to seek, are likely to differ from bureaucrats with expenditures to control. Party organizers who must tend to local activists are apt to differ from parliamentary party politicians with broader electorates to whom they must appeal.[3] As we have seen repeatedly in earlier chapters, policymakers of the Left—whether bureaucrats or politicians—differ systematically from their more conservative colleagues. Surely, the more microscopically we view the policy process, the more variations we are likely to discover among bureaucrats and among politicians. The two groups rarely confront each other en bloc; alignments around the table are usually based on other considerations. Nevertheless, the broad contrasts in background, in values, in outlook, and in behavior that emerge from our interviews with bureaucrats and politicians, particularly in Europe, are too consistent and coherent to be ignored.

## Lessons from Case Studies

Others before us have studied the roles of bureaucrats and politicians in the policy process, drawing evidence from case studies that are necessarily more impressionistic than our surveys, but also more closely tied to the immediate context of policy decision. The significance of our findings can be enhanced by linking them to the conclusions of the rich case literature. Let us consider several successive phases of the policy process, from initiation to implementation.

Studies of *policy initiation* throughout the West almost invariably stress the influence of top-level bureaucrats. One of us summarized these analyses in an earlier report:

> Public bureaucracies, staffed largely by permanent civil servants, are responsible for the vast majority of policy initiatives taken by governments. Discretion, not merely for deciding individual cases, but

for crafting the content of most legislation, has passed from the legislature to the executive. Bureaucrats, monopolizing as they do much of the available information about the shortcomings of existing policies, as well as much of the technical expertise necessary to design practical alternatives, have gained a predominant influence over the evolution of the agenda for decision.[4]

Policy activism by bureaucrats is sometimes said to be a peculiarly American phenomenon, the result of idiosyncratic governing institutions and a relatively inchoate political base. However, Hugh Heclo's superb study of social policy development in Sweden and Britain reveals that the activist civil servant is "a pervasive policy phenomenon rather than the exception." His account of the crucial role of civil servants in policy initiation is worth citing at some length.

The place of civil servants in the development of modern social policy has been crucial. . . . While parties and interest groups did occasionally play extremely important parts, it was the civil services that provided the most constant analysis and review underlying most courses of government action. Parties and interest groups typically required a dramatic stimulus, such as a spurt in unemployment, to arouse their interest, but administrative attention remained relatively strong throughout these fluctuations . . .

Apart from the persistence of influence, the substantive administrative effect on policy content has been immense. Insofar as policy has evolved as a corrective to social conditions, civil servants have played a leading role in identifying these conditions and framing concrete alternatives to deal with them . . .

As the first social policy initiatives have become established, the full scope of administrative influence has come into play in both Britain and Sweden. Social policy has most frequently evolved as a corrective less to social conditions as such and more to the perceived failings of previous policy. To officials has fallen the task of gathering, coding, storing, and interpreting policy experience. A policy "problem" may involve public demands and/or conflicting alternatives presented by competing political parties, and/or a group's definition of its own injured interest; it always involves the government bureaucracy's own conception of what it has been doing.[5]

As Heclo acknowledges, party politicians are occasionally responsible for policy initiatives and, as we shall see later, even the initiatives of civil servants usually occur within broad parameters established by political leaders. Nevertheless, in this first critical phase of policy development, most observers now agree, bureaucrats are usually more prominent than politicians.

A second important aspect of the policy process is *conflict management,* the task of assembling a sufficiently broad coalition of interests to assure acceptance of a new measure. Politicians play a more important role in conflict management than in policy initiation, particularly when the conflicts to be managed are expressed in the public arenas of parliament and party. However, it is increasingly recognized that in more private settings bureaucrats play a crucial role in winning support or at least acquiescence from organized interests.

Referring to the American experience, Francis Rourke writes that "bureaucratic policy-making in [domestic] areas commonly represents a reconciliation of conflicting group interests as much as it does the application of expertise toward the solution of particular problems." He also asserts that "executive agencies in European states have historically had less reason and less opportunity to engage in direct political activity of the sort that is so common in the United States,"[6] but European case studies suggest that today bureaucrats are no less important in conflict management there. Indeed, at least in some countries, the advent of "corporatist pluralism" has overshadowed the traditional role of elected politicians as representatives and brokers of interests. The following description of Norway by Per Laegreid and Johan Olsen is typical:

> A "two-tier" system has been institutionalized as the territorial channel of representation has been supplemented by a "corporate" channel. During the last decades the bureaucratic demand for "distance" from affected groups has been replaced by a norm of participation by such groups in policymaking processes. The main participants in this channel are top civil servants, representatives of organized interests, and experts from institutions of research and higher learning. Elected politicians participate only rarely.[7]

In actuality, through congressional committees American politicians probably play a more important role in these "subgovernments" than their counterparts in Europe.

So effectively do bureaucrats engage in conflict management that the term *pressure group* is often misleading in its implication that such organizations are doing the pressuring. Close observers of the interaction between government officials and interest groups have discovered that the officials exert influence at least as often as they receive it. In England, for example, the "Whitehall consensus" is said to represent a subtle kind of control by the civil service over interest articulation by outside groups. Richard Rose notes that the responsibility for mobilizing public and parliamentary support for policy initiatives still lies with leading politicians, but he adds that "consensus mongering" among the interests most directly affected is now the province of civil servants.[8] All this is, of course, quite consistent with our Image III.

These subgovernments involving bureaucrats, interest-group representatives, experts, and occasionally politicians are typically highly segmented by functional area—agricultural policy, health care, and so on. As a result, "conflicts usually evolve between segments, or between a segment and institutions trying to coordinate across segments and sectors."[9] Therefore, a third important aspect of policymaking involves *coordination and tradeoffs across issue areas*. B. Guy Peters has stressed the importance of this step in the policy process "in which the numerous proposals coming from numerous departments, agencies, or bureaus are brought into direct confrontation, and decisions must then be made about the priorities of government in pursuing one as opposed to the other. The expression of these priorities may involve legislative time, publicity, or legal clout, but, most often, they involve money as expressed in the public budget. These allocative decisions are perhaps as important if not more important than the development of policy ideas in the final determination of policy."[10]

In these crucial processes of planning, coordination, and budgeting, civil servants appear to be increasingly important, although conflicts often pit bureaucratic agencies against one another.[11] When these conflicts expand beyond the control of civil servants, political leaders are likely to be called on to make choices. Although less is known about patterns of influence in this realm than in other areas of policymaking, the potential influence of politicians is probably highest in the allocative phase of the policy process.

As we explained in Chapter 1, we have generally ignored *implementation* in our discussion of policymaking by bureaucrats and politicians, primarily because for the most part this topic lies outside the clouded area of joint responsibility. However, implementation is by no means an automatic or mechanical phase of the policy process. Quite apart from the well-known difficulties in ensuring that government actually does what it has decided to do, lessons learned while administering current policy are a powerful contributing factor in the evolution of new policy.[12] Thus, any rounded assessment of the relative influence of bureaucrats and politicians must note the predominance of bureaucrats in this area too.[13]

Our account of the roles of politicians and bureaucrats in the several phases of the policy process has so far highlighted the influence of civil servants. They seem to dominate policy initiation and implementation, and they have gained substantial responsibility for conflict management and even for allocative decisions. However, this sketch would remain inaccurate if we were to ignore some important political constraints with which civil servants must reckon.

Fundamentally, most descriptions of policymaking in Western nations concur that policy must be acceptable to the top political leadership, as embodied in the ruling party or parties. The norms of representative democracy, which (as we have seen) are widely accepted by policymaking elites, endow elected politicians with a monopoly on one essential ingredient in policymaking—legitimacy as the final decision-making authority. However expert and imaginative a civil servant in substantive terms, however skilled in winning consent from organized interests, however adept in coordinating his initiatives with others, however successful in implementation, he needs endorsement from political leaders for his actions. Constitutionally, politicians are everywhere empowered to reject the counsel of bureaucrats, although such rejection is infrequent in practice. Policymaking is thus a kind of dialectic, in which the "law of anticipated reactions" normally governs the behavior of bureaucrats. Consequently, in broad political and ideological terms most major policies reflect the preferences of party and parliamentary majorities.

In his cross-national study of housing policy Bruce Headey, for example, rejects the common view that "whether one political party or another wins office makes precious little difference to policy decisions, let alone to social and economic conditions. In view of such comment it is significant to report that parties appear to have made a vast difference to housing programmes and conditions in Sweden, the UK, and the US."[14] Similarly, Renate Mayntz reports from Germany that "federal bureaucrats do not need the [political] executive's attention and cooperation in policy development, but they depend fully on it for subsequent endorsement and support. This never forgotten dependence motivates federal bureaucrats to take not only the executive's expressed wishes, but also his likely preferences and the constraints to which his decisions are subject very seriously as guidelines for their everyday work."[15] This dialectical relationship is well captured by a passage from one of our own interviews with a German civil servant.

We are not here to receive orders, mentally to click our heels, and to say "Jawohl!"—that's not why we are here. On the contrary, if [senior civil servants] have a different conception [of the problem]—and they should always have a political conception—they must under certain circumstances use their conception in conjunction with their expertise and simply say, "But I would propose thus and such for this reason." And if the minister says, "No, politically we can't do that on account of these reasons," then all right, it will be done as proposed [by the minister]. It must be this way, because the minister is the responsible official, who must have the last word. That can't be avoided.

In short, politicians deserve a considerable share of the praise—and the blame—for what the bureaucracy does. As James Q. Wilson has pointed out in the American context:

If our bureaucracy often serves special interests and is subject to no central direction, it is because our legislature often serves special interests and is subject to no central leadership. For Congress to complain of what it has created and it maintains is, to be charitable, misleading.[16]

As we noted in Chapter 1, in many countries the relationship between bureaucratic and political participants in policymaking is complicated by several personnel patterns that blur conventional boundaries. First, incumbents of key bureaucratic posts are often chosen with some attention to political credentials as well as to substantive expertise. This pattern is most familiar in the United States, but a similar (though more subtle) sort of selection seems to occur in other countries as well. It is hardly accidental that at the time of our interviews in Sweden, ministry officials responsible for policy initiation were much more likely to be Social Democrats than were administrators in the boards and public authorities. It is equally significant that the ideological complexion of the top ranks of the German civil service became more progressive following the change of government in 1969, and that Gaullists vastly outnumber Leftists among our French higher civil servants. Neither in Europe nor in the United States do these phenomena (at least at the national level) necessarily represent party patronage of the cruder sort. Rather, they reflect for the most part the understandable efforts of political leaders to ensure that their closest bureaucratic collaborators are broadly sympathetic to the political and ideological orientations of the government in power. Such mechanisms can mitigate the threat of purely bureaucratic predominance in policymaking.

On the other hand, another sort of career pattern might represent the gradual extension of bureaucratic influence. In many countries career bureaucrats constitute a substantial fraction of the political elite, both in parliament and in the cabinet. Such a tendency is clearly marked in the French Fifth Republic. As Jean-Louis Quermonne has observed,

> One could schematize the hierarchical pyramid of the political class by the increase in the percentage of members of the administration as one moves up in the hierarchy: from 34–41 percent in the National Assembly, from 41–65 percent in the government, the proportion of civil servants would rise to 100 percent at the top of the government and of the State.[17]

Less dramatic, but still significant tendencies for bureaucrats to enter politics exist in Sweden, the Netherlands, Germany, and elsewhere. Indeed, comparatively speaking, the Anglo-American democracies are quite unusual in the relative insignificance of the bureaucratic channel into the political elite.

Without specially designed studies over time of the attitudes and behavior of policymakers who pass from one category to another, it is impossible to judge whether ex-bureaucrats in politics are better seen as subversives or as turncoats. Certainly they complicate the issue of the relative influence of politicians and bureaucrats. Vincent Wright has aptly summarized the French case:

> The line between politics and administration in France is singularly blurred because the lines between politicians and bureaucrats are often confused: it is perfectly possible for a member of a *grands corps* to be at the same time an active politician, a member of a *cabinet* and Mayor (roles which place him in some kind of political and administrative no-man's land). Often it is extremely difficult to discover how decisions are made.[18]

Although we have hazarded some generalizations about the respective roles of politicians and bureaucrats based on case studies of the policy process, it is important to keep in mind that patterns of influence vary from issue to issue, from era to era, and from country to country. For example, the autonomy of civil servants in policymaking is probably greater on narrower issues that arouse little controversy. "The more politicized the decision becomes, the more the influence of civil servants is likely to be reduced."[19]

Cross-national variation in the respective roles of bureaucrats and politicians has long been a staple topic of comparative political analysis. Such differences are traceable to many factors, including constitutional provisions, developmental sequences, and party systems. Precise comparisons of patterns of bureaucratic and political power in various countries are not available, and our own research was not designed to provide evidence of this sort. Nevertheless, among our seven nations, our impression (based on the available secondary literature, as well as our interviews) is that bureaucratic influence is highest in France, followed by England. Among the remaining European countries, the influence of parliamentary and party politicians seems to be highest in Germany.[20]

Across the Atlantic in the United States, policy decisions are reached in a setting of splintered and penetrable institutions. In a country without a strong state tradition, lacking in central authority, possessed of a virile individualistic ideology, and lacking well-developed parties, decision making is highly political and depends on policy entrepreneurs. Congress has ready access to its own experts, independent of the executive branch. Together with the committee system, these resources have given the United States the most technically knowledgeable parliamentarians in the world, and more than elsewhere they share in the critical phase of policy initiation.[21] American bureaucrats are required to play a more overtly political game than any of their European counterparts: in the absence of clear and strongly organized party will to carry out an organized agenda, politicians and bureaucrats in this country often promote their own agendas, encouraged by the fluidity of the policy environment. To be sure, bureaucrats on both sides of the Atlantic can be activists, but the nature of their activism differs. Activist bureaucrats in Europe play an executive game in order to push their definitions of policy, whereas their American counterparts need to play both executive and legislative games. In America, ambidexterity is a useful trait because there is more than one pot to stir.

Although the relationship between politicians and bureaucrats in Western polities has competitive features, it is *not* fundamentally one of zero-sum conflict, in which any gain for politicians is a loss for bureaucrats and vice versa. Both can make important contributions to public policy and, conversely, both can be weak and ineffective. For example, our impression is that both politicians and bureaucrats are influential participants in the evolution of Swedish policy. By contrast, neither Italian politicians nor Italian bureaucrats seem to have succeeded in producing adequate policy responses to the multiple challenges facing that system. In general, we share Heclo's view that for better *and* for worse bureaucrats and politicians are interdependent participants in the policy process:

> Government performance (in the sense of both negative constraints and the positive use of bureaucracy) can be thought of as the product of political leadership times bureaucratic power. A product rather than merely a sum is at stake because, depending on how politicians and bureaucrats are linked, either one can diminish or magnify the impact of the other on total performance.[22]

### Evaluating Bureaucrats and Politicians as Policymakers

Direct conflict between bureaucrats and politicians is occasionally cited as a basic problem of modern government. One analyst of Leon Blum's Popular Front government in France (1936–1937) has argued that "a root cause of Blum's failure, and an explanation for the cautious conservatism of his government's actions, stems from the inherent resistance to innovation of the conservatively biased career civil service which the Socialist government proved unable to counter by the one means available to it— finding the personnel appropriate to its policies."[23] Nearly half a century later, at the other end of the ideological spectrum, some leading members of the government of Margaret Thatcher would unconsciously echo this complaint, castigating the British civil service for failing to adjust to the new Conservative policies. However, the record of policymaking in most Western nations suggests that in fact few issues pit politicians against bureaucrats in frontal combat."Virtually no battles follow such lines."[24] Close analyses of policy processes typically reveal fluid alignments that vary with the issues at stake and find politicians and civil servants on both sides. Only on occasional issues involving the organization of government itself are the stakes so structured that politicians or bureaucrats will act on the basis of the commonality of their craft.

Despite all this, it remains important to ask about the relative predominance of bureaucrats and politicians in the policy process. In the sport of baseball, all teams have batters and pitchers, but the outcome of any given game depends on the prowess of the individuals playing those positions. Still, to understand the sport and its strategies and how they may be changing, we need to know about the relationship between batters and pitchers. Similarly, to understand the process of government, how it may be changing, and how strategies for influencing policy are affected, we need to know about the relationship between politicians and bureaucrats. The real issue is not whether a bureaucratic cabal is obstructing politicians, or whether politicians have gained the upper hand over bureaucrats. Instead, we need to ask about the advantages and disadvantages of bureaucratic and political modes of decision making—about the characteristic blind spots and biases (and conversely, the characteristic contributions and insights) of bureaucrats and politicians as policymakers, recognizing that both are important actors in Western governance—and are likely to remain so for the foreseeable future. Our research, coupled with the case studies we have been discussing, provides a basis for beginning to address these important evaluative issues.

EFFECTIVENESS AND RESPONSIVENESS   "Governing and democracy are warring concepts," says Samuel P. Huntington,[25] and yet we want governments to be both effective and responsive. One broad contrast between bureaucratic and political approaches to policymaking, supported by much of our evidence, suggests that bureaucrats are oriented toward efficient problem solving, whereas politicians seek to ensure that policies meet popular demands.

Virtually all top bureaucrats in Western democracies have received an advanced, highly selective, often scientific or technical education, and most have spent an apprenticeship of several decades in national government, acquiring practical experience with the details of policy and administration. As policymakers they focus on the managerial and technical problem-solving aspects of their role. In analyzing policy they discuss specifics, not abstract ideals, and they stress technical and administrative feasibility as a central criterion for judging alternatives. To be sure, none of this guarantees that they will produce effective policy. However, our findings show that each of the traits just enumerated distinguishes bureaucrats from politicians, and it seems reasonable to conclude that bureaucrats are better suited to provide dispassionate expertise. Policy analysis and debate tied firmly to the facts is more likely to occur in a bureaucratic than in a political context. As Rourke has put the point, "Bureaucracy is a governmental habitat in which expertise finds a wealth of opportunities to assert itself and to influence policy . . . The truth of the matter is that a great many policy judgments hinge on technical advice that only professional personnel can supply."[26]

On the other hand, parliamentary elites are leavened by significant numbers of persons from more modest backgrounds, in part because educational credentials are somewhat less crucial for a political career and in part because some political parties provide special access for working-class spokesmen. More of the career of the average politician has been spent outside the rarefied atmosphere of the national capital, and he continues to have much more frequent contact with local groups and ordinary citizens. Politicians consider the expression of particularized grievances an important part of their role, and they stress responsiveness to public opinion as an important norm, not only for themselves but for administrators as well. The basic political values of the average politician are more egalitarian and even populist. They are more sympathetic than most bureaucrats to the idea of involving citizens in self-government, and they are somewhat more supportive of the institutions of pluralist democracy. For all these reasons, we believe, politicians are better suited than bureaucrats to furnish sensitivity to popular discontent.[27]

Politicians and bureaucrats tune in to different stimuli. The "sensors" of politicians key in on signals from the grass roots and are more likely to detect sociopolitical problems. The sensors of bureaucrats are tuned to knowledge-driven and technology-driven changes, including changes in "social technology," as Heclo's study of social policy illustrates. Trying to adapt to changes in energy supplies and technologies is the forte of bureaucrats, but dealing with burdens of cost distribution is the natural turf of politicians. Bureaucrats and politicians gravitate naturally toward different definitions of the same problem. When politicians speak about social justice or individual freedom, bureaucrats are likely to think in terms of the actuarial aspects of social insurance or cost-benefit analyses of market regulation.

A striking illustration of the insensitivity of many bureaucrats to redistributive issues emerged from one of our pretest interviews with a British civil servant. "What are the sources of poverty in modern society," we asked, "and what can be done about it?" To our surprise he responded quickly that poverty was a tractable issue on its way to being resolved. Civil service experts even now were readying a computer program for analyzing income distribution, he explained, and when the necessary raw data had been gathered and processed, they would be able to determine the proper amount of income to be redistributed via the tax and welfare systems.

Startled at the implication that there was some objectively "proper" distribution of income, we asked whether this was not an exquisitely political issue. Not so, he assured us.

If we had the full facts in front of us, there would not be any significant divergence between different governments—and that's all I'm concerned about—between one government and the next, there would not be much disagreement about the choices to be made. Of course, the politicians try to pretend there are big differences between them, and you've still got your extremists on either side who continue to shout out the old slogans for electoral advantage, but fortunately we only have elections every five years.

Thinking perhaps of similar incidents in his own experience, a British MP once wrote that "one of the reasons why it is better to be governed by politicians than by civil servants is that civil servants are apt to disguise their value judgments as judgments of fact. Politicians are slightly more honest about bringing theirs into the open."[28] It must be added, of course, that politicians occasionally commit the opposite error of dismissing real issues of fact as merely differences of opinion and interest.

For all these reasons, policymaking by bureaucrats and policymaking by politicians exhibit different weaknesses and involve different dilemmas. The moral dilemma posed by bureaucratic policymaking is power without responsibility; the dilemma of policymaking by politicians is power without competence. Excessively bureaucratic policymaking may lead to a crisis of legitimacy, but excessively political policymaking threatens a crisis of effectiveness.

Some of these differences between bureaucratic and political modes of decision making are illustrated in Gary Freeman's excellent comparison of French and British policy toward immigration.

> Decisions about French policy on immigration were taken primarily by civil servants, planners, and Ministers, not by Deputies. The way these decision makers thought, talked, and acted about immigration is strongly parallel to what one expects of actors in a technocratic system.
>
> There was a powerful tendency for those officials with responsibility for immigration policy to emphasize the technical and economic aspects of the problem. They tended to talk in terms of planning goals, demographic trends and imperatives, and manpower forecasts and needs. They seldom discussed what might be called the human, political, or social sides of the phenomenon. The idea that an imported minority labor force might become dissatisfied and demand a modicum of political representation seems never to have occurred to those who set about creating such a group . . .

The predominance of the economic planning perspective on immigration helped retard the development of a significant public debate over the direction of that policy. Fine distinctions between the number of skilled workers needed in the construction trades and the probable rate of peasant movement to the cities are not the stuff of political conflict . . . Faced with the inherently controversial proposition of bringing in large numbers of non-European workers to live in France, those who directed policy came to frame the discussion in the least controversial, most technical, and most boring terms possible. They did this in order to avoid public reaction, to be sure, but they also acted in the way that was most normal and meaningful for them. In other words, . . . this . . . is the natural consequence of the manner in which the officials in charge of those policies approached public affairs.

In Britain, by contrast, Freeman continues,

almost all major policy departures were contained in Acts of Parliament. Those that were not . . . were still presented in that forum and debated. The centrality of the Commons in the process meant that decisions were made in a highly political atmosphere, with more or less full and open debate. This gave opponents of immigration and Back-Bench dissidents the opportunity to expound their views to the public. Whatever the merits of such an arrangement, it is certainly not conducive to quiet, unobtrusive decision making.[29]

BALANCE AND ENTHUSIASM   Framing the contrast between bureaucratic and political modes of policymaking in terms of effectiveness and responsiveness evokes Image II, but the results of our surveys, as well as the evidence from case studies, make clear that this is not a sufficient account of the contributions of bureaucrats and politicians. Responsiveness is not just a matter of yes or no. As Image III suggests, we need to ask "Responsive to whom, and with what élan?"

Both in their role conceptions and in their styles of policy analysis, we found, bureaucrats show a special predilection for mediating interests and minimizing conflicts. Ideologically, their consistent centrism leads them to shun radical change and tinker at the margins of the status quo. These inclinations are reinforced by the heavy concentration of their personal contacts within the closed world of their department and its organized clientele. Given these traits, policymaking by bureaucrats is likely to be characterized by continuity, stability, and predictability.

The role conceptions and political styles of politicians point in a very different direction. They see themselves as advocates, partisans, and tribunes. Analyzing policy, they emphasize ideals and doctrines, and they do not hesitate to take sides in social conflicts, blaming some groups and defending the interests of others. Their ideologies are full-blooded and partisan, and they articulate coherent alternatives to current policies. Their sensitivity to less sectoral interests is reflected in their close ties to political parties and to the grass roots. Their special contributions to policymaking include direction, energy, and a modicum of idealism.

Bureaucrats are equilibrators under conditions with well-defined parameters. Their solutions are not so comprehensive as those of politicians, nor are they founded in broader visions of society. As Michael Gordon says of the British civil service,

> Whether known as "civilized skepticism," "weary disillusionment," or, more extremely, "pathological cynicism," the bureaucratic ethos makes its habitués unreceptive to proposals that involve more than the slightest of incremental changes . . . In default of partisan enthusiasm, the incentives to creativity wane in a bureaucracy, and policy programs are viewed more and more in opportunistic terms.[30]

Rarely do they favor great change (or great restoration, for that matter), because their view is largely focused on the highway ahead rather than on the surrounding landscape. Concerned more with "doing" than with "dreaming," they are biased toward the status quo; as Richard Rose notes, "by definition, the status quo is 'do-able,' because it is already being done."[31] In a static world this approach to problem solving might be quite effective, for it allows progress by successive approximation; but in a changing world of novel challenges, the bureaucratic slogan of "no risky experiments" is, ironically, risky.

The bureaucrat's concern to accommodate established interests exacerbates many of these defects. As John P. Roche and Stephen Sachs wrote:

> The bureaucrat approaches a policy question with a predisposition towards harmony; he is prepared to compromise in order to promote unity and cohesion within the organization and to broaden its external appeal. He considers policy, if not a mere expedient with which to build up organizational strength, no more than a flexible expression of intentions which can be modified as required by "practical" needs.[32]

The more structured the policy environment, the more the bureaucrat tends toward equilibration and equivocation. Narrowing one's angle of vision to a limited number of organized interests does facilitate consensus mongering, but often at the expense of ignoring conflicting interests in the broader society. An overriding commitment to harmony means having to accommodate to any interest that is well enough organized to have gained entrance to departmental consultations. The result may be what Samuel Beer terms *pluralistic stagnation,* in which  vested interests can stall any innovative policy proposal, particularly one with redistributive implications. In a "zero-sum society" like that foreseen by Lester Thurow, where (at least in the short run) "the essence of problem solving is loss allocation," bureaucratic policymaking may simply mean paralysis.[33]

In contrast to this indictment, policymaking by politicians appears to have certain advantages. Willing to risk conflict, the politician is more open to creative innovation. As Roche and Sachs suggest, "The bureaucrat seeks to extend the area of compromise; the enthusiast [politician], the area of principle . . . Against the sceptical patience of the bureaucrat, he pits his passion and his chiliastic dedication . . . If we believe with Max Weber that only by reaching out for the impossible has man attained the possible, it is the enthusiast who may bring [the polity] to the fullest realization of its own potentialities."[34]

However, the politician's approach has grave inconveniences for the commonweal. "His firm belief in the basic articles of his credo may lead him to be dogmatic and doctrinaire and into unfortunate excesses . . . With his fervour and sense of righteousness, he can easily become a prisoner of his own presuppositions with the result that the actual world becomes a handmaiden of his abstractions."[35] Even less messianic politicians are typically insensitive to the practical problems of implementing their ideals. Once a bill has been passed (or merely a press release issued), the politician is ready to move on to the next "hot" topic. The lessons that bureaucrats learn from administrative feedback too often are lost on the politician. If the problem with bureaucrats is that they ignore new issues, the problem with politicians is that they forget old ones. For politicians, tomorrow has a figurative meaning; for bureaucrats, a literal one.

Without bureaucrats, governments are liable to flounder, to have desires but no discipline, to see problems and frustrations without pausing long enough to construct workable solutions. Policymaking solely by politicians would lack what Heclo calls *neutral competence*—that amalgam of bureaucratic virtues that "helps to avoid gratuitous conflicts that would use up resources and relations needed for more important issues," that "temper[s] boldness with the recognition that [the bureaucrats] will have to live with the consequences of misplaced boldness."[36] Energy and enthusiasm unchecked by a recognition of the need for compromise may produce a deadlock of unresolvable conflict. If bureaucratic policymaking carried to an extreme threatens a crisis of stagnation, purely political policymaking risks a crisis of frenzy.

Some of these contrasting vices and virtues of bureaucratic and political decision making are nicely illustrated in Lennart Lundqvist's study of American and Swedish responses to air pollution. In the politicized environment of American decision making, Lundqvist argues,

> Policy decisions were made in very swift fashion because policymakers wanted to join the popular environmental bandwagon. Later, there was less unanimity and more conflict. The speed of policymaking slowed down and became characterized by bargaining and deliberate efforts to build majorities around compromise formulas . . .

> In the United States, the first phase witnessed an obsession with radical goals and a seeming neglect for the availability of means to achieve these proud objectives. The competitive bandwagon atmosphere induced policymakers to engage in policy escalation and speculative augmentation beyond implementative capability. In the second more adversary and less unequivocal phase, policy content was marked by incrementalism.

In Sweden, however,

> clean air policymaking was for the most part a very long, drawn-out process. The style was less competitive, and the issue never became as divisive as in the United States. Swedish clean air politics has been marked by deliberate efforts to reach compromises acceptable to all interests concerned . . .

> Swedish clean air policy has been marked by an obsession with means and resources rather than goals. Instead of going for what they *wanted* to do, the policymakers went for what they *could* do. Policy choice and change throughout has been marked by incrementalism, by a gradual adjustment of objectives to available means and resources.

Yet if bureaucratic modes of decision making are more likely to pay homage to the reality principle than are political modes, it should further be noted, just as our distinction between political and bureaucratic styles of decision making implies, that

> the Swedish administrators could engage in negotiations with polluters to find an acceptable formula for policy implementation . . . One

is left with the impression that this consensual and cozy context provides less incentive for vigorous enforcement than does the adversary American context.[37]

A CREATIVE DIALOGUE   If bureaucrats and politicians each wear special blinders, they also each have special virtues. A fundamental issue, then, is how to make best use of the unique qualities that each group brings to the policy process. For while there are endemic tensions between the orientations of bureaucrats and the orientations of politicians, the central question we address here is not one of conquest—of who can be made stronger and who weaker. The issue instead is how the inherent tension between these perspectives on policymaking can be made more creative.

While the mix of these outlooks does not depend exclusively on the nature of the institutional relationship between politicians and bureaucrats, this relationship can have a major impact on the policy process and its products. As we noted back in Chapter 1, there are signs that the distinctions between bureaucrats and politicians, already altered from the more traditional conceptions embodied in Image I and Image II, are becoming further blurred. The movement toward politico-administrative hybrids may well accelerate as more burdens are placed on coordinating policy activity with political needs.[38] Even today this trend is fairly well advanced in the United States—a setting that defies many of the role-based generalizations we have developed in this book—and over the last decade or so a similar tendency has become more visible in Germany as well. Expertise and politics mix in Washington and (to a lesser extent) in Bonn among both sets of elites.

The development of politico-administrative hybrids (adumbrated in Image IV) imbues administrators with the spirit of politics and inclines politicians to ask questions of technique and detail. As yet, it is not clear whether this still nascent trend will foster government that is both effective and responsive, both balanced and enthusiastic, or whether it will only mean that bureaucrats and politicians will stumble over one another in laying claim to the same turf.

A few speculations may be hazarded on the basis of the German and American experience. First, it does not seem to be the case that politicization of the upper strata of the bureaucracy necessarily reduces expertise; in fact, many of the political appointees in Germany and in the United States have professional credentials that more than match those of career civil servants.

On the other hand, over the long run, greater reliance on political credentials for administrative appointments might lead to excessive partisanship in day-to-day administrative decisions—particularly if the parties themselves are very strong, as they are in Germany today. K. H. F. Dyson reports some evidence of this sort of *Parteibuch* ("party-book") administration in German local government. Ironically, a second danger posed by a trend toward Image IV hybrids is the domination of the parties by an elite that is rooted in the official administration. Here too Dyson reports a growing bureaucratization of German legislatures and party leadership at the local levels.[39] (This phenomenon is analogous to the concerns occasionally expressed in the United States that congressional staffers are coming to dominate the legislative process.) So far, in West Germany at least, these dangers have been held in check at the federal level, but the trends are too recent for the long-term dangers to be dismissed out of hand.

In the United States, home of the politico-administrative hybrid, the relationship between bureaucrats and politicians oscillates between collision and collusion. At the symbolic level, bureaucrats frequently are fair game for congressional politicians, whose authority they are said to usurp; aggressive assertions of bureaucratic authority can lead to face-offs. At the operational level, however, excessive collusion marks the relationship between bureaucrats and politicians, as each seeks to insulate his interests from the threat of system-wide coordination.

If trends toward merger of the two roles cannot be said to ensure a proper balance between political and bureaucratic perspectives, might a strict division of labor provide a solution? Here again although confident generalization is impossible, the experiences of Italy and Britain are not comforting. At the formal level bureaucrats and politicians in Italy agree that their roles are quite distinct, but at the practical level they are fundamentally estranged from one another. The basic perspectives of the two groups in Rome seem so different, and their distrust of one another is so great, that it is difficult to imagine satisfactory working relations evolving.

Mutual respect between politicians and bureaucrats, and a fairly clear sense of the division of labor, are characteristic of Britain. However, the policy performance of British government in recent decades has hardly been fully satisfactory. Indeed, after reviewing the German case, one British observer concludes that "a sense of shared responsibility—combined with the presence of organizational and policy skills at the top, produced by the interaction of political and administrative careers—

helps explain the generally better performance of German than of British governments in recent years."[40] Commented another critic of the British system:

> Certainly officials were loyal in the general sense of supporting ministerial policy decisions that were taken against their advice and they administered those decisions in good faith and as effectively as they could. All the same, the underlying nagging question that remained was whether the executive machine was so structured that ministers had many informed ideas of their *own*, could count on their being *rigorously* analyzed in concrete policy situations by officials *sympathetic* to them, and could be sure of getting a *wide range* of divergent views framed, if need be, by *bold, imaginative* advisers.[41]

It is clear that no single formula has yet been discovered for ensuring a creative dialogue between politicians and bureaucrats, nor are we as yet certain how such a dialogue would affect policy performance. We believe, however, that our multiple and conflicting criteria for a satisfactory policy process are most likely to be satisfied if politicians and bureaucrats augment one another's diverse strengths and share a mutual appreciation for their separate perspectives. In a well-ordered polity, politicians and bureaucrats each can do what they are best able to do: politicians articulate society's dreams, and bureaucrats help bring them gingerly to earth.

Notes

Prior Publications

Index

# Notes

## 1 Introduction

1. Max Weber, "Politics as a Vocation," in *From Max Weber: Essays in Sociology,* ed. and trans. H. H. Gerth and C. Wright Mills (New York: Oxford University Press, 1958), pp. 77–128.

2. See Robert D. Putnam, *The Comparative Study of Political Elites* (Englewood Cliffs, N.J.: Prentice-Hall, 1976), pp. 173–190 and 205–208, for relevant evidence. As noted there, and as Weber had recognized, the United States does not fully fit this account. The characteristics of the U.S. political elite have been more stable over this century—partly because the capture of political power by middle-class party politicians occurred much earlier in this country, partly because American national parties never achieved the strength and unity of modern European parties. American peculiarities are discussed later in this chapter.

3. Eric Damgaard, "The Political Role of Nonpolitical Bureaucrats in Denmark," in *The Mandarins of Western Europe: The Political Role of Top Civil Servants,* ed. Mattei Dogan (New York: Halsted Press, 1975), p. 276; Morris P. Fiorina, *Congress: Keystone of the Washington Establishment* (New Haven: Yale University Press, 1977), p. 93.

4. G. E. Aylmer, *The King's Servants: The Civil Service of Charles I, 1625–1642* (New York: Columbia University Press, 1961), p. 10, as cited in Alfred Diamant, "The Bureaucratic Model: Max Weber Rejected, Rediscovered, Reformed," in *Papers in Comparative Public Administration,* ed. Ferrel Heady and Sybil L. Stokes (Ann Arbor: University of Michigan, Institute of Public Administration, 1963), p. 85.

5. On the central role of parties and bureaucracies in contemporary conceptions of political development, see Ferrel Heady, *Comparative Public Administration,* rev. 2nd ed. (New York: Marcel Dekker, 1979), pp. 79–126, and the vast literature cited there.

*265*

6. A useful overview of much of this literature is that of B. Guy Peters, *The Politics of Bureaucracy* (New York: Longman, 1978); for the U.S. case see Lewis C. Mainzer, *Political Bureaucracy* (Glenview, Ill.: Scott, Foresman, 1973).

7. Woodrow Wilson, "The Study of Administration," *Political Science Quarterly*, 2 (June 1887): 209–210, as cited in Peters, *The Politics of Bureaucracy*, p. 4.

8. See Mainzer, *Political Bureaucracy*, p. 69.

9. Luther W. Gulick, "Notes on the Theory of Organization," in *Papers on the Science of Administration*, ed. Luther W. Gulick and Lyndall Urwick (New York: Columbia University, Institute of Public Administration, 1937), p. 10.

10. Heady, *Comparative Public Administration*, pp. 387–388; Samuel Krislov, *Representative Bureaucracy* (Englewood Cliffs, N.J.: Prentice-Hall, 1974), p. 288.

11. Peters, *The Politics of Bureaucracy*, pp. 137–138.

12. As cited in Diamant, "The Bureaucratic Model," p. 85.

13. For early statements of this point see Carl J. Friedrich, "Public Policy and the Nature of Administrative Responsibility," in *Public Policy*, ed. Carl J. Friedrich and E. S. Mason (Cambridge, Mass.: Harvard University Press, 1940); and Paul H. Appleby, *Policy and Administration* (University: University of Alabama Press, 1949).

14. Peter Shore, *Entitled to Know* (London: MacGibbon & Kee, 1966), p. 153, as cited in Richard Rose, "The Variability of Party Government: A Theoretical and Empirical Critique," *Political Studies*, 17 (December 1969): 428.

15. As cited in Diamant, "The Bureaucratic Model," p. 80.

16. See Gerhard Loewenberg and Samuel C. Patterson, *Comparing Legislatures* (Boston: Little, Brown, 1979), pp. 142–143; Renate Mayntz and Fritz W. Scharpf, *Policy-making in the German Federal Bureaucracy* (Amsterdam: Elsevier, 1975), p. 67; and Rose, "The Variability of Party Government."

17. Francis E. Rourke, *Bureaucracy, Politics, and Public Policy*, rev. ed. (Boston: Little, Brown, 1976), p. 184.

18. Because this question was put to politicians in Britain and Germany only, the figures in the text are limited to those two countries. However, there is no reason to believe that they are in any way unrepresentative.

19. Herbert A. Simon, *Administrative Behavior*, 2nd ed. (New York: Macmillan, 1957), pp. xii, 57–58, 197.

20. Fritz Morstein Marx, *The Administrative State* (Chicago: University of Chicago Press, 1957), pp. 41 and 25.

21. Karl Mannheim, *Ideology and Utopia* (New York: Harcourt, Brace & World, 1946), p. 105.

22. Glendon Schubert, *The Public Interest* (Glencoe, Ill.: Free Press, 1960).

23. Morstein Marx, *The Administrative State*, pp. 137–138.

24. See Putnam, *Comparative Study*, pp. 205–207.

25. Francis E. Rourke, ed., *Bureaucratic Power and National Politics* (Boston: Little, Brown, 1965), p. 187.

26. Rourke, *Bureaucracy, Politics, and Public Policy*, p. 75.

27. Pendleton Herring, *Public Administration and the Public Interest* (New York: McGraw-Hill, 1936) as cited in Emmette S. Redford, *Democracy in the*

*Administrative State* (New York: Oxford University Press, 1969), pp. 189–190.

28. Norton E. Long, "Power and Administration," *Public Administration Review,* 9 (Autumn 1949): 257–264; Rourke, *Bureaucracy, Politics, and Public Policy,* pp. 73–74.

29. Mayntz and Scharpf, *Policy-making,* p. 132.

30. James B. Christoph, "High Civil Servants and the Politics of Consensualism in Great Britain," in Dogan, *The Mandarins,* p. 47.

31. Richard Rose, *The Problem of Party Government* (New York: Free Press, 1974), pp. 418–419.

32. Colin Campbell and George J. Szablowski, *The Super-Bureaucrats: Structure and Behavior in Central Agencies* (Toronto: Macmillan of Canada, 1979), p. 201.

33. Christoph, "High Civil Servants," p. 29.

34. Mattei Dogan, "The Political Power of the Western Mandarins: Introduction," in Dogan, *The Mandarins,* p. 17; Roland Ruffieux, "The Political Influence of Senior Civil Servants in Switzerland," in *The Mandarins,* pp. 246–247; Vincent Wright, "Politics and Administration under the French Fifth Republic," *Political Studies* 22 (March 1974): 58; John Higley, Karl Erik Brofoss, and Knut Groholt, "Top Civil Servants and the National Budget in Norway," in *The Mandarins,* p. 262.

35. Mayntz and Scharpf, *Policy-making,* p. 136.

36. Samuel P. Huntington, "Congressional Responses to the Twentieth Century," in *The Congress and America's Future,* ed. David B. Truman (Englewood Cliffs, N.J.: Prentice-Hall, 1965), p. 30.

37. Damgaard, "The Political Role of Nonpolitical Bureaucrats," p. 291.

38. The question was posed only in Britain; 36 percent of the MPs agreed without reservation, compared to 15 percent of the civil servants.

39. C. H. Sisson, *The Spirit of British Administration* (London: Faber, 1959), p. 23, as cited in Rose, *Party Government,* p. 423.

40. Morstein Marx, *The Administrative State,* p. 102.

41. As cited in Loewenberg and Patterson, *Comparing Legislatures,* p. 20.

42. Christoph, "High Civil Servants," p. 48.

43. Sisson, *Spirit,* p. 23, as cited in Rose, *Party Government,* pp. 423–424.

44. Mayntz and Scharpf, *Policy-making,* p. 71.

45. Rose, *Party Government,* p. 480.

46. Bruce W. Headey, "A Typology of Ministers: Implications for Minister–Civil Servant Relationships in Britain," in Dogan, *The Mandarins,* p. 83.

47. Mayntz and Scharpf, *Policy-making,* p. 74.

48. Ibid., p. 162.

49. Ibid., pp. 74–75, 153–157.

50. Mainzer, *Political Bureaucracy,* p. 115.

51. Rose, "The Variability of Party Government," p. 442.

52. See Samuel H. Beer, "Political Overload and Federalism," *Polity* 10 (Fall 1977): 5–17; and Gerhard Lehmbruch, "Liberal Corporatism and Party Government," *Comparative Political Studies* 10 (April 1977): 91–126.

53. Lehmbruch, "Liberal Corporatism," pp. 117–118, 122.

54. Cited in Dogan, *The Mandarins,* p. 20.

55. Mayntz and Scharpf, *Policy-making,* p. 92.
56. Dogan, *The Mandarins,* p. 20.
57. Rose, *Party Government,* p. 387.
58. Headey, "Typology of Ministers," p. 69.
59. Campbell and Szablowski, *The Super-Bureaucrats,* p. 78.
60. Alfred Diamant, "Tradition and Innovation in French Administration," *Comparative Political Studies* 1 (July 1968): 255.
61. Interestingly, the same phraseology has been used to describe trends in Germany (for example, Nevil Johnson, *Government in the Federal Republic of Germany* [Oxford: Pergamon Press, 1973], as cited in Dogan, *The Mandarins,* p. 15); France (for instance, Wright, "Politics and Administration"); and the United States (Hugh Heclo, *A Government of Strangers* [Washington, D.C.: Brookings Institution, 1977], pp. 65–76).
62. See Dogan, *The Mandarins,* pp. 14–15; Wright, "Politics and Administration," pp. 48–49; Jeanne Siwek-Pouydesseau, "French Ministerial Staffs," in *The Mandarins,* pp. 196–209; and Ezra Suleiman, *Politics, Power, and Bureaucracy in France: The Administrative Elite* (Princeton, N.J.: Princeton University Press, 1974).
63. See, for example, Heady, *Comparative Public Administration,* pp. 219–220.
64. See Rose, *Party Government.*
65. Mayntz and Scharpf, *Policy-making,* pp. 85–86.
66. Campbell and Szablowski, *The Super-Bureaucrats.*
67. For a fuller account of our Swedish findings, see Thomas J. Anton, *Administered Politics: Elite Political Culture in Sweden* (Boston: Martinus Nijhoff, 1980).
68. Heclo, *Government of Strangers,* pp. 34–36.
69. Ibid., p. 40.
70. Ibid., p. 82.
71. Loewenberg and Patterson, *Comparing Legislatures,* p. 164.
72. Naturally, some ministers and former ministers appear in our parliamentary samples, but in numbers too scant for us to generalize with any confidence.
73. Suleiman, *Politics, Power, and Bureaucracy.*
74. Higley, Brofoss, and Groholt, "Top Civil Servants," p. 252.
75. Huntington, "Congressional Responses."
76. For several methodological reasons involving problems of translation, sampling, and coding, we are less certain of the precision of our cross-national comparisons than of our cross-role comparisons. For example, on a question about the desirability of expanding popular participation in politics and government, we are somewhat more confident in the comparison between British politicians and British civil servants or between Italian politicians and Italian civil servants than we are in the comparison between British and Italian politicians or between British and Italian civil servants. This book focuses on the more reliable of the two types of comparison.
77. Richard E. Neustadt, *Presidential Power: The Politics of Leadership* (New York: Wiley, 1960), p. 33.

78. Samuel P. Huntington, *Political Order in Changing Societies* (New Haven: Yale University Press, 1968), p. 110.

79. Loewenberg and Patterson, *Comparing Legislatures,* p. 142.

80. Charles Hyneman, *Bureaucracy in a Democracy* (New York: Harper and Brothers, 1950), as cited in Mainzer, *Political Bureaucracy,* pp. 76–77.

81. See, for example, J. Leiper Freeman, *The Political Process* (New York: Random House, 1955).

82. Norton E. Long, "Power and Administration," in *Bureaucractic Power,* ed. Francis E. Rourke, 2nd ed. (Boston: Little, Brown, 1972), p. 7.

83. Rourke, *Bureaucracy, Politics and Public Policy,* pp. 73–74.

84. Norton E. Long, "Bureaucracy and Constitutionalism," *American Political Science Review,* 46 (September 1952): 808–818; and Rourke, *Bureaucracy, Politics, and Public Policy,* p. 154.

85. In some respects institutional analysis might lead us to expect the German Federal Republic to be more like the United States than are other European systems—that is, that distinctions between bureaucrats and politicians might be somewhat weaker there than elsewhere in Europe. Among the justifications for this speculation are (1) the more powerful and independent role of the Bundestag in national policymaking, and (2) the prominence of committed partisans in the upper reaches of the federal bureaucracy. On the former point, see Loewenberg and Patterson, *Comparing Legislatures;* on the latter, see Robert D. Putnam, "The Political Attitudes of Senior Civil Servants in Western Europe: A Preliminary Report," *British Journal of Political Science,* 3 (July 1973): 257–290; and Mayntz and Scharpf, *Policy-making.* Nevertheless, the main contrast we wish to stress is that between Europe and America.

## 2  Strategy of Inquiry

1. This does not mean that other elites or forces in society are not also significant influences in these matters. Nor, certainly, is it implied that governments are the sole wielders of power in society. In constitutional systems government is but one force, albeit a constantly involved one, among a constellation of forces. The more powerfully organized the state is to give direction, potentially—but only potentially—the greater the influence bureaucrats or politicians may be able to wield. Conversely, the more easily penetrated the state is and the more decision-making is dispersed, the more reasonable it seems that nonpublic elites will exert substantial influence over decisions and policy agendas. The interdependent relationship between interest groups and the state remains, however, a very murky area. See Paul M. Sacks, "State Structure and the Asymmetrical Society: An Approach to Public Policy in Britain," *Comparative Politics,* 12 (April 1980): 349–376.

2. In two countries, Sweden and the United States, we did not interview high-fliers as such. In the United States, the absence of a strong central personnel office in combination with the reluctance of senior officials to clearly specify their likely successors led us to cease identifying high-fliers to be interviewed. In all likelihood, many of the American equivalents of the British high-fliers are lo-

cated in staff positions (rough equivalents of the French ministerial cabinets), in agencies of the Executive Office of the President, and in the institutional world bridging public and private domains. Trying to determine who these personnel are in the United States, as contrasted with Britain where individuals were identified through the Civil Service Department, in itself tells us a great deal about the two administrative systems, the styles of administration, and the role of career civil servants within them. In Sweden, many of the high-fliers are, in effect, already high-level civil servants in the small policy-developing ministries.

3. Another reason may be that, except in Britain, high-fliers were identified by the senior incumbents we interviewed. It is certainly possible that these officials identified younger civil servants much like themselves.

4. The one exception was Sweden, where 18 percent of our sample came from agencies principally devoted to defense and foreign affairs. Some officials elsewhere were engaged in tasks largely international in character, but not located within foreign or defense ministries; they also fell into the net cast by our sampling frame.

5. Formally speaking, our respondents were sampled from the following levels: Britain, deputy secretary and under secretary; France, *directeur generale;* Germany, *Abteilungsleiter* and *Unterabteilungsleiter;* Italy, *direttore generale* and *ispettore generale;* Netherlands, *directeur generaal* and *directeur;* the more complex Swedish and American samples are described in the text. Our British sample includes eighteen members of what were then termed the "specialist classes"— lawyers, engineers, scientific officers, and so on—groups that were subsequently merged with the generalist "administrative class."

6. In addition to the conspicuous dualism of the American and Swedish samples, there is a complication with regard to the German sample. The structure of German administration in the Federal Republic also has produced a tendency toward dualism; as in Sweden, the ministries in Bonn are small and oriented to policy development, with many of the traditional implementing activities taking place in the *Länder* (states). Our decision to interview only federal officials means that relatively few of our German civil servants are responsible for administration only.

7. Adam Przeworski and Henry Teune, *The Logic of Comparative Social Inquiry* (New York: Wiley, 1970), p. 131. The logic of comparative analysis, in this particular sense, is explicated by Przeworski and Teune: simply put, their argument is that explanatory structures must be specified across populations so that variations or similarities across those populations can be accounted for by generic indicators.

8. See Sidney Verba, Norman H. Nie, and Jae-on Kim, *Participation and Political Equality: A Seven-Nation Comparison* (Cambridge: Cambridge University Press, 1978), pp. 42–43. Conversely, if differences are found across nations, cultural variation may be relevant. See David J. Elkins and Richard E. B. Simeon, "A Cause in Search of Its Effect, or What Does Political Culture Explain?" *Comparative Politics,* 11 (January 1979): 127–146.

9. For an example of this genre see Hugh Heclo, *Modern Social Politics in*

*Britain and Sweden: From Relief to Income Maintenance* (New Haven: Yale University Press, 1974).

10. An early and now classic study is, of course, Richard T. LaPiere, "Attitudes vs. Actions," *Social Forces,* 13 (October 1934–May 1935): 230–237. Regrettably, the results of the LaPiere study (which discovered that hotel managers were far more likely to reject a Chinese traveler when application was made in writing than when the traveler arrived in person) have been erroneously interpreted to mean that behavior is not influenced by beliefs. For the LaPiere investigation uncovered but one component of belief, namely that of affect. LaPiere's evidence justifies some skepticism about the connection between beliefs and behavior, but it surely does not justify a generalization that there is no connection.

11. See Donald D. Searing, "Measuring Politicians' Values: Administration and Assessment of a Ranking Technique in the British House of Commons," *American Political Science Review,* 72 (March 1978): 65–79.

12. At least this is the position of consistency theorists of attitudes. See, for instance, Martin Fishbein, ed., *Readings in Attitude Theory and Measurement* (New York: Wiley, 1967), esp. part 3.

13. For an amplification of such arguments see Gabriel A. Almond, "The Intellectual History of The Civic Culture Concept," in *The Civic Culture Revisited,* ed. Gabriel A. Almond and Sidney Verba (Boston: Little, Brown, 1980), pp. 1–36; see also Bert A. Rockman, *Studying Elite Political Culture: Problems in Design and Interpretation* (Pittsburgh: University Center for International Studies, 1976).

14. A panel study of Italian regional elites found, for instance, that basic ideological orientations exhibit high stability over time. See Robert D. Putnam, Robert Leonardi, and Raffaella Y. Nanetti, "Attitude Stability Among Italian Elites," *American Journal of Political Science,* 23 (August 1979): 463–494.

15. See Joel D. Aberbach, James D. Chesney, and Bert A. Rockman, "Exploring Elite Political Attitudes: Some Methodological Lessons," *Political Methodology,* 2 (Winter 1975): 1–28. Quotation on p. 3. See also Lewis Dexter, *Elite and Specialized Interviewing* (Evanston, Ill.: Northwestern University Press, 1970).

16. Knut Groholt and John Higley, "National Elite Surveys: Some Experiences from Norway," *Acta Sociologica,* 15 (no. 2, 1972): 176.

17. Ibid.

18. Sidney Verba, "Cross-National Survey Research: The Problem of Credibility," in *Comparative Methods in Sociology: Essays on Trends and Applications,* ed. Ivan Vallier (Berkeley: University of California Press, 1971), p. 321.

19. For the American component of the study see Aberbach et al., "Exploring Elite Political Attitudes." For reinforcing evidence from other investigations see Putnam et al., "Attitude Stability," and Groholt and Higley, "National Elite Surveys."

20. As reported in Putnam et al., "Attitude Stability."

21. It should be noted, however, that the coders of the British, German, Italian, and Swedish data met together on a regular basis in order to minimize this

problem (and others), and that they usually were joined by the coding supervisor of the American congressional study, as well as the French coders.

22. For the French data a sample of about 25 percent of the interviews was double coded. For the Dutch data, the figure is about 33 percent. Budgetary shortfalls prevented complete double coding in these two studies.

23. For a detailed description of the procedures used in one of the country studies, see Aberbach et al., "Exploring Elite Political Attitudes." As the data presented in table 3 of the article indicate, the more manifest the coding items (that is, the more they measure direct responses to particular items), the higher the reliability coefficients.

24. Thomas J. Anton, *Administered Politics: Elite Political Culture in Sweden* (Boston: Martinus Nijhoff, 1980), p. 187.

25. See J. J. Richardson, "Policy-Making and Rationality in Sweden: The Case of Transport," *British Journal of Political Science*, 9 (July 1979): 341–353.

26. See especially Ronald F. Inglehart, "The Silent Revolution in Europe: Intergenerational Change in Post-Industrial Societies," *American Political Science Review*, 65 (December 1971): 991–1017.

27. For much of the following discussion see *Annual Register: World Events, A Review of the Year 1969* (London: Longmans, Green), and the *Annual Registers* for 1970, 1971, and 1973.

28. For a more detailed discussion of this point see Robert D. Putnam, "The Political Attitudes of Senior Civil Servants in Western Europe: A Preliminary Report," *British Journal of Political Science*, 3 (July 1973): 281–284.

29. For evidence of Dutch mass public "radicalism" see Inglehart, "The Silent Revolution."

30. See Anton, *Administered Politics.*

31. See Joel D. Aberbach and Bert A. Rockman, "Clashing Beliefs Within the Executive Branch: The Nixon Administration Bureaucracy," *American Political Science Review*, 70 (June 1976): 458–460.

### 3  Paths to the Top

1. This fact is well established in the literature on the subject. See Robert D. Putnam, *The Comparative Study of Political Elites* (Englewood Cliffs, N.J.: Prentice-Hall, 1976), pp. 21–44, and sources cited therein.

2. Information on gender is not available for our French samples.

3. Higher-level professionals and managers include, for example, doctors, lawyers, company directors, administrators with more than twenty-five subordinates, and large landowners; middle-level professionals and managers include teachers, pharmacists, shop owners with four to nine employees, and owners of medium-sized farms.

4. Our scheme for classifying occupational social status is drawn from David Butler and Donald Stokes, *Political Change in Britain* (New York: St. Martin's Press, 1969). For evidence on the cross-national comparability of the occupational status of our respondents and their recruitment-pool peers see table 4.1 in Peter N. Blau and Otis Dudley Duncan, *The American Occupational Structure* (New York: Wiley, 1967), pp. 122–123.

5. In some of our countries these gross educational figures mask further differentiation between the bureaucratic and political samples. In Britain, for example, 66 percent of the administrators are graduates of Oxbridge, compared to only 37 percent of the MPs. However, in the United States, only 3 percent of the career civil servants attended Ivy League schools as undergraduates, compared to 16 percent of the political executives and 10 percent of the congressmen. See Joel D. Aberbach and Bert A. Rockman, "The Overlapping Worlds of American Federal Executives and Congressmen," *British Journal of Political Science,* 7 (January 1977): 29.

6. Evidence on the changing composition of elites in advanced industrial nations shows that the importance of educational credentials has risen quite sharply in recent decades. See Putnam, *The Comparative Study of Political Elites,* pp. 205–214.

7. We conjecture that legal education on the Continent may be associated with a rather formal, legalistic approach to public problems, with particularly significant consequences for the bureaucracies of Germany and Italy. On the other hand, American career officials should find technical-scientific approaches congenial, while the British bureaucracy should be marked by the generalist tendencies of the humanities and social sciences. A case-by-case, bargaining approach ought to be most prevalent among the American and British parliamentarians. These conjectures are tempered by a recognition that styles of policymaking probably are more deeply affected by on-the-job training than by university education.

For an examination of the links in our data between type of education and political outlook, see Robert D. Putnam, "Elite Transformation in Advanced Industrial Societies: An Empirical Assessment of the Theory of Technocracy," *Comparative Political Studies,* 10 (October 1977): 383–412.

8. The political profiles are most certainly different because a Republican administration was selecting the appointees, but the social-status differences would probably hold no matter which party had done the recruiting. See, for example, the data in table A.4 in Dean E. Mann's study of *The Assistant Secretaries* (Washington, D.C.: Brookings Institution, 1965), p. 291. The differences in educational levels between appointees of the Truman, Eisenhower, and Kennedy administrations are trivial. In addition, Mann reports definite bias toward Ivy League and prestige private institutions for undergraduate and especially graduate work in all three administrations (p. 20), findings that parallel our own (Aberbach and Rockman, "Overlapping Worlds"), especially when we recall that our data include respondents below the level of assistant secretary.

9. Entirely apart from this exclusiveness in terms of social strata, one vertical or sectoral discriminant is also worth noting. Although farmers were numerically very important in the social structure of virtually all our countries in the previous generation, only 8 percent of the elites are the sons of farm workers or farm owners, large or small. The recent American president and Swedish prime minister notwithstanding, farm children rarely make it to the top of modern democratic political systems.

10. This is especially the case when the educational requirements for entry into the elite stress a general liberal education rather than one that has yielded

technical or specialized skills. The "traditional ideal" of the classically educated bureaucrat is captured by Lord Macaulay's statement in 1854: "We believe that men who have engaged up to twenty-one or twenty-two in studies which have no immediate connection with the business of any profession, and of which the effect is merely to open, to invigorate, and to enrich the mind, will generally be found in the business of every profession superior to men who have, at eighteen or nineteen, devoted themselves to the special studies of their calling." Cited in Richard Rose, *Politics in England* (Boston: Little, Brown, 1964), p. 94. Our data indicate that more liberally educated elites do have higher-status social backgrounds than the technically educated. Therefore, when a classical education serves as a filter to the top, as has traditionally been the case in the British bureaucracy, social bias is almost assured, because of the types of people who tend to pursue a classical education (those from the leisure class).

11. See Putnam, *The Comparative Study of Political Elites*, pp. 28–32, and the studies cited therein.

12. See Georg Busch, "Inequality of Educational Opportunity by Social Origin in Higher Education," in *Education, Inequality, and Life Chances* (Paris: Organization for Economic Cooperation and Development, 1975), vol. 1, pp. 159–181.

13. These gross generalizations must be qualified by reference to some national peculiarities. Posteducational social bias seems to be especially sharp in French and Italian administrative recruitment, as well as in French parliamentary recruitment (at least in the special circumstances just after 1968). In these three cases, all the arrows in Figure 3–1 are quite strong.

14. This generalization is not true for our French sample, but recall that that sample underrepresents left-wing, working class parties.

15. A difference between U.S. career and political executives illustrates this point nicely. Three percent of the civil service sample are members of minority groups, whereas 16 percent of the recently recruited political executives are members of such groups.

16. For a discussion of this index of inequality, see Hayward R. Alker, Jr., and Bruce M. Russett, "On Measuring Inequality," *Behavioral Science,* 9 (July 1964): 207–218. For an interesting and ingenious more recent illustration of this technique applied to the study of elite composition, see John D. Nagle, *System and Succession: The Social Bases of Political Elite Recruitment* (Austin: University of Texas Press, 1977). Nagle reports somewhat higher indexes of inequality for German and American political elites than those reported here, but his analysis is restricted to the occupations of the politicians, whereas we consider their social origins. Since politicians tend to be quite upwardly mobile, their current social status is significantly higher (and hence less egalitarian) than their class of origin.

17. See Ezra Suleiman, *Politics, Power, and Bureaucracy in France: The Administrative Elite* (Princeton, N.J.: Princeton University Press, 1974), pp. 63–67.

18. Ibid., pp. 55–56.

19. For a fuller discussion see Putnam, *The Comparative Study of Political Elites,* pp. 46–70.

20. This measure excludes prior service in related posts in state or local government or in national politics outside the government or parliament. Moreover,

it disregards possible interruptions of government service. The first of these qualifications means that our data tend to underestimate the importance of apprenticeship in roles outside national government. This is a special problem in the case of parliamentary elites, many of whom have held preparliamentary political positions. Except in the case of American political executives, the second qualification is less important in practical terms, since relatively few respondents in the other samples have ever left national government once having arrived.

21. For evidence on the special attitudes of the German bureaucrats see Bärbel Steinkemper, *Klassische und politische Bürokraten in der Ministerialverwaltung der Bundesrepublik Deutschland* (Cologne: Carl Heymanns, 1974); Hans-Günter Steinkemper, *Amtsträger im Grenzbereich zwischen Regierung und Verwaltung: Ein Beitrag zur Problematik der Institution des politischen Beamten in der Bundesexekutive* (Frankfurt: Peter D. Lang, 1980); and Robert D. Putnam, "The Political Attitudes of Senior Civil Servants in Western Europe: A Preliminary Report," *British Journal of Political Science,* 3 (July 1973): 257–290.

22. Kenneth Prewitt, "Political Socialization and Leadership Selection," *Annals of the American Academy of Political and Social Science,* 361 (September 1965): 100, 105.

23. To simplify the calculation of these correlation coefficients between party sympathies that refer to different political epochs and to partially transformed party systems, we have collapsed party preference at both the mass and elite levels in each country into a single Left-Center-Right trichotomy. Data were not obtained on parental party preference in the U.S. congressional interviews, nor on respondents' party preferences among Italian bureaucrats. Self-described independents were excluded from the analysis; including them would lower the correlations for the bureaucratic elites still further.

24. See Putnam, *The Comparative Study of Political Elites,* pp. 93–94. We shall show in Chapter 5 that particularly among politicians, party preference and political ideology are correlated. Party preference is a better variable to use in this chapter, because we have comparable data for the political elites and the mass publics.

25. Data on bureaucrats' party preferences were not collected in Italy. To ensure comparability, we included only the data for American career civil servants in calculating Figure 3–4. Data for France and for American political executives are discussed in the text. Data were not collected for the fathers of American congressmen.

26. Respondents who declared no party preference were excluded from the analysis. Parties were classified as follows. Britain: Left = Labour; Center = Liberal; Right = Conservative. Germany: Left = SPD (Social Democratic), KPD (Communist); Center = FDP (Free Democratic); Right = CDU (Christian Democratic Union), CSU (Christian Social Union), NSDAP (Nazi). Netherlands: Left = PSP (Pacifist Socialist), PPR (Radical), PVDA (Labor), D'66 (Democrats 1966), CPN (Communist); Center = ARP (Anti-Revolutionary), CHU (Christian Historical Union), KVP (Catholic People's); Right = VVD (People's party for Freedom and Democracy—Liberals), VVP (People's Liberal), BP (Farmers'), SGP (Political Reformed). United States: Left = Democratic; Right = Republican.

27. The fathers of American political executives had a mean party preference score of 2.24 and their recruitment-pool peers averaged 2.06. The executives themselves scored 2.46, clearly to the right of their fathers and peers. The comparable figures for France are 2.60 for bureaucrats, 2.23 for their peers, and 2.00 for the bureaucrats' fathers.

28. Samples of younger politicians and bureaucrats were interviewed in Britain, France, Germany, and Italy; younger bureaucrats, but not younger politicians, were also interviewed in the Netherlands.

29. See note 6.

30. We note in passing that some evidence from our surveys hints that in ideological and philosophical terms the younger generation diverges markedly from the senior sample. Demographic stability does not necessarily imply attitudinal or behavioral stability. See Putnam, "The Political Attitudes of Senior Civil Servants," and evidence in Chapter 6 of this book for age-related attitudes toward democracy.

### 4  Roles and Styles in Policymaking

1. Max Weber, "Bureaucracy," in *From Max Weber: Essays in Sociology* ed. and trans. H. H. Gerth and C. Wright Mills (New York: Oxford University Press, 1958), p. 201.

2. See, for instance, Frederick W. Taylor, *The Principles of Scientific Management* (New York: W. W. Norton, 1967). In a revealing passage, Taylor (pp. 142–143) claims:

Scientific management will mean . . . the elimination of almost all causes for dispute and disagreement . . . What constitutes a fair day's work will be a question for scientific investigation, instead of a subject to be bargained and haggled over . . . But more than all other causes, the close intimate cooperation, the constant personal contact between the two sides, will tend to diminish friction and discontent. It is difficult for two people whose interests are the same . . . to keep up a quarrel.

3. See Woodrow Wilson, "The Study of Administration," *Political Science Quarterly,* 2 (June 1887): 209–210.

4. Two other role foci, those of *spectator* and *careerist,* were included, but seemed to tap characteristics so passive that very few respondents were coded as having emphasized them.

5. Max Weber, "Politics as a Vocation," in *From Max Weber,* p. 101.

6. Ibid., p. 117.

7. Among American bureaucrats, for example, only 14 percent claimed to serve only the public in general. Similar findings among administrators in several American states and the Canadian province of Ontario are shown in Robert S. Friedman, Bernard W. Klein, and John H. Romani, "Administrative Agencies and the Publics They Serve," *Public Administration Review,* 26 (September 1966): 192–204.

8. For an interesting typology of interest-group relationships with the bureaucracy, see B. Guy Peters, "Insiders and Outsiders: The Politics of Pressure

Group Influence on Bureaucracy," *Administration and Society,* 9 (August 1977): 191–218.

9. For Rose's discussion of this concept, see Richard Rose, "The Variability of Party Government: A Theoretical and Empirical Critique," *Political Studies,* 17 (December 1969): 413–445, esp. 441–445.

10. The distinction between "partisans" and "integrators" is discussed by William Gamson. See his *Power and Discontent* (Homewood, Ill.: Dorsey Press, 1968), esp. chap. 1.

11. A similar distinction between "policy-proposing" civil servants in ministries and "implementing" civil servants in boards and authorities exists within the Swedish sample. However, rank-order agreement between them with regard to role focus is nearly perfect (Spearman's rho = .97). Although the Swedish ministry officials are rough equivalents of the American political executives, they are much more different from Swedish MPs in role focus rankings than are American bureaucrats from American members of Congress. In short, the convergence in role focus between politicians and bureaucrats is unique to the United States.

12. For an initial attempt at answering this question, see Joel D. Aberbach and Bert A. Rockman, "The Overlapping Worlds of American Federal Executives and Congressmen," *British Journal of Political Science,* 7 (January 1977): 23–47.

13. See Wallace Sayre, "Bureaucracies: Some Contrasts in Systems," *Indian Journal of Public Administration,* 10 (April–June 1964): 219–229.

14. As part of an excellent and more general discussion of the impact of subgovernments on political authority, see Richard Rose, "Governments against Sub-Governments: A European Perspective on Washington," in *Presidents and Prime Ministers,* ed. Richard Rose and Ezra N. Suleiman (Washington, D.C.: American Enterprise Institute, 1980), pp. 284–347.

15. Ibid., esp. pp. 334–347.

16. In 1973 approximately 38 percent of the members of the German Bundestag were government officials on leave. See Arnold J. Heidenheimer and Donald P. Kommer, *The Governments of Germany,* 4th ed. (New York: Thomas Y. Crowell, 1975), p. 189. And approximately 18 percent of the members of the lower chamber of the Dutch States General were government officials. See Gordon L. Weil, *The Benelux Nations: The Politics of Small Country Democracies* (New York: Holt, Rinehart and Winston, 1970), pp. 136–139.

According to our own sample estimates, 30 percent of German MPs have a civil service background, as do 21 percent of Dutch MPs, 13 percent of Italian deputati, 3 percent of British MPs, and no U.S. congressmen. French and Swedish data are not available for this particular characteristic; however, it is estimated that in France about 15 percent of the deputies elected in 1973 have a civil service background. See Henry W. Ehrmann, *Politics in France,* 3rd ed. (Boston: Little, Brown, 1976), p. 165.

17. In Germany, for example, the gamma coefficient between civil service background and technical role focus is −.08, but in Italy it is .79 and in the Netherlands .42.

18. A classic statement of this position argues that the bureaucracy in the

United States often serves to represent interests that lack adequate voice on Capitol Hill or in the White House. See Norton E. Long, *The Polity* (Chicago: Rand McNally, 1962), p. 71.

19. The best-known claim of this sort is made by Robert A. Dahl. See his *Preface to Democratic Theory* (Chicago: University of Chicago Press, 1956).

20. David B. Truman, "The American System in Crisis," in *Political Elites in a Democracy,* ed. Peter Bachrach (New York: Lieber-Atherton, 1971), p. 57.

21. The term "segmented responsiveness" comes from Charles E. Gilbert, "The Framework of Administrative Responsibility," *Journal of Politics,* 21 (August 1959): 373–407.

Thomas J. Anton and Samuel H. Beer have separately traced the impact of segmented responsiveness on federal assistance programs and each has noted the tendency for policymaking to become increasingly centralized while the political decision makers themselves become increasingly responsive to local and parochial interests as a basis for defining formulas. See, for instance, Anton's "Federal Assistance Programs: The Politics of System Transformation," paper presented at the Urban Choice and State Power Conference, Center for International Studies, Cornell University, June 1–4, 1977; also Beer's "In Search of a New Public Philosophy," in *The New American Political System,* ed. Anthony King (Washington, D.C.: American Enterprise Institute, 1978), pp. 5–44.

22. Lennart J. Lundqvist, "Clean Air Policies in the United States and Sweden: What Matters Most, Technology, Economics, or Politics?" paper presented at the annual meeting of the American Political Science Association, Washington, D.C., August 31–September 3, 1979.

23. Convergent evidence bearing on this astonishing finding can be found in Aberbach and Rockman, "Overlapping Worlds," p. 38. The authors report that the correlation between political party identification and political ideology is stronger among American bureaucrats than politicians. To some extent this is accounted for by the regional factor within the Democratic party and, indeed, the correlation between party and ideology improves appreciably once Southern Democrats are removed from the analysis. However, even allowing for the regional factor fails to push the party-ideology correlation among members of Congress beyond the magnitude obtained among American bureaucrats!

24. See Thomas E. Mann, *Unsafe at Any Margin: Interpreting Congressional Returns* (Washington, D.C.: American Enterprise Institute, 1978).

25. Schwarz asserts that many British MPs "are constituency-oriented in the sense of performing service tasks for their constituents." See "The Impact of Constituency on the Behavior of British Conservative MPs: An Analysis of the Formative Stages of Issue Development," *Comparative Political Studies,* 8 (April 1975): 88. Also see Bruce E. Cain, John A. Ferejohn, and Morris P. Fiorina, "The House is Not a Home: British MPs in Their Constituencies," *Legislative Studies Quarterly,* 4 (November 1979): 501–523.

26. There is, of course, a veritable deluge of literature on the "vanishing marginals" phenomenon in the House of Representatives and an equally substantial emphasis upon trying to explain it. The explanations offered tend to focus on the increased sensitivity of members to packaging themselves favorably before

their constituents through the performance of casework, as well as gaining bene-fits for their districts. The core of this theory is David Mayhew, *Congress: The Electoral Connection* (New Haven: Yale University Press, 1974).

27. Anton, "Federal Assistance Programs." Beer, of course, also points to the lack of partisanship in such distributive issues and the irrelevance, therefore, of the old New Deal alignment with respect to the lines of cleavage surrounding them. See his "In Search of a New Public Philosophy."

28. See Ross Clayton and Ron Gilbert, "Perspectives on Public Managers: Their Implications for Public Service Delivery Systems," *Public Management,* 51 (November 1971): 8–13; and Michael M. Harmon, "Normative Theory and Pub-lic Administration: Some Suggestions for a Redefinition of Administrative Re-sponsibility," in *Toward a New Public Administration: The Minnowbrook Perspec-tive,* ed. Frank Marini (New York: Chandler, 1971), pp. 172–185.

29. Renate Mayntz and Fritz W. Scharpf, *Policy-Making in the German Fed-eral Bureaucracy* (Amsterdam: Elsevier, 1975), pp. 98–99.

30. Among notable discussions on this point are Volker Ronge, "The Politi-cization of Administration in Advanced Capitalist Societies," *Political Studies,* 22 (March 1974): 86–93; Theodore Lowi, *The End of Liberalism* (New York: W. W. Norton, 1969); Ezra Suleiman, *Politics, Power, and Bureaucracy in France: The Administrative Elite* (Princeton, N.J.: Princeton University Press, 1974); and Colin Campbell and George J. Szablowski, *The Super-Bureaucrats: Structure and Be-havior in Central Agencies* (Toronto: MacMillan of Canada, 1979).

31. See especially Ronge, "The Politicization of Administration," and Rob-ert D. Putnam, "The Political Attitudes of Senior Civil Servants in Britain, Ger-many, and Italy," in *The Mandarins of Western Europe: The Political Role of Top Civil Servants,* ed. Mattei Dogan (New York: Halsted Press, 1975), pp. 87–128.

## 5   The Compass of Elite Ideology

1. For a part of this terminological debate see Chaim I. Waxman, ed., *The End of Ideology Debate* (New York: Funk & Wagnalls, 1968); Robert D. Putnam, "Studying Elite Political Culture: The Case of 'Ideology,'" *American Political Science Review,* 65 (September 1971): 651–681; and Willard A. Mullins, "On the Concept of Ideology in Political Science," *American Political Science Review,* 66 (June 1972): 1–13.

2. Joseph LaPalombara, "Decline of Ideology: A Dissent and an Interpre-tation," in Waxman, *End of Ideology Debate,* p. 320.

3. Robert A. Haber, "The End of Ideology as Ideology," in Waxman, *End of Ideology Debate,* p. 186.

4. See Robert D. Putnam, *The Comparative Study of Political Elites* (Engle-wood Cliffs, N.J.: Prentice-Hall, 1976), pp. 87–91, and the studies cited therein.

5. George F. Bishop and Kathleen A. Frankovic, "Ideological Consensus and Constraint among Party Leaders and Followers in the 1978 Election," paper presented at the annual meeting of the American Political Science Association, Washington, D.C., August 31–September 3, 1979.

6. On the United States see Allen H. Barton, "Consensus and Conflict

among American Leaders," *Public Opinion Quarterly,* 3 (Winter 1973–74): 507–530.

7. Fritz Morstein Marx, *The Administrative State: An Introduction to Bureaucracy* (Chicago: University of Chicago Press, 1957), p. 162.

8. Swedish data are omitted, since information on this variable is not available for Swedish politicians.

9. These patterns are confirmed by other ideological measures from our American interviews, and we are confident of the transatlantic contrast drawn here. Unfortunately the overlap in ideological measures between the European and American data sets is quite limited, so our direct evidence of the contrast is limited to that in Table 5–1. For further discussion, see Joel D. Aberbach and Bert A. Rockman, "The Overlapping Worlds of American Federal Executives and Congressmen," *British Journal of Political Science,* 7 (January 1977): 23–47, esp. pp. 37–38.

10. The results presented in the text and in Table 5–2 are drawn from a principal-components analysis, with pairwise deletion of missing data to maximize the number of available cases. Results from alternative factoring methods, including listwise deletion of missing data, are essentially identical. The first factor to be extracted, with an eigenvalue of 2.91, accounts for 58 percent of the common variance; the second factor, with an eigenvalue of 0.74, accounts for only 15 percent of the common variance and thus falls far below the conventional cutoff point for factor extraction.

11. Philip E. Converse, "The Nature of Belief Systems in Mass Publics," in *Ideology and Discontent,* ed. David E. Apter (New York: Free Press, 1964), pp. 206–261.

12. The statistical problem here has been understood by many analysts, but the first published work to address the issue in the context of research on belief systems, and to propose a technique for avoiding the problem, is that of Allen H. Barton and R. Wayne Parsons, "Measuring Belief System Structure," *Public Opinion Quarterly,* 41 (Summer 1977): 159–180. We are much indebted to their work. Barton and Parsons confirm Converse's substantive findings with their alternative methodology.

13. Operationally speaking, we follow the technique outlined by Barton and Parsons, "Measuring Belief System Structure," pp. 164–170. Each respondent's score on each of the five core variables is normalized in terms of our total sample. (This is tantamount to allowing our entire set of bureaucrats and politicians to determine what counts as a "centrist" or "extreme" response on a given variable.) Then for each respondent we calculate the standard deviation across his five Z-scores; the higher that standard deviation, the lower his ideological consistency. To minimize missing data problems, in our final analysis we have eliminated the variable dealing with government economic planning, and we have ignored missing data on not more than one additional variable. This procedure enables us to estimate ideological consistency for a considerably larger number of respondents, but it does not affect our conclusions in any substantive way. Unfortunately, Swedish and American data are available on too few of the core variables for us to include those two national samples in the analysis.

14. With one exception we find no difference in ideological consistency across our national samples. Both our French samples, however, earned slightly *lower* consistency ratings. Analogously, the intercorrelations among the core variables were somewhat lower in both French samples than elsewhere. Although a full exploration of this national peculiarity lies outside our scope here, it seems to result from a somewhat larger number of respondents in France who couple a desire for important social reform with a preference for more laissez-faire government. This somewhat anomalous pattern of responses might be seen in retrospect as an anticipation of the Giscard-Barre line that emerged in 1977. Although this interpretation is admittedly ad hoc, it illustrates that "inconsistent" response patterns need not be unintelligible or unintelligent.

15. This composite measure is based on factor scores from the factor analysis reported in Table 5–2. In order to maximize the number of cases and samples available for subsequent analysis, the factor score was computed on the basis of whatever core variables were not missing for a given respondent. In comparison with the results of a more conservative strategy—eliminating any respondent for whom one or more of the core variables was missing—our strategy produces slightly lower correlations between the ideological index and other variables. In effect, by misclassifying a few respondents on the basis of an abbreviated set of answers, our technique slightly understates the degree to which Left-Right ideology is related to other aspects of a policymaker's outlook and behavior. A detailed analysis, however, reveals no significant distortions introduced by this treatment of missing data, and our approach expands the generalizability of our results to a wider sample. In particular, we are able to include American and Swedish politicians (for whom only one of the five core variables is available) and American and Swedish bureaucrats (for whom only two are typically available).

For the rest of the sample, four or five of the core variables are available. Following the general strategy of this book, each of the most important analyses has been conducted on each national sample separately. Naturally, the clarity of the patterns varies from sample to sample; but with only two exceptions, the major generalizations reported in the text are uniformly confirmed by these country-by-country analyses. The French patterns are generally weaker than those in the other European countries, probably because, as stated in note 14, the ideological domain is somewhat less unidimensional in our French samples. The more important and persistent exception, as we note when appropriate, is the United States. The peculiarity of America is, of course, a recurrent theme of this book.

16. See Robert D. Putnam, "Bureaucrats and Politicians: Contending Elites in the Policy Process," in *Perspectives on Public Policy-Making,* ed. William B. Gwyn and George C. Edwards III, *Tulane Studies in Political Science,* vol. 15 (New Orleans: Tulane University Press, 1975), pp. 185–189.

17. Bear in mind that "extremist" here is a relative term. As members of their respective national elites, very few of our respondents are extremists in the more full-blooded journalistic sense.

18. This distinction between having an ideology and thinking ideologically is no mere play on words. We find no correlation between levels of conceptualization and ideological consistency, as defined earlier. Some people—especially

centrists and bureaucrats, and most especially, centrist bureaucrats—seem to have a real aversion to abstract, deductive discourse about public affairs. Yet their ideological stance on public issues is no less coherent and predictable.

19. Politicians in Germany, Italy, and the Netherlands were asked initially about the two or three biggest problems facing their country; one of those nominated was then chosen for more detailed discussion.

20. For economy and clarity we present our findings in this chapter in a tabular, percentage format, as in Table 5–3, based on arbitrary trichotomization of our Left-Right composite measure at $\pm 0.5$ standard deviation from the global mean. Statistical afficionados will recognize that a more sophisticated approach would be to retain the full range of the dependent and independent variables, employing a multiple-regression framework and using beta-weights to compare the effects of role and ideology. In fact, we have carried out precisely that technique in parallel to all the analyses reported here, confirming our results without exception.

For the variables and samples studied here, the crude percentage differences reported in Table 5–3 (and elsewhere) are numerically quite similar to the relevant beta-weights. For example, in a multiple regression predicting policy reformism from role (politician/bureaucrat) and ideology (full factor score), the beta for role was .33 and the beta for ideology was .27; these compare to mean percentage differences of 29 percent for role and 23 percent for ideology.

21. We have here another instance of the constrained-variance (or "fighting-weight") problem. Because our bureaucratic sample shows much less ideological variance than our political sample, correlation coefficients measure poorly the relative impact among bureaucrats and politicians of ideology on other variables, such as policy reformism. For example, the correlation between the Left-Right factor score and the policy reformism variable is $r = .18$ for bureaucrats and $r = .33$ for politicians, falsely suggesting that ideology is only weakly related to policy reformism among bureaucrats. Strictly speaking, the proper technique for avoiding this problem of constrained variance is to calculate *un*standardized regression coefficients. In this instance, for example, the relevant figures are $b = .32$ for bureaucrats and $b = .35$ for politicians, indicating essentially no difference in the potency of the ideological variable in the two samples. In all analyses presented in this chapter the results of the parallel regression analyses are substantively identical to the simple percentage differences used in our tables. We prefer to present percentages on grounds of wider intelligibility.

22. Because the United States frequently departs from European patterns in our data, we should note that ideology has at least as powerful an impact on desires for the future among our American respondents as anywhere else.

23. Ralf Dahrendorf, *Class and Class Conflict in Industrial Society* (Stanford, Calif.: Stanford University Press, 1959), p. 284. The earlier quotation is at p. 64.

24. William A. Gamson, *Power and Discontent* (Homewood, Ill.: Dorsey Press, 1968), p. 18.

25. Alexander L. George, "The 'Operational Code': A Neglected Approach to the Study of Political Leaders and Decision-Making," *International Studies Quarterly,* 13 (June 1969): 190–222.

26. The mean intercorrelation among these three items across the entire sample was $r = .29$. One point was given for an "agree" response, three points for "agree with reservations," seven for "disagree with reservations," and nine for "disagree." The IPC is simply the respondent's mean score on the three items.

27. Statistically, this index is the respondent's score on the only factor to emerge from a principal-components analysis of our five items. The mean intercorrelation among the five is $r = .30$, and the individual loadings on the principal factor are all $.67 \pm .05$. This index is closely related to the Index of Tolerance for Politics referred to elsewhere in reports of our research; for present purposes we have deleted one item, dealing with the mutual interference between politicians and bureaucrats, because it was worded quite differently for the two samples.

28. Our category of "centrists" is contaminated to some extent by people whose responses on the five core variables were relatively inconsistent, for a combination of rightist answers on some questions and leftist answers on others averages out to a muddled middle. If we purge these more incoherent or idiosyncratic respondents from the analysis and look only at "consistent centrists," the distinctive profile of our centrist politicians becomes even sharper. For example, among politicians who indicate a high degree of support for the institutions of pluralist politics, only 5 percent are consistent centrists; among those politicians showing least support for pluralist politics, 51 percent are consistent centrists!

29. Country-by-country analyses generally confirm these patterns. Even among American bureaucrats, ideology and images of the governing process seem to be correlated, with Leftists showing more sensitivity to social and political conflict and endorsing a more *engagé* role for civil servants. Our French data hint at the same pattern although, as indicated earlier, our basic ideological variables do not segregate contrasting groups of policymakers as clearly in France as elsewhere.

30. Allan Kornberg, *Canadian Legislative Behavior* (New York: Holt, Rinehart and Winston, 1967), p. 137, n. 5. For additional studies of the party-ideology linkage in a wide range of countries, see Putnam, *Comparative Study*, pp. 88–89.

31. Max Weber, "Politics as a Vocation," in *From Max Weber: Essays in Sociology*, ed. and trans. H. H. Gerth and C. Wright Mills (New York: Oxford University Press, 1958), p. 95.

32. These figures exclude Italy and Sweden, where we did not succeed in collecting information on the bureaucrats' party affiliation. The role difference in strength of the party-ideology tie is found in every other European country. In fact, in France there is essentially no such correlation at all among our bureaucratic respondents. Nearly half the French civil servants we interviewed expressed no party preference, and nearly two-thirds of the rest declared themselves Gaullist. This partisan homogeneity, coupled with the French ideological idiosyncracies noted earlier, helps explain the absence of a party-ideology link in our French bureaucratic data.

The only other national anomaly is the United States, where the party-ideology link is actually weaker among politicians than among bureaucrats. As we have discussed elsewhere (Aberbach and Rockman, "Overlapping Worlds," p. 38), regional factors within the dominant Democratic party disturb a straightforward connection between party and ideology among members of Congress.

When the relation between party and attitudes along the Left-Right dimension is examined for Northern Congressmen only, it rises closer to the level of our other parliamentary elites and approaches the strength of the equivalent tie among American bureaucrats.

33. Figure 5–6 is based on a pair of regression analyses, predicting ideology from political party separately for politicians and bureaucrats. Parties here are arrayed along a standard Left-Right continuum; see Ronald Inglehart and Hans D. Klingemann, "Party Identification, Ideological Preference, and the Left-Right Dimension Among Western Mass Publics," in *Party Identification and Beyond*, ed. Ian Budge, Ivor Crewe, and Dennis Fairlie (London: John Wiley, 1976), pp. 243–273, for an empirically based Left-Right ranking of European parties.

34. So few bureaucrats identify with political parties at the extremes that our inferences there must be quite cautious, based on linear extensions of the trends visible in our data.

35. These correlations are particularly striking given the crudeness of the available indicators and the range of political systems included in our calculations. Because of the diversity of the parties mentioned—forty-five of them in the countries for which we have relevant data—we have simply classified them into Left, center, and Right, as described in Chapter 3, note 16. Social class is measured on a six-point occupational scale. Urbanism is a seven-point ranking of the size of the respondent's home town. As is well known, errors in each of these measures tend to attenuate artificially the observed correlations. The same broad pattern is found within each of the countries for which we have data on paternal partisanship for both politicians and bureaucrats, that is, excluding Sweden and the United States. Among European voters, religion is generally an even stronger predictor of party choice than social class and urbanism, but unfortunately we did not ask about the religious preferences of our respondents' fathers.

36. This observed difference in the power of social antecedents to explain ideology among politicians and bureaucrats is quite independent of the differences in the distribution of their respective scores on the independent variables. In short, the "fighting-weight" problem does not invalidate our conclusions here.

37. This pattern is very robust, occurring quite distinctly in each of our national samples. (We lack all information on the fathers of our Swedish politicians, so the analysis cannot be carried out there.) The United States is only a partial exception: in neither American sample is there a significant correlation between ideology and parental social class. That is hardly surprising, since historically social class has been a relatively weak predictor of partisanship in the American electorate. On the other hand, urbanism (of childhood home) is a fairly strong predictor of ideology among congressmen ($r = .37$), but not among bureaucrats ($r = -.07$). Thus, within the limits of the available data, it seems true in the United States, as in Europe, that the ideology of politicians is more deeply rooted sociologically than the ideology of bureaucrats.

38. For a useful introduction to this technique see Herbert B. Asher, *Causal Modeling*, Sage University Paper series on Quantitative Applications in the Social Sciences, no. 07-003 (Beverly Hills, Calif.: Sage Publications, 1976). The size of the coefficient beside each arrow in Figure 5–7 indicates the relative impor-

tance of that direct linkage, controlling for all other variables explicitly included in the diagram. The *direction* of the arrows is established not by the statistical analysis, but rather by theoretical assumption. The curved line linking urbanism and social class reflects the fact (not analyzed here) that in our samples respondents from larger cities tended to have slightly higher social origins.

39. We distinguish here between the ministries of health, education, welfare, housing, and labor, on the one hand, and all other ministries, on the other. The correlation between this dichotomous variable and ideology is $r = .28$ in the United States and $r = .33$ in Germany. Similar correlations elsewhere do not reach statistical significance.

40. Richard Rose, *The Problem of Party Government* (London: Macmillan), p. 418, emphasis added.

41. Morstein Marx, *The Administrative State*, pp. 161-162.

42. As quoted in Richard Rose, "Models of Governing," *Comparative Politics*, 5 (July 1973): 491.

43. Rose, *Party Government*, pp. 423-424.

44. Ironically, the one bit of hard evidence that our measures of ideology actually predict behavior comes from the United States. As we have reported elsewhere, among our congressional respondents our ideological scale is significantly correlated with roll call voting patterns, see Aberbach and Rockman, "Overlapping Worlds," p. 37. Unfortunately, we do not have suitable independent measures of the behavior of our bureaucratic respondents, and in Europe party discipline vitiates the usefulness of parliamentary voting as a measure of individual behavior.

45. Francis E. Rourke, *Bureaucracy, Politics, and Public Policy*, rev. ed. (Boston: Little, Brown, 1976), p. 154.

### 6  Democrats, Pluralists, Populists, and Others

1. Robert Michels, *Political Parties: A Sociological Study of the Oligarchical Tendencies of Modern Democracy* (New York: Collier Books, 1962), p. 364.

2. V. O. Key, Jr., *Public Opinion and American Democracy* (New York: Knopf, 1961), p. 491.

3. J. R. Pennock, *Democratic Political Theory* (Princeton, N.J.: Princeton University Press, 1979), p. 244.

4. See A. D. Lindsay, *The Modern Democratic State* (New York: Oxford University Press, 1947).

5. Giovanni Sartori, *Democratic Theory* (Detroit: Wayne State University Press, 1962), p. 5.

6. George H. Sabine, "The Two Democratic Traditions," *Philosophical Review*, 61 (1952): 457.

7. Pennock, *Democratic Political Theory*, p. 16.

8. Robert A. Dahl, *Polyarchy: Participation and Opposition* (New Haven: Yale University Press, 1971), pp. 4-5.

9. Among the German bureaucrats we interviewed in 1970, 31 percent had entered the national civil service before 1945; for Italian bureaucrats, the figure

was 92 percent! Of our German politicians, 42 percent said they became "actively interested" in politics prior to 1945; for Italian politicians, the figure was 65 percent, although most were referring to the period of the Resistance between 1943 and 1945. Of course, our point is not that all these people are (or were) crypto-Nazis or crypto-Fascists, but rather that their induction into politics and government did not take place under normal democratic conditions.

10. Robert D. Putnam, *The Beliefs of Politicians: Ideology, Conflict and Democracy in Britain and Italy* (New Haven: Yale University Press, 1973), p. 205.

11. These questions were asked only in Britain, Germany, Italy, and of Swedish civil servants. Lacking comparable evidence from Swedish politicians, we exclude the Swedish data entirely from our analyses here.

12. To add immediacy and realism, we phrased these items for the most part as descriptions of contemporary politics in the respondent's own country. ("The general welfare *of the country* is seriously endangered by . . . interest groups"; parties and parliament do not "guarantee reasonably satisfactory public policy *in this country*," and so on; emphasis added.) The questions implicitly asked the respondent to compare the current situation in his country with his own values, and thus to reveal his underlying standards. Since reasonable observers might assess differently the costs of pluralism in various contemporary political systems, without thereby differing in their personal commitment to democracy, cross-national comparisons of responses to these items are somewhat problematic. However, comparisons within a single country—between politicians and bureaucrats, for example—are not vitiated by this potential methodological difficulty, and by replicating within each national sample the analyses reported here, we have in effect controlled for possible bias.

13. For a full presentation of the responses to all our individual questionnaire items in each country, see Samuel J. Eldersveld, Sonja Hubée-Boonzaaijer, and Jan Kooiman, "Elite Perceptions of the Political Process in the Netherlands, Looked at in Comparative Perspective," in *The Mandarins of Western Europe: The Political Role of Top Civil Servants,* ed. Mattei Dogan (New York: Halsted Press, 1975), pp. 129–161.

14. Ralf Dahrendorf, *Society and Democracy in Germany* (Garden City, N.Y.: Doubleday, 1969), pp. 138–140. Dahrendorf makes the further empirical claim that aversion to conflict is characteristic of German political thought, helping to explain Germany's historical inability to sustain democratic institutions. As a historical account, this proposition is persuasive, but as an account of contemporary German elite attitudes, our evidence is that it is quite false. Indeed, none of our national samples expressed as much tolerance for social and political conflict as the Germans. To take a single example, 73 percent of the Germans agreed that "it is social conflicts that bring about progress in modern society," as compared with 61 percent of the British, 40 percent of the Dutch, and 14 percent of the Swedish civil servants! Whether these results reflect the long-term effects of Bonn's low-temperature, stable politics or an appreciation of Dahrendorf's widely read defense of the salubrity of social conflict, they do underline the importance of historical transformations of political culture.

15. The precise wording of this question varied somewhat from country to

country. In Britain, we asked whether conflict was "a sign of social health or social illness." In the Netherlands and for most of the German interviews, the alternatives were "useful . . . harmful," while the usual phrasing in Italy was "normal . . . pathological." In many cases the respondent himself raised the normative issue without prompting during the more general discussion of social conflict and consensus.

16. The Pluralism Index should not be confused with one of its components, the Index of Support for Pluralist Institutions, which is based only on five closed questionnaire items. The results in Table 6–2 are derived from a principal-components factor analysis with pairwise deletion of missing data, in order to maximize the number of available cases. The first factor to be extracted, with eigenvalue of 1.81, accounts for 36 percent of the common variance; as shown in the table, the average correlation between this factor and the five component variables is .58. (The full analysis reveals a second factor, with an eigenvalue of 1.34; this factor represents the independent clustering of the two conflict items, distinct from the other measures of support for liberty and pluralism.) The Pluralism Index is simply the respondent's score on the first factor; in order to maximize the number of cases available for subsequent analysis, up to two variables were allowed to be missing for any given respondent.

17. The fact that scores on the Pluralism Index, and on the Populism Index to be introduced later, are distributed in a bell-shaped curve is an artifact of the normalization that occurs during factor analysis. Nevertheless, the two indexes do accurately rank-order respondents, given their responses to the component items.

18. We have divided the Pluralism and Populism factor scores at ± 0.5, which is roughly equivalent to dividing the total distribution into thirds.

19. For a more detailed account of our Dutch findings, see Samuel J. Eldersveld, Jan Kooiman and Theo van der Tak, *Bestuur en Beleid* (Assen, Netherlands: Van Gorcum, 1980).

20. Robert D. Putnam, "The Political Attitudes of Senior Civil Servants in Western Europe: A Preliminary Report," *British Journal of Political Science*, 3 (July 1973): 279.

21. A principal-components factor analysis of these six items found an average communality of .31. In fact, the Elitism Index is a simple additive index of the six items, but this is correlated $r = .95$ with the scores on this first factor. For the full range of responses on these six items see Eldersveld, Hubée-Boonzaaijer, and Kooiman, "Elite Perceptions."

22. A single factor with an eigenvalue of 2.10 emerges from a principal-components analysis of these four items; it accounts for 52 percent of the total common variance; as Table 6–4 shows, the average correlation between this factor and the four component variables is .72. The Populism Index is the respondent's score on this factor, with up to two variables allowed to be missing for any given respondent.

23. On the one measure for which we have comparable data for our American bureaucratic sample (the question about increased popular participation), the Americans are nearly as enthusiastic egalitarians as the Swedes. For further in-

formation on the American case, see Joel D. Aberbach and Bert A. Rockman, "Administrators' Beliefs About the Role of the Public: The Case of American Federal Executives," *Western Political Quarterly,* 31 (December 1978): 502–522.

24. Despite this anomaly, it remains true within each of our four countries that (a) politicians are more concentrated than bureaucrats in the lower right-hand, prodemocratic corner, and (b) bureaucrats are more concentrated than politicians in the upper left-hand, antidemocratic corner and in the lower left-hand, "nineteenth-century-liberal" corner. Not surprisingly, these role differences are considerably stronger in Italy than elsewhere. Interestingly, "nineteenth-century liberals" are considerably more common in Britain than elsewhere, particularly among British civil servants, 44 percent of whom fall into this category.

25. For simplicity's sake, we present our findings here in terms of the bivariate relationship between the Pluralism Index and other variables. However, these patterns are very robust and persist under numerous controls. Because pluralism is itself correlated with populism and (as we shall describe later) with Left-Right ideology, we have ascertained that the distinctive characteristics of "the pluralist syndrome" cohere, even with ideology and populism held constant. We have also confirmed that with a few minor exceptions the pattern appears separately within each nation-role subsample—among Italian politicians, among Swedish bureaucrats, and so on.

26. The precise format of this series of questions varied somewhat from country to country, but only in the Netherlands were we unable to make a summary assessment of the respondent's political reformism. The data presented in this section are, as usual, based on all available national samples combined, but in each case we have also confirmed that the patterns exist in essentially the same form within each country considered separately.

27. This variable is theoretically and operationally quite distinct from the parallel measure of attitudes to the existing *social* order that we introduced in Chapter 5. Nevertheless, the two measures are empirically correlated, as discussed in the text.

28. Robert R. Palmer, *The Age of Democratic Revolutions: A Political Theory of Europe and America, 1760–1800* (Princeton, N.J.: Princeton University Press, 1959). We anticipated that this connection between ideology and support for democratic values might be reversed on the extreme left, since extremists of any ilk are often thought to be antidemocratic. However, we could discover no such pattern. Two obvious test cases would be the Communist leaders of France and Italy. Some scholars have questioned whether Italian Communist politicians are really as antidemocratic as is sometimes alleged; see, for example, Robert D. Putnam, "The Italian Communist Politician," in *Communism in Italy and France,* ed. Donald L. M. Blackmer and Sidney Tarrow (Princeton, N.J.: Princeton University Press, 1975). In any event, according to our measures, Communist politicians in Italy are more committed to both populism and pluralism than their counterparts in any other party. On the other hand, French Communists might have looked rather different; unfortunately we lack data on this point.

29. Dahl, *Polyarchy,* p. 167.

30. A somewhat different version—the "disgruntlement hypothesis"—would

imply that aspirants who find themselves, for whatever reason, excluded from the councils of the great generalize their resentment to the whole democratic system. Our data seem to exclude this hypothesis; controlling for our respondents' levels of professional satisfaction does little to wash out the correlation between contacts and democratic attitudes. For other evidence that in Western democracies support for democratic norms is positively correlated with political involvement, see the studies cited in Robert D. Putnam, *The Comparative Study of Political Elites* (Englewood Cliffs, N.J.: Prentice-Hall, 1976), p. 116.

31. J. L. Talmon, *Origins of Totalitarian Democracy* (London: Secker and Warburg, 1955).

32. Pennock, *Democratic Political Theory,* pp. 16-58.

### 7  Interactions at the Top

1. W. Lloyd Warner, Paul P. Van Riper, Norman H. Martin, and Orvis F. Collins, *The American Federal Executive* (New Haven: Yale University Press, 1963), pp. 238-239.

2. See particularly Volker Ronge, "The Politicization of Administration in Advanced Capitalist Societies," *Political Studies,* 22 (March 1974): 86-93.

3. Robert D. Putnam, "The Political Attitudes of Senior Civil Servants in Britain, Germany, and Italy," in *The Mandarins of Western Europe: The Political Role of Top Civil Servants,* ed. Mattei Dogan (New York: Halsted Press, 1975), pp. 88-90.

4. For example, Thomas Cronin's distinction between "inside" and "outside" cabinet posts in the United States carries with it a distinctive pattern of interactions for cabinet secretaries. Richard Rose draws a similar distinction within the British government among those ministries having policies central to the prime minister's interests, and those having relative autonomy but little possibility of commanding much attention from the prime minister. See Thomas E. Cronin, *The State of the Presidency* (Boston: Little, Brown, 1975), pp. 188-201; and Richard Rose, "British Government: The Job at the Top," in *Presidents and Prime Ministers: Giving Direction to Government,* ed. Richard Rose and Ezra Suleiman (Washington: American Enterprise Institute, 1980), pp. 1-49.

5. A number of our questions along these lines were not asked of the Swedish and American respondents either, although the two samples have been included in the analysis wherever we have comparable data.

6. In Sweden a five-point scale was used. Therefore the Swedish data are excluded from that part of the analysis comparing mean scores. Recoding the scale scores of responses from the other countries to accord with the measurement procedure used in Sweden reveals that excluding the Swedish data from pooled computations makes no significant difference in any reported results.

7. Among bureaucrats, three samples—British, German, and Italian—have been coded on all items. Dutch bureaucrats are missing on "cabinet office," which is a matter of constitutional design rather than our oversight. The Americans are missing primarily on contacts with bureaucrats inside their departments, and the Swedes have been coded only on contacts with citizens, MPs, party

leaders, and ministers. In the Swedish case, a large number of sociometric questions were asked, but not many were precisely comparable with those asked elsewhere.

The British, German, Italian, and Dutch samples are also the most completely covered on all of the items for MPs, and the Swedish and American the least.

The consequence, which is far more significant for the bureaucratic than the parliamentary samples, is that multivariate analyses typically are based on the four nations—Britain, Germany, Italy, and the Netherlands—with the most comparable data. This is especially so with regard to our use of factor scores as indexes to distinguish patterns of contact behavior among bureaucrats. The advantages of multivariate analysis conflict here with the cross-national generalizability we want. Therefore, bivariate analyses with all contact items utilizing the full data set are presented wherever feasible, along with the analyses employing factor scores. As the reader will see, the basic relationships remain undisturbed.

8. Organizational identity, therefore, is likely to be strongest at, or even below, the department level. According to this hypothesis, the perception of problems and their preferred solutions will relate most solidly to the activities and goals of the most localized subunits. For evidence see Herbert A. Simon, *Administrative Behavior,* 3rd ed. (New York: Free Press, 1976), pp. 309–314; and Robert Axelrod, "Bureaucratic Decision-Making in the Military Assistance Program: Some Empirical Findings," in *Readings in American Foreign Policy: A Bureaucratic Perspective,* ed. Morton H. Halperin and Arnold Kanter (Boston: Little, Brown, 1973), pp. 154–171.

Departmental and subunit particularism may be attenuated by recruitment practices designed to mold administrators' orientations to the administrative system itself, by personnel policies that shift administrators across departments with some frequency, and by centripetal political institutions that diminish opportunities for sustaining and nurturing specific departmental or subunit interests.

9. James Q. Wilson, *Political Organizations* (New York: Basic Books, 1973), p. 345.

The higher reported frequency of contacts with interest groups by bureaucrats than by politicians obtains despite the fact that politicians were asked about "groups and organizations" generally, whereas bureaucrats were asked only about "groups interested in the activities of your department."

10. In speaking of British MPs, for example, Schwarz asserts that many of them "are constituency-oriented in the sense of performing service tasks for their constituents." See John E. Schwarz, "The Impact of Constituency on the Behavior of British Conservative MPs: An Analysis of the Formative Stages of Issue Development," *Comparative Political Studies,* 8 (April 1975): 88.

11. Samuel P. Huntington, "Congressional Responses to the Twentieth Century," in *The Congress and America's Future,* ed. David B. Truman (Englewood Cliffs, N.J.: Prentice-Hall, 1965), p. 25.

12. See especially on this point Ronge, "The Politicization of Administration."

13. See Robert K. Merton, "Patterns of Influence: Local and Cosmopolitan Influentials," in *Social Theory and Social Structure*, rev. ed., ed. R. K. Merton (New York: Free Press, 1968), pp. 441–474; also Joel D. Aberbach and Bert A. Rockman, "The Overlapping Worlds of American Federal Executives and Congressmen," *British Journal of Political Science*, 7 (January 1977): 23–47; Andrew Hacker, "The Elected and the Anointed: Two American Elites," *American Political Science Review*, 55 (September 1961): 539–549; Huntington, "Congressional Responses"; Robert D. Putnam, "Bureaucrats and Politicians: Contending Elites in the Policy Process," in *Perspectives on Public Policy-Making*, ed. William B. Gwyn and George C. Edwards III, *Tulane Studies in Political Science*, vol. 15 (New Orleans: Tulane University Press, 1975), pp. 179–202; and Edward Shils, "The Legislator and His Environment," *University of Chicago Law Review*, 18 (1950–51): 571–584.

14. Putnam, "Political Attitudes of Senior Civil Servants," pp. 88–90.

15. However, the close-ended three-variable Index of Programmatic Commitment (IPC) is correlated strongly with the Index of Tolerance for Politics (ITP) ($r = .49$), but only weakly with the Advocacy-Neutrality scale ($r = .14$), and virtually not at all with the Gray Area ($r = .05$). Among the three measures of attitudes to politics, only the Gray Area is significantly correlated with administrative rank, and that correlation is very modest ($r = .15$).

16. In this regard especially, see Hugh Heclo, *Modern Social Politics in Britain and Sweden: From Relief to Income Maintenance* (New Haven: Yale University Press, 1974). As Heclo concludes, the energies that bureaucrats can provide are transmitted as ideas for adjusting and correcting current policies.

17. A version of the hybrid is celebrated in the American literature as being responsive to outside forces while at the same time acting as an advocate of causes. For a compendium of such statements see Frank Mariani, ed., *Toward a New Public Administration: The Minnowbrook Perspective* (San Francisco: Chandler Publishing, 1971). The American version emphasizes "democratic" and "responsive" aspects of administration and in this may be culturally biased. For a hybrid model elsewhere that accords more closely with the policy coordinating and proposing roles suggested by our data, see Colin Campbell and George J. Szablowski, *The Super-Bureaucrats: Structure and Behavior in Central Agencies* (Toronto: Macmillan of Canada, 1979).

18. By pooling the distribution on rank across the national samples (calibrated for each national sample) and dividing at the mean of the distribution, we created a dichotomized measure of rank that minimizes variation in its meaning across national samples.

19. For a description of this function in Britain, see Hugh Heclo and Aaron Wildavsky, *The Private Government of Public Money* (Berkeley: University of California Press, 1974).

20. The term "peers" in Table 7–7 is somewhat misleading, since it is based in each country on an item listing a specific organizational level (for example, undersecretary in Britain). Our lower-ranking respondents were typically at that level themselves, whereas our higher-ranking respondents were typically one level higher. The relevant correlation in Table 7–7 ($-.27$) simply indicates that

the lower-ranking bureaucrats have more contact at their own level than with their superiors.

21. Because the "in-out" party variable had to be reconstructed on a country-by-country basis, the correlation coefficient presented is a *mean* of the country correlations.

22. See, for example, Andrew S. McFarland, *Power and Leadership in Pluralist Systems* (Stanford, Calif.: Stanford University Press, 1969), esp. pp. 15–31. Case studies particularly tend to heighten an awareness of the complexity of causal forces in the process of decision making. For recent evidence of a resurgence of the British parliament, see John E. Schwarz, "Exploring a New Role in Policy Making: The British House of Commons in the 1970s," *American Political Science Review,* 74 (March 1980): 23–37.

23. Harold Seidman, *Politics, Position, and Power: The Dynamics of Federal Organization,* 2nd ed. (New York: Oxford University Press, 1975), p. 139. Eugene McGregor notes also that in the United States "career mobility patterns reinforce . . . bureau autonomy by restricting civil service careers to a series of coterminous professional groupings and administrative-political boundaries." See Eugene P. McGregor, Jr., "Politics and the Career Mobility of Bureaucrats," *American Political Science Review,* 68 (March 1974): 26.

24. See Joel D. Aberbach and Bert A. Rockman, "Bureaucrats and Clientele Groups: A View from Capitol Hill," *American Journal of Political Science,* 22 (November 1978): 818–832; Roger H. Davidson, "Breaking Up Those 'Cozy Triangles': An Impossible Dream?" in *Legislative Reform and Public Policy,* ed. Susan Welch and John G. Peters (New York: Praeger, 1977); Morris P. Fiorina, *Congress: Keystone of the Washington Establishment* (New Haven: Yale University Press, 1977); and Randall B. Ripley and Grace A. Franklin, *Congress, the Bureaucracy, and Public Policy* (Homewood, Ill.: Dorsey Press, 1976).

25. More than half the British civil servants have served in more than one department. The British show the highest level of lateral mobility of any national sample, and the Swedes the next highest.

26. For a somewhat contrary view, see Michael R. Gordon, "Civil Servants, Politicians, and Parties: Shortcomings in the British Policy Process," *Comparative Politics,* 4 (October 1971): 29–58. However, Gordon does not deny that administrative fragmentation is less pronounced in Britain than in the United States or Germany, for example.

27. See Johnson, *Government in the Federal Republic,* esp. pp. 53–64 and 88–97; Gerhard Loewenberg and Samuel C. Patterson, *Comparing Legislatures* (Boston: Little, Brown, 1979), esp. pp. 35–38; Gerhard Loewenberg, *Parliament in the German Political System* (Ithaca, N.Y.: Cornell University Press, 1967); and T. Alexander Smith, *The Comparative Policy Process* (Santa Barbara, Calif.: Clio Books, 1975), esp. pp. 18–20. Nearly two-fifths (38 percent) of the members of the Bundestag in our sample have civil service backgrounds, by far the greatest proportion of any of the national legislative samples. Moreover, considerable emphasis is placed upon work within parliamentary committees. In Heidenheimer's words:

Most of the Bundestag's real legislative work is done in committees . . . And the committees have emerged as powerful centers, in which interest groups frequently reject or rewrite bills submitted by the executive agencies . . . Thus the parties try to fill their committee places with experts, many of them ex-officials and interest group representatives who can compete with civil servants in their own technical and legal language.

See Arnold J. Heidenheimer, *The Governments of Germany,* 3rd. ed. (New York: Thomas Y. Crowell, 1971), p. 175.

28. Johnson, *Government in the Federal Republic,* pp. 150, 86.

29. Putnam, "Political Attitudes of Senior Civil Servants," pp. 99-109. For further evidence that the federal bureaucracy in Germany has become more "political" in an openly partisan sense, and especially more tolerant toward pluralism, see Bärbel Steinkemper, *Klassische und politische Bürokraten in der Ministerialverwaltung der Bundesrepublik Deutschland* (Cologne: Carl Heymanns, 1974).

30. For other evidence see Putnam, "Bureaucrats and Politicians," and Aberbach and Rockman, "Overlapping Worlds."

31. Putnam, "Political Attitudes of Civil Servants"; Sabino Cassese, "Lights and Shadows of the Higher Civil Service in Italy," paper presented at a conference sponsored by the Centro de Investigaciones Sociologicas in Madrid, December 1980, on the role of higher civil servants in central governments.

32. Cassese, "Lights and Shadows," p. 1.

33. Robert Leonardi, Rafaella Nanetti, and Gianfranco Pasquino, "Institutionalization of Parliament and Parliamentarization of Parties in Italy," *Legislative Studies Quarterly,* 3 (February 1978): 179. Morstein Marx observes that the politicization of the civil service tends to occur in the absence of prospective alternation in the government. Fritz Morstein Marx, *The Administrative State* (Chicago: University of Chicago Press, 1957), p. 170.

34. Sidney Tarrow observes that Communist mayors often "cited evidence of their aggressive efforts to get help from non-Communist deputies, senators, and provincial councillors." One PCI mayor is quoted as saying: "To get 70 million lire for my community, I had the help of two Christian Democratic deputies. If I got the money right away, it was thanks to their interest." See Sidney Tarrow, "Party Activists in Public Office: Comparison at the Local Level in Italy and France," in *Communism in Italy and France,* ed. Donald L. Blackmer and Sidney Tarrow (Princeton, N.J.: Princeton University Press, 1973), pp. 155-156. The classic argument on this matter has been made by Joseph LaPalombara in his *Interest Groups in Italian Politics* (Princeton, N.J.: Princeton University Press, 1964). LaPalombara (p. 139) quotes an Italian bureaucrat as saying:

As far as the political party affiliation of the deputy is concerned, the only party that counts at the moment in public administration is Christian Democracy. We find little need to pay attention to the demands or the threats of the other political parties, or their representatives, or their deputies, or their senators.

35. As Tomasson writes: "It is doubtful whether the legislative process of any modern government institutionalizes compromise, investigation, and consultation with interested parties to the degree that Sweden does." Richard F. Tomasson, *Sweden: Prototype of Modern Society* (New York: Random House, 1970), p. 23.

36. Consider, for instance, the following remarks by a leading scholar of government in the Federal Republic of Germany:

The cabinet principle has been submerged in the Bonn Republic and is far less significant than in Britain where a collegiate government still predominates in form and to a large extent in practice . . .

Departmentalism has been reinforced by the lack of central personnel management and rotation of officials between ministries. Moreover, within ministries there is great emphasis on the basic working units or bureaux . . . There is little counterweight to this organizational bias at Chancellor and Cabinet levels; sometimes it is lacking even within ministries. The pressure is to maximize activities within departments at the bureaux level rather than to relate them to broader governmental goals. Initiative tends to come primarily from below, from bureaux which often reflect established social and economic interests.

K. H. F. Dyson, "Planning and the Federal Chancellor's Office in the West German Federal Government," *Political Studies,* 21 (September 1973): 351.

37. From this perspective British civil servants are not necessarily less political in their behavior than, for example, their German or American peers. Rather, a diverse set of power centers allows conflict, in the language of E. E. Schattschneider, to be socialized more readily (*The Semi-Sovereign People: A Realist's View of Democracy in America* [New York: Holt, Rinehart and Winston, 1960]). A relatively closed system characterized by anonymity and stringent rules regarding the use of official information means that bureaucrats must be exceptionally artful and judicious in the politics of persuading their superiors to see things as they wish them to be seen. By contrast, diverse centers of power provide the politically astute administrator with more tools to bring about favorable outcomes or to lessen the probability of unfavorable ones. For a vivid contrast of the American and British administrative systems in this regard, see Wallace B. Sayre, "Bureaucracies: Some Contrasts in Systems," *Indian Journal of Public Administration,* 10 (April–June 1964): 219–229.

38. This conclusion is more nuanced and (we now think) more accurate than the position implied in Putnam, "Political Attitudes of Senior Civil Servants."

## 8    Energy and Equilibrium in the Policy Process

1. This listing is borrowed from Joseph L. Nyomarkay and William W. Lammers, "The Passing of Liberal Polities: Changes in Political Career Patterns in Five Nations, 1868–1978," paper presented at the annual meeting of the American Political Science Association, Washington, D.C., August 31–September 3, 1979, p. 3. The sources cited include Bell, *The Coming of Post-Industrial Society* (New York: Basic Books, 1973); Lasch, "Take Me to Your Leader," *New York Review of Books* (October 18, 1973), p. 66; Blau, *Bureaucracy in Modern Society* (New York: Random House, 1956), pp. 107–108; Jacoby, *The Bureaucratization of the World* (Berkeley: University of California Press, 1973), pp. 162, 198 ff.; Benveniste, *The Politics of Expertise* (Berkeley: Glendessary Press, 1972), pp. 195 ff.; Straussman, *The Limits of Technocratic Politics* (New Brunswick, N.J.: Transaction Books, 1978), p. 12; Meynaud, *Technocracy* (New York: Free Press,

1968), p. 62; Suleiman, *Elites in French Society* (Princeton, N.J.: Princeton University Press, 1978), p. 161; and Touraine, *The Post-Industrial Society* (New York: Random House, 1971), pp. 28–29.

2. Vincent Wright, "Politics and Administration Under the French Fifth Republic," *Political Studies,* 22 (March 1974): 44–65.

3. For evidence suggesting the former, see Joel D. Aberbach and Bert A. Rockman, "Clashing Beliefs Within the Executive Branch: The Nixon Administration Bureaucracy," *American Political Science Review,* 70 (June 1976): 456–468; and for evidence suggesting the latter, see John D. May, "Opinion Structure of Political Parties: The Special Law of Curvilinear Disparity," *Political Studies,* 21 (June 1973): 135–151.

4. Robert D. Putnam, "The Political Attitudes of Senior Civil Servants in Western Europe: A Preliminary Report," *British Journal of Political Science* 3 (July 1973): 257.

5. Hugh Heclo, *Modern Social Policies in Britain and Sweden: From Relief to Income Maintenance* (New Haven: Yale University Press, 1974), pp. 301–303. For similar evidence see James B. Christoph, "High Civil Servants and the Politics of Consensualism in Great Britain," and John Higley, Karl Erik Brofoss, and Knut Groholt, "Top Civil Servants and the National Budget in Norway," in *The Mandarins of Western Europe: The Political Role of Top Civil Servants,* ed. Mattei Dogan (New York: Halsted Press, 1975), pp. 25–62, 252–274; Michael Gordon, "Civil Servants, Politicians, and Parties: Shortcomings in the British Policy Process," *Comparative Politics,* 4 (October 1971): 29–58; Renate Mayntz and Fritz Scharpf, *Policy-making in the German Federal Bureaucracy* (Amsterdam: Elsevier, 1975); Richard Rose, "The Variability of Party Government: A Theoretical and Empirical Critique," *Political Studies,* 17 (December 1969): 413–445; Alberta Sbragia, "Not All Roads Lead To Rome: Housing Policy in the Italian Unitary State," *British Journal of Political Science,* 9 (July 1979): 315–339; Ezra N. Suleiman, *Politics, Power, and Bureaucracy in France: The Administrative Elite* (Princeton, N.J.: Princeton University Press, 1974); Wright, "Politics and Administration."

Also very useful as reviews of the relevant case literature on the policy process are the following papers presented at a conference sponsored by the Centro de Investigaciones Sociologicas in Madrid, December 1980, on the role of higher civil servants in central governments: Carlos R. Alba, "Spanish Top Civil Servants: Francoism and After"; Sabino Cassese, "Lights and Shadows of the Higher Civil Service in Italy"; Per Laegreid and Johan P. Olsen, "Top Civil Servants in Norway"; Renate Mayntz, "German Federal Bureaucrats: A Functional Elite between Politics and Administration"; T. J. Pempel, "Organizing for Efficiency: The Higher Civil Service in Japan"; Richard Rose, "The Political Status of Higher Civil Servants in Britain"; Ezra N. Suleiman, "Bureaucrats, Politics, and Policy-making in France"; and Arturo Valenzuela, "Parties, Politics, and the State in Chile: The Higher Civil Service." (These papers are to be published in a volume edited by Suleiman and Alba.)

6. Francis E. Rourke, *Bureaucracy, Politics, and Public Policy,* rev. ed. (Boston: Little, Brown, 1976), pp. 73–75.

7. Laegreid and Olsen, "Top Civil Servants," p. 30.

8. Rose, "Political Status of Higher Civil Servants," pp. 6, 33–34; J. P. Nettl, "Consensus or Elite Domination: The Case of Business," *Political Studies,* 13 (1965): 41. See also Heclo, *Modern Social Policies,* and Bruce Headey, *Housing Policy in the Developed Economy* (London: Croom Helm, 1978), pp. 238–240.

9. Laegreid and Olsen, "Top Civil Servants," pp. 33–34.

10. B. Guy Peters, "Bureaucracy, Politics, and Public Policy," *Comparative Politics,* 11 (April 1979): 349.

11. For studies of this phase see Hugh Heclo and Aaron Wildavsky, *The Private Government of Public Money* (Berkeley: University of California Press, 1974); Aaron Wildavsky, *The Politics of the Budgetary Process,* 2nd ed. (Boston: Little, Brown, 1974); and Higley, Brofoss, and Groholt, "Top Civil Servants."

12. See especially Heclo, *Modern Social Policies.*

13. To be sure, politicians may exert a very powerful influence on the outcome of individual cases, but in the aggregate, the role of bureaucrats in the application of current policy is surely more important.

14. Headey, *Housing Policy,* p. 235. Other observers, though ascribing considerable significance to the impact of parties on policy, note that "parties are not always equipped to compete with bureaucracies and interest groups." Arnold J. Heidenheimer, Hugh Heclo, and Carolyn Teich Adams, *Comparative Public Policy: The Politics of Social Choice in Europe and America* (New York: St. Martin's Press, 1975), p. 53.

15. Mayntz, "German Federal Bureaucrats," p. 39.

16. James Q. Wilson, "The Rise of the Bureaucratic State," in *The American Commonwealth—1976,* ed. Nathan Glazer and Irving Kristol (New York: Basic Books, 1976), p. 103.

17. Jean-Louis Quermonne, "Politisation de l'administration ou fonctionnarisation de la politique," paper presented at the Conference on Administration and Politics in France under the Fifth Republic, Paris, November 30–December 1, 1979, p. 16, as cited in Suleiman, "Bureaucrats, Politics, and Policy-Making," p. 31.

18. Wright, "Politics and Administration," p. 65.

19. Laegreid and Olsen, "Top Civil Servants," p. 34. They point out that if controversy tends to reduce the influence of civil servants, then conflict aversion and a willingness to seek compromise may not be simply an aspect of a bureaucratic mentality, but instead a rational power-maximizing strategy.

20. On the role of parties, parliament, and the bureaucracy in German policymaking, see Nevil Johnson, *Government in the Federal Republic of Germany* (Oxford: Pergamon Press, 1973); K. H. F. Dyson, *Party, State, and Bureaucracy in Western Germany* (Beverly Hills, Calif.: Sage Publications, 1977); and Mayntz and Scharpf, *Policy-making.*

21. Jack L. Walker, "Setting the Agenda of the U.S. Senate: A Theory of Problem Selection," *British Journal of Political Science,* 7 (July 1977): 423–445.

22. Hugh Heclo, *A Government of Strangers: Executive Politics in Washington* (Washington, D.C.: Brookings Institution, 1977), p. 7. Heclo and Aaron Wildavsky made the same point in their study of the British Exchequer (*Private Gov-*

*ernment of Public Money,* p. 373), speaking of the relationship between politicians and bureaucrats: "Virtually every point of potential conflict is also a point of unavoidable mutual dependence."

23. Irwin M. Wall, "Socialists and Bureaucrats: The Blum Government and the French Administration, 1936–1937," *International Review of Social History,* 19 (1974): 326, as cited in Suleiman, "Bureaucrats, Politics, and Policy-Making," p. 6.

24. Laegreid and Olsen, "Top Civil Servants," p. 32.

25. Samuel P. Huntington, "The United States," in Michel Crozier, Samuel P. Huntington, and Joji Watanuki, *The Crisis of Democracy* (New York: New York University Press, 1975), pp. 50–118.

26. Rourke, *Bureaucracy, Politics, and Public Policy,* pp. 132–133.

27. Sometimes it has been argued, at least in the United States, that the bureaucracy is actually more representative than the legislature. The classic statement of this view is Norton E. Long, "Bureaucracy and Constitutionalism," *American Political Science Review,* 46 (September 1952): 808–818. We know of no empirical evidence to sustain this thesis, and surely our own does not. See also Lee Sigelman and William G. Vanderbok, "The Saving Grace? Bureaucratic Power and American Democracy," *Polity* 10 (Spring 1978): 440–447.

28. David Marquandt, "A War of Ideologies," *New Society* (London), 17 (February 18, 1971): 279.

29. Gary P. Freeman, *Immigrant Labor and Racial Conflict in Industrial Societies* (Princeton, N.J.: Princeton University Press, 1979), pp. 115–118.

30. Gordon, "Civil Servants, Politicians, and Parties," p. 54.

31. Rose, "Political Status of Higher Civil Servants," p. 33.

32. John P. Roche and Stephen Sachs, "The Bureaucrat and the Enthusiast," *Western Political Quarterly,* 8 (1955), as reprinted in *Policy-Making in Britain,* ed. Richard Rose (New York: Free Press, 1969), p. 84. Strictly speaking, this sparkling essay deals not with bureaucrats and politicians as government policymakers, but with two types of leaders of social movements; nevertheless, many of its assertions fit remarkably well with our own findings.

33. Samuel H. Beer, "Political Overload and Federalism," *Polity,* 10 (Fall 1977): 5–17; Lester C. Thurow, *The Zero-Sum Society* (New York: Basic Books, 1980), p. 12.

34. Roche and Sachs, "Bureaucrat and Enthusiast," pp. 86, 89, 92. To make clear the parallel to our concern here with government policymaking, we have substituted "the polity" for "the movement" in the passage cited.

35. Ibid., pp. 91–92.

36. Hugh Heclo, "OMB and the Presidency—the Problem of 'Neutral Competence,'" *The Public Interest,* 38 (Winter 1975): 82.

37. Lennart Lundqvist, *The Hare and the Tortoise: Clean Air Policies in the United States and Sweden* (Ann Arbor: University of Michigan Press, 1980), pp. 185, 196.

38. Laegreid and Olsen offer an intriguing alternative hypothesis, using Norway as an example. They believe that slower growth and the emergence of such cultural issues as abortion will reduce social consensus and politicize policy

discussions in the years ahead. "A likely result is that the Storting [Parliament] and political parties [will] become increasingly influential, and that ministers will emphasize their party affiliation more than their administrative position ... The role of civil servants will be weakened as issues become more politicized, and as there is less agreement on who should be considered experts" ("Top Civil Servants," p. 38).

39. Dyson, *Party, State, and Bureaucracy*, pp. 20–50.

40. Ibid., p. 63.

41. Gordon, "Civil Servants, Politicians, and Parties," p. 31 (italics in original).

# Prior Publications
# from the University of Michigan
# Comparative Elites Project

Thomas J. Anton, Claes Linde, and Anders Mellbourn, "Bureaucrats in Politics: A Profile of the Swedish Administrative Elite," *Canadian Public Administration,* 16 (Winter 1973): 627–651.

Robert D. Putnam, "The Political Attitudes of Senior Civil Servants in Western Europe: A Preliminary Report," *British Journal of Political Science,* 3 (July 1973):257–290, reprinted in *The Mandarins of Western Europe: The Political Role of Top Civil Servants,* ed. Mattei Dogan (New York: Halsted Press, 1975).

John Waterbury, "Endemic and Planned Corruption in a Monarchical Regime," *World Politics,* 16 (July 1973): 533–565.

Joel D. Aberbach, James D. Chesney, and Bert A. Rockman, "Exploring Elite Political Attitudes: Some Methodological Lessons," *Political Methodology,* 2 (1975): 1–28.

Samuel J. Eldersveld, Sonja Hubée-Boonzaaijer, and Jan Kooiman, "Elite Perceptions of the Political Process in the Netherlands, Looked at in Comparative Perspective," in Dogan, *The Mandarins.*

Robert D. Putnam, "Bureaucrats and Politicians: Contending Elites in the Policy Process," in *Perspectives on Public Policy-Making,* ed. William B. Gwyn and George C. Edwards III, *Tulane Studies in Political Science,* vol. 15 (New Orleans: Tulane University Press, 1975), pp. 179–202.

Joel D. Aberbach and Bert A. Rockman, "Clashing Beliefs within the Executive Branch: The Nixon Administration Bureaucracy," *American Political Science Review,* 70 (June 1976): 456–468.

Bert Rockman, *Studying Elite Political Culture: Problems in Design and Interpretation* (Pittsburgh: University Center for International Studies, 1976).

Joel D. Aberbach and Bert A. Rockman, "The Overlapping Worlds of American

Federal Executives and Congressmen," *British Journal of Political Science,* 7 (January 1977): 23–47.

Robert D. Putnam, "Elite Transformation in Advanced Industrial Societies: An Empirical Assessment of the Theory of Technocracy," *Comparative Political Studies,* 10 (October 1977): 383–412.

Joel D. Aberbach and Bert A. Rockman, "Administrators' Beliefs about the Role of the Public: The Case of American Federal Executives," *Western Political Quarterly,* 31 (December 1978): 502–522.

Joel D. Aberbach and Bert A. Rockman, "Bureaucrats and Clientele Groups: A View from Capital Hill," *American Journal of Political Science,* 22 (November 1978): 818–832.

Anders Mellbourn, *Byråkratins ansikten* (Stockholm: Publica LiberFörlag, 1979).

Thomas J. Anton, *Administered Politics: Elite Political Culture in Sweden* (Boston: Martinus Nijhoff, 1980).

Samuel J. Eldersveld, Jan Kooiman, and Theo van der Tak, *Bestuur en Beleid* (Assen, Netherlands: Van Gorcum, 1980).

Samuel J. Eldersveld, "Political Elite Linkages in the Dutch Consociational System," in *Political Parties and Linkage,* ed. Kay Lawson (New Haven: Yale University Press, 1980).

Samuel J. Eldersveld, Jan Kooiman, and Theo van der Tak, *The World of Dutch Elites: Images of MPs and Higher Civil Servants* (Ann Arbor: University of Michigan Press, 1981).

# Index

Administrators, politicians and bureaucrats as, 4–21. *See also* Roles; Styles
Affirmative action, 61
Age: and tenure of elites, 68–72, 78, 79, 201–202; as factor in pluralism and populism, 200–202
Andrarchy, 47
Anton, Thomas J., 278
Aristotle, 141
Aylmer, G. E., 3

Barre, Raymond, 85
Barton, Allen H., 280
Beer, Samuel H., 14, 258, 278
Behavior: beliefs and, 30–33, 46–47; perceptions of roles and, 86
Beliefs: behavior and, 30–33, 46–47; procedures for testing effects of social background, 75–76. *See also* Democracy; Ideology
Bell, Daniel, 238
Benn, Anthony Wedgwood, 13
Bentham, Jeremy, 171
Benveniste, Guy, 238
Bevan, Aneurin, 12
Blau, Peter, 238
Blum, Leon, 252
Brandt, Willy, 17, 40
Bundestag, 17, 40, 98, 101, 231–232

Bureaucracy: modern, emergence, 1; tasks, 2–3; legitimacy, European and American contrasted, 23; guild vs. entrepreneurial systems of recruitment, 67–68, 70, 81–82; commitment to bureaucratic convention, by ideology, 151–153; rapid expansion and democratic principles, 170–171; role in democracy, 174; contact patterns, 212–216; structure and bureaucrats' contact patterns, 224–227; fragmentation and bureaucrats' contact patterns, 228–229
Bureaucrats: permanent, rise, 1–2; in Third World systems, 3; and relation to politicians, images, 4–21, 238–239, 241; preferred traits, 12; and "superbureaucrats," 18; overlap with politicians, 20–23, 84–86, 91–94, 111–114, 239–244; and cross-national differences, 21–22; composition of samples, 24–29; social origins and educational backgrounds, 47–67, 78–81; geographic origins, 65–67, 78, 80; career lines, 67–72, 174, 249–250; age and tenure, 68–72, 78, 79; political origins and current loyalties, 72–78, 160–164; changes in social and political composition, 78–83; role foci, 86–91, 97;